D1534815

ASSET ALLOCATION

A Handbook of

PORTFOLIO POLICIES, STRATEGIES & TACTICS

Edited by

Robert D. Arnott
President and Chief Investment Officer, First Quadrant

Frank J. Fabozzi, CFA
Visiting Professor, Alfred P. Sloan School of Management
Massachusetts Institute of Technology
and Managing Editor, *The Journal of Portfolio Management*

Probus Publishing Company
Chicago, Illinois

Library of Congress Cataloging in Publication Data Available

ISBN 1-55738-013-9

Printed in the United States of America

1 2 3 4 5 6 7 8 9 0

DEDICATION

To my wonderful son, Robin, born in the same month as this project; and to my wife, Bobbi, whose patience with my long hours permitted this book to become a reality.

Robert D. Arnott

To my wife Dessa.

Frank J. Fabozzi

Contents

SECTION THREE
TACTICAL ASSET ALLOCATION

Contributors

Keith P. Ambachtsheer, *Keith P. Ambachtsheer & Associates, Inc.*

Robert D. Arnott, *First Quadrant Corporation*

Richard M. Bookstaber, *Morgan Stanley & Co., Inc.*

Peter L. Bernstein, *Peter L. Bernstein, Inc.*

Roger G. Clarke, *TSA Capital Management*

Charles H. DuBois, *Citicorp Investment Management*

Jeremy J. Evnine, *Wells Fargo Investment Advisors*

Frank J. Fabozzi, *Massachusetts Institute of Technology* and *Journal of Portfolio Management*

H. Gifford Fong, *Gifford Fong Associates*

Gary L. Gastineau, *Salomon Brothers Inc*

Laurie S. Goodman, *Goldman Sachs & Co.*

Roy D. Henriksson, *Salomon Brothers Inc*

Roger D. Ibbotson, *Ibbotson Associates, Inc.*

William S. Krasker, *Salomon Brothers Inc*

Adrian Lee, *J. P. Morgan Investment Management, Inc., London*

Martin L. Leibowitz, *Salomon Brothers Inc*

William J. Marshall, *Franklin Savings Bank*

William F. Sharpe, *Stanford University*

Laurence B. Siegel, *Ibbotson Associates, Inc.*

Oldrich A. Vasicek, *Gifford Fong Associates*

CHAPTER 1

Introduction: The Many Dimensions of the Asset Allocation Decision

ROBERT D. ARNOTT
PRESIDENT & CHIEF INVESTMENT OFFICER
FIRST QUADRANT

FRANK J. FABOZZI, PH.D., C.F.A.
VISITING PROFESSOR
SLOAN SCHOOL OF MANAGEMENT
MASSACHUSETTS INSTITUTE OF TECHNOLOGY
AND MANAGING EDITOR
THE JOURNAL OF PORTFOLIO MANAGEMENT

Asset allocation. Everyone's talking about it, but what is it and what are people doing? One of the puzzles in asset allocation is that the asset allocation decision is *not* one decision. Much of the confusion and mystique that surrounds asset allocation stems directly from this fact. The term "asset allocation" means different things to different people in different contexts. Asset allocation can loosely be divided into three categories: *policy* asset allocation, *tactical* asset allocation, and *dynamic* strategies for asset allocation, designed to reshape the return distribution. Most of the attention in this book is focused on the first two

1

categories, but there are many variants on each of the three themes, which deserve a brief overview.

POLICY ASSET ALLOCATION

The policy asset mix decision can loosely be characterized as a long-term asset allocation decision, in which the investor seeks to assess an appropriate long-term "normal" asset mix which represents an ideal blend of controlled risk and enhanced return. The strategies which offer the greatest prospects for strong long-term rewards tend to be inherently risky strategies. The strategies which offer the greatest safety tend to offer only modest return opportunities. The balancing of these conflicting goals is what we call "policy" asset allocation.

Even within this definition of policy asset allocation, there are many considerations which the investor must address. Policy asset allocation is the balancing of risk and reward in assessing a long-term "normal" asset mix. But *what* risks and *what* rewards are to be contemplated in this evaluation? For the investor with a short investment horizon and a need to preserve capital, the relevant definition of risk is very different from a long-horizon investor such as a pension fund or an endowment fund. Ironically, the lowest risk strategy for a short-horizon investor may be a high-risk strategy for a long-horizon investor. This somewhat surprising fact is explored from several angles throughout the opening section of the book, which focuses on policy asset allocation.

For many investors, there is more than one definition of risk which may have a bearing on the policy asset allocation decision. For example, the pension sponsor needs to be concerned with volatility of assets, volatility of liabilities, volatility of the surplus (or difference between assets and liabilities), volatility of the expense ratio or contribution rate for funding the pension plan, as well as a handful of other factors. But risk is not just volatility. Under the new pension accounting guidelines for United States-based corporations, risk also can be defined in terms of shortfall. After all, upside risk is a risk that no one fears. But downside risk is to be avoided. Notably in pension management, there is the need to avoid any risk of a net, unfunded liability. No pension officer wants to be tagged as the individual responsible for a new liability appearing on the balance sheet!

In assessing the policy asset allocation, there is even a host of different tools at the investor's disposal. Should the investor use optimization techniques? Should optimization techniques with a shortfall constraint be the basis for the policy asset mix decision? How does the suitable policy mix shift with different investor circumstances? All of these are questions which can and must be addressed in assessing the policy asset allocation decision.

DYNAMIC STRATEGIES

Some of the more intriguing and controversial strategies to emerge in recent years are the "dynamic" strategies, in which the asset mix is mechanistically shifted in response to changing market conditions. The most well-publicized variant of these dynamic strategies would certainly be portfolio insurance. However, dynamic strategies can be used for a whole host of purposes which go well beyond simple portfolio insurance, for all of its potential merits or demerits. In essence, these dynamic strategies enable the investor to reshape the entire return distribution. By dynamically shifting the asset mix, investors can control both downside risk and surplus volatility; can directly build a "shortfall constraint" into their strategy; and in essence can reshape the return distribution as they see fit. Dynamic strategies are notable for their mechanistic nature and for their potential impact on policy asset allocation. They are mechanistic in the sense that any action in the capital markets triggers a prescribed reaction in the portfolio of assets.

Dynamic strategies have an interesting implication for the policy asset allocation decision. If a dynamic strategy is employed, it can represent a long-term policy asset allocation *response* to changing market conditions. Many advocates of portfolio insurance have also been advocates of a more aggressive asset allocation stance, leaning more heavily towards equities in response to the protection offered by portfolio insurance. Other investment practitioners have argued for the opposite strategy: selling portfolio insurance. Such a process would involve boosting equity exposure after a decline and lowering it after a rally, thereby ostensibly providing a "built-in" policy response to changing market conditions. Such strategies clearly provide greatly increased flexibility in investment management and greatly improved control over the nature of the portfolio, *if the dynamic strategy can be implemented at a reasonable cost*. This last issue has been the focal point of much of the controversy regarding dynamic strategies in the wake of the October 1987 market crash.

TACTICAL ASSET ALLOCATION

Once the policy asset allocation has been established, and once the use of dynamic strategies, if any, has been decided upon, the investor can turn attention to the issue of tactical asset allocation. Here again things are not as simple as they would appear on the surface. Tactical asset allocation is not a single, clearly defined strategy. There are many variations and nuances involved in building a tactical allocation process.

Attention might first be paid to the whole puzzle of semantics. One of the problems in reviewing the concepts of asset allocation is that the same terms are often used for different concepts. The term "dynamic asset allocation" has been used to refer to some of the dynamic strategies noted above, as well as to tactical asset allocation. The term "strategic asset allocation" has been used to refer to the long-term policy decision and to intermediate-term efforts to strategically position the portfolio to benefit from major market moves, as well as to aggressive tactical strategies. Even the words "normal asset allocation" convey a stability which is not consistent with the real world. As an investor's risk expectations and tolerance for risk change, the normal or policy asset allocation may change. It is critical in exploring asset allocation issues to know what *element* of the asset allocation decision is the subject of discussion, and to know *in what context* the words "asset allocation" are being used.

Tactical asset allocation broadly refers to active strategies which seek to enhance performance by opportunistically shifting the asset mix of a portfolio in response to the changing patterns of reward available in the capital markets. Notably, tactical asset allocation tends to refer to disciplined processes for evaluating prospective rates of return on various asset classes and establishing an asset allocation response intended to capture higher rewards. In the various implementations of tactical asset allocation, there are different investment horizons and different mechanisms for evaluating the asset allocation decision. These also merit a brief review.

Tactical asset allocation can refer to either an intermediate-term or a short-term process. There are tactical processes which seek to measure the relative attractiveness of the major asset classes and which seek to participate in major movements in the stock or bond markets. Other approaches are more short-term in nature, designed to capture short-term movements in the markets. The shared attributes of these tactical asset allocation processes are several:

- They tend to be objective processes, based on analytic tools, such as regression analysis or optimization, rather than relying on subjective judgment.
- They tend to be driven primarily by objective measures of prospective values within an asset class. We *know* the yield on cash, we *know* the yield on maturity to long bonds, and the earning yield on the stock market represents a reasonable and objective proxy for long-term rewards available in stocks. These objective measures of reward lead to an inherently value-oriented process.
- Tactical asset allocation processes tend to buy after a market decline and sell after a market rise. As such, they can tend to be inherently contrarian. By objectively measuring which asset classes are offering the greatest prospective rewards, tactical asset allocation disciplines measure which asset classes are most out of favor. In so doing, they steer investments into unloved asset classes. These assets are priced to reflect the fact that they are out of favor and the corresponding fact that investors demand a premium reward for an out-of-favor investment. *Therein lies the effectiveness of tactical asset allocation disciplines.*

The types of tactical asset allocation disciplines cover a wide spectrum. Some are simple, objective comparisons of available rates of return. Others seek to enhance the timeliness of these value-driven decisions by incorporating macro-economic measures, sentiment measures, volatility measures and even technical measures. In essence, the users of these more elaborate approaches would argue that, just as an undervalued stock can get more undervalued, so too an undervalued asset class can grow more undervalued. The investor who buys an asset as soon as it becomes undervalued does less well than the investor who buys that same asset class shortly before it finally rebounds.

THE ASSET ALLOCATION DECISIONS

In conclusion, we should reiterate that there is not one asset allocation decision, but many. In this book, we seek to assemble some of the best thinking in the investment world today on the subject of asset allocation. To be sure, there are many fine practitioners and theoreticians whose ideas do not appear in this volume. Regrettably, it is not possible to assemble all of the worthy asset allocation thinking in a single volume. Nonetheless, we believe we have selected some of the ideas and some of the thinkers who have been important, creative contributors to the whole field of asset allocation.

CHAPTER 2

Overview of the Total Asset Allocation Problem*

PETER L. BERNSTEIN
PRESIDENT
PETER L. BERNSTEIN, INC.
AND EDITOR
THE JOURNAL OF PORTFOLIO MANAGEMENT

Before the process of asset allocation begins—in fact, even before the definition of the related liability structure begins—investors must answer four questions. The answers to these questions are not obvious to any of us. In fact, we do not ask these questions of ourselves frequently enough. Some of us never ask them. Nevertheless, answers to these questions are essential if asset allocation is going to deliver the results expected, instead of just random surprises.

The four questions are:

1. Who is the owner of the assets and why does it matter? The owner of the assets determines the character of the liabilities that the assets are supposed to fund.
2. What are the assets and why does it matter? The conventional breakdown into asset classes hides a veritable tangle of hybrid securities and disparate parts whose reality is different from their appearance and whose covariances are fluid or obscure.

---

*This chapter is adapted from a paper that appeared in the *Financial Analysts Journal*, March-April, 1987.

3. Who are the managers and why does it matter? How closely are the owners of the assets with multimanager structures really controlling the risks of the total portfolio?
4. Is diversification itself dead and why does it matter? Portfolio insurance and other forms of dynamic hedging strategies are doing strange things to the types of orthodox diversification techniques that usually come under the heading of asset allocation.

WHO IS THE OWNER OF THE ASSETS?

Portfolio managers tend to become so fascinated with assets that they forget that assets have no reason for being except to fund liabilities. If we never had any liabilities, we would have no need for assets. As soon as we assume any kind of obligation, however, the search for appropriate assets to fund that obligation begins.

The manner in which we deploy the assets under management—the urgency for high rates of return, the consequences of loss, the time horizon that is acceptable—will therefore depend totally on the owner of those assets. Different owners have different liability structures, which means that the urgency for high rates of return, the consequences of loss, and the acceptable time horizon will clearly vary from one owner to another.

The proverbial widow has to worry about losses, because the time horizon for recouping is short; high returns have to be a secondary consideration. A young executive on the make has the luxury of plenty of time and opportunity to recoup losses and can therefore invest aggressively. Pension funds have long time horizons but the sponsor of a fund may worry about having to make good on losses or about covariances between asset returns and the fund's liabilities, so that some blend of these three considerations is most likely.

In many cases, the ownership of the assets is obscure rather than simple. An elderly widow may think one way, but her hungry heirs may encourage her to follow aggressive investment policies to suit their own time horizon and urgencies for high returns. The conflicts of interest between the income beneficiaries of a trust and the remaindermen are all too familiar. A young executive may have more than just a few immediate liabilities with impatient creditors acting like proxy owners of his assets.

The corporate pension fund presents even more complex questions of ownership. The debate over who owns the fund's assets continues without clear resolution, but the appropriate allocation of assets will also lack definition until we have resolved the debate over ownership.

Are the employees of the corporation the owners of the assets? Or are they simply creditors?

The employees have the senior claim on the assets. They have lent their deferred wages to the corporation and have a further contractual claim on future compensation. The assets of the pension fund are collateral to secure these claims.

Followed to its logical conclusion, this view reveals the employees as the ultimate owners of the assets in the pension fund. The sole objective of the employees is to be as certain as possible that their claims are secure. Like our proverbial widow, they will be willing to minimize return in exchange for the comfortable feeling that the plan is, first and foremost, minimizing risk.

I would argue that this view holds even through the new reality that pension funds own an increasing share of corporate sponsors themselves. This puts the employees in an odd conflict of interest with themselves, but their dominant interest must continue to be the safety rather than the rate of return of the pension fund.

What about the stockholders? The stockholders own the residual interest in the pension fund, even if we can debate their ownership in the portion of the fund required to collateralize the pension obligations. As a result of the bull market of the 1980s in stocks and bonds, many of those residual interests have become substantial interests relative to the assets of the corporation as a whole.

The goal of the stockholders is to minimize pension expense and to maximize their residual interest in the fund—perhaps with a view to subsequent recapture for the corporation as a whole. This approach is the only one consistent with the stockholders' objective of maximizing the long-run value of the corporation.

In the extreme, furthermore, the stockholders have the right to put the liabilities of the pension fund to the Pension Benefit Guaranty Corporation. This means that the stockholders are perfectly willing to brush off the consequences of loss and to accept higher risks than the employees would accept: the stockholders, rather than the beneficiaries of the fund, will enjoy the fruits of the higher returns that the greater risks are expected to provide.

But there is a third guest at the party—management. The pension officer, the chief financial officer, the chief executive officer, and often the board of directors also have a stake in the performance of the fund. In addition, these are the people—not the employees or the stockholders—who make the hands-on decisions that determine the risk/reward tradeoffs in the pension fund.

These people are employees and often stockholders as well, but the pension officer and the CFO have a separate role to play. They know that senior management looks to the performance of the pension fund as a measure of their performance for the corporation. The future career of the pension officer and the CFO brightens or dims as, calendar quarter by calendar quarter, the fund results roll in. Their time horizon is much shorter than the time horizon of the employees or the stockholders.

Management likes good results, of course. But management also wants results that are *smooth*. Surprises are jarring and raise questions that may be difficult to answer. Smooth results lead to easy and confident extrapolation. This means that high returns are nice for management but volatility is anathema. Such views lead to partiality toward portfolio insurance or broad diversification and other forms of bet-hedging, even at the expense of maximizing returns.

Who are the owners of the pension fund? How can we decide which asset allocation strategy to select until we know the answer?

WHAT ARE THE ASSETS?

Even if we think we know how to allocate the assets appropriately, how much do we know about the essential nature of what we are allocating? The conventional breakdown of stocks, bonds and paper, now frequently expanded to include non-US securities, real estate and venture capital, is a dangerous oversimplification of reality.

The conventional taxonomy of assets is intrinsically dirty. Most assets are hybrids. As we look deeper, we find that what we call equities and bonds and short-term paper are in fact complex combinations of options—puts and calls—and zero-coupon riskless bonds. These three elements are the atoms from which we form the enormous variety of molecules to which we assign familiar names, but whose performance is going to reflect their essential natures.

For example, we can replicate the performance of put options simply by combining risky assets and risk-free assets in a systematic manner.

A conventional asset class breakdown would disguise our ownership of a synthetic put. We can also go the other way. By combining risky assets with the right combination of puts and calls, the portfolio will mimic the performance of a risk-free asset, but our asset allocation breakdown would show no risk-free asset in the portfolio.

Consider a portfolio that consists only of equities. What do the stockholders really own? They share a claim on the assets with the creditors. The creditors have the prior claim. Therefore, the stockholders do not really own the assets. They own a put that they have purchased from the creditors—an option that gives the stockholders the right to walk away from their debts and leave the creditors holding the bag. The price that the stockholders pay for this option depends on the same variables that determine the price of any option—the strike price, the time to expiration, and the volatility of the underlying assets.

Looked at from the other side, the creditors own a call on the residual assets. Therefore, corporate bonds are in reality a riskless security plus this call option or subject to the stockholders' exercise of their put option. This means that corporate bonds, even AAA bonds, have a significant equity element and will respond to changes in equity expectations as well as to changes in interest rates. It is no wonder, then, that stock index futures will often hedge bond portfolios more efficiently than Treasury bond futures can hedge them.

The difficulty with asset allocation classification procedures reaches beyond the complexities of asset structure. Conventional breakdowns are incomplete, because they hide the covariances among asset returns that are so essential to the whole process of portfolio formation. Common factor themes run right across all asset classes—inflation, fear/greed, the role of the United States in the world, and oil prices are just a few examples of such common factors.

I pointed out above that corporate bonds are a combination of a risk-free asset and equity features. The point works in reverse. Most stocks have at least some degree of interest sensitivity, and many stocks have a high degree of interest sensitivity.

The essential nature of an equity is best seen when you peel it like an onion. The outer layer is the dominating influence of the stock market itself, so that each individual stock is a microcosm of an index fund. Then comes each stock's own specific responses, as well as a variety of covariances with subgroups of stocks or common economic factors. As interest rates are among the most powerful common factors that influence stock returns, each individual stock is not only a microcosm of a stock index fund, but also a microcosm of a bond index fund!

Unfortunately, the opposite is true. We have just considered asset classes that share covariances with other asset classes. Some so-called asset classes, however, have such low covariance among their component parts that they do not deserve the name of an asset class.

We talk about international investing as though putting assets outside the United States meant depositing them in some kind of identifiable basket of stocks. A recent Salomon Brothers study of international investing shows that this is a serious misconception.[1] Independent movements among 28 national markets are more the rule than the exception. More than 60 out of 784 intermarket correlations are negative and most are less than $+0.10$. The U.S. correlations with the other 27 countries range all the way from -0.03 (Thailand) to 0.64 (Canada).

We also treat real estate as a homogeneous asset class, and with as little justification. A paper by Grissom, Kuhle, and Walther shows significant differences in both risk and return among office buildings, residential real estate, shopping centers and industrial properties.[2] The same paper and a paper by Froland, Grolow, and Sampson[3] demonstrates that the real estate markets in different parts of the country also have low covariances with one another.

Even within the stock market itself, the pieces are uncomfortably disparate. According to Ibbotson Associates,[4] small stock returns correlate negatively with bond returns and positively with inflation. Large capitalization stocks do the opposite. Are "stocks" a hedge against inflation? Small stocks had an annual standard deviation of 36.0% from 1926 through 1985, while large stocks show only 21.2%. How risky are "stocks"?

Yes, the conventional taxonomy of assets is intrinsically dirty.

[1]*International Equity Analysis*, Salomon Brothers Inc, New York, June 1987.

[2]Terry V. Grissom, James L. Kuhle, and Carl H. Walter, "Diversification Works in Real Estate, Too," *The Journal of Portfolio Management*, Winter 1987, pp. 66–71.

[3]Charles Froland, Robert Grolow, and Richard Sampson, "The Market Risk of Real Estate," *The Journal of Portfolio Management*, Spring 1986, pp. 12–19.

[4]*Stocks, Bonds, Bills, and Inflation: 1986 Yearbook*, Ibbotson Associates, Chicago, 1986, p. 32.

WHO ARE THE MANAGERS?

By this question, I mean: Who is really managing the show?

The easy answer is that the owner of the assets or the owners's designated agent—say, the pension officer—is managing the show. These people do have the *responsibility,* but do they in reality have the authority? Or is the authority so dissipated among the individual portfolio management organizations that *no one* is managing the show? This arrangement seems to be most frequently the case.

What are all these people supposed to be doing? The goal of portfolio management is to select and arrange assets that will assure the payment of all explicit and implicit liabilities as they come due. Only minor modifications are needed to make this simple statement fit all possible kinds of investors. To the extent that investors ignore this definition and pursue different goals, those investors are probably taking either more risk than they have to take or less risk than they should take.[5]

Liabilities, like assets, have variable values; even nominally fixed assets and liabilities have variable real values. Therefore, the process of minimizing risk is the process of matching the variability of the assets to the variability of the liabilities. Risk begins where mismatch begins.

How closely can the owner of the assets, or the owner's agent, control for mismatch in an environment where the number of separate portfolio managers significantly exceeds one? Can there be any control at all, when each management organization is pursuing its own duration and other risk control strategies in accordance with its own assigned asset class, its own investment style, its own market expectations and its overwhelming drive to provide higher returns than its peers provide? If everybody landed on the appropriate setting of the risk dial, the coincidence would be nothing short of amazing.

For example, let us assume that stocks are relatively insensitive to interest rates at some moment in time. Does the asset owner then make certain that the fixed-income managers hold a preponderance of long-term bonds, even against the better judgment of those managers, so as to offset the lack of exposure to interest rate variability in the stock

---

[5]For an emphatic and systematic defense of this view of the goals of portfolio management and the meaning of risk, see Robert H. Jeffrey, "A New Paradigm for Portfolio Risk," *The Journal of Portfolio Management,* Fall 1984, pp. 33–40.

portfolio? Or, conversely, if the equity portfolio managers have composed a portfolio that has high interest sensitivity, will the total allocation to fixed-income or the duration of the fixed-income share of the total portfolio reflect that fact?

The essence of prudent portfolio management is to hedge bets—don't put all the eggs in one basket, and seek out asset groups with negative covariances. We do this with the full expectation that some baskets will provide better returns than others. Indeed, we explicitly select some assets to underperform under most likely conditions and to outperform only when our primary bets go haywire. In other words, we pray and hope that the assets that hedge our primary bets will underperform, because we will have made the wrong primary bet if the hedging asset does better.

How can the owners of the assets preserve this crucial hedging structure, when they parcel out the assets to different managers, all of whom justify their very existence by aiming to outperform their competitors? Can the owners tell Manager A or Manager B to underperform—that is, to posture their share of the portfolio so that it will perform well only under low-probability outcomes? Is there a manager who would accept an account under those constraints?

In recent years, for example, both bonds and stocks have been effective hedges against disinflation. This means that you needed only one of these two assets, not both. But if both expectations and liability structures ordained a heavy overweight in common stocks for your portfolio, then how would you have protected against an outbreak of inflation? An instruction to the fixed-income managers to hold cnly short-term paper would do the trick. How do you tell your fixed-income manager to hang in at the short end at a time when bond returns are going through the roof?

Who are the managers? The lines of authority in the management structure are more crooked than most people recognize.

IS DIVERSIFICATION DEAD?

The question perhaps overstates the issue, but let us consider the full implications for asset allocation of substituting portfolio insurance for diversification. The transformation is profound.

We employ diversification as the cornerstone of asset allocation, as I mentioned above, for reasons of prudence. We want to avoid putting all our eggs in one basket and tend to shun different baskets with identical characteristics. Put another way, diversification is an explicit sacrifice of return maximization to assure survival if something goes wrong with our primary bets.

Portfolio insurance, at first glance, appears to be a logical substitute for diversification. The goal of portfolio insurance is also to sacrifice some upside potential in order to assure survival.

Two critical differences separate these two risk-reducing strategies, however.

First, portfolio insurance sets a minimum amount below which the insured assets or asset/liability surplus will not fall. Diversification merely promises to reduce downside risks, not to eliminate them. That is, portfolio insurance explicitly defines the risky and the riskless asset; diversification is less firm on the matter of definition, assuming simply that not all of the assets will do badly at the same time.

Second, portfolio insurance is an active strategy—or a dynamic strategy, to use the popular buzzword—while diversification is passive. In theory, insured portfolios should vary their mix between the risky and the riskless asset with every market movement, no matter how small; in practice the activity does tend to be high. Diversified portfolios, on the other hand, are much more inclined to be buy-and-hold.

As a result of these two distinctions, the underlying assumptions of the strategies are fundamentally different. The consequences for both the portfolio and the markets are also fundamentally different.

Diversification is an explicit recognition of uncertainty and makes no definite judgments about how investors are going to behave in the future. Diversification is therefore a probability-driven strategy.

Portfolio insurance, on the other hand, embodies a clear statement about the intentions of other investors. The owners of insured portfolios fully expect uninsured investors to oblige by holding the cash reserves of the insured investors until needed and then by providing the insured investors with those cash reserves as called upon to do so. The uninsured investors are also expected to provide the insured investors with the risky asset on demand.

For portfolio insurance to provide what it is purported to provide, the probabilities must be 100% that uninsured investors will play their proper role without hesitation. Portfolio insurance is therefore a certainty-driven strategy.

The consequences of these two strategies for market volatility are clear enough and too familiar to warrant repetition here. Nevertheless, in light of the distinctions that I have set forth, these consequences appear even more significant.

The more modest pretensions of diversification make it likely that diversification as a means of reducing risk will never lose its luster. As long as there are assets that covary negatively, or only slightly positively, with other assets, diversification will make sense. Asset allocation will then have to deal with a broad menu of assets.

Portfolio insurance concentrates on only two assets, carefully predetermined. To the extent that its assumptions about the behavior of uninsured investors turn out to be less than 100% correct, however, portfolio insurance can end up only chasing its own tail. The refusal of uninsured investors to play their appointed role will increase the volatility of prices of risky assets and drive insured portfolios to sell or buy even more aggressively than they would have traded in the first place.

OVERVIEW OR UNDERVIEW?

Before the investor gets down to the nitty-gritty of asset allocation, a myriad of issues must be determined. Who owns the assets to be allocated and how does that owner want to structure the risk exposure? What are the assets intrinsically as opposed to how they are labeled? Who will manage the show and make certain that risks are hedged as they are supposed to be hedged? Are the underlying assumptions of diversification or portfolio insurance consistent with all of the above?

In short, the overview of asset allocation must begin with an underview—a thorough examination of the very guts of the matter in terms of ownership, the intrinsic nature of the assets themselves, risk control mechanisms, and basic assumptions about market behavior. Only after settling these issues can the investor proceed to consider how to allocate the assets.

SECTION ONE

Policy Asset Mix

CHAPTER 3

Defining and Managing Pension Fund Risk*

ROBERT D. ARNOTT
PRESIDENT & CHIEF INVESTMENT OFFICER
FIRST QUADRANT

PETER L. BERNSTEIN
PRESIDENT
PETER L. BERNSTEIN INC.
AND EDITOR
THE JOURNAL OF PORTFOLIO MANAGEMENT

The way we manage risks is ultimately going to depend on how we define those risks. This is often a more complicated task than it appears to be at first glance. Risk is such a many-headed monster that selecting the right head to focus on can be a major challenge.

Although the analysis that we offer here relates specifically to pension fund risk, the development of our argument and the issues that we raise lend themselves to broad generalizations. The precise definition of the risks we face is critically important, and risk management must be exquisitely sensitive to that definition.

Corporate executives have traditionally defined pension fund risk in

*This chapter is an adaptation and expansion of Robert D. Arnott and Peter L. Bernstein, "The Right Way to Manage Your Pension Fund," *Harvard Business Review,* January/February 1988. Copyright 1988 by the President and Fellows of Harvard University.

terms of the trade-off between risk and return on the *assets* accumulated to fund pension obligations. Although there has been a slowly growing recognition that this focus on asset risk was much too narrowly defined, there has also been strong resistance to breaking deep-seated habits.

Assets do not exist in a vacuum, seeking return and avoiding risk for their own sakes. This may seem obvious when stated in so many words, but it has taken the arrival of Financial Accounting Standards Board Statement 87 (FASB 87) to bring the variability of pension fund *liabilities* to front and center. FASB 87 focuses on the pension fund *surplus*—the difference between the assets and the liabilities. This focus has been reinforced by the Omnibus Budget Reconciliation Act (OBRA) of 1987. OBRA adds legal weight to the FASB accounting guidelines, by mandating pension contribution rates and Pension Benefit Guaranty Corporation (PBGC) insurance premiums which are sensitive to the pension funding ratio. The result is a belated awakening to the simple idea that the assets need to have some systematic relationship to the character of the liabilities that they fund.

Nevertheless, the implications of new notions are frequently subtle, and the response of pension fund strategies to FASB 87 and to OBRA is no exception. At most corporations, the definition of pension fund risk has shifted, but remains flawed because it remains oversimplified. This means that the restructuring of those funds may still be inappropriate in terms of the "true" risks of the pension plan. The oversimplification arises from paying too much attention to the interest sensitivity of the pension surplus, a result of FASB 87's emphasis on defining the surplus in terms of the interest sensitivity of the fund's actuarial liabilities.

These considerations are highly significant in their impact on corporate profitability and financial health. Pension fund assets have accumulated to a point where they tend to loom large relative to the total pool of assets in the corporation. Their variability and their rate of return have a meaningful influence on the company's bottom line; under FASB 87, their relationship to the liabilities of the pension fund may become visible on the published balance sheet as well.

Senior management should seek to achieve two objectives. First, the pension fund deserves as much attention as any significant operating division. Second, senior management must begin to analyze pension fund decisions in the context of potential long-term returns *measured against the true impact on corporate risk.*

THE CONVENTIONAL VIEW OF PENSION FUND RISK

As pension funds began to assume importance among corporate assets—say, over the past quarter century—pension fund management focused on the trade-off between the expected returns on their investments and the volatility of those returns. The idea was to maximize return consistent with some control over the magnitude of year-to-year, and sometimes even quarter-to-quarter, variations in the rate of return.

Volatility was of concern for three reasons:

1. First, all other things being equal, volatility tends to reduce returns over the long run. To put it simply, if you lose 50%, you have to gain 100% to break even.
2. Second, even if you believe that the assets you select can return enough to overcome the drag imposed by variability, the variability by its very nature creates uncertainty as to what the assets will be worth when liabilities come due.
3. Finally, corporate managements tend to like smooth numbers. Irregular numbers raise questions that most people would be just as happy to avoid.

The traditional approach, therefore, was to seek the highest possible return at an acceptable level of volatility or, alternatively, to minimize volatility at any given level of expected return. This view of risk and reward was described in an array such as that shown in Exhibit 1, which plots expected asset returns on the vertical axis and variability of asset returns on the horizontal axis. The array runs from cash at the low end to stocks at the high end.

Putting all your eggs in one basket is never optimal. By employing the magic of diversification to reduce variability, you can obtain more expected return per unit of risk or reduce the risk per unit of expected return by combining assets instead of selecting just one. That process results in the curve known in investment parlance as the "efficient frontier." This curve shows the best return that can be achieved through diversification at any given level of risk.

The popularity of this approach to pension fund management rested on its simplicity, its familiarity and its convenience. It became a total expression of the culture of the pension fund world in the 1970s. The evaluation of assets based on market levels fits the intuitive idea of

EXHIBIT 1:
RISK AND REWARD—THE TRADITIONAL PERSPECTIVE

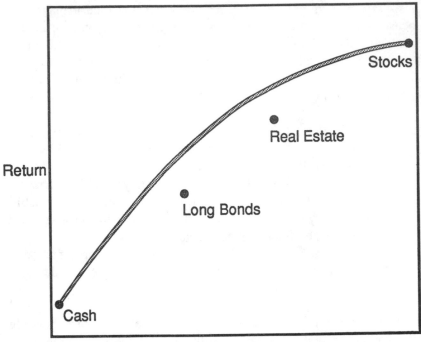

what investing a pension fund is all about. As Exhibit 2 suggests, other important variables—future contributions to the fund, estimated future wage growth and the discount rate used to calculate net present values were all determined by the actuary, were independent of movements in the capital markets and were changed infrequently.

This traditional view of pension risk suggests that pension plans with low tolerance for risk will tend to locate themselves toward the left-hand side of the frontier, with more in bonds and cash and less in stocks. Those with a greater willingness to bear risk in the search for higher returns will locate themselves toward the right, with heavier concentrations in the riskier assets like stocks and real estate.

As is evident in Exhibit 3, the slope of the efficient frontier is relatively flat in the zones where most funds position themselves. This feature of the frontier would lead us to conclude that most funds are

EXHIBIT 2:
RISK AND REWARD—TRANSITION TO FASB–87

	Traditional	*FASN–87*

Assets	Variable:
	   Market-Driven
		Variable:
		   Market-Driven

Asset Growth	Fixed*	Fixed*
NPV Liability Components		
Wage Growth	Fixed*	Fixed*
Discount Rate	Fixed*	Variable: Market-Driven

*Set by actuary.

EXHIBIT 3:
RISK AND REWARD: THE TRADITIONAL PERSPECTIVE—
OBSERVED RISK TOLERANCE

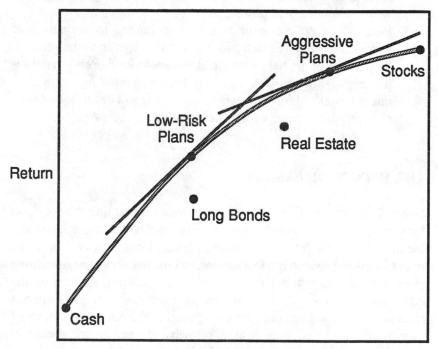

highly tolerant of risk, because a curve with only a slight upward slope means that these funds will accept a large increase in risk for a modest increment in expected return.

This view of pension risk and reward is unrealistic for three reasons:

1. First, corporate pension fund sponsors tend to be prudent, careful investors, with risk tolerances that cover a wide range from conservative to moderately aggressive. They take their fiduciary responsibility seriously. Relatively few have risk tolerances as high as Exhibit 3 suggests.
2. Furthermore, this traditional perspective is silent on the subject of liabilities—it tells management nothing about where they should position themselves on the frontier. It provides information only on what the shape of the frontier is like. Corporations with a mature workforce or with unique business risks should hardly want to be on the same point of the frontier or at the same level of risk tolerance as corporations with a young workforce or with stable earnings power.
3. Finally, the definition of risk here is limited to variability of expected returns on assets, with no attention given to the variability patterns of the liabilities the assets are to fund. Pension liabilities are highly sensitive to many factors, including changes in interest rates, which suggests rather a different definition of pension risk from what we see here.

THE IMPACT OF FASB 87

FASB 87 brings the liabilities into the picture by putting the focus on the *surplus* of the pension fund—the difference between the assets and the liabilities. This introduces an extra level of complexity. The value of the assets is easy enough to measure, but the liabilities are something else again. As shown in Exhibit 2, the major change induced by the accounting standard has been to mandate the use of market interest rates on long-term bonds for the calculation of the net present value of those liabilities. Projections of asset growth and wage growth remain in the domain of the actuary. (See Exhibit 4.)

EXHIBIT 4:
WHAT ARE FASB 87 AND THE OBRA?

FASB 87 is the recent ruling by the Financial Accounting Standards Board relating to pension accounting. For many corporations, FASB ruling #87 will have more impact on corporate earnings than any other ruling to date. FASB 87 mandates that:

- For both reported earnings and balance sheet calculations, pension accounting for defined benefit plans must estimate liability by applying a *market* interest rate to the expected obligations served by the pension plan, in order to determine the net present value of those obligations. This means that as market interest rates move, so too does the liability. If market rates rise, the net present value of future obligations declines, and vice versa.
- For those defined benefit plans with an underfunded pension plan (i.e., the net present value of the liability exceeds the assets in the plan), the liability side of the balance sheet must include this unfunded pension liability.
- *Changes* in the surplus for the pension plan, if larger than 10% of plan assets or liabilities, must be reflected in the *earnings* statement in the form of operating earnings. This takes the form of an allowance for changes in pension contributions, amortizd to compensate for the change in pension surplus. Whether or not the corporation chooses to actually change their pension contribution rate, FASB 87 requires the corporation to treat reported earnings as if contributions are adjusted to reflect a change in the pension surplus.

The Omnibus Budget Reconciliation Act of 1987 (OBRA) is a recent legislative initiative which reinforces the FASB 87 interpretation of liabilities. OBRA mandates that:

- Pension contributions for an underfunded pension plan (with an ABO funding ratio below 100%) must accelerate contributions to the pension plan. The underfunded liability must be amortized over a period of just five years.
- A pension sponsor with an ABO funding ratio in excess of 150% must cease pension contributions.
- Underfunded pension plans must pay a significantly increased insurance premium to the Pension Benefit Guarantee Corporation (PBGC). Because of a conservative definition of the discount rate used to calculate liabilities, this applies to pension plans with a funding ratio below approximately 125%.

EXHIBIT 4: (continued)
WHAT ARE FASB 87 AND THE OBRA?

These two sets of rulings may have a profound effect in shortening the investment horizon of the corporate pension sponsor. For the pension fund that slides from marginal funding into underfunded territory, many ills are visited upon the corporation: pension expense rises, thereby reducing reported corporate earnings; contributions to the pension plan must sharply accelerate; PBGC insurance premiums rise rapidly; and, last but not least, a new liability appears on the balance sheet. The stipulation that contributions must cease for well-funded plans will also have a potentially serious effect. Without contributions, the well-funded pension plans will gradually be forced down to ABO funding ratios which will result in some vulnerability to the adverse consequences detailed above. The net result may be a gradual but long-term shift in the direction of more conservative pension management policies in order to prevent the pension plan from adversely affecting corporate management or earnings. If this shift to conservatism takes place, it would be at the cost of reducing long-term rates of return for pension management and increasing the long-term cost of pension plans.

DEFINED BENEFIT VERSUS DEFINED CONTRIBUTION

Clearly, neither ruling applies to defined *contribution* plans which make up some 30% of all pension assets. If a corporation offers a defined contribution plan to their employees, there is no pension surplus or unfunded liability. A defined contribution plan involves a contractual commitment to contribute a certain amount of money to a pension plan, with no guarantee as to how much money will be in the plan at retirement and no guarantee as to the annual retirement benefit that the employee will receive. A defined *benefit* plan does the opposite. While it makes no guarantee as to the amount of contribution which the corporation will make, it does guarantee a defined annual retirement benefit to the employee.

In a defined contribution plan, the employee bears all market risk and captures all of the reward in the event of strong markets. In a defined benefit plan, the corporation bears the market risk: if the performance is disappointing, the corporation must suffer the penalty of increased pension contribution costs, hence increased labor costs. If results are strong, the corporation reaps the benefit in the form of reduced pension contributions, hence reduced labor costs. These new regulations have an important impact on the balance sheet and earnings statement for any company which has a defined benefit pension plan.

The rationale for the insistence on market-determined discount rates is simple enough. Actuarial valuations tend to lag reality and aim, like many other features of corporate bookkeeping, at smooth changes. The capital markets are anything but smooth, but their view of the appropriate discount rate is immediate and inescapable. In addition, the markets are undoubtedly more accurate than the view, no matter how judicious, of a single individual or organization aiming to be conservative, avoiding frequent changes and shunning disruptive numbers.

The consequence of this redefinition of risk is profound. If the objective is to maximize the excess of assets over liabilities, while seeking to minimize the *variability* of that excess, then we have to ask which assets best match the variability pattern of the liabilities. As FASB 87 treats the liabilities as fixed obligations, discounted at a market interest rate, this is equivalent to asking, "Which assets act most like long-term bonds?" The answer is obvious. As we shall see shortly, the answer is perhaps too obvious.

The immediate implication of FASB 87 is that long-term bonds are the lowest risk asset, replacing cash in that enviable spot. Therefore, we have to redraw our chart showing the trade-off between risk and expected return. The result appears in Exhibit 5. The expected rates of return are the same, but the riskiness of the assets has changed.

In the context of the FASB 87 definition of surplus valuation, the chart tells us that any asset with variable income or whose principal value does not move closely with the bond market will be a risky asset. At the extreme, cash becomes anathema, with its low expected return and high variability of income; its much-vaunted stability of principal does no good in hedging liabilities whose principal value can vary widely over time.

The clear implication of this shift in viewpoint is that bonds provide the risk-minimizing choice for pension funds, at an attractive long-term rate of return. Other assets can still make good sense, but at a considerable increase in risk. In fact, the simplicity of the analysis presented here is so attractive that one may be sorely tempted to pronounce the problem of pension fund investment solved and to turn one's attention to more pressing matters.

This is precisely the wrong conclusion to reach. FASB 87 suggests an unduly simplistic view of pension risk, which is only one step in the right direction. Compelling reasons to favor other assets exist for many funds, although not for all.

EXHIBIT 5:
RISK AND REWARD: THE FASB–87 PERSPECTIVE—
OBSERVED RISK TOLERANCE

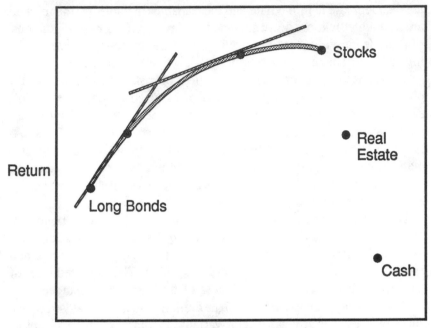

Variability of Fund Surplus
(assets minus present value of liabilities)

The search, and the justification for, an appropriate framework for pension management depend upon the manner in which we define pension fund risk. If pension fund risk is related solely to the variability in the discount rate used to calculate net present values, then bonds are the asset of choice. Any alternative *must* be justified only on the basis of a substantial return enhancement. When we widen the definition of risk, on the other hand, assets with variable rather than fixed-income streams can become the low-risk assets.

The critical question then becomes how to determine whether discount rate variability should be the dominant consideration in the definition of pension fund risk.

ANALYZING THE CHARACTERISTICS OF THE LIABILITIES

The attraction of bonds is greatest where the interest sensitivity of the liabilities is highest. Or, put a little differently, the attraction of bonds is greatest where the dollar amount of the liabilities, like the dollar amount of the bond coupon payments, is fixed. Under those circumstances, the only factor influencing the present value—and the ultimate obligation—of the liabilities is the relevant rate of interest.

The obligation to cover pensions for retirees meets this criterion most precisely. This is an amount that the actuaries can estimate with great accuracy. Unless the corporation assumes an obligation to protect its retirees from inflation, the retiree liability is as close to a fixed and predetermined sum as can be found in the universe of pension liabilities.

This is why the dedicated bond portfolio has attracted such a large following in recent years. Here was an opportunity to create an exact match between assets and liabilities. The primary attraction was the elimination of risk, made possible by the use of immunization and other forms of cash-matching techniques to make a perfect asset/liability match.

By "elimination of risk," we do not refer to return variability as such, but rather to the risk of having insufficient assets to meet the obligation as it comes due. This is, indeed, the only rational definition of risk; everything else is a variation on that theme. With interest rates so high in the late 1970s and the early 1980s, the dedication of income-matched bond portfolios to meet the obligations for retired lives (and the use of annuities to permit plan termination), enabled corporate management to free up pension assets for other uses.

As it happens, the definition of the Accumulated Benefit Obligation (ABO) is remarkably similar to this retiree liability. FASB 87 defines this ABO liability as the amount to be paid to retirees and present employees assuming immediate termination of the pension plan. Essentially, this is the same as defining the size of an annuity to be purchased for these employees at retirement, with the size of the annuity to be determined on the basis of today's wages and today's "years of service."

This definition of the liability, as with the liability for retirees alone, creates a fixed nominal total pension liability. The present value of the liability so defined is the Accumulated Benefit Obligation. This present value of liabilities is deducted from the value of the pension assets to determine the ABO pension surplus.

Although an important improvement over the simplistic actuarial discount rate structures of the past, this model is also unrealistic once we look beyond the Accumulated Benefit Obligation. Indeed, to some extent, it is even unrealistic within the confines of that obligation as defined under FASB 87. Three problems intervene:

1. The duration of the bond portfolio may not be as long as the duration of the liabilities. That is, the flow of coupon payments and ultimately the return of principal may arrive sooner than the time needed to fully pay off the liabilities of the ABO, which may stretch far into the future. If that incoming cash cannot be reinvested at the same or a higher rate of interest than the rate paid on the original investment, the bond portfolio will fail to cover these obligations as they come due. This risk is known as reinvestment risk.

2. Many corporations assume the responsibility of providing their retirees with at least partial protection against inflationary inroads into the purchasing power of their pensions. A pension fund invested totally in long-term bonds will clearly not address this *implicit* component of the liability.

3. Finally, and most important, the ABO contains the unrealistic assumption of immediate pension plan termination. Growth in wages and assets between the present date and retirement are ignored, and only the current years of service, rather than the years of service at retirement, are reflected in the ABO. To make matters even more unrealistic, the ABO also assumes that no new workers enter the workforce between now and the retirement of the present workforce. Implicitly, FASB 87 assumes that all of these additional obligations are addressed through future expense provisions.

THE IMPLICATIONS OF THE PROJECTED BENEFIT OBLIGATION

Corporate managements obviously realize that their pension liability goes well beyond the ABO. Active employees are going to earn higher wages in the future, which may grow faster or slower than the actuarial assumption, and will typically receive their pensions based on final pay. Asset growth also may be greater or less than the rate assumed by the actuary. Estimates of these uncertain but critical magnitudes must be added to the ABO to derive the true total pension liability, which is known as the Projected Benefit Obligation (PBO).

Many different factors will influence the actual size of the PBO. The dominant factors on wage growth will be inflation, productivity change and the fortunes of the company in question.

Over the long run, wages tend to keep pace with changes in the cost of living, even if the match is inexact. Much of the benefit of productivity improvement has been shared between workers and stockholders, with customers receiving an additional portion in the form of lower or less rapidly increasing prices. Even with high inflation and high productivity growth, an unprofitable company will be unable to keep compensation in pace with these forces; but a highly profitable company may treat its employees even better than inflation and productivity alone would warrant.

From this viewpoint, a 100% long-term bond portfolio may not be the risk-minimizing asset for hedging against the possibility of ending up with insufficient money to fund the true pension obligations. We now must seek assets, some with fixed-income returns, but many with variable-income returns, with the variability approximating as closely as possible the variability of inflation and productivity change. In addition, we should seek assets that diversify the inherent risks of the company in question, so that the company can pay its pensioners even if it falls on ill-fortune before or during their retirement.

Exhibit 6 provides some insight into how the income flows of stocks, bonds and cash have moved in relation to wage rates over the past thirty-odd years. The individual sections of the figure trace the path of hourly nominal compensation in the nonfarm business sector and the income flow from dividends, bond interest and Treasury bills.

The section on dividend income assumes simply that the fund bought the Standard & Poor's 500 Stock Composite Index at the beginning of 1954 and held it through to the end of 1986. We can see that dividends failed to keep pace with the growth in hourly compensation, primarily because of the steady shortfall from 1967 to 1976. Nevertheless, dividends have just about tracked the rise in hourly wage rates during the period since 1976, which includes the most virulent of the inflation years.

EXHIBIT 6:
HOW HOURLY COMPENSATION FARED AGAINST DIVIDEND AND
INTEREST INCOME AND TREASURY BILLS: 1954–1986

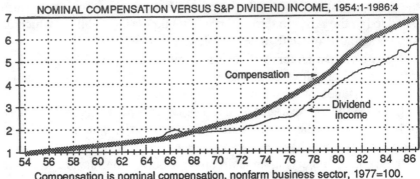

NOMINAL COMPENSATION VERSUS S&P DIVIDEND INCOME, 1954:1-1986:4

Compensation is nominal compensation, nonfarm business sector, 1977=100.
Dividend income is trailing 4-quarter dividends on S&P 500 Composite.
1954:1 = 1 for both series.

NOMINAL COMPENSATION VERSUS LONG-TERM INTEREST INCOME, 1954:1-1986:4

Compensation is nominal compensation, nonfarm business sector, 1977=100.
Interest income is calculated interest on corporate bond portfolio.
1954:1 = 1 for both series.

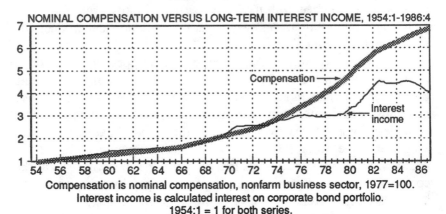

NOMINAL COMPENSATION VERSUS ANNUAL RETURNS ON TREASURY BILLS, 1954:1-1986:4

Compensation is nominal compensation, nonfarm business sector, 1977=100.
Bill returns are year-over-year returns on 90-day Treasury bills.
1954:1 = 1 for both series.

Our plot for long-term bond interest gives bonds the benefit of the doubt, but even so the mismatch between changes in bond income and wages after 1975 is painfully clear. Here we dropped the assumption of just one initial investment in 1954 and assumed that new money came into the pension fund each year and was invested in bonds at the rate of interest prevailing at the time of purchase.[1] The larger the inflow of new corporate contributions relative to the pool of monies already invested in the pension fund, the more closely the flow of interest income will keep up with inflation. But even so, it is evident that bonds are a miserable hedge against the inflation and productivity growth that drive wage increases.

A pension fund with a higher cash flow than we have assumed, or a younger fund started, say, in the early 1970s instead of the early 1950s, would have shown more favorable results. Note, however, that our equity graph assumed that no additional money came in after the fund was started in 1954, but dividends still provided an excellent hedge against wage growth.

The third section of Exhibit 6 also assumes just one investment in 1954, which was continuously rolled over into new Treasury bills every quarter. Here the variability of the income stream is the most visible feature. Nevertheless, the total flow of income from this hypothetical Treasury bill portfolio was the highest of the three shown here, comfortably above the cumulative total of the nominal compensation curve.

Note that Treasury bills represent a much better fit for the incremental PBO than for the ABO. Even though cash equivalents do not fluctuate in value with the net present value of the liabilities, they do provide a very good immunization against inflation. If cash is held for retirement benefits, with income reinvested, it can be expected to grow with inflation and hence with the magnitude of retirement benefits. If the corpus of that investment, rather than the income generated by the Treasury bills, is then distributed to pay retirement benefits, then Treasury bills actually represent a good fit with the incremental PBO. However, this good fit is only from the vantage point of risk. The long-term rates of return for cash equivalents remain low. Thus, for the incremental PBO, cash remains an unattractive asset.

---

[1]The calculations assume that new money contributed each year was equal to 10% of the total asset value at the end of the preceding year, including interest earned in that year. This is a rough approximation of reality. If we had treated the bond simulation like the others, without any adjustment for fresh inflows of cash, the interest income number would never have budged above 1. This is what would have happened with a bond purchase in 1954 and no subsequent purchases at the higher interest rates that developed later.

Although these graphs are meant only to be suggestive, their suggestions are significant. The emphasis on covariance with bond interest, as stipulated in FASB 87, becomes a dangerous oversimplification when the incremental liabilities of the Projected Benefit Obligation, above and beyond the ABO liabilities, are taken into consideration. Protection against the risk that the earnings of the pension fund will fail to cover the Projected Benefit Obligation requires a combination of assets—like equities—whose income flow is somehow related to the pressures of inflation and is also related to productivity change.

HOW TO BALANCE THE ABO AND THE INCREMENTAL PBO IN PENSION FUND RISK

Treasury bills, common stocks, and other variable return assets may do a better job than bonds in hedging the long-term risks inherent in wage growth assumptions, but they have two important disadvantages. First, their income flows are too variable to fund the retirees or the Accumulated Benefit Obligation. Second, they are only partially interest sensitive, and sometimes correlate negatively with changes in long-term interest rates, which means that they add unwanted variability to the pension fund surplus, as defined under FASB 87—a central component of that surplus is the net present value of the liabilities, which are highly sensitive to interest rates.

The task of senior management in determining how best to hedge pension fund risk, therefore, is to weigh as accurately as possible the relative importance of the advantages and disadvantages of each type of asset. In essence, this involves employing fixed-income assets to fund fixed-dollar obligations, where the estimate of the liability has a high degree of certainty, and employing variable-income assets to fund variable-dollar obligations, where the estimate of the liability has a high degree of uncertainty.

The best way to look at this problem is to make separate estimates of the ABO and the PBO and examine the size of the spread between the two, the incremental PBO. The more mature the plan, or the more mature the workforce, the smaller that spread is likely to be. In other words, the pension liability for a mature workforce, being by definition closer to maturity than a young workforce, lends itself more readily to certainty in the estimation process. In many such cases, the ABO can exceed 90% of the total PBO, leading to a relatively well-defined nominal liability. Mature plans, therefore, will have an incentive to favor long-term bonds at the expense of stocks or cash equivalents. Long-term bonds can provide certainty of return to cover the certainty of the liability. In addition, long-term bonds will provide maximum stability to the pension fund surplus within the definitions and reporting requirements of FASB 87.

Conversely, emerging plans, associated with younger or faster growing companies, will have a higher PBO liability relative to the ABO and therefore will have an incentive to hold a more aggressive asset mix, with a stronger relationship with future wage growth. In such a case, equities will tend to dominate.

This preference for equities is likely to hold true for reasons beyond the ability of dividends to keep pace with inflation and to reflect productivity improvements as well. Pension plans that cover young workers will start paying significant sums in pensions only in the far distant future. Reinvestment risk is minimized by matching the horizon of the liabilities. Equities can represent a good fit, because the principal is never repaid and because the cash return is expected to grow larger with the passage of time.

So far so good. Life is not quite this simple, however. We have yet to consider the conflict between the short run and the long run in pension planning, as well as the difference between variability in rates of return—essentially asset price variability—and variability in flows of income in each asset. Return variability and the short-run/long-run conflicts are interrelated.

In the short run, stability in the pension fund surplus is important because of its impact on current profitability and the balance sheet. The framers of FASB 87 knew what they were about in trying to arrive at a better definition of the influence of the pension fund on earnings and financial well-being. In the long run, on the other hand, stability of the surplus is not nearly as important as its size. The corporation would like to have something left over to accommodate reduced contributions during periods of earnings weakness. In essence, the pension plan acts as a tax-deferred savings plan, or an "IRA" for the corporation, right down to the penalty for early withdrawal.

The assets that best assure a surplus over the Projected Benefit Obligation in the long run are the riskiest in the short run, in that they add variability to the pension fund surplus. Stocks, for example, have the clear lead for matching the attributes of the longest-term liabilities, but their short-run returns are highly variable and only weakly correlat-

ed with interest rates. At the other end of the spectrum, cash equivalents tend to have low returns that are frequently correlated negatively
with returns on bonds.

A graphic display of these dilemmas appears in Exhibit 7. Here the
chart relates to the Accumulated Benefit Obligation and repeats the
array shown in Exhibit 5. This is essentially the short-run view of the
matter. The expected rates of return are the same as in the original array
in Exhibit 1. The risks, however, relate primarily to the sensitivity of
asset returns to interest rates, because it is interest rates that determine
the net present values of the liabilities, and we want to stabilize the
relationship between the assets and the net present values of the liabilities—that is, the surplus—in the short run.

EXHIBIT 7:
RISK AND REWARD—THE ABO

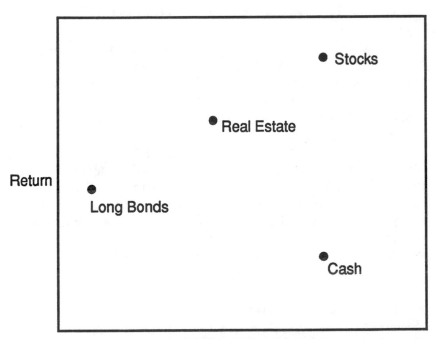

Variability of Fund Surplus
(assets minus present value of liabilities)

Exhibit 8 shows what happens when we introduce the incremental Projected Benefit Obligation into our deliberations and begin to take a longer-run view. The variable-income assets now become less risky; the fixed-income assets become riskier. In plain English, this means that the variable-income assets increase management's confidence in their ability to fund the PBO, while bonds would not be the almost "risk-free" assets that they are for the ABO.

The shift in viewpoint is critical. Now we direct our attention to the ultimate future size of the liabilities, not just to their sensitivity to interest rates, which determine only their actuarial net present values. In other words, minimizing the long-run variability of the pension fund surplus depends upon our ability to fund the PBO rather than merely

EXHIBIT 8:
RISK AND REWARD—PBO–ABO

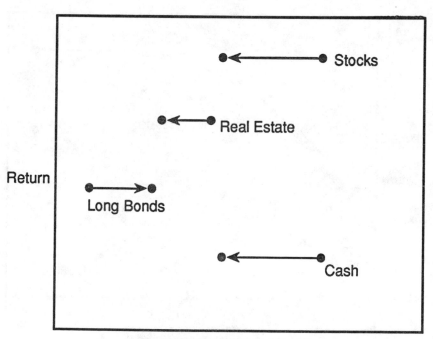

Variability of Fund Surplus
(assets minus present value of liabilities)

minimizing the short-run variability of the ABO surplus.

Finally, Exhibits 9A and 9B demonstrate the differing choices available to mature and early growth funds. We show the location of the assets for the mature pension plan in Exhibit 9A and for the young plan in Exhibit 9B. Once again, we construct an efficient frontier composed of combinations of assets rather than portfolios of single assets.

The mature fund would take dangerously larger risks for each increment of return by moving very far from a bond portfolio. The fixed nature of the obligations makes anything other than fixed-income assets highly risky. The slope of the risk/return relationship is steep at the left-hand side, in the low-risk tolerance zone where this fund belongs.

EXHIBIT 9A:
"TRUE" RISK AND REWARD—THE MATURE PLAN
(ABO DOMINATES)

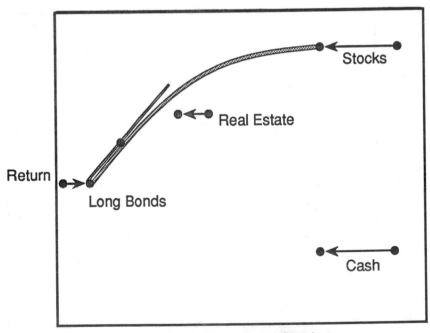

Variability of Fund Surplus
(assets minus present value of liabilities)

EXHIBIT 9B:
RISK AND REWARD—THE EARLY GROWTH PLAN
(PBO ›› ABO)

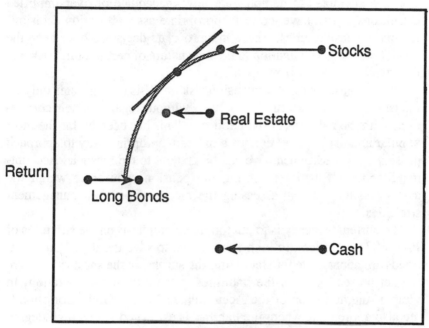

Variability of Fund Surplus
(assets minus present value of liabilities)

In Exhibit 9B, the riskiness of variable-income assets declines as we lengthen the time horizon that is appropriate to a younger fund, while the riskiness of bonds increases. This fund has a greater appetite for riskier securities as we conventionally classify them. It will locate itself further out to the right on the efficient frontier, where the slope is flatter, as befits a fund with a higher risk tolerance. Indeed, even with the same risk tolerance (measured by the slope of the risk tolerance line) as the mature plan, the younger plan would use more stocks and real estate to match the greater sensitivity of liabilities to inflation or productivity growth.

SUMMARY

We began this analysis with the assertion that the management of risk depends criticially on the manner in which we define risk. This discussion has attempted to demonstrate how inadequate or oversimplified definitions of risk have led to inappropriate asset allocation decisions for many pension funds. These inappropriate decisions have been the result of inadequate attention to the *true* nature of pension fund risk and the many forces that play upon it.

The simplest approach to pension risk analysis concentrates only on the riskiness of the assets themselves, without regard to their correlations with the riskiness of the liabilities. This has been by far the most popular approach, but it remains a most inappropriate way to approach pension fund management. We can be grateful to the Financial Accounting Standards Board for forcing the pension sponsor to weigh the assets *and* liabilities in assessing the merits of pension management strategies.

The current tendency is to put too much emphasis on the strictures of FASB 87 and to look to long-term bonds to save the day. Long-term bonds are appropriate for stabilizing the surplus in the short run, where the net present value of the liabilities is the crucial consideration. In view of the definition of the Accumulated Benefit Obligation, bonds are also appropriate where the liability is estimated with a high degree of certainty, as in the case of retired lives or a pension fund for a mature workforce.

On the other hand, there is a danger in viewing all pension funds in these terms. Sometimes there is a temptation to go in that direction just because of the simplicity of relating the variability of the assets to the variability of the present values. Sometimes this temptation arises from a slavish devotion to the short run, where the desire for smoothness and consistency can easily dominate the acceptance of the variability that is inescapable in achieving high longer-run returns.

In reality, the size of the pensions that the corporation pays in future years will have relatively little to do with today's level of long-term interest rates. In reality, therefore, the future value of the pension obligation is going to be far more important than today's present value. The corporation that seeks to have a surplus in its pension fund in the future had better consider the risks likely to arise in the future, not just the immediate risks.

But that warning applies to all risk management. You do not buy life insurance on a building or fire insurance on a senior executive. You do not take out a 30-year term life policy on a 55-year-old executive or a 6-month maintenance agreement on a brand new mainframe computer. Insurance policies are matched to the nature and time horizon of the risks. The pension fund example is different from these examples only in its complexities, but then all corporations face many risks of equivalent complexity. They deserve equivalent analysis.

CHAPTER 4

Risk and Return: Implications for the Asset Mix

LAURENCE B. SIEGEL
MANAGING DIRECTOR
IBBOTSON ASSOCIATES, INC.

ROGER G. IBBOTSON
PROFESSOR IN PRACTICE OF FINANCE
YALE SCHOOL OF MANAGEMENT
AND PRESIDENT
IBBOTSON ASSOCIATES, INC.

The asset mix decision evolves from the interaction of two sets of factors: the investment objective, such as building wealth or funding an obligation stream; and the characteristics of the assets themselves. This chapter focuses on the asset characteristics.

First we present historical returns on the principal asset classes of the U.S. economy in the risk-premium or "building block" framework originally set forth by Ibbotson and Sinquefield.[1] Second, we use the

---

[1]Roger G. Ibbotson and Rex A. Sinquefield, *Stocks, Bonds, Bills, and Inflation: The Past and The Future*, 1982 edition, Institute of Chartered Financial Analysts, Charlottesville, VA, 1982. First book edition, 1977. First publication, *Journal of Business* 49:1 (January 1976), 11–47 (historical returns) and *Journal of Business* 49:3 (July 1976), 313–338 (forecasts of the future).

historical data to form conclusions about the rewards (in the form of return) for taking systematic risks. These conclusions are shaped into probabilistic forecasts of return distribution for assets taken alone, and for asset mixes (portfolios). Third, we note the dilemma faced by many investors in pursuing more than one investment objective at the same time, and discuss the role of asset allocation and portfolio insurance in that dilemma. Finally, we discuss new approaches to the estimation of risk and return, including Arbitrage Pricing Theory and a macro-economic model of future asset returns. We address the impact of risk and return on the asset allocation decision more or less continuously throughout the chapter, as the various issues unfold.

HISTORICAL AND FORECAST ASSET RETURNS

Stocks, Bonds, Bills, and Inflation

The historical returns presented here are not only interesting in themselves, but have broad implications for forecasting, which is the essence of the asset allocation process. Specifically, the expected return on an asset is seen to be related to its risk. The year-by-year returns also provide a perspective on portfolio insurance, by demonstrating the probability of a year's return on an asset class falling below a prespecified minimum.

Return data were collected for 1926–1986 on the principal asset classes of the U.S. economy—common stocks (represented by the Standard & Poor's 500, or S&P for short); small-company stocks; long-term government bonds; Treasury bills; and consumer goods (inflation);[2] Exhibit 1 graphically depicts the growth of a dollar invested at year-end 1925 in each of the asset classes; yearly changes in the index levels translate to annual returns. Exhibit 2 presents summary statistics of the returns used to generate Exhibit 2.

The equity series (S&P stocks and small-company stocks) have the highest average returns but are the most variable, or risky. The fixed-income series (government and corporate bonds, and Treasury bills) have lower returns and are less risky.

---

[2]The data in Exhibits 1, 2 and 3 are from Ibbotson and Sinquefield (*op. cit*), updated in *Stocks, Bonds, Bills, and Inflation 1987 Yearbook*, Ibbotson Associates, Inc. [8 South Michigan Ave., Chicago, IL 60637], 1987. The Ibbotson Associates yearbook also contains a series for corporate bonds, and includes monthly and annual total returns and return indices, component and inflation-adjusted series, statistical analysis, and methodology.

EXHIBIT 1:
WEALTH INDICES OF INVESTMENTS IN THE U.S. CAPITAL MARKETS,
1926–1986

Source: Ibbotson Associates, Chicago.

EXHIBIT 2:
BASIC SERIES: TOTAL ANNUAL RETURNS (1926–1986)

SERIES	GEOMETRIC MEAN	ARITHMETIC MEAN	STANDARD DEVIATION	DISTRIBUTION
COMMON STOCKS	10.0%	12.1%	21.2%	
SMALL STOCKS	12.5	18.2	36.0	
LONG TERM CORPORATE BONDS	5.0	5.3	8.5	
LONG TERM GOVERNMENT BONDS	4.4	4.7	8.6	
U.S. TREASURY BILLS	3.5	3.5	3.4	
INFLATION	3.0	3.1	4.9	

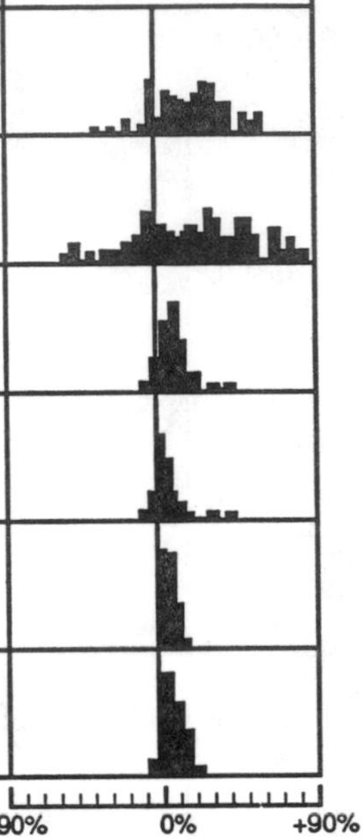

-90%   0%   +90%

Analyzing Asset Returns: A Risk Premium or "Building Block" Approach

By taking the difference between two return series, we can derive the risk premium realized from taking a given incremental risk. Exhibit 3 presents summary statistics for four risk premium series. The equity risk premium, for example, represents the average additional return, or reward, earned by investors in S&P stocks for taking the incremental risk of stocks relative to Treasury bills. Because investors conform their expectations to that which proves over time to be realizable, this equity risk premium is a good estimate of the forward-looking risk premium. It may thus be used as the equity risk premium in the traditional version of the Capital Asset Pricing Model.[3]

Other rewards for taking risk are evident from Exhibit 3. Over the 61-year period studied, small company stocks have systematically[4] rewarded investors for taking the additional risk of small (relative to large) stocks with a 3.9% additional compound annual return. Likewise, corporate bonds provide a return incremental to that of default-free government bonds. Government bonds, in turn, provide a return incremental to that of Treasury bills, which are also free of price fluctuation risk.

Given these observations, we can construct a simple model of expected return and risk on practically any asset or mix of assets.[5] For

---

[3]The Capital Asset Pricing Model (CAPM) was originally set forth in William F. Sharpe, "Capital Asset Prices: A Theory of Market Equilibrium under Conditions of Risk," *Journal of Finance* 19 (September 1964), 425–442; and in John Lintner, "The Valuation of Risk Assets and the Selection of Risky Investments in Stock Portfolios and Capital Budgets," *Review of Economics and Statistics* 47 (February 1965), 13–37. Many variants have appeared since the CAPM was first presented.

In the traditional or Sharpe-Lintner CAPM, the beta of a stock is multiplied by the equity risk premium to arrive at the stock's expected return in excess of the current short-term riskless yield. (The beta of a stock, in this context, is the slope parameter from regression of a stock's excess returns on the market excess returns. The excess return is the return in excess of the short-term riskless return.)

We regard the Sharpe-Lintner model as primarily useful for estimating the short-term expected return on a stock. The long-term expected return is estimated using a similar method, but where the current long-term Treasury yield is taken as the riskless rate, and historical yield (not total) returns on long-term Treasury bonds are taken as the historical riskless return series, for calculating both the equity risk premium and the stock's beta.

Asserting that long-term bonds are riskless requires some elucidation. Long-term bonds, of course, fluctuate in price over time. However, they are riskless to the holder with a time horizon that matches the payments of principal and (if any) coupons on the bond. Such holders form the likely (or highest-bidding) clientele for these bonds, and are thus likely to be the price-determining investors for them. The fact that the yield curve slopes upward on average, after controlling for anticipated changes in inflation, suggests that this assertion is not precisely true.

[4]Risks that are consistently rewarded on average over time by higher returns are known as *systematic*. In the traditional CAPM framework, only beta risk is systematic; all other risks can be eliminated by diversification and are thus unsystematic and unrewarded. We believe that a variety of risks are systematic.

[5]Other assets—foreign securities, real estate, different maturities and qualities of bonds, etc.— are also amenable to the risk premium approach set forth here. One would typically compare historical returns on the desired asset to returns on a reference asset. A reference asset is one differing from the desired asset in one risk dimension but otherwise similar. Thus one could (for example) derive a risk premium for Japanese stocks in excess of the return on U.S. stocks.

EXHIBIT 3:
DERIVED SERIES: SUMMARY STATISTICS OF ANNUAL COMPONENT RETURNS (1926–1986)

SERIES	GEOMETRIC MEAN	ARITHMETIC MEAN	STANDARD DEVIATION	DISTRIBUTION
EQUITY RISK PREMIA stocks - bills	6.3%	8.6%	21.7%	
SMALL STOCK PREMIA small stocks - stocks	3.9	6.0	22.2	
DEFAULT PREMIA LT corps - LT govts	0.6	0.6	3.2	
HORIZON PREMIA LT govts - bills	0.9	1.2	8.5	

-90%   0%   +90%

example, the expected return on a long-term corporate bond is the sum of the expected inflation rate, real riskless rate, horizon premium and default premium. Because in this approach the expected return on an asset is the sum of numerous arithmetic parts, the approach may be characterized as a "building block" approach.

Forecasting the Market: The Use of Historical Data to Estimate Probability Distributions of Asset Returns

The expected return on an asset is the *mean* of the probability distribution of future returns on the asset. It is as important to know the *distribution* of possible future returns as to know the mean or expectancy.

An example is provided in Exhibit 4. The one-year return on the stock market is modeled as the one-year Treasury-bill yield, which is regarded as certain, plus a risk premium which is uncertain with an arithmetic mean return of 8.6% and a standard deviation of 21.7% (from Exhibit 4). Since historical equity risk premia have been distributed roughly lognormally[6] (as contrasted with normally), a lognormal distribution is assumed for the future also. The percentiles in Exhibit 4 indicate the probability of the stock market performing worse than the indicated return. For example, the 95th percentile return is +51.0%; this indicates that the market has a 95% probability of returning 51% or less in the next year, and a 5% probability of returning more.

Estimation of probability distributions for asset returns can be carried over multiple years, as shown in the rightmost two columns of Exhibit 4, which give return distributions over a 20-year horizon.

EXHIBIT 4:
FORECAST DISTRIBUTIONS OF STOCK MARKET (S&P 500)
TOTAL RETURNS AS OF DECEMBER 31, 1986

Percentile of Market Performance	One-Year Forecasts		Twenty-Year Forecasts	
	Compound Annual Return in Percent	Future Value of $1 Invested Today	Compound Annual Return in Percent	Future Value of $1 Invested Today
95th	51.0%	$1.51	20.9%	$44.39
90th	41.2	1.41	19.1	32.82
75th	26.1	1.26	16.1	19.79
50th (median)	11.3	1.11	12.9	11.30
25th	−1.8	0.98	9.8	6.45
10th	−12.3	0.88	7.0	3.89
5th	−18.0	0.82	5.4	2.88

---

[6]A lognormal distribution is one in which the logarithms of the return relatives are distributed normally. The return relative is equal to one plus the return. That is, for a return of 15% or 0.15, the return relative is 1.15.

Notice that the distribution of compound annual rates of return "tightens" as one goes from few to many years, while the distribution of ending wealth values "broadens."

These estimated rates of return, or forecasts, are of course not intended to beat the market. Rather, they are estimates of what the market itself is expecting or forecasting—in a sense, "market consensus forecasts."

Asset Allocation Basics: Probability Distributions of Returns for Asset Mixes

The method used to forecast distributions of asset returns in the foregoing section can also be used for asset *mixes*. The mean of the distribution for a mix of (say) stocks and bonds is simply the weighted average of the mean for stocks and the mean for bonds, where the proportion of each aset in the mix is used as the weight. However, the standard deviation of returns is a function of not only the assets' individual standard deviations and weights in the mix but also of the *correlation coefficient* between the two assets. Specifically, the lower the correlation between the assets, the greater the reduction in the standard deviation below the weighted average of the assets' individual standard deviations. This reduction of portfolio standard deviation is known as the gain from diversification.

Exhibit 5 shows the probability distribution of one-year returns for stocks, bonds, and portfolio mixes containing both assets. At the most elementary level, one can choose which of the six portfolios shown best fits one's tolerance for risk and desire for return. The results shown in Exhibit 5 are typical of those provided by the asset allocation tools currently in use.[7]

---

[7]Most asset allocation software, including William F. Sharpe's *Asset Allocation Tools* (available from Ibbotson Associates), also contains a mean-variance (Markowitz) optimizer, which identifies asset mixes lying on the efficient frontier. In our simplified example (where the only assets are stocks and bonds), all of the portfolios shown are on the efficient frontier. In the real world, however, with multiple assets, these sample portfolios are not necessarily efficient.

EXHIBIT 5:
FORECAST DISTRIBUTIONS OF ONE-YEAR TOTAL RETURNS ON STOCK/BOND PORTFOLIO MIXES AS OF DECEMBER 31, 1986 (RETURNS IN PERCENT)

Percentile of Market Performance	% Stocks: % Bonds:	Portfolio Mixes					
		100 0	80 20	60 40	40 60	20 80	0 100
95th		51.0%	42.6%	34.8%	28.3%	23.9%	22.7%
90th		41.2	34.8	28.9	24.0	20.6	19.6
75th		26.1	22.9	19.8	17.2	15.3	14.4
50th (median)		11.3	10.8	10.3	9.7	9.2	8.7
25th		−1.8	0.2	1.9	3.2	3.7	3.0
10th		−12.3	−8.6	−5.5	−2.9	−1.6	−2.2
5th		−18.0	−13.6	−9.7	−6.5	−4.8	−5.3

Note: Stocks are presented by the S&P 500. Bonds are represented by a portfolio of long-term, high-grade corporate bonds.

ACHIEVING MULTIPLE INVESTMENT OBJECTIVES

The Institutional Investor's Policy Dilemma

The primary asset classes of the economy—stocks, bonds, cash, real estate and so forth—meet the needs of the investor who has one specific objective. If the objective is to fund an obligation stream, matching of cash flows to obligations is achievable (within parameters of error) by means of bond dedication and/or immunization. For taxable corporations sponsoring tax-exempt pension plans, such strategies also have the advantage of arbitraging against the tax code.[8] If the investor's goal is to build wealth, the asset allocation decision is distilled to a question of risk tolerance, and perhaps illiquidity tolerance.[9]

Most institutional investors do not, however, have such clearly defined goals. Pension plan sponsors, for example, get to keep some or all of market profits in excess of defined benefits, giving them an incentive to act like wealth builders. Yet they must avoid underfunding their obligation stream.

With primary assets as defined above,[10] simultaneously maximizing returns and minimizing the probability of underfunding is *impossible*. The closest that one can come is to avoid compromising either investment goal too much, by taking a middle position. The familiar 60/40 stock/bond mix for corporate pension plans (or 40/60 for public sector plans) probably results from this need to compromise. Another upshot of the portfolio manager's dilemma is the continuing debate on what the goal of fiduciary investment should be—to build wealth or to fund specific obligations.

---

[8]As was pointed out in Fischer Black, "The Tax Consequences of Long-Run Pension Policy," *Financial Analysts Journal*, July–August 1980, 1–28, and Irwin Tepper, "Taxation and Corporate Pension Policy," *Journal of Finance* 36 (March 1981), 1–14, a corporation can borrow (with tax deductible interest) to buy bonds for its pension fund (with tax exempt interest). A riskless tax arbitrage is thus achieved. We would point out that the corporation need not specifically borrow for the purpose of buying bonds. It need only be indebted. In that sense, the Black-Tepper arbitrage is almost universally if unwittingly used.

[9]The short-horizon wealth builder may have the same risk tolerance as the long-horizon wealth builder, yet hold very different portfolios. The long-horizon portfolio would almost certainly contain real estate. The illiquidity of real estate does not hurt the long-horizon investor. However, other investors shun illiquid assets, driving their prices down and returns up. Hence, the investor with a high illiquidity tolerance will earn higher returns.

[10]Portfolios of stocks, bonds, cash, and real estate typically have return distributions approximating the lognormal.

Portfolio Insurance and Its Impact on Asset Allocation

The recent explosion of derivative securities (futures and options) and portfolio insurance strategies dependent on such securities has made it possible to pursue two investment goals simultaneously. The most common strategy is to "buy" protection against outcomes below a prespecified floor—portfolio insurance. Of course, there are many variations on this theme, elaborated elsewhere in this book.[11] The common thread is that by using derivative securities, the investor can construct a probability distribution that is different from the lognormal or bell-curve distribution that characterizes almost all portfolios of primary asset classes.

The effect of portfolio insurance on the probability distribution of returns is made clear by Exhibit 6. We construct a simple example where the portfolio is composed of the S&P and the floor is a total return of zero. In this example, where portfolio insurance works properly, the probability of a negative outcome is zero for the insured portfolio. However, the return is lower for each positive (i.e., possible) outcome.

Unfortunately, portfolio insurance does not always work properly. Portfolio insurance theoretically requires a continuous distribution of market returns; of course, the market actually moves in discrete rather than continuous price jumps, but when the jumps are small, portfolio insurance works well. However, when there are *large* jumps in market levels, as in the crash of October 1987, portfolio insurance fails to protect against losses. This outcome is analogous to other forms of insurance, which do not pay off when the catastrophe insured against is sufficiently widespread or extreme.[12]

Taken alone (apart from the portfolio it insures), portfolio insurance is an asset with a negative expected return and negative risk. These attributes are shared with all kinds of insurance. While a negative expected return is easy enough to understand, negative risk is tougher. How can the risk of any asset be less than zero? It can in a portfolio

---

[11]See Chapter 10.

[12]The cost of portfolio insurance is consequently unknown. Were portfolio insurance to be executed using an actual rather than a synthetic put, its price could be observed in an auction market. This price would become very high in volatile markets. The authors thank John A. DeTore, Jr. of Wellington Management for this and other insights.

EXHIBIT 6:
FORECAST DISTRIBUTIONS OF ONE-YEAR TOTAL RETURNS ON UNINSURED AND INSURED S&P 500 STOCK PORTFOLIOS AS OF DECEMBER 31, 1986 (RETURNS IN PERCENT)

Percentile of Market Performance	Uninsured S&P Portfolio	Insured S&P Portfolio where Floor is a Total Return of Zero
95th	51.0%	46.0%
90th	41.2	36.2
75th	26.1	21.1
50th (median)	11.3	6.3
25th	−1.8	0.0
10th	−12.3	0.0
5th	−18.0	0.0

Note: Portfolio insurance is assumed to have a cost of 5% per year in any year with a stock market total return of 5% or more. In years with a stock market total return between zero and 5%, the cost is equal to the total return, so that the total return after costs on the insured portfolio is zero.

context, where insurance assets "gobble up" the risk of other assets—in effect, having negative risk.

While portfolio insurance, and other strategies to reconfigure the probability distribution of portfolio returns, make it easier to achieve diverse investment goals, they make the mathematics of asset allocation more difficult. An ideal asset allocation tool for today's complex markets would treat portfolio insurance (or insured portfolios) as an asset class. Futures, options and dynamic strategies with the effect of reconfiguring portfolio return distributions would also be treated as asset classes.

ALTERNATIVE APPROACHES TO RISK AND RETURN

What's Wrong with the Capital Asset Pricing Model?

The Capital Asset Pricing Model (CAPM), which inspired the risk premium analysis set forth above, has contributed greatly to the understanding of risk and return since its inception in the 1960s. It does not, however, explain the returns on stocks as well as might be desired. There have been periods in which low beta stocks outperformed high beta stocks in rising markets, contrary to what the CAPM predicts. Stocks are also sensitive to factors other than economy risk (the risk that beta measures). Interest rates, for example, play a large role in determining the returns of some stocks, while specific prices, such as those of oil, farm products or gold, determine the returns of others.

Outside the stock market, the CAPM fails more broadly. Bond prices are affected by the general level of interest rates, the credit risk of the particular bond and refunding risk (the right, if any, of the borrower to "call" or prepay the principal). Real estate returns are affected by taxes and illiquidity. Foreign securities have their own set of risks, which do not map well into the the CAPM framework.

A Call for a New Equilibrium Theory

Researchers have noted these issues repeatedly, usually addressing each problem in isolation. Attempting to integrate these issues, Ibbotson, Diermeier and Siegel[13] called for a "new equilibrium theory" (NET) in which the expected return on an asset, that is, its cost of capital, is literally the sum of all capital costs. Capital costs include non-risk costs and risk costs. Examples of non-risk costs are illiquidity costs and taxes; information, transaction and search costs; maintenance, insurance and storage costs; and nonpecuniary costs and benefits (negative costs). The cost of taking on a given risk may be thought of as the amount an investor would pay to get the risk to go away. An asset may have any number of risks.

NET has not become a prominent method of estimating expected returns for several reasons. It is not a theory, but a call for a theory. There is no mathematical formula associated with it. The risk and non-risk costs are difficult to quantify. However, NET induces researchers to think of the expected return on an asset in terms of all of its risk and non-risk attributes, not just of beta risk. Moreover, NET allows one to think of all assets, including human capital as well as stocks, bonds, bills, real estate and other conventional and unconventional assets in a single, unified framework.

---

[13]Roger G. Ibbotson, Jeffrey J. Diermeier, and Laurence B. Siegel, "The Demand for Capital Market Returns: A New Equilibrium Theory," *Financial Analysts Journal* 40:1 (January/February 1984), 22–33.

Arbitrage Pricing Theory (APT)

A formal theory, proposed in the mid-1970s by Stephen Ross,[14] looks at the multiple risks associated with holding a given asset. Because the theory assumes perfect arbitrage conditions (i.e., that disequilibrium profit opportunities will be arbitraged away), it is labeled Arbitrage Pricing Theory (APT). APT states that the expected return on an asset is the sum of the payoffs for an indeterminate number of risk factors, where the amount of each risk factor contained in a given asset is estimated. Of the asset pricing theories that have been proposed since the CAPM, APT is by far the most helpful in furthering the understanding of risk and return, at least within the equity markets.

Micro-APT

The development of APT as a theory has spawned considerable research in identifying the risks of asset classes (such as stocks) and in estimating the amount of each risk inherent in a given asset. One approach has been to identify microeconomic, or, more specifically, financial market factors that affect asset returns.

Our research indicates that for stocks in the U.S. stock market, the expected return is described by a stock's comovement with five return series: the aggregate stock market, large capitalization stocks (where capitalization is defined as price times shares outstanding), small capitalization stocks, high cash-flow-to-price ratio stocks and low cash-flow-to-price ratio stocks.[15] This finding is useful in forecasting returns on individual stocks, although not necessarily for allocating assets between the stock market and alternative investments. We anticipate that as research continues (by us and others), additional microeconomic factors will be discovered.

Macro-APT

By looking at the "real economy," or asset side of the macroeconomic balance sheet, it is possible to relate expected returns in the financial

---

[14]Stephen A. Ross, "The Arbitrage Pricing Theory of Capital Asset Pricing," *Journal of Economic Theory*, (December 1976), 341–360.

[15]See *APT!™*, *Alcar's Financial Policy Information Service*, The Alcar Group Inc. [5215 Old Orchard Road, Skokie, IL 60077]; and Roger G. Ibbotson, Stephen A. Ross, and Richard Roll, *The Cost of Capital Quarterly*, forthcoming, Ibbotson Associates, 1988.

markets to macroeconomic variables.[16] We label this approach macro-APT.[16]

Chen, Roll and Ross[17] added considerably to the understanding of equity markets by focusing on the effect of exogenous forces on stocks. In their framework, exogenous forces include both macroeconomic forces and conditions in financial markets other than the stock market. They concluded that stock returns were a function of: (1) the growth rate in industrial production; (2) the change in expected inflation; (3) unanticipated inflation; (4) unanticipated change in the bond default premium; and (5) unanticipated change in the bond horizon premium.

The implications of this result for asset allocation are ill-defined but suggest interesting possibilities. Although Chen, Roll and Ross studied individual stock behavior, it is reasonable to suppose a similar model could be constructed for portfolios, including the whole asset class of stocks. Bonds, cash, real estate, and other asset classes would presumably have very different responses to macroeconomic conditions. (The macro-APT analysis of other asset classes would probably use different sets of variables.) From such results, an asset allocation decision framework could be developed.

A Macroeconomic Asset Allocation Model

In formulating a model for the asset allocation decision that would reflect current knowledge and allow for active as well as passive decision making, we drew on the macroeconomy. We recast the market model regression for stocks in macroeconomic terms:[18]

---

[16]In the macroeconomic balance sheet, the real economy (the set of productive or "return-generating" businesses) makes up the asset side. Financial instruments constitute claims against these assets and hence make up the liability side. From the macroeconomic point of view, returns to the asset side govern—on average over time—returns to the financial-market claims. See Jeffrey J. Diermeier, Roger G. Ibbotson, and Laurence B. Siegel, "The Supply of Capital Market Returns," *Financial Analysts Journal* 40:2 (March/April 1984), 74–80.

[17]Nai-fu Chen, Richard Roll, and Stephen A. Ross, "Economic Forces and the Stock Market," *Journal of Business* 59:3 (July 1986), 383–403.

[18]Stock market or beta risk was called economy risk as early as 1964 (see Sharpe, *op cit.*). We regard the primary risk being priced in the stock market as economy (represented by production) risk, on the asset side of the macroeconomic balance sheet, with beta risk being the reflection of that risk on the liability or financial-market side.

$$R_{s,t} = a + b\,(\Delta GNP_{t+1}) + \tilde{\varepsilon}$$

where

$R_{s,t}$ is the return on the stock market in period t

a is the intercept

b is the slope parameter or loading factor representing the effect of next-period change in GNP on stock returns

$\tilde{\varepsilon}$ is an error term with a mean of zero (ideally distributed unit normal)

We express the relationship between bond yields and inflation as follows:

$$\Delta Y_t = a + b(\Delta I_t) + \tilde{\varepsilon}$$

where

ΔY_t is the change in yield on a bond over period t

a is the intercept

b is the slope parameter, representing the effect of the change in inflation on bond yields

ΔI_t is the change in the inflation rate over period t

$\tilde{\varepsilon}$ is the error term

We have examined these relationships over historical time. We determined that if an investor had had perfect foresight about the next period's GNP and inflation rate, his or her results from active asset allocation using this model would have dramatically beat a fixed-weight or other passive strategy. We believe that with far less than perfect macroeconomic foresight, an investor can use this model actively to allocate funds among asset classes.

Operating the model of expected returns described above is simple.

The investor inputs a forecast for GNP and the change in the inflation rate. The model thus translates a set of macroeconomic forecasts into expected returns for stocks and bonds. The asset-class expected returns are then inserted into an optimizer, along with their standard deviations and cross-correlation, to determine an efficient frontier. The asset mix that matches the investor's risk tolerance is selected.

The efficient frontier moves over time as different forecasts of GNP and inflation rate changes are input. Given a fixed risk tolerance, the desired asset mix changes. The investor actively implements the macroeconomic forecasts by transacting so as to hold the asset mix indicated by the optimizer.

The model can be further refined. Stocks almost certainly have an inflation loading factor as well as a GNP loading factor. Asset classes treatable by the model include small-company stocks (considered a separate class), foreign stocks and bonds and cash equivalents. For each asset class, a GNP loading factor and/or an inflation loading factor can be empirically determined. With this broader spectrum of asset classes, the model is both inclusive of the opportunity set faced by institutional investors and active with respect to the allocation of assets in the portfolio.

SUMMARY

As noted at the beginning, the asset mix decision results from the interaction of asset characteristics and investor needs. With regard to the former, we have seen that return over the long run (1926–1986) is related to the risk taken, comparing across asset classes. The return—both historical and expected—on any asset can be characterized as the sum of the returns on various component parts of the asset's return. Such a "building block" approach enables probabilistic forecasts to be made.

On the investor's side, we pointed out the dual nature of the investment manager's responsibility: to fund obligations and to build wealth. A portfolio designed to maximize the probability of funding obligations would consist only of bonds and would be fully dedicated, while one designed to maximize terminal wealth would consist only of stocks and other high-return, high-risk investments. Balanced portfolio mixes, as well as strategies such as portfolio insurance, are methods of addressing both objectives at the same time.

CHAPTER 5

Integrating Business Planning with Pension Fund Planning*

KEITH P. AMBACHTSHEER
KEITH P. AMBACHTSHEER & ASSOCIATES, INC.

In the beginning, employer pensions were unfunded gratuities. In the last few decades, they have evolved into legal funded property. In more recent years, the dollar value of this pension property has mushroomed, often elevating the pension plan into one of the largest "businesses" of the employer. This chapter looks at the implications of this development for the plan sponsor. Specifically, the chapter examines the financial connections between plan sponsors, pension plans and plan members. The nature of these financial connections have a good deal to say about how pension fund asset mix policy should be established. This is demonstrated by the cases of ALPHA Corporation, a private sector employer, and the Public Sector Retirement System, a pension plan sponsored by a public sector entity. Trustees for both pension plans make asset mix policy decisions in the chapter, in each case keeping the legitimate interests of plan members *and* the plan sponsor in mind.

---

*Much of the case material in this chapter appears in Keith P. Ambachtsheer, "In Defense of A 60/40 Asset Mix For Pension Funds," *Financial Analysts Journal*, September-October 1987.

PENSIONS AS GRATUITIES

The concept of employer pensions has been around since the beginning of this century. But until relatively recently, pensions were gratuities, pure and simple. That is, they represented unilateral decisions by employers to bestow financial benefits on long service employees *without any legal obligation to do so*. Slowly, over time, these "gratuity" arrangements started to be codified and to evolve into contractual arrangements between employers and their (current and former) employees.

According to Paul Halbrecht, here's where things stood in the 1950s:[1]

Pension plans contain inherent limitations on the security they offer:

— the liability is limited to the size of the fund . . . and the degree of funding varies widely
— the employer has the right to unilaterally modify or terminate the plan
— actually receiving a pension is often dependent on restrictive conditions not clearly communicated to plan members
— employees have no say in any governance or administrative matters related to the plan

[*Halbrecht concludes*] . . . taken together, these provisions leave the employee very much dependent on the continued solvency and good will of the employer for any actual pension benefits.

Legislation during the 1960s and 1970s[2] did much to enhance the property rights of plan members through a standardization of vesting requirements, funding requirements, disclosure requirements and a government guaranty that a minimum benefit would be paid.

---

[1]Paul Halbrecht, *Pension Funds and Economic Power*, The Twentieth Century Fund, New York, 1959.

[2]The federal and provincial Pension Benefits Acts were written in the mid-1960s in Canada. The Employee Retirement Income Security Act (ERISA) was enacted by the U.S. Congress in 1974.

[3]The most common implicit understanding in pure defined benefit plans is for the employer to provide post-retirement inflation protection on a "best efforts" basis. Over the last 10 years, this has typically meant inflation related updates of about 50% of the increase in the CPI. Some

PENSIONS AS PROPERTY

Both the economic evolution of employer/employee total compensation arrangements and the aforementioned legislation has led to an ability to categorize pension arrangements today into one of three categories:

1. *Asset-based Pension Arrangements.* The employer agrees to contribute a regular amount (usually a fixed percentage of current pay) into an employee investment account. The employee's pension is based on the size of the life annuity that the accumulated value of the pension investment account can purchase on retirement.

2. *Pure Defined Benefit Pension Arrangements.* The employer agrees to pay a defined pension (usually based on earnings and years of service) regardless of how the pension fund performs. Such arrangements are usually non-contributory. If the employee is required to contribute, it is at a fixed rate which will not vary with subsequent pension fund investment performance.

3 *Shared Risk Defined Benefit Pension Arrangements.* The employer agrees to pay a defined pension, but the employee agrees to pay a proportionate share of the contributions required to help finance ultimate benefits. Here *both* the employer and employee contribution rates will vary with pension fund investment performance.

Most plan members in North America are covered by arrangements that are legally pure defined benefit plans. While relatively few are *explicitly* covered under shared risk defined benefit arrangements, some private sector and many public sector employment plans implicitly operate on this basis.[3] In this chapter we look at the asset allocation

observers argue that, at some point, this regular *"ad hocing"* eventually becomes an obligation to continue to do so. All this raises some interesting questions with respect to accounting treatment as well. FASB Statements 87 and 88 and CICA Handbook Section 3460 set out how defined benefit pension plans are to be treated in corporate financial statements in the U.S.A. and Canada respectively. Their appearance has created somewhat of a dilemma for many chief financial officers: do you let the accounting rules drive the economics of your pension plan, or do you make the economics drive the rules? CFOs making the latter choice are finding there are ways to make the rules (and the accountants who wrote them) fit the economics *where the CFO has thought through the economics.* This chapter endeavors to contribute to that thinking-through process.

implications of *both* the "pure" and "shared risk" defined benefit pension arrangements.

There is an important aspect of pure defined benefit pension plans that the legislation of the 1960s and the 1970s did *not* address. This aspect continues to be a major impediment to the formulation of focused, unambiguous pension fund asset mix policies under this type of pension arrangement. The reality of this type of plan is that there are, at any point in time, not one but *two* legitimate pension liabilities. We refer to them as the "legal termination liability" and the "economic going-concern liability."

TWO LEGITIMATE LIABILITY DEFINITIONS

The reason why there are two legitimate liability definitions in defined benefit employer pension plans is simple. It is because once a plan exists, the employer has the option to either continue the plan, or to terminate it. And in that option lies a great anomaly in corporate and public finance. Why? Because for a typical defined benefit pension plan, *the "best estimate" continuation liability at any point in time has a much greater value than the termination liability.*

Recently, Ippolito provided a vivid example of the potential value disparity between the two liabilities.[4] He estimated that for a typical 55-year-old worker the "economic going-concern" pension liability might be at least 2.7 times the value of the "termination" liability. Similarly, Ezra and Ambachtsheer reported a median 3:1 ratio between these two liability levels in a sample of 146 defined benefit plans.[5]

The reason for the disparity is simple. The "economic going-concern" liability reflects an assumption that the pension benefits accruing will actually be paid out over time and that the nominal dollar value of the benefit payments over time will reflect actual inflation experience over time. By contrast, the "termination" liability simply reflects the price of a basket of fixed dollar current and deferred life annuities. These annuities, priced at current interest rates, would be just sufficient

---

[4]Richard A. Ippolito, "The Economic Burden of Corporate Pension Liabilities," *Financial Analysts Journal*, January–February 1986. His book, *Pensions, Economics, and Public Policy* (Dow Jones-Irwin 1986), further elaborates on the distinction between what Ippolito calls "true" and "legal" pension liabilities.

[5]D. Don Ezra and Keith P. Ambachtsheer, "Pension Funds: Rich or Poor?," *Financial Analysts Journal*, March–April 1985.

to discharge pension obligations earned to date based on today's compensation rates.

This chapter does not examine the economic, legal and even moral issues surrounding the going-concern/termination value disparity[6]. It simply takes this disparity as a "given" and focuses instead on the *investment implications* of these two possible views of pure defined benefit pension liabilities.

THE TERMINATION VIEW OF PURE DEFINED BENEFIT PENSION LIABILITIES

Much of the recent literature on balance sheet management in the context of defined benefit pension plans focuses on the investment implications of taking the *termination* view of pure defined benefit pension liabilities.[7]

The logic of a pension fund asset allocation framework with a "termination liabilities" focus proceeds from two critical assumptions:

1. The pension liability relevant for making asset allocation decisions is the plan "termination liability."
2. The plan "termination liability" is fixed in normal terms.

---

[6]Ippolito, for example, argues that if workers forego the present value-equivalent of ongoing rather than termination benefits as the non-current portion of a total compensation package, there is an implicit contract to provide ongoing benefits (see also footnote 3). Terminated employees and/or their unions have made this argument in a number of court cases arising out of plan terminations. In a recent case in Ontario where an employer had already received the termination surplus, the court ordered the money to be returned to the trustees until it ruled on the merits of the employees' case. An out-of-court settlement resulted with the employer and plan members splitting the termination surplus 50%/50%. The recent Blessitt vs. Dixie Engine decision by the United States Court of Appeals suggests the courts are also starting to change their thinking on termination pension benefits.

[7]See, for example, Martin L. Leibowitz, "The Dedicated Bond Portfolio in Pension Funds— Part I: Motivations and Basics," *Financial Analysts Journal*, January–February 1986; Martin L. Leibowitz, "The Dedicated Bond Portfolio in Pension Funds—Part II: Immunization, Horizon Matching, and Contingent Procedures," *Financial Analysts Journal*, March–April 1986; Martin L. Leibowitz, "Total Portfolio Duration: A New Perspective on Asset Allocation," *Financial Analysts Journal*, September–October 1986; Martin L. Leibowitz, "Pension Fund Asset Allocation through Surplus Management," *Financial Analysts Journal*, March–April 1987; and Martin L. Leibowitz, "Liability Returns: A New Look at Asset Allocation," *The Journal of Portfolio Management*, Winter 1987.

Making these two assumptions is not without merit. After all, regulations require trusteed pension funds to be managed ". . . solely in the interest of plan beneficiaries. . . ." Taken literally, this means the only role of the pension fund is to ensure there is enough money available to pay the accrued pension debt if, for some reason, the plan sponsor either can't or no longer wants to. And if the plan sponsor can't or no longer wants to pay, the plan is clearly in a termination situation.

As for the "termination liability" being fixed in nominal terms, this is still the standard legal and accounting interpretation of what is owed in the plan windup case. That is, that there is no legally enforceable obligation to provide a termination *quid pro quo* for any explicit or implicit understanding that the plan, as a going-concern, was to provide inflation-related benefits.[8]

THE INVESTMENT IMPLICATIONS OF THE TERMINATION VIEW OF PENSION LIABILITIES

A nice feature of the "termination liabilities" formulation of the pension fund asset allocation problem is that there is a "risk free" asset. This risk free asset is likely to be a long duration, default free, fixed rate bond portfolio. Why? Fixed dollar pension plan termination liabilities can be discharged with the purchase of a portfolio of current and deferred annuities. Depending on the mix of active and retired lives and their respective age distributions, the duration of such a portfolio might be somewhere between 10 and 15 years.[9]

Liabilities with this duration are well within the duration reach of an asset portfolio of zero-coupon bonds. By matching asset and liability durations, any existing "termination surplus" (plan assets in excess of the plan "termination liability") can be locked in. In the "termination" framework, both short-term debt securities and stocks are risky. Both have nominal interest rate-related durations that are far too short. In addition, stock prices move up or down for reasons totally unrelated to changes in interest rates.

---

[8]But see footnote 6. It might be unwise to assume that the current status of the plan termination surplus ownership issue is permanent.

[9]Leibowitz calculates durations of about 6 years for retireds and 13 years for actives in the sample pension plan he uses. See Leibowitz, "Liability Returns: A New Look at Asset Allocation," *The Journal of Portfolio Management*, Winter 1987.

PENSION PLAN SPONSORS AND THE "TERMINATION LIABILITY" FRAMEWORK

Despite the logic of the "termination" view of pension liabilities, very few pension funds have 100% bond asset mix policies. The fact that actual pension fund asset mixes deviate significantly from the risk-free portfolio suggested by the "termination liability" framework can be explained by one of two reasons:

1. Plan sponsors use the "legal termination liability" framework but willingly assume considerable balance sheet risk in framing their asset mix policies.
2. Plan sponsors don't use the "nominal termination liability" framework in framing their asset mix policies.

Reason #1 doesn't strike us as very plausible. We don't perceive pension plan sponsors in aggregate to be aggressive risk takers in managing pension plan balance sheets.

Reason #2 seems more plausible. That is, plan sponsors rightly or wrongly don't accept the two critical assumptions about "time" (i.e., finite-life pension liabilities—and hence assets) and "the nature of the pension promise" (i.e., nominal rather than inflation-sensitive) behind the "termination" view of pension liabilites. A variation on this theme is that many (especially public sector) employers believe they do in fact not have the right (moral if not legal) to unilaterally terminate an in-place defined benefit plan.

Reason #2 is supported by a study by Malley and Jayson.[10] Their surveys and interviews with financial executives indicated much more of a "going-concern" mentality rather than a "termination" mentality, among respondents in making funding and investment policy decisions.

Further support for the second interpretation comes from the fact that the funding process focuses on ongoing rather than termination

---

[10]Susan L. Malley and Susan Jayson, "Why Do Financial Executives Manage Pension Funds the Way They Do?," *Financial Analysts Journal*, November–December 1986. In my book (Keith P. Ambachtsheer, *Pension Funds and the Bottom Line*, Dow Jones-Irwin 1986) I also make the fundamental assumption that employer pension plans are "going-concern" financial entities, and should be managed that way.

pension benefits. Given the former require two or three times the amount of dollars to fund than the latter, plan assets tend to exceed the termination liability by multiples of two or three in a typical plan.[11] Thus for most plans, solvency is not the central issue. Instead, *the central issue is to earn a high long-term rate of return* on a pool of assets the value of which easily matches that of some of the plan sponsor's main line businesses.

PENSION PLAN SPONSORS, "TIME," AND "THE PENSION PROMISE"

What happens to the asset allocation question when ongoing rather than termination assumptions are made about "time" and "the nature of the pension promise"? The assumptions now become:

1. The pension liability relevant for making pension fund asset allocation decisions is *not* the "legal termination liability," but the "economic, going-concern liability."
2. The plan "economic, going-concern liability" is *not* fixed in nominal terms. It is highly inflation-sensitive.

With these assumptions, the pension fund is much more likely to be viewed as a *permanent* tax-exempt capital pool, the return on which can be used to help discharge pension debt when it falls due. As to what direction the answer to the asset allocation question might now take us, there are five considerations. We list them as questions a plan sponsor might ask:

- How do we view long-term capital market prospects?
- Is it clear that risk-related return gains in the pension fund indeed do translate into reduced employer contributions?
- While a plan termination is not expected, how would we "settle" with our current and former employees if it did occur?
- How concerned are we about shorter term fluctuations in the economic and/or accounting values of plan assets and plan liabili-

---

[11]See footnote 5.

ties, and hence the plan surplus (economic and/or accounting) position?[12]

- To what degree are we prepared to/can we integrate the main business and the pension plan balance sheet for capital structure and tax planning purposes?

We expand on these five questions for asset allocation against "economic, going-concern pension liabilities" in Exhibit 1.

PENSION PLAN SPONSORS AND THE "ECONOMIC GOING-CONCERN LIABILITY" FRAMEWORK

When the pension investment problem shifts from a termination context to a long-term, ongoing context, some interesting things happen. "Risk" measured by the exposure of the "termination surplus" (plan assets in excess of the plan termination liability) to changes in long-term bond yields (i.e., the "termination" formulation) is no longer relevant.

"Risk" now is related to *actual* real return experience in relation to *anticipated* real return experience. On a 3% real return basis, a 20% of payroll contribution rate might be needed to support plan benefit payments equal to 70% of final earnings, and maintained in real terms over the life of the pensioner. But if a 6% real return is earned instead, the required contribution rate might be halved—into the 10% area. Thus, real return uncertainty translates directly into "contribution rate risk."

Who bears this "contribution rate risk"? That depends very much on what the pension "deal" is between the employer and the employees. In a fully indexed, non-contributory "pure" defined benefit plan, which is being funded with, say, a 20% of payroll contribution rate, "contribution rate risk" is fully borne by the employer.

If the pension fund earns a 3% real rate of return, there will be a

---

[12]This question brings to the fore the issue of whether economics will drive accounting or accounting will drive economics. We have already conceded that there will be cases where the economics dictate a "termination" rather than "going-concern" view of the world. In these latter cases, shorter term fluctuations in the value of the plan termination surplus are likely to be important. Hence, paying a premium to insure its value becomes a potentially attractive economic proposition.

EXHIBIT 1:
FIVE ASSET ALLOCATION CONSIDERATIONS

Consideration	Commentary
1. Long-Term Capital-Market Prospects	● Are there reasons to believe the historical structure of risk premiums will/will not be paid in the future? How do our views on this impact our choice of normal asset mix policy?
2. The "Going-Concern Deal"	● How are pension fund gains (i.e., return in excess of the risk-free long-term liability discount rate) to be distributed between the plan sponsor and plan beneficiaries? What about pension fund losses (i.e., return shortfalls)?
	● What do the answers to these questions tell us about how aggressive an asset mix policy to adopt?
3. The "Termination Deal"	● While we plan to run the business and the fund as going-concerns, there are a number of possible windup scenarios (i.e., conversion to a money purchase plan, corporate takeover/reorganization, bankruptcy). Will we *really* only pay plan members the absolute legal minimum? Or do we have a contract (explicit or implicit) to pay more?
	● How does this "more" manifest itself? As the absolute legal minimum plus a share of the termination surplus? As an expected inflation-related or "excess interest"-related increment to the legal minimum?
4. Fluctuations in the Value of Plan Assets and Liabilities	● Are shorter-term fluctuations in the economic (i.e., "real") value of plan assets and plan liabilities of major concern to us? If yes, why? What about fluctuations in the *accounting* value of assets and liabilities? If yes, why?
5. Degree of Business and Plan Integration	● We realize that full integration would have the pension fund invested in the most heavily taxed securities, with whatever offsets are needed on the main business balance sheet to give us the integrated asset/liability structure we want.
	● Are we prepared to live with the potential consequences of full integration (i.e., strange-looking non-integrated main business and pension balance sheets, possibly inquiries from the tax authorities and rating agencies)?

long-term balance between plan assets and plan (economic, going-concern) liabilities. If the fund earns more, assets grow faster than liabilities and the contribution rate can fall below 20%. If the fund earns less, assets grow slower than liabilities, and the contribution rate must rise about 20%.[13]

WHAT IS THE "GOING-CONCERN PENSION DEAL"?

What about more typical private sector cases where, for example, a final earnings formula (possibly up to 50% of final pay) ensures pre-retirement indexation, but post-retirement indexation is "*ad hoc*" and is not explicitly being pre-funded? Is the amount by which pensions are updated now dependent on pension fund performance? If there *is* a connection, you have a risk-sharing situation between the plan sponsor and plan members.

What about arrangements where the employer and the employees have agreed to split contributions, say 50%/50%, regardless of whether they amount to 5%, 10%, or 20% of pay? Now a risk-sharing situation exists *explicitly*. Thus, the plan member's risk exposure, like that of the plan sponsor, could also be in the form of contribution rate uncertainty, or it could be more direct in the form of real benefit payments uncertainty.[14]

This discussion on the nature of the pension "deal" is not peripheral, but in fact central to the pension fund asset allocation question. Probably the most fundamental requirement in the investment management profession is the "Know Your Client" rule. The obvious extension of this rule in the case of employer pension plans is to identify the finan-

---

[13]This leverage of the long-term real return on assets on the required contribution rate reflects the long duration of "economic going-concern" pension liabiliites: durations in excess of 20 years are not uncommon. The numbers used are illustrative only. PC-based pension liability valuation systems now exist to do such calculations for specific plans in minutes, if not seconds.

[14]Once one begins to study what actual pension "deals" exist between specific employers and their current and inactive employees, the popular notion that there are only two possible "deals" between them (i.e., pure defined benefit or pure defined contribution or asset-based) shatters very quickly. There are in fact many "deals." Unfortunately, employers and employees don't always have the same view of what the "deal" is. Even more unfortunately, rather than solving disputes through arbitration or even the courts, politicians are sometimes brought into these disputes. If this involvement ends up constraining the range of compensation formula options open to employers and employees by law, economic efficiency will suffer. This problem is compounded when the government is itself a large employer (as is usually the case).

cial risks and rewards inherent in any defined benefit pension arrangement and how they are to be shared by stakeholders.

From the perspective of framing an asset mix policy, there is ideally only one stakeholder: either the plan sponsor (i.e., the pure defined benefit plan case) or the plan member (i.e., the asset-based plan case). With either, it is clear who the "client" is. If the "pension deal" involves some sharing of investment gains and losses between these two parties, the determination of an appropriate asset mix policy must reflect this reality.

AN ASSET ALLOCATION CHECKLIST

To systematically analyze the sometimes conflicting forces impacting on long-term pension fund asset allocation, a checklist is useful. The checklist in Exhibit 2 addresses four of the five key going-concern asset allocation questions we posed above. For the sake of realism, both a private sector plan sponsor and a public sector plan sponsor are represented: the former on behalf of the ALPHA Corporation pension plan (a pure defined benefit case), the latter on behalf of the PSRS (Public Sector Retirement System, a shared risk defined benefit case).[15] Neither plan sponsor is real, but their situations are realistic. We address the "capital market prospects" question separately later in the chapter.

The Checklist Responses: Implication for Asset Mix Policy

The checklist responses contain strong messages for asset mix policy. If the ALPHA and PSRS responses are representative for private and public sector plan sponsors,[16] the implications are:

1. The long-term nature of pension fund investing is confirmed in the sense that the primary planning mode is "ongoing," rather

---

[15]Readers wanting more detail on ALPHA Corporation are referred to my book *Pension Funds and the Bottom Line*. We believe its pension "deal" to be quite reflective of many actual U.S. and Canadian private sector pension "deals." The reason for introducing a public sector employer separately is to show that this pension "deal" may be quite different than in the private sector. While the actual "deal" described is hypothetical, it in fact reflects that of at least two large Canadian public sector employer pension plans quite closely.

[16]We have already indicated that we believe they are. See footnotes 10 and 15.

EXHIBIT 2:
ASSET ALLOCATION CHECKLIST

I. THE "GOING-CONCERN DEAL"

ALPHA

- benefit accruals formally indexed, pre-retirement up to 50% of final pay . . . *"ad hoc"* post-retirement (60% of CPI is target) updates . . . no explicit tie between pension fund performance and inflation updates

- the plan is non-contributory and is being funded on a 7.5%/6.0% basis (investment return/wage growth), leading to a 8% "normal" contribution rate . . . inflation updates do not increase the contribution rate unless the updated funding target exceeds the value of plan assets . . . contribution rate reduced if plan assets exceed funding target by a certain percentage

PSRS

- benefit accruals formally indexed, pre-retirement up to 70% of final pay . . . post retirement updates tied to pension fund performance (return in excess of 3% becomes inflation update subject to a 100% of CPI upper bound and a 0% of CPI lower bound)

- the plan is contributory (50%/50%), and is being funded on a 3.0%/1.5% (investment return/wage growth) basis, leading to a 20% "normal" contribution rate . . . this contribution rate is adjusted up or down depending on plan economic funded status (i.e., plan assets at market, plan liabilities estimated on a 3.0%/1.5% return/salary increase basis)

II. THE "TERMINATION DEAL"

ALPHA

- in a voluntary plan termination situation, ALPHA would offer plan members the better of two calculations—the present value of projected benefits calculated on a 7.5% basis for inactive liabilities and a 7.5%/6.0% basis for actives . . . the alternative calculation for actives is the accumulated value of contributions, credited the risk-free rate of interest . . . ALPHA would own any asset surplus or owe any asset deficiency

PSRS

- this situation has not been explicitly contemplated . . . any termination settlement would have to be negotiated between the government and the unions involved (such negotiations would likely lead to a settlement based on the 3.0%/1.5% experience assumptions basis, with any asset surplus or deficiency split 50%/50%)

III. ASSET AND LIABILITY VALUE FLUCTUATIONS

ALPHA

- ALPHA recognizes that on a going-concern economic basis, it should include a 2.5% (i.e., 60% of 4%) inflation factor, implying the use of 5.0%/3.5% experience assumptions to estimate the going-concern economic liability . . . plan assets will fluctuate depending on their sensitivity to changes in economic expectations and capital market psychology

- ALPHA's management is satisfied that the new accounting rules can be employed in such a way that the financial status of its retirement system can be represented in an unbiased way, and that through the available smoothing mechanisms no year-to-year surprises will be encountered

PSRS

- calculated on a 3.0%/1.5% basis, the going-concern liability will progress smoothly over time . . . plan assets will fluctuate depending on their sensitivity to changes in economic expectations and capital market psychology

- the new private sector accounting rules are irrelevant to the PSRS situation . . . however, asset value smoothing will be used for disclosure and contribution rate calculation purposes

IV. MAIN BUSINESS/PENSION PLAN PLANNING AND BALANCE SHEET INTEGRATION

ALPHA

- ALPHA wants to focus on "cashflow integration" rather than "tax structure integration"—in other words, it does not want to have to make extra contributions when it is least able to do so (i.e., liabilities rising faster than expected as the value of plan assets and corporate earnings are falling)

PSRS

- Government is interested in the correlation between tax revenues and the required pension plan contribution . . . it wants to avoid the need to make extra contributions at a time when tax revenues are falling (i.e., as tax revenues are falling, and plan assets are falling, plan liabilities are rising faster than expected)

EXHIBIT 2: (continued)
ASSET ALLOCATION CHECKLIST

- ALPHA understands the tax arbitrage argument but has decided not to "play" it—in other words, it has decided not to reshuffle corporate and pension assets and liabilities between the main business and pension plan balance sheets, mainly because such activity would signal the corporation is engaged in a form of not-easy-to-explain form of gaming the tax authorities and because it believes financial analysts and rating agencies might misinterpret such moves

- the tax arbitrage consideration is irrelevant in the PSRS context unless the issuance of tax-exempt bonds is a realistic option

than "termination." A corollary is that any segmentation of the liabilities into "retired lives" and "actives" is unnecessary and possibly even misleading.[17]

2. Investment risk, whether viewed in its "ongoing" or "termination" dimensions, has a "real" rather than "nominal" focus because pension benefits have a "real" rather than a "nominal" focus:

   (a) in its "ongoing" dimension, risk relates to the impact of negative real returns on future contribution rates

   (b) in its "termination" dimension, risk relates to the volatility of the market value of pension assets in relation to the settlement value of the pension liability . . . this liability will *not* necessarily be sensitive to changes in nominal interest rates, depending on the nature of the "termination" deal

   (c) in either dimension, risks may be *shared* rather than borne purely by either the plan sponsor or plan members

3. Despite the long-term nature of pension fund investing, shorter-term changes in the economic going-concern balance sheet matter because:

   (a) such changes trigger changes in contribution rates and hence the disposition of future stakeholder (i.e., plan sponsor, plan member, or both) cashflows

   (b) such changes affect the value of the plan sponsor's own securities and hence its cost of debt and equity capital

   (c) if there *is* a plan termination, settlement could be related to the economic rather than the legal termination liability.

4. There is a strong basis for looking at the relationship between the nature and source of sponsor cashflows and pension fund returns. For example, if sponsor cashflows are negatively affected by changes in the inflation rate, that is all the more reason to invest

---

[17]Active lives/retired lives segmentation was of course central to the "retired lives immunization" wave that swept the pension industry a few years ago. For "retired lives immunization" to make economic sense, one of two conditions must hold: (1) the plan sponsor must be willing to literally discharge its obligations to inactive plan members through the purchase of annuities, or (2) the plan sponsor must be certain that pensions-in-pay will never be adjusted for actual inflation experience. In fact, while we are not aware of precise statistics on the prevalence of these conditions, the vast majority of plan sponsors have *not* bought their way out of their retired lives obligations, and the vast majority of plan sponsors *do* provide inflation-related updates to pensions-in-pay.

in inflation hedges in the pension fund. Conversely, if sponsor cashflows are more negatively impacted by economic recession, more emphasis should go to putting recession hedges in the pension fund.

CAPITAL MARKETS PROSPECTS

Capital market prospects matter in the "economic going-concern" planning context because this context recognizes that ongoing pension benefit payments can come from only two sources: (1) contributions into the pension fund and (2) investment earnings on those contributions. Further, the more there is of the latter, the less there has to be of the former. We suggested above, for example, that an incremental 300 basis points of pension fund return could *halve* required contribution rate for a typical defined benefit pension plan.

What *are* reasonable long-term capital market prospects today? Answers to this question always reflect a blend of historical experience, the structure of capital markets yields and prices at the point in time the question is posed, and any forward-looking judgments the forecaster is prepared to make at that point in time. The numbers in Exhibit 3 reflect "equilibrium" long-term capital markets prospects in the spirit of the work done by Ibbotson, Siegel, Brinson, Diermeier, Schlarbaum, et. al.[18]

Capital Market Prospect Implications

On a prospective returns basis, equity-oriented investments should permit a pension plan to meet its obligations with the lowest contribution rate over the long run. Within the equity investment sphere, common stocks offer liquidity at the price of somewhat lower prospec-

---

[18]For a fully developed set of capital markets expectations using this history/current prices/ forward-looking judgments blend, see Gary P. Brinson, Jeffrey J. Diermeier, and Gary G. Schlarbaum, "A Composite Portfolio Benchmark for Pension Plans," *Financial Analysts Journal*, March–April 1986; and Roger Ibbotson and Laurence Siegel, "The World Market Wealth Portfolio," *Journal of Portfolio Management*, Winter 1983. The numbers used in this article were developed using the "equilibrium" framework described in these articles. Not surprisingly, our numbers bear a close resemblance to those published in the 1986 *FAJ* article cited above.

EXHIBIT 3:
LONG-TERM REAL RETURN PROSPECTS

	Long-Term Real Return Implication
1. By its very nature, a properly invested, diversified pool of *venture capital* investments should always have the best long-term return prospects. Studies suggest 15% real return experience is common over the last 10 years:	15%
2. Diversified pools of commercial *real estate* are being priced on a 7% cash yield basis in mid-1987. It is not unreasonable to project maintenance of the purchasing power of this cash yield over the long-term through increased rents:	7%
3. *Common stock* prices have now been bid up to a point where it is difficult to see the long-term historical 7% real return prospectively. A 3½% cash yield plus 2½% long-term real economic growth prospects lead to real return prospects of:	6%
4. *Long bonds* still offer historically high real return prospects measured against current inflation experience, without strong views as to whether long-term inflation will average out above or below today's experience, the prospect is:	3.5%
5. *T-bills* also still offer historically high real returns today. But real returns over the long-term should decline back to more normal levels.	1.5%

tive returns relative to real estate and considerably lower returns in relation to venture capital.

We noted above that in a going-concern mode, downdrafts in pension plan assets values still matter. Such downdrafts can lead to higher contribution rates, can affect the value of plan sponsor securities (and hence its cost of capital) and decrease the benefit security of plan members.

When are diversified portfolios of equity investments most likely to suffer material downward revisions in value? During periods of high stock valuation followed by a major decline in economic activity; likely a time when inflation rates are falling, long-term interest rates on high quality bonds are falling and hence the prices of these bonds are rising. *Thus, in a going-concern mode, the rationale for high-quality bonds is not immunization, but fund capital value and income protection during periods of sharply falling equity values and equity-related earnings.*

For example, $1 invested in stocks in 1929 would have been worth 36 cents four years later (while there are no numbers for real estate or venture capital for this period, investors no doubt suffered major losses in these equity classes as well).[19] Over that same four-year period, $1 invested in long bonds would have increased to $1.19. The consumer price index dropped 20% in the 1929-1932 time period. *A 40% stocks/ 60% bonds asset mix would have roughly maintained the real value of a pension fund over this four-year period.*

BONDS AND INFLATION RISK

While bonds can save a pension fund during unanticipated major declines in economic activity, they can seriously erode the real value of pension assets and income during periods of rising inflation. For example, $1 invested in long bonds in 1978 would have been worth 98 cents four years later. But with the CPI rising 48% over the 1978–1981 period, the loss in *real* terms was more like 50%. A $1 invested in stocks over the same four-year period would have increased to $2.19. *Again, a 40% stocks/60% bonds asset mix would have roughly maintained the real value of the pension fund over this four-year period.*

Is the 40% stocks/60% bonds mix *the* minimum risk (against economic going-concern liabilities) pension fund asset mix policy for all seasons then? Not necessarily. In the stagflation world of the mid-1970s, stocks and bonds *both* had negative real rates of return. During this period only exposure to real estate, venture capital, and foreign investments would have maintained the real value and real investment income of the pension fund.[20]

---

[19]The 1929–1932 and 1978–1981 examples were developed from Canadian capital markets and inflation experience using the *Canadian Economic Statistics* database of the Canadian Institute of Actuaries. While the numbers would have been somewhat different with U.S. data, the conclusions would not.

[20]Our observations, of course, relate to the underlying covariance structures of real rates of return. If covariance structures shift with changes in economic eras (from a period rising inflation to deflation, for example), covariance statistics generated over periods which include more than one such era will have no predictive content. We believe that much can be learned by carefully studying actual capital markets behavior within pre-defined periods of economic history and, conversely, by studying the economic environment during pre-defined periods of capital markets history.

A FORWARD-LOOKING ASSET MIX POLICY

Having already ranked the eligible asset classes in terms of long-term return prospects, long-term asset mix policy becomes a question of real return *risk* and how to best defend against it. We postulate how a diversified equity-oriented portfolio (say, 10% venture capital, 30% real estate, 40% domestic stocks, 20% foreign stocks), and a high-quality long bond portfolio (say, 20-year zero coupons) might perform in three "bad news" scenarios below. The three "bad news" scenarios are generalizations of the 1929–1932 (deflation), late 1960's to mid-1970's (stagflation), and 1978–81 (rising inflation) periods. Implications for three 80/20, 60/40, 40/60) equity/bond mixes are also shown in Exhibit 4.[21]

EXHIBIT 4:
WAYS IN WHICH THINGS MIGHT GO WRONG OVER THE NEXT 4 YEARS

Possible "Bad News" Scenarios	100% Equity	100% Bonds	80%/20%	60%/40%	40%/60%
Deflation	−40%	+60%	−20%	0%	+20%
Stagflation	+10%	−10%	6%	2%	−2%
Rising Inflation	+10%	−50%	−2%	−14%	−26%

Note: Numbers reflect cumulative four-year real returns.

Based on Exhibit 4, the following are observed:

1. Clearly, the "swing" scenarios are Deflation and Rising Inflation. Here is where the diversified equity-oriented portfolio and the long bond portfolio real return projections have to be at least of the right order of magnitude.
2. The projections *are* consistent with capital markets experience during periods of economic conditions similar to those being

---

[21]For the reasons set out in footnote 20, we continue with the "scenario approach" to look at prospective "economic going-concern" balance sheet risk and contribution rate risk for sponsors of defined benefit pension plans. Readers are invited to put their *own* estimates into Exhibit 4 to see if such estimates would change any of the six observations based on Exhibit 4.

postulated. Recall that the equity portfolio has only 40% domestic common stocks in it. We would have been considerably more uncertain about equities in all three scenarios without the equity portfolio's 60% exposure to venture capital, real estate and foreign stocks.

3. While *the 100% bond portfolio* might be risk-minimizing against "legal termination pension liabilities," it *is at least as risky as a 100% equity-oriented portfolio* against "economic going-concern pension liabilities." These latter liabilities do *not* decline or rise in line with rising or falling nominal interest rates.

4. The risk-minimizing (in the sense of balancing off deflation and rising inflation bad news) asset mix policy against "economic going-concern pension liabilities" is no longer 40%/60%. This balance is now struck at about 70%/30% if (a) the deflation and rising inflation outcomes are deemed to be equally likely, and (b) the "pain" of about a 10% decline in the real value of pension assets is the same in both Deflation and Rising Inflation.

5. Would the use of T-bills help get the downside get back to a 0% real rate of return. This is equivalent to asking if shortening the duration of the bond portfolio would be of help. The answer is "Yes." By reducing the equity weighting back to 40% and reducing the duration of the bond component from 20 years to about 3 years, prospective real return equivalence in deflation and rising inflation is reestablished at 0%.

6. In terms of prospective long-term real return (taking weighted averages from Exhibit 3), the 70%/30% equity/long bond mix works out to 6.1% versus 4.0% on the 40%/10%/50% equity/bond/T-bill mix. *This 210 basis points return differential translates into a potential 30%/40% differential in the contribution rate required to support a typical defined benefit pension plan.*[22]

Will the ALPHA Corporation Pension Plan and the Public Service Retirement System Trustees adopt the 70%/30% asset mix policy? Or

---

[22]To arrive at the fifth and sixth observations, we assumed that T-bills might do about 20% cumulatively over 4 years in deflation and 0% in rising inflation. By 40/10/50 we mean a 40% equity-oriented/10% long bond/50% T-bill mix—implying about a 3-year duration for the 60% debt portion. The conversion of the 210 basis point return differential into a 30–40% contribution rate differential is again just suggestive of the order of magnitude involved. (See footnote 13 for more on this long-term return/contribution rate sensitivity.)

the more conservative 40%/10%/50% policy? Or something in between? We turn to these questions next.

DELIBERATIONS AT ALPHA CORPORATION

ALPHA's plan is a pure non-contributory defined benefit pension plan.
Appropriately then, plan governance is under the control of ALPHA
Corporation, with its management required to behave prudently and to
have due regard for their obligation to maintain plan solvency. Exhibit
5 details their asset mix policy deliberations.

EXHIBIT 5:
ALPHA CORPORATION PENSION PLAN

THE ASSET ALLOCATION CHECKLIST

I.   *The "Going-Concern Deal"*

- The plan as a "final earnings"-based benefit formula and ALPHA has a
  long history of providing *ad hoc* inflation updates averaging 60% of
  CPI. These two factors together suggest ALPHA should look at risk and
  return in real terms on the asset side of the balance sheet.

- The plan is non-contributory, and there is no ambiguity that good investment results lead directly to lower plan contributions by the employer, just as bad investment results will lead to higher contributions by the
  employer.

II.   *The "Termination Deal"*

- In any plan termination other than corporate bankruptcy, the "settlement value" of accrued pensions would be above the "legal termination
  liability" and would not fluctuate in line with fluctuations in long bond
  values and yields. The probability of plan termination is judged to be
  very low.

III. *Asset and Liability Value Fluctuations*

- ALPHA management deems the "economic going-concern" balance
  sheet to be the one which will guide their asset mix policy decision. The
  plan now has about a 15% "going-concern" asset cushion (of course,
  its "legal termination" asset cushion is considerably larger). ALPHA
  policy is to increase the corporate contribution rate if the "going-concern" cushion goes negative.

- ALPHA management is well aware that it might be appropriate or even necessary to report different asset and liability numbers to the regulatory authorities and in its financial statements. These numbers will likely be a smoothed blend of the "legal termination" and "economic going-concern" balance sheets.

IV. *Degree of Main Business/Pension Plan Decisions Integration*

- The key question for management here is whether ALPHA's main business would fare worse in the deflation or rising inflation scenario (if one was decidedly worse for ALPHA than the other, it would be logical to "buy" protection against it in the pension fund). After considerable deliberation, they decided the main business would be equally hurt by deflation or rising inflation—assuming the latter brought with it significant increases in real labor costs. Also, they decided they were not prepared to guess whether one scenario was more likely to occur than the other. In conclusion, they decided they would *not* bias their asset mix policy decision due either consideration.

- Management also decided not to engage in any pension plan—related tax arbitrage by reshuffling main business and pension plan assets and liabilities in an attempt to reduce corporate taxes payable.

V. *Capital Markets Prospects*

- A diversified equity-oriented policy has a long-term prospective real return in the 6%/7% range. But even when combined with a 30% long bond position, such an asset mix policy could lead to declines in the real value of the pension fund in the 10% range over the next four years.

- Better downside protection involves jointly reducing equity exposure and the duration of the debt component fund.

THE ASSET ALLOCATION DECISION

The combination of Alpha Corporation's going-concern focus, a healthy "going-concern" pension plan balance sheet, and the potential of being able to fund a competitive pension plan with a long-term contribution rate in the 4% of pay area, lead Alpha to decide to pursue the 70%/30% asset mix policy. The 70% equity component is diversified across venture capital, real estate and domestic and foreign stocks. The 30% debt component is to be in long duration, high-quality bonds.

AT THE PUBLIC SECTOR RETIREMENT SYSTEM

Unlike the ALPHA Corporation situation, investment risks and rewards are shared in the Public Sector Retirement System. They are shared by the taxpaying public, active public sector employees and inactive/retired public sector employees. The composition of the Board of Trustees reflects this risk-sharing reality. Exhibit 6 sets out their asset mix policy deliberations.

EXHIBIT 6:
PUBLIC SECTOR RETIREMENT SYSTEM

THE ASSET ALLOCATION CHECKLIST

I.   *The "Going-Concern Deal"*

- The pension plan as a "final earnings"-based benefit formula. The plan also has a post-retirement inflation update formula tied to pension fund performance (return in excess of 3% becomes the inflation update subject to a 100% of CPI upper bound and a 0% of CPI lower bound). Thus, risk and return should be analyzed in both nominal and real terms on the asset side of the balance sheet.

- Plan contributions are shared 50%/50% by the employer and active employees. Thus, through the contribution formula and through the link between inflation updates and pension fund performance, all stakeholders share in both good and poor investment performance.

II. *The "Termination Deal"*

- There is no formal agreement in place as to what would happen in case of a plan termination. But with the best estimate of the "going-concern" liability outstripping the value of plan assets by 30%, negotiations would surely focus on how much the—"settlement value" of the benefits exceeded the value of plan assets. But with no intent on the part of the employer to terminate, all this is very hypothetical.

III. *Asset and Liability Fluctuations*

- With the liability being calculated on a 3% discount rate basis, it will progress smoothly (assuming a steady-state plan membership size and composition) over time. The plan asset value in relation to this "economic going-concern" liability value is material because the gap between the two affects the contribution rate. The "normal" contribution rate is 20% of pay. But the *actual* current contribution rate is 25% (12.5% each for the employer and the employees) of pay, reflecting the amortization of the sizable unfunded past service liability. Poor investment experience would widen the asset-liability gap further, further increasing the required contribution rate for the employer and active employees.

- Poor investment experience also affects pensioners. If the nominal fund return is below 3%, pensioners get no inflation update regardless of what the actual inflation rate was over the measurement period. Pensions-in-pay are updated for inflation experience by the amount fund return exceeds 3%, up to a maximum of 100% of CPI. Thus, possible asset mix policy choices have to be tested for impact on inflation updates to pensioners.*

IV. *Degree of Government/Pension Plan Decisions Integration*

- In assessing if deflation and rising inflation would be equally problematic "bad news" scenarios for the government (i.e., the plan sponsor in this case), the decision was "No." Deflation would decidedly be the worse of these two bad worlds. In this scenario, the government would be faced with falling tax revenues and rising demands in its financial resources, while still being obliged to make interest payments on its outstanding high-coupon long-term debt.

- While active employees feel they would be equally hurt by a rising contribution rate in the two "bad news" outcomes, pensioners fear the rising inflation scenario more. It is in this scenario they run the risk that pension fund returns won't be adequate to protect the real value of their pension.

V. *Capital Markets Prospects*

- While the prospective long-term 6%/7% real rate of return associated with the 100% equity-oriented policy is very attractive, the consequences of a deflation outcome with this policy are unacceptable to the employer (i.e., the government). The government believes the plan has to trade off some long term return for better deflation protection by lowering equity exposure and increasing long bond exposure.

---

*There is an interesting debate in progress on this question of how to best provide formal inflation protection for retired plan members. One school would tie the formula directly to the CPI. The other would, as in the PSRS example, tie it to capital market returns. The argument here is that pensioners should also bear at least some of the risk associated with formally (as opposed to *ad hoc*) providing inflation protection.

THE ASSET ALLOCATION DECISION

The trustees of the public sector retirement system agree to set the asset mix policy at 50%/50%. The 50% equity component is to be diversified across venture capital, real estate and domestic and foreign stocks. The 50% debt component is to be in medium duration, high-quality bonds. This policy should eventually move the joint employer-employee contribution rate from the current 25% of pay to an eventual 10% of pay. Pensions should be maintained in real terms in all but the worst inflation scenario.

ASSET ALLOCATION DECISION DETAILS

There is more to ALPHA's and PSRS's asset mix policy decisions than appears in Exhibits 5 and 6. For example, the degree of "give" in the policies will have to be decided, with special emphasis on whether any attempt is to be made to shift the asset mix based on shorter term market anticipations. If the answer is "Yes," the double question, "Who will do it with how much money?," will require a lot of careful study. Other chapters in this book study these questions in detail.[23]

Another important consideration is the plan's likely evolving liquidity needs. Even in a "going-concern" mode, material changes in the size and composition of plan membership, and in the relationship between money flowing into the plan and out of the plan, can take place. Such potential changes also need careful study. It is not acceptable for a pension plan to have the perfect long-term asset mix policy but not to be able to write checks when it has to because it has no cash!

THE IMPORTANCE OF INTEGRATION

This chapter has placed pension fund asset allocation in a broader economic context. Such a broader context forces consideration of the nature of the pension "deal" between the employer and its current and former employees. It also forces a decision as to which of the two

---

[23]Much has been written about the distinction between the establishment of a "normal" asset mix policy (the subject of this chapter) and tactical asset allocation or market timing. See, for example Chapter 7. The point made here is that market timing should not be confused with deciding on target asset mix policy weights in the context of investing against "economic going-concern" pension liabilities.

possible planning modes, "termination" or "going-concern" is to dominate the asset mix policy decision.

In a "termination" planning mode, a classic bond immunization strategy is a feasible policy option. Interestingly, such a strategy, on a different level, also immunizes any possible economic interaction between a plan sponsor's main business and its pension "business."

A "going-concern" planning mode recognizes that, unless the pension plan really *is* shut down, the pension fund is an ongoing "money spinner" which helps to finance pension obligations when they fall due. As this chapter has shown, pension fund asset allocation decisions in this latter context become, for plan sponsors, important *financial policy decisions*. Hence, they can no longer be made in isolation. They must be integrated into the plan sponsor's overall financial strategy.

CHAPTER 6

Inflation, Interest Rates, and Pension Liabilities*

LAURIE S. GOODMAN
VICE PRESIDENT
FINANCIAL STRATEGIES GROUP
GOLDMAN SACHS & CO.

WILLIAM J. MARSHALL**
SENIOR VICE PRESIDENT
FRANKLIN SAVINGS BANK

INFLATION RISK AND INTEREST RATE RISK

Pension fund managers have historically been concerned about the effects on their pension obligations of detrimental movements in both inflation and interest rates. They realize that they can address interest rate risk by acquiring long-term bonds with the appropriate interest rate

---

*The authors would like to thank Fischer Black, Dennis Kass, Jose Scheinkman, Irwin Tepper, and Robert Zink for their helpful comments and insights; Jennifer Nissen for her valuable assistance in preparing the numerical examples; and Emmanuel Roman for his empirical research on the relationship between anticipated inflation and interest rates.

**Dr. Marshall was a Vice President in the Fixed Income Division at Goldman Sachs & Co. at the time this chapter was written.

sensitivities. But many managers believe that by holding fixed income assets, they will increase the vulnerability of their funds to the effects of inflation. That is, rising prices mean higher wages, which result in higher pension benefits. While their pension obligations vary *directly* with inflation, however, the returns to a long-term bond portfolio vary *inversely* with inflation. Thus, in this conventional view, hedging interest rate risk is inconsistent with hedging inflation risk.

In this chapter we show that pension fund managers can address inflation risk and interest rate risk simultaneously. While it is true that wage levels—and therefore pension benefits—rise more rapidly as the inflation rate goes up, the conventional view neglects the effect of anticipated inflation on interest rates. In fact, rising anticipated inflation rates cause current and expected future interest rates to increase as well. Thus, a larger discount factor must be applied to future benefits, reducing the present value of pension liabilities. Indeed, as our analysis in this chapter suggests, this negative effect on pension liabilities overwhelms the positive effect from higher wage levels.

We develop these ideas in more detail in the next section, in which we present a theoretical sensitivity analysis of the impact on pension liability value of changes—anticipated and unanticipated—in inflation and of changes in the real rate of interest.

To supplement this theoretical analysis, we present a simulation in the third section based on historical evidence. If the effect of inflation on pension liabilities was channeled primarily through higher wages and salaries, we would expect to see a positive correlation between levels of inflation and pension liabilities from period to period. *In fact, empirical evidence suggests that inflation and pension liabilities are negatively related.* This supports our proposition that inflation transmits its primary effect on pension liabilities through interest rates rather than wage levels.

In the fourth section we discuss how fund managers might address the inflation and interest rate risk in pension liabilities using fixed income instruments. Readers should realize that while this chapter treats two major elements of the asset allocation decision—inflation and interest rate risk—other influences are also important, including variations in employment and real wages over time. Although these considerations are beyond the scope of this chapter, they cannot be ignored.

ANALYSIS

We will use stylized examples to isolate the impact of inflation on pension liabilities. Our analysis considers exclusively the pension liabilities owed to active workers (active lives). This is because pension fund sponsors are concerned about the impact of inflation on the salaries of active workers. By contrast, for retired workers (retired lives) in plans without COLAs, inflation has no effect other than its operation through interest rates.

Consider a so-called "final pay plan"—a plan in which benefits are based on salary at retirement.[1] The representative active member of this plan has been with the firm 20 years and has 10 years to go until retirement. While the worker is older than the average member of the plan, he is representative for purposes of calculating the typical pension plan liability, because benefit obligations are weighted by length of service. The plan expects to pay the representative individual for 17 years after retirement. The worker is paid 40% of his final salary in each retirement year if he leaves the firm this year, and there are no cost of living allowances in retirement. This is based on a benefit formula of 2% of his final salary per year of service (20). Of relevance to calculating the pension liability is his period of time with the firm to *date*, rather than to retirement.

Calculating the Pension Liability

Our analysis uses the projected benefit obligation (PBO) as a proxy for the economic pension liability. We use the PBO because it is one reasonable measure of the pension obligation of a going concern.[2] In addition, the PBO is the accounting measure of liability that is used to calculate pension expense and funded status for the firm's financial reports under FASB-87.

---

[1] This represents a slight simplification of reality since most final pay plans base benefits on a worker's average pay during the last 3 to 5 years of service.

[2] An alternative measure of pension liabilities is the accumulated benefit obligation (ABO). This is the existing liability of the pension plan, based on current salary and past service. It does not include an adjustment for the effect of future salary increases. We focus on the PBO, as inflation would be expected to be more important in this measure.

The PBO measures the pension obligation based on service to date, projected mortality, and anticipated salary growth. The dependence on future salary growth arises because most plans base benefits on average salary over some period just prior to retirement.

The PBO is not the only measure of the true economic obligation of every firm. In truth, the perception of the obligation may vary from firm to firm, as do economic circumstances. Nevertheless, the PBO suits our purpose well by isolating the effects we wish to analyze— inflation and interest rate risks.

To determine the PBO for an active worker, we need to calculate the value at retirement of the benefit stream and discount its value back to the present. We will do so using equations (1) - (4):

$$\text{Current Wage} \times \text{Inflation Adjustment} = \text{Retirement Wage} \quad (1)$$

$$\text{Retirement Wage} \times \text{Benefit Formula} = \text{Annual Benefit} \quad (2)$$

$$\text{Annual Benefit} \times \text{Annuity Factor} = \text{Value at Retirement of Benefit Stream} \quad (3)$$

$$\text{Value at Retirement of Benefit Stream} \times \text{Discount Factor} = \text{Present Value of Pension Liability} \quad (4)$$

Assuming the current wage is \$20,000, inflation is 5%, and the interest rate is 8.15%, we can use the above equations to calculate the value of the PBO.

From equation (1):
Current Wage	=	\$20,000
Inflation Adjustment	=	$1.629 \ (= 1.08^{10})$
Retirement Wage	=	\$32,578

From equation (2):
Retirement Wage	=	\$32,578
Benefit Formula	=	0.4
Annual Benefit	=	\$13,031

From equation (3):

Annual Benefit	= $13,031
Annuity Factor	= 9.031
Value at Retirement of Benefit Stream	= $117,685

From equation (4):

Value at Retirement of Benefit Stream	= $117,685
Discount Factor	= .457 ($= 1.0815^{-10}$)
Present Value of Pension Liability	= $53,760

We show this result in column (1) of Exhibit 1. We can now put equations (1) - (4) together to obtain equation (5):

$$\text{Present Value of Pension Liability} =$$

$$\begin{array}{ccccccccc} \text{Current} & \times & \text{Inflation} & \times & \text{Benefit} & \times & \text{Annuity} & \times & \text{Discount} \quad (5) \\ \text{Wage} & & \text{Adjustment} & & \text{Formula} & & \text{Factor} & & \text{Factor} \end{array}$$

In terms of our example:

$$\$53,760 = \$20,000 \times 1.629 \times .04 \times 9.031 \times .457$$

Calculating Interest Rate and Inflation Sensitivity

We can think of inflation as being composed of anticipated and unanticipated inflation. In like manner, we can think of nominal, or observable, interest rates as being composed of two parts: a "real" rate of interest that is ultimately based on the productivity of capital, and the anticipated rate of inflation. Any change in anticipated inflation is reflected in a change in nominal interest rates as well. We explain these relationships more fully in Exhibit 2.

Thus, we can conceive of three different shocks to the system: (1) unanticipated inflation, (2) a change in anticipated inflation, and (3) a change in the real rate of interest. We consider the effect on the pension obligation of each of these in turn, beginning with unanticipated infla-

EXHIBIT 1:
INTEREST RATE AND INFLATION SENSITIVITY OF PENSION LIABILITIES WITHOUT COLAS

	(1) Base Case	(2) 1pp* Rise in Unanticipated Inflation	(3) 1 pp Rise in the Real Rate of Interest	(4) 1 pp Rise in Anticipated Inflation	(5) 1pp Rise in Unanticipated and Anticipated Inflation
Current wage	20,000	20,200	20,000	20,000	20,200
Inflation adjustment until retirement	1.629	1.629	1.629	1.791	1.791
Benefit formula	.4	.4	.4	.4	.4
Annuity factor (retirement-death)	9.031	9.031	8.435	8.446	8.446
Discount factor (retirement-present)	.457	.467	.415	.416	.416
Present value of pension liability	53,760	54,297	45,587	50,275	50,275
Percent change from base case	0	1.0%	−15.2%	−6.5%	−5.5%
Duration of pension liability with respect to shock (years)		−1.0	15.2	6.5	5.5

*pp = percentage point.

EXHIBIT 2:
INFLATION AND INTEREST RATES: DEFINITIONS AND CONCEPTS

Inflation:	Rate of change in the general level of prices
Anticipated inflation	The generally expected future rate of inflation.
Inflation risk:	
Unanticipated inflation:	Any difference between actual and anticipated inflation.
Change in anticipated inflation:	Any change in the forecast of future inflation.
Nominal interest rate:	The real rate of interest plus the anticipated rate of inflation.
Interest rate risk:	The risk of changes in the nominal interest rate. To a first order approximation, this can be decomposed as follows:

$$\begin{matrix} \text{\% Change in Nominal} \\ \text{Interest Rate} \end{matrix} = \begin{matrix} \text{\% Change in Real} \\ \text{Interest Rate} \end{matrix} + \begin{matrix} \text{\% Change in} \\ \text{Anticipated Inflation} \end{matrix}$$

Thus, as a first order approximation, a 1 percentage point change in either real interest rates or anticipated inflation causes a 1 percentage point change in the nominal intereste rate.

---

tion. For simplicity, we assume a flat yield curve. Interest rate changes affect all sectors of the yield curve in a parallel manner.

Changes in Unanticipated Inflation In our example, we will assume that an unanticipated change in the inflation rate results in a corresponding wage change but leaves all other relevant variables intact. That is, an unexpected price shock that raises the price level by 1% will boost the current wage level by 1% and leave all nominal and real interest rates unchanged. Thus, the pension liability will also change by 1%, as we show in Exhibit 1. We can say that since a 1 percentage point increase in unanticipated inflation[3] causes a 1% *rise* in pension liabili-

---

[3]Unanticipated inflation has an expected value of zero. Since an unexpected 1% surge in the price level implies an addition of 1 percentage point to the inflation rate, we can refer to this as a 1 percentage point "change in unanticipated inflation."

ties, the PBO has a price sensitivity, or effective modified duration of −1 year with respect to unanticipated inflation. As we shall see in the section "Implications for Assessing Interest Rate Sensitivity," PBO duration is a critical number for the fund manager to know in managing interest rate risk by establishing a duration match or deliberate mismatch.

Of course, it is a bit artificial to consider a change in unanticipated inflation in isolation. If inflation is higher in one year than in the previous year, there will generally be an increase in inflation expectations that will have an impact on nominal interest rates. We will take that into account later in this chapter.

Changes in the Real Rate of Interest We will now consider a 1 percentage point rise in the real rate of interest.[4] As column (3) of Exhibit 1 shows, this increase will be reflected in the annuity factor and the discount factor. That is, the value of the benefit stream as of the date of retirement is lower than in the base case, and its present value is lower still. As you would expect, if interest rates rise, the benefit stream payable between years 10 and 27 will be worth considerably (15.2%) less today. Thus, the PBO has a duration of 15.2 years with respect to changes in the real rate of interest.

Changes in Anticipated Inflation We now consider the effect of changes in anticipated inflation. That change will affect three components of the PBO calculation: the inflation adjustment, the annuity factor, and the discount factor. Note from column 4 of Exhibit 1 that overall, a 1 percentage point rise in anticipated inflation with no initial price shock will cause a 6.5% fall in the value of the pension liability. As you would expect intuitively, the inflation adjustment and the discount factor are completely offsetting. That is, the inflation adjustment for salaries is 6% rather than 5%, but the discount rate used is commen-

---

[4] A 1% rise in the real rate of interest will be associated with slightly more than a 1% rise in nominal rate of interest. The interest rate is given by the equation below.

$$\text{Interest rate} = (1 + \text{real rate}) \times (1 + \text{anticipated inflation}) - 1$$
$$= \text{real rate} + \text{anticipated inflation rate} + \text{real rate} \times \text{anticipated inflation rate}$$

Thus, if the real rate is 3% and the anticipated inflation rate is 5%, the interest rate will be 8.15%. If real interest rates go up to 4%, the nominal interest rate will go up to 9.20%.

surately higher.[5] Because our example does not provide for cost of living allowances after retirement begins, there is no further inflation adjustment beyond that point. However, the annuity factor is lower.

We now consider a 1 percentage point change in anticipated inflation resulting from a 1% shock to the price level. This will affect four components of our calculation: the current wage, the inflation adjustment, the annuity factor, and the discount factor. This will cause a 5.5% fall in the value of the pension liabilities, as we can see in column (5) of Exhibit 1, which is a combination of columns (2) and (4). We show this result graphically in Exhibit 3. The increase in the current wage and the inflation adjustment shift the pension obligation up from point A to point B. However, increases in the annuity and discount factors shift the new benefit schedule down to point C.

Summing Up the Basic Example The change in the value of the pension liabilities depends very much on the nature of the shock. In our basic example, which excludes cost of living adjustments after retirement, a one-time 1% shock to the price level—with no effect on inflation expectations—expands pension liabilities by 1%. A 1 percentage point increase in real rates will cause pension liabilities to contract by 15.27%. A 1 percentage point change in anticipated inflation will shrink pension liabilities by 6.5%. A 1 percentage point rise in both anticipated and unanticipated inflation will cause a 5.5% reduction in the value of pension liabilities. The basic lesson of this example is that a surge in inflation affecting both wages and interest rates will have the net effect of reducing the PBO.

We are now ready to consider two modifications to the above analysis. We will first examine a benefit plan with cost of living allowances, and we will then allow for the partial transmission of a price level shock to inflation expectations.

---

[5]A 1 percentage point change in anticipated inflation from 5% to 6% will cause the nominal rate of interest to rise from 8.15% to 9.18%. This is because the nominal rate of interest is the rate of anticipated inflation (6%) plus the real rate (3%) plus the rate of anticipated inflation times the real rate (.18%), as explained in footnote 3. The effects of the inflation adjustment and the discount factor are offsetting because $(1.05)/(1.05)(1.03)$ is equivalent to $(1.06)/(1.06)(1.03)$.

EXHIBIT 3:
EFFECT OF RISE IN ANTICIPATED AND UNANTICIPATED INFLATION ON PENSION LIABILITIES

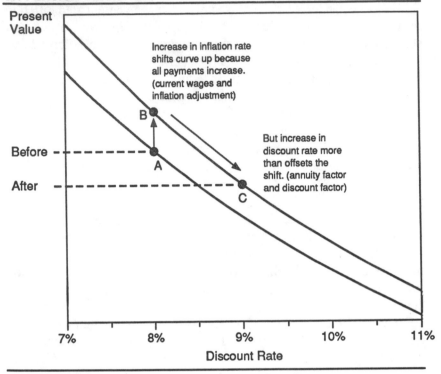

Adding Cost of Living Allowances

We can easily revise the above analysis to allow for automatic cost of living allowances (COLAs) after retirement. A full COLA ensures that the income of retirees goes up by the rate of change in the price level. A retiree would receive higher pension payments each year in order to maintain constant purchasing power of these payments during the retirement period.

In terms of our analysis, the benefit formulas in equations (1) - (4) remains unchanged. The annuity factor in equation (3), however, takes on a new meaning. It is now the present value of the annuity with the provision that the amount to be paid each year in retirement will grow by the anticipated inflation rate. Column (1) of Exhibit 4 shows the present value of the pension liabilities with a COLA. This is much

EXHIBIT 4:
INTEREST RATE AND INFLATION SENSITIVITY OF PENSION LIABILITIES WITH COLAS

	(1) Base Case	(2) 1pp Rise in Unanticipated Inflation	(3) 1pp Rise in Real Rate	(4) 1 pp Rise in Anticipated Inflation	(5) 1pp Rise in Unanticipated and Anticipated Inflation
Current wage	20,000	20,200	20,000	20,000	20,200
Inflation adjustment	1.629	1.627	1.629	1.791	1.791
Benefit formula	.4	.4	.4	.4	.4
Annuity factor	13.166	13.166	13.166	13.166	13.166
Discount factor	.457	.457	.415	.416	.416
Present value of pension liability	$ 78,375	79,158	65,750	78,375	79,158
Percentage change from base-case		+1.0%	−23.8%	0	+1.0%
Duration of pension liability (years)		−1.0	+23.8	0	−1.0

higher than the base case value in our basic example of Exhibit 1. The difference comes from the increase in the annuity factor to 13.166 with a COLA, from 9.031 without a COLA.

As Exhibit 4 shows, a 1 percentage point increase in unanticipated inflation, causing no rise in inflation expectations, will boost pension liabilities by 1%. A 1 percentage point rise in the real interest rate will decrease pension liabilities by 16.1%. These results are consistent with those in Exhibit 1.

The major difference arising from the COLA appears in column (4) of Exhibit 4: a 1 percentage point increase in anticipated inflation will not change pension liabilities. It is clear that wages are fully indexed for inflation before retirement and benefits are fully indexed for inflation after retirement. This fully offsets the reduction in the discount factor. Thus, a rise in inflation expectations will have no effect on pension liabilities. This result contrasts with that of the basic example with no COLAs, in which a 1 percentage point increase in anticipated inflation substantially reduces the PBO.

In sum, for a pension plan with COLAs, combining a 1 percentage point rise in unanticipated inflation with a 1 percentage point rise in anticipated inflation will produce a 1% rise in the level of pension liabilities, as indicated by column (5) of Exhibit 4. This is because COLAs serve to neutralize the interest rate effect of anticipated inflation on pension liabilities.

For many pension plans, cost of living increases are optional rather than mandatory. Nonetheless, these managers feel a moral obligation to partially make up for inflation. These plans can be viewed as combinations of a plan with a COLA and a plan without. For example, a plan with a 50% make-up rule can be looked upon as having 50% of its liabilities subject to COLAs and 50% not subject to COLAs. In terms of our analysis, a 1 percentage point rise in anticipated inflation would produce a change in pension liabilities of $[1/2 \, (-6.5) + 1/2 \, (0)] = -3.25\%$. A 1 percentage point rise in unanticipated and anticipated inflation would cause a change in pension liabilities of $[1/2 \, (-5.5) + 1/2 \, (1)] = -2.25\%$.

Transmission of Unanticipated Inflation

For the case without COLAs, we have shown that if there is no effect on future inflation expectations, a 1 percentage point increase in unanticipated inflation will cause pension liabilities to rise by 1%. If a 1 percentage point increase in unanticipated inflation causes a 1 percentage point rise in inflation expectations, the effect will be a drop in pension liabilities of 5.5%.

We refer to the effect of unanticipated inflation on subsequent expectations as the rate of transmission of unanticipated inflation. The two cases outlined above are actually polar cases of this phenomenon—0% transmission and 100% transmission. We can easily consider other possibilities. For a 1 percentage point rise in unanticipated inflation and an 80% transmission rate, we have a current wage of $20,200 versus $20,000 in the base case. The new rate of anticipated inflation is 5.8% rather than 5.0%, and the new nominal interest rate is 8.974. Thus, the inflation adjustment is 1.757 rather than 1.629. The annuity factor is 8.558 rather than 9.031, and the discount factor is .423 rather than .457. The drop in the pension liability is 4.29%. We can perform the same calculations for other transmission rates.

We show the results of these calculations in Exhibit 5. Clearly, as the transmission rate rises, the effect on the pension liability become larger in absolute value and more negative.

Summarizing the Theoretical Analysis

The results of our analysis indicate that the effect of inflation on pension liabilities may be far different from that suggested by the conventional wisdom. In our examples, a once and for all 1 percentage point shock to the price level with no changes in inflation expectations will cause a 1% rise in pension liabilities. A 1 percentage point rise in unanticipated and anticipated inflation will be reflected in nominal interest rates, causing a sharp *drop* in the liabilities of pension plans without COLAs. With a COLA, this effect disappears. If the transmission between unanticipated and anticipated inflation is less than 100%, as we generally expect it will be, a rise in unanticipated inflation will cause a fall in pension liabilities, but the effect in terms of absolute value will be less than in the 100% transmission case (a decline of 5.5%). In short, inflation expectations are transmitted into pension liabilities both *directly* and indirectly through interest rates. The magnitude of the indirect transmission is far greater than the magnitude of the direct transmission.

EXHIBIT 5:
PRICE SHOCKS AND CHANGES IN ANTICIPATED INFLATION RATES

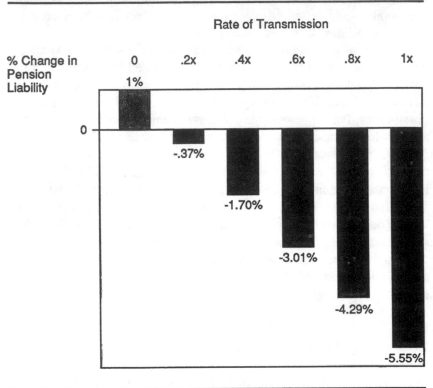

SIMULATION RESULTS USING HISTORICAL DATA

We showed in the previous section that the effect of inflation on pension fund liabilities depends on the extent to which inflation is anticipated and is hence reflected in interest rates. The more that it is, the greater is the net reduction in pension liabilities from an increase in inflation. In this section we will reinforce this point with the results of a simulation study using historical data. The study establishes that after we have accounted for interest rate risk, little residual risk from inflation remains.

Our simulation study used a data series on pension liabilities developed at Goldman Sachs.[6] This series measures the PBO during 1957-86, assuming that FASB 87 has been in effect the whole period. It takes into account both active workers and retirees. The study assumes a constant work force size and, for each year in question, a constant future real rate of interest. The assumption of a constant real interest rate is consistent with the accounting treatment of the PBO, although it is not consistent with economic reality in the short or medium term.

The year-to-year changes in this PBO series are based solely on inflation and interest rate risk. Wages are varied each year according to the actual inflation rate (changes in the Consumer Price Index). The discount rate used for the liabilities is the prevailing 20-year Treasury rate. The anticipated inflation rate is the discount rate (the Treasury bond rate) less the assumed 3% constant real rate. The series does not take into account year-to-year variations in the size of the workforce, the number of hours worked, or changes in productivity.

To determine the relative importance of interest rate risk and inflation risk for pension liabilities, we look at the correlation between this simulated PBO and inflation risk, and between the PBO and interest rate risk, based on annual data from 1957 through 1986. Exhibit 6 presents these results. The correlation between the PBO and the return on a long Treasury instrument is .97. This finding suggests that 94% of the variation in the PBO could have been hedged using long Treasury securities [.94 = (.97)^2]. The correlation between the PBO and inflation is negative, suggesting that the (negative) effects of anticipated inflation operating through interest rates outweighed the (positive) effects of unanticipated inflation alone.

We now use this result to see how closely an immunized bond portfolio would have tracked the PBO. We know the standard deviation of the annual percentage changes in the PBO is 9.27%. The standard deviation of the annual returns on the 20-year Treasury is 11.07%. We construct an immunized bond portfolio consisting solely of 20-year Treasuries. Equation (6) gives the weighting of the immunized bond portfolio.

---

[6]The data was developed jointly by Goldman Sachs and Irwin Tepper Associates. A similar set of data, the Goldman Sachs Pension Liability Indexes, will be published on a regular basis.

Weighting of
Immunized Bond =
Portfolio

Correlation of the PBO with the return on
20-year Treasury
$$\frac{\times \text{ Standard Deviation of PBO Changes}}{\text{Standard Deviation of 20-year Treasury Returns}} \quad (6)$$

In terms of our numbers,

Weighting of
Immunized Bond $= (.97) \times (9.72)/(11.07) = .85$
Portfolio

Thus, for each dollar in the pension liability, we use .85 market value of a 20-year bond to create an immunized portfolio. Exhibit 7 shows the performance of the immunized bond portfolio and the simulated PBO year by year since 1957. As you can see, they track closely.

Exhibit 8 decomposes the unanticipated change in the simulated PBO into two sources: variation corresponding to the performance of the immunized bond portfolio attributable to interest rate changes, and a residual variation attributable to unanticipated inflation. These residuals tend to be extremely small. The standard deviation of the PBO

EXHIBIT 6:
HISTORICAL EVIDENCE CORRELATION MATRIX

	PBO	Inflation	Yield	Treasury Return	S&P 500 Return
PBO	1				
Inflation	−.18	1			
T-bill yield	.19	.69	1		
Return on long Treasury	.97	−.22	.21	1	
Return on S&P 500	.13	−.23	−.07	.13	1

EXHIBIT 7:
INTEREST RATE AND PENSION LIABILITIES

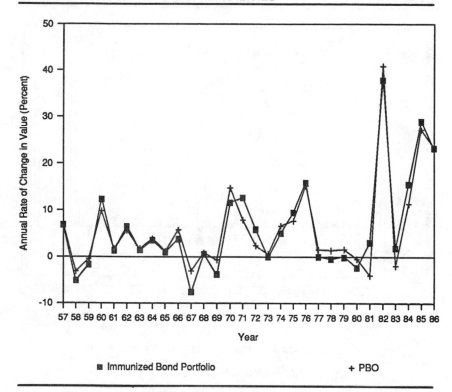

changes is 9.72%. The standard deviation of the immunized portfolio is 9.42%, and the standard deviation of the residual is 2.39%.[7]

These figures should be interpreted cautiously; the simulated PBO series takes into account only inflation and interest rate risk. Moreover, the PBO is constructed assuming that wage inflation moves together with price inflation and that real rates of interest are constant. If either of these assumptions were relaxed, the immunized portfolio would track less well. In addition, variations in the PBO will occur in real life

---

[7]This can be seen more easily in terms of variances, as the variance of the PBO is the variance of the immunized portfolio plus the variance of the residual. The variance of the PBO is 94.47. The variance of the immunized portfolio is $[(.851) \times (11.07)]^2 = 88.74$. The variance of the residual is $[94.47 - 88.74] = 5.73$.

EXHIBIT 8:
COMPONENTS OF PENSION LIABILITY (PBO) VOLATILITY

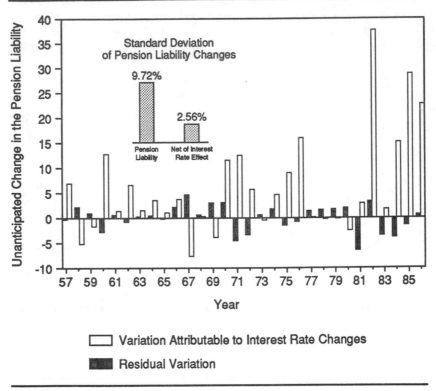

Variation Attributable to Interest Rate Changes

Residual Variation

because of year-to-year variations in employment. Over the longer term, demographic changes and changes in pension plan provisions are also highly important.

Despite these caveats, we may safely conclude from this work that interest rates are an important channel for the transmission of inflation to pension liabilities. Once the interest rate is netted out, the residual risk of the *stylized* PBO series is on the small order of 5% of the total variation. If we took into account the considerations discussed in the previous paragraph, variations in interest rates would probably explain less than the remaining 95% of the year-to-year variation in the PBO. Nevertheless, the explanatory power of the residual resulting from unanticipated inflation would continue to be low.

IMPLICATIONS FOR ASSESSING INTEREST RATE SENSITIVITY

The analysis presented earlier in this chapter demonstrated that pension plans have different durations with respect to anticipated inflation and real rate risk. In our basic example, the duration of the pension liability was 6.5 years with respect to anticipated inflation and 23 years with respect to changes in the real rate of interest.

Historical Duration

The historical duration of a pension liability is a weighted average of duration attributed to variations in real interest rates and anticipated inflation. The weight for each source is the historical proportion of nominal interest rate changes attributed to variation in that source. Thus, the duration of the pension liability is calculated as follows:

Implied duration of   =   Duration from   ×   Proportion of
  pension liability   changes caused by   interest rate changes
                          anticipated inflation   caused by
                                               anticipated inflation

+ Duration from changes caused × Proportion of changes caused
   by the real rate of interest   by the real rate of interest

Or, in terms of our example, if 84% of the changes in nominal interest rates were due to changes in anticipated inflation,

Historical duration of   = $(6.5 \times .84) + (15.2 \times .16) = 7.89$
pension liability (no COLAs)

The actual historical evidence suggests that the correct weighting is 71.3% anticipated inflation risk and 28.7% real rate risk. Thus the historical duration of the pension liabilities of active workers is 9.00 years $(6.5 \times .713) + (15.2 + .287)$.

The methodology we use for calculating the source of the variation in interest rates is relatively straightforward. Since neither anticipated inflation nor the real rate of interest is directly observable, we derived this result by constructing an annual series for both variables for 1958–86. We used a simple model suggesting that anticipated inflation is a function of long-run average inflation and the inflation in the preceding period. Thus, if inflation was higher than anticipated one year, anticipated inflation the next year would be lower than actual rate the previous year but higher than the previous year's expected rate. This series has a standard deviation of 2.96% and a variance of 8.79%. For our real interest rate series, we took the difference between Treasury-bill yields and the anticipated inflation series calculated from our model. This series has a standard deviation of 2.06% and a variance of 4.26%. Using these figures and taking into account the correlation of $-.2$ between anticipated inflation and real interest rates, we can show that 71.3% of this duration can be attributed to variations in anticipated inflation and 28.7% to variations in real interest rates.[8] Thus, historically, asset durations should have been weighted slightly over 2/3 by the duration of anticipated inflation and slightly under 1/3 by the real rate duration. The derivations are shown in the Appendix.

Some Complications

Two types of problems may arise in assessing the interest rate sensitivity of pension liabilities. First, while one can do a historical analysis of the proportion of nominal interest rate changes caused by changes in anticipated inflation versus changes in real rates, it does not mean that the historical result will hold in the future. Thus, it is important that a pension fund manager assess the interest rate sensitivity in light of his expectations as to the source of a change in nominal rates. If, for example, a money manager believes that 95% of next year's variation in nominal rates will be caused by changes in anticipated inflation, the correct duration for him to hedge is $(6.5)(.95) + (15.2)(.05) = 6.935$ years.

Second, it is possible that a pension fund manager will have an

---

[8]We explain the mathematics in the Appendix. This slight negative correlation between anticipated inflation and real interest rates holds up regardless of how we calculate the anticipated inflation series—using a simple model, a more complicated model allowing for longer lags, or a perfect foresight model. With monthly data the correlation will be much more negative. See, for example, Robert Litterman and Laurence Weiss, "Money, Real Interest Rates, and Output: A Reinterpretation of Postwar U.S. Data," *Econometrica*, Volume 53, No. 1, Janaury 1985.

asymmetric view of the world. For example, he may believe that current real rates are abnormally high, so that any increase in nominal interest rates will be due to a rise in anticipated inflation, whereas a decrease in nominal rates will be due to a fall in the real rate of interest. To hedge this risk, he must use an immunized asset portfolio in combination with options. We can clarify this point with a numerical example.

Assume that a pension fund has liabilities of $100 million and assets of $100 million. The duration of the asset portfolio is 6.5 years. The fund manager believes that over the next quarter nominal interest rates will either move up 100 basis points or move down 100 basis points—any interest rate increase will result from anticipated inflation, and any interest rate decrease will result from declining real rates.

At the end of the quarter, the assets will be worth $93.5 million if (nominal) rates have gone up and $106.5 million if rates have gone down. But the pension liabilities will be worth $93.5 million if rates have gone up and $115.2 million if rates have gone down (the liability duration is 6.5 years with respect to anticipated inflation changes and 15.2 years with respect to real rate changes). Thus, the pension fund will be underfunded by $8.7 million if rates fall by 100 basis points. To address this possibility, the pension fund manager must buy call options that will pay off $8.7 million if rates go down by 100 basis points.

An alternative strategy for the pension fund manager would be to fund with assets that have a duration of 15.2 years. If rates go down 100 basis points, the pension fund would have $115.2 million of liabilities and $115.2 million of assets. If rates go up 100 basis points, the fund would have $84.8 million of assets and $93.5 million of liabilities—an underfunding of $8.7 million. The manager could alleviate this risk by purchasing put options that pay off $8.7 million if rates go up 100 basis points.

In sum, the duration of pension liabilities is more complicated than has previously been recognized. It depends critically on whether the source of the change in nominal interest rates is a change in real rates or a change in inflation expectations. A duration matched position would involve evaluating the relative probability of a change in real rates and a change in anticipated inflation, calculating the implied duration of the pension liabilities, and using that figure as the duration to be hedged. If the pension fund manager's expectations are asymmetric, the position must, of necessity, involve options.

CONCLUSIONS AND CAVEATS

This analysis has shown that by addressing interest rate risk, pension fund managers are also taking into account most of the inflation risk in pension liabilities. This is because interest rates are an important channel for the transmission of inflation to pension liabilities. Thus, pension fund managers need not worry that by addressing the interest rate risk they are ignoring the effects of inflation. The two can be dealt with simultaneously.

One implication of our analysis is the necessity for pension fund managers to develop a view on the sources of possible movements in nominal interest rates. While managers typically make predictions of inflation and interest rates, it is not likely that they explicitly break this forecast down into changes in the real rate versus anticipated inflation. This breakdown, however, is inherent in the projection of nominal interest rates and inflation; the real rate forecast is roughly the difference between the two. That is, if a fund manager expected inflation to go up by 2 percentage points (change in anticipated inflation) and nominal interest rates to rise by 3 percentage points, then he is implicitly forecasting a real rate increase of 1 percentage point.

In making use of the analysis in this chapter, the reader should keep in mind that its scope is limited to a consideration of changes in inflation and interest rates. While these are of critical importance, there are other elements that also go into the asset allocation decision for a pension portfolio. These include, for example, changes in the size of the company's workforce in response to macroeconomic forces, the less-than-perfect correlation between wage inflation and price inflation, and perhaps demographic trends and changes in pension benefits over time. When pension fund managers address changes in their pension liabilities from one year to the next, they cannot ignore these considerations.

We recognize that all the above influences are important in asset allocation decisions. Moreover, our research has shown that there is no single magic formula that provides answers for all pension plans. Rather, optimal asset allocation depends to a large extent on the objectives and risk profit of the pension fund manager.

APPENDIX
WEIGHTING THE HEDGE

We want to calculate the duration of assets that will best hedge the interest rate risk in the PBO. In terms of mathematical notation, we want to minimize the squared differences between change in assets and changes in the PBO. We can write:

$$\text{Min } E \ (\Delta A - \Delta PBO)^2 \tag{A-1}$$

where E is the expected value operator and A represents the assets of the pension plan. For a first order change in interest rate, we may rewrite (A-1):

$$\text{Min } E \ (D_A \ (\Delta r_1 + \Delta r_2) - D_1 \ (\Delta r_1) - D_2 \ (\Delta r_2))^2 \tag{A-2}$$

where the real interest rate is defined as the 1-year Treasury rate minus anticipated inflation, and:

D_A is the duration of assets

D_1 is duration of the PBO with respect to unanticipated inflation

Δr_1 is the change in anticipated inflation

D_2 is the duration of the PBO with respect to the real rate of interest

Δr_2 in change in the real rate of interest

$\Delta r_1 + \Delta r_2$ is the change in the nominal interest rate

Simplifying (A-2), we obtain:

$$\text{Min } [(D_A - D_1)^2 \times \sigma_1{}^2 + (D_A - D_2)^2 \times \sigma_2{}^2 \\ + 2 \ (D_A - D_1)(D_A - D_2) \times \rho \sigma_1 \ \sigma_2] \tag{A-3}$$

where σ_1 is the standard deviation of changes in anticipated inflation

σ_2 is the standard deviation of change in the real rate

ρ is the correlation between anticipated inflation and the real rate of interest

Differentiating and solving A-3, we find

$$(D_A - D_1)(\sigma_1^2 + \rho\sigma_1\sigma_2) = -(D_A - D_2)(\sigma_2^2 + \rho\sigma_1\sigma_2) \qquad \text{(A-4)}$$

In final form:

$$D_A = D_1 \frac{\rho_1^2 + \rho\sigma_1\sigma_2}{\sigma_1^2 + \sigma_2^2 + 2\rho\sigma_1\sigma_2} + D_2 \frac{\sigma_2^2 + \rho\sigma_1\sigma_2}{\sigma_1^2 + \sigma_2^2 + \rho\sigma_1\sigma_2} \qquad \text{(A-5)}$$

Note that $(\sigma_1^2 + \sigma_2^2 + 2\rho\sigma_1\sigma_2)$ is the variance of 1-year Treasury yields.

Using historical numbers, we have $\sigma_1 = 2.96$, $\sigma_1^2 = 8.79$, $\sigma_2 = 2.06$, $\sigma_2^2 = 4.26$ and $\rho = -.2$. Applying these to equation A-5, we can calculate the duration of the pension assets:

$$D_A (\rho = -.2) = 6.5 \ \frac{8.79 - 1.22}{10.61} + 23 \frac{4.26 - 1.22}{10.61} = 11.22 \text{ years}$$

The first term of this calculation represents 71.3% of the total, the second term 28.7%.

CHAPTER 7

Policy Asset Mix, Tactical Asset Allocation, and Portfolio Insurance*

WILLIAM F. SHARPE
TIMKEN PROFESSOR OF FINANCE
GRADUATE SCHOOL OF BUSINESS
STANFORD UNIVERSITY

Previous chapters in this section have discussed methods for choosing a policy asset mix. Such procedures, sometimes termed "strategic asset allocation," have been used for well over a decade. Section Three of this book deals with approaches to tactical asset allocation. These, too, have been in use for several years (initially, under the title "market timing models"). Section Two discusses surplus management, optimization, and portfolio insurance methods, the most recent in the list of procedures for asset allocation.

This chapter is intended to help the reader understand the similarities and differences among these methods. It does so by providing an overview of a general approach to asset allocation—one that subsumes the traditional procedures as special cases. We begin with a description

*Much of this chapter is taken from William F. Sharpe "Integrated Asset Allocation," *Financial Analysts' Journal*, September/October 1987. I am grateful to the Financial Analysts' Federation for permission to publish it here.

of the overall approach, termed *Integrated Asset Allocation*. Next we discuss alternative objectives for asset allocation analyses. Since many studies are limited to two asset classes, we treat such cases in some detail. Finally, we describe the three traditional types of asset allocation analysis.

INTEGRATED ASSET ALLOCATION

Exhibit 1 shows the major steps involved in asset allocation. Boxes on the left are concerned with the capital markets. Those on the right are specific to an investor. Those in the middle bring together aspects of the capital markets and the investor's circumstances to determine the investor's asset mix and its performance.

The process begins at the top and proceeds downward. Then it begins all over again.

Box I1 shows the things that matter to an investor—the current values of assets and liabilities and, by implication, net worth. An individual investor's net worth is his or her *wealth*; a pension fund's net worth is the plan *surplus*.

Net worth will generally determine an investor's current tolerance for risk, shown in box I3. The relationship between the investor's circumstances (box I1) and risk tolerance (box I3) can be portrayed by a *risk tolerance function*. It is shown in box I2.

Box C1 shows the current state of the capital markets. Included are such things as current and historic levels of stock and bond indices, past and projected dividends and earnings. Such information provides major inputs for predictions of the expected returns and risks of various asset classes and the correlations among their returns (shown in box C3). Some procedure must be used to translate capital market conditions (box C1) into predictions about asset returns (box C3). It is shown in box C2.

Given an investor's risk tolerance (box I3) and predictions concerning asset expected returns, risks and correlations (box C3), an *optimizer* can be employed to determine the most appropriate asset mix (box M2). Depending on such things as the number of assets, the optimizer (shown in box M1) could be a simple rule of thumb, a mathematical function, or a full-scale quadratic program.

Box M3 shows actual returns. Given the investor's asset mix at the *beginning* of a period (box M2), the asset returns during the period

EXHIBIT 1:
INTEGRATED ASSET ALLOCATION

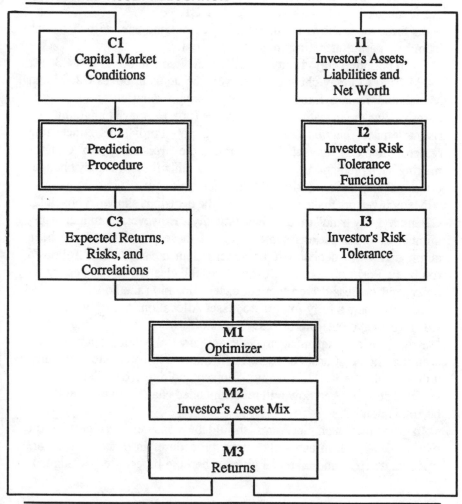

(box M3) determine the values of the investor's assets at the beginning of the *next* period. And, given the nature of the investor's liabilities at the beginning of a period, changes in capital markets (including returns on fixed-income obligations) and accrual of new obligations determine the investor's liabilities at the beginning of the next period. Returns in one period thus influence the investor's assets, liabilities and net worth at the beginning of the next period, as shown by the "feedback loop" from box M3 to box I1.

Returns during a period also constitute part of the overall capital market conditions at the beginning of the next period. This is shown by the feedback loop from box M3 to box C1.

As these loops show, the process is a continuing one, with decisions from one period affecting those of the next.

From period to period, any (or all) of the items in boxes C1, C3, I1, I3, M2 and M3 may change. However, the items in boxes C2, I2 and M1 should remain fixed, since they contain *decision rules* (procedures). Thus the investor's risk tolerance (box I3) may change, but the risk tolerance *function* (box I2) should not. Predictions concerning returns (box C3) may change, but not the *procedure* (box C2) for making such predictions. The optimal asset mix (box M2) may change, but not the *optimizer* (box M1) that determines it.

Many investors make some or all of the decisions shown in boxes I2, C2 and M1 "by hand" (and/or heuristically). However, in an increasing number of organizations some or all of these procedures have been automated, with decision rules specified in advance, then followed routinely. Portfolio insurance procedures fall clearly in this category, as do certain process-driven tactical asset allocation methods.

To implement a fully Integrated Asset Allocation, one only (!) has to fill in (or leave out) the boxes.

Key decisions that must precede any asset allocation analysis concern the choice of asset classes. How many will be considered? How will each be defined? How will current holdings be related to the selected classes? And how will recommended changes in asset holdings be implemented?

In principle, such decisions should be considered as part of the overall design of an asset allocation procedure. In practice, they are often made first, and taken as given when the procedure is designed.

ASSET ALLOCATION OBJECTIVES

To find an optimal asset mix, an optimizer must have an explicit *objective function*. Typically this involves the risk and expected value of some key attribute.

In an integrated asset allocation analysis, the attribute is the investor's *net worth* at some future date. Optimization thus deals with *expected future net worth* and the *standard deviation of future net worth*.

Traditional analyses often concentrate on the value of the investor's *assets* at some point in the future. Optimization then deals with the *expected return* and *standard deviation of return* on current assets.

The nature of the objective function must also be reflected in the measure of risk tolerance, which indicates the investor's willingness to accept greater risk in order to obtain a greater expected reward. In many analyses, risk tolerance is typically concerned with the tradeoff between expected return and standard deviation of return. In an integrated asset allocation analysis, it measures the investor's willingness to take on added *net worth risk* in order to increase *expected net worth*.

"Asset only" analyses can be considered special cases of integrated asset allocation in which liabilities equal zero (or are positive, but not subject to uncertainty).

TWO-ASSET ALLOCATION

The remainder of this chapter will focus on cases in which only two assets are considered and liabilities equal zero. Many asset allocation analyses conform to these restrictions, and we will discuss such approaches in this context.

The chapter appendix analyzes conditions for an optimal asset mix under the general conditions in which multiple asset classes and liabilities are considered.

When only two assets are involved, the relationship between the inputs and the optimal asset mix is particularly simple. Let the assets be S (e.g., stocks) and B (e.g., bonds or bills). As shown in the appendix, the optimal (dollar) amount to be invested in S can be computed as:

$$D_S = k_0 W + k_1 ART$$

where k_0 and k_1 are parameters, W is the investor's current net worth, and *ART* is his or her *absolute risk tolerance*.

To determine the proportion of assets invested in stocks, both sides of the equation can be divided by W, giving:

$$\frac{D_S}{W} = k_0 + k_1 \frac{ART}{W}$$

The latter ratio is termed the investor's *relative risk tolerance*. Representing this by *RRT*, and using the standard notation X_S to represent the relative amount invested in stocks, gives:

$$X_S = k_0 + k_1 RRT$$

If asset B is riskless, the value of k_0 becomes zero, giving:

$$D_S = k_1 ART$$

and

$$X_S = k_1 RRT$$

The appendix shows that the values of k_0 and k_1 depend on the expected returns and risks of the assets and on the estimated correlation between their returns. Of particular importance is the fact that k_1 is proportional to the difference in expected returns on the two assets:

$$k_1 = \frac{E_S - E_B}{k_2}$$

where k_2 depends (as does k_0) solely on the risks of the two assets and on the estimated correlation between their returns.

To avoid excess notation, no indication of time has been included in the equations. Each value is assumed to be relevant for the single period over which a decision is to be made. As will be seen, traditional approaches to asset allocation make different assumptions concerning the constancy of various aspects of these relationships over time.

CHOOSING A POLICY ASSET MIX

Previous chapters have decribed key aspects associated with the choice of a policy asset mix. Here, we outline the steps involved in traditional formal approaches to such a decision.

Exhibit 2 portrays a typical strategic or policy asset allocation analysis in terms comparable to those used for the more general Integrated Asset Allocation.

EXHIBIT 2:
STRATEGIC ASSET ALLOCATION

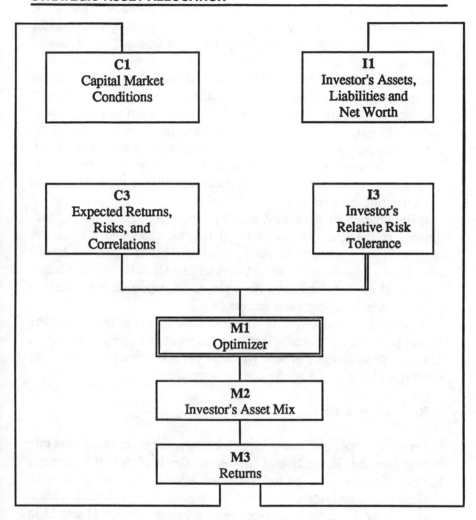

Strategic asset allocation studies are usually done episodically (e.g., once every three years). Relatively few asset mixes are considered (e.g., bond/stock combinations with 0,10,20, . . . 100% invested in stocks). An analysis (typically using Monte Carlo simulation) is performed to determine the likely range of outcomes associated with each mix. Typical outcomes analyzed are pension contributions over the next five years, pension surplus five years hence, and so on.

When the analysis is complete, the investor is asked to examine the ranges of outcomes associated with each of the mixes, then choose the preferred one. This constitutes the "policy," "long-run," or "strategic" asset mix.

In the vast majority of such analyses, each mix is expressed in terms of the percentage of total value invested in each asset class. Such an approach can be termed a *constant mix strategy*. It differs from a "buy-and-hold" strategy in that transactions are required to periodically re-balance the mix after market moves change relative asset values. Al-though liabilities are usually included in the simulation results, no explicit attempt is made to alter the asset mix to take the nature of the liabilities into account.

Policy studies almost always employ "long-run" capital market con-ditions. In particular, asset expected returns, risks and correlations remain constant throughout the simulation. This is portrayed by the absence of a connection between boxes C1 and C3 in Exhibit 2. Chang-ing capital market conditions from period to period do not influence predictions concerning asset returns.

In the case of two assets, if predictions are constant, the parameters k_0 and k_1 in our equations will remain the same from period to period. Letting the subscript t denote the time period, the equation for the proportion invested in stocks can be written as:

$$X_t = k_0 + k_1 RRT_t$$

For each set of simulations in such a study, the percentage asset mix is held constant. In the case of two assets, this implies that X_t remains the same from period to period. As the equation shows, this can only be optimal if the investor's *relative risk tolerance* is unchanged. This is portrayed by the absence of a connection between boxes I1 and I3 in Exhibit 2 and by the use of the term *relative* risk tolerance in box I3. Changing circumstances from period to period do not influence the investor's (relative) attitude toward risk.

Each of the possible strategies considered in a policy study can be represented by a different level of relative risk tolerance. The smaller the tolerance for risk, the more conservative the asset mix. The analysis is framed in terms of asset mix. However, by selecting one of the constant asset mixes, the investor provides important information about his or her risk tolerance.

TACTICAL ASSET ALLOCATION

Tactical procedures, described in the chapters of Section Three, are applied routinely, as part of continuing asset management. Their goal is to take advantage of inefficiencies in the relative prices of securities in different asset classes.

Early tactical asset allocators switched funds between bonds and stocks. Many now use bonds, stocks and cash equivalents, and a few employ multiple asset classes as well as global diversification. Examples can be found in Section Three.

Exhibit 3 portrays a typical tactical asset allocation analysis in terms comparable to those used earlier.

Explicitly or implicitly, tactical procedures assume that the investor's relative risk tolerance is unaffected by changes in his or her circumstances. As in Exhibit 2, this is portrayed by the absence of a connection between boxes I1 and I3 and by the use of the term *relative risk tolerance* in box I3.

Tactical changes in asset mix are driven by changes in predictions concerning asset returns. In simpler systems, only predictions of expected returns on stocks and bonds change. In more complex systems, predicted expected returns, risks and even correlations change.

In "two-way" systems, the percent invested in stocks is related linearly to the spread between the expected returns of stocks and bonds. This can be seen to follow directly from the assumed conditions. Given constant estimates of risks and correlation, the parameters k_0 and k_2 in our equations remain the same from period to period. Assuming constant relative risk tolerance, and letting the subscript t denote time, gives:

$$X_{st} = k_0 + \frac{RRT}{k_2} (E_{st} - E_{bt})$$

In practice, tactical asset allocation systems are often "contrarian" in nature. Typically, the expected return on stocks is based on the relationship between the current level of a stock market index and projec-

EXHIBIT 3:
TACTICAL ASSET ALLOCATION

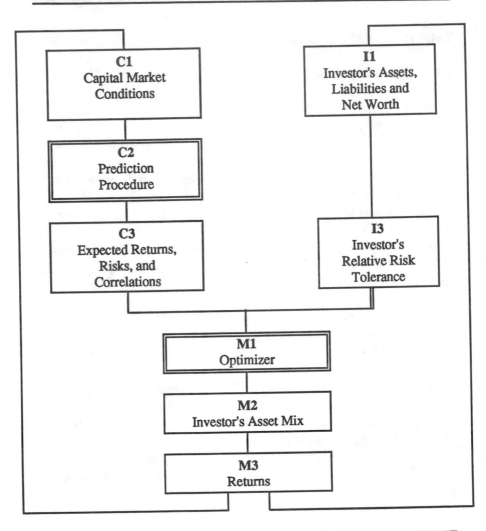

tions of dividends for its component stocks. Variations in projected dividends are usually smaller than the corresponding variations in stock prices. Thus expected returns tend to fall when prices rise, leading to a decrease in stock holdings.

Changes in asset expected returns, risks and correlations would take place in even the most efficient security markets. However, tactical asset allocation procedures typically operate on the assumption that markets overreact to information. In this sense, they base decisions on deviant beliefs, rather than those of the consensus of investors.

PORTFOLIO INSURANCE

Portfolio insurance procedures are described in the chapters in Section Two. They are generally applied routinely, as part of continuing asset management. In principle, they are intended to better adapt long-run results to an investor's objectives, without attempting to "time" the market. In practice, they are sometimes used for "closet" market timing. We focus here on the principle.

Exhibit 4 portrays an insured asset allocation procedure in the terms used earlier.

The earliest forms of portfolio insurance involved dynamic changes in asset allocation designed to replicate effects obtainable with certain option positions. For example, one might replicate the outcomes obtained by holding a portfolio plus a one-year put option written on that portfolio. Equivalently, one might replicate the outcomes obtained by holding a one-year Treasury bill plus a one-year call option on the portfolio. In either case, the striking price of the option would represent a floor below which the value of the investor's assets at the specified horizon date should not fall. Such procedures are described in detail in Section Two.

We will term an approach of this type *option-based portfolio insurance*.

Most portfolio insurance strategies allocate assets between two major classes (e.g., stocks and Treasury bills). In essence, such an approach provides a rule which relates the appropriate asset mix to the excess of the current value of the investor's net worth over a desired *floor*. The relationship is similar to that shown in Figure 5. The horizontal axis plots the current value of the "cushion" (asset value minus floor value) and the vertical axis the dollar amount to be invested in the risky asset (e.g., stocks). In an option-based insurance procedure, the floor at any given time is the present value of the desired floor at the horizon date. When assets fall to that value, nothing is invested in the risky asset. As asset value increases, the amount invested in the risky asset can increase, reaching the total value of the assets as an upper limit.

EXHIBIT 4:
INSURED ASSET ALLOCATION

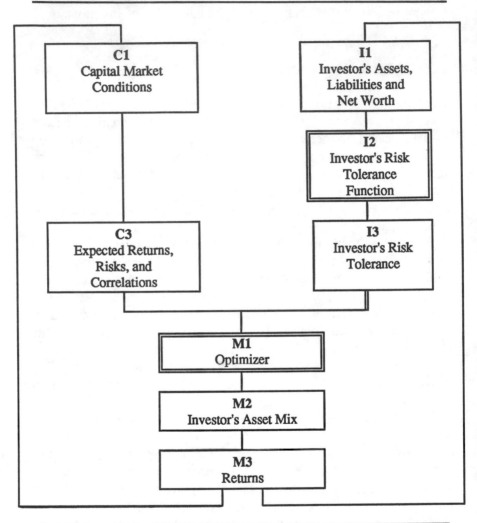

Option-based portfolio insurance strategies require the amount invested in the risky asset to be a function of both the current value of the asset cushion and the time remaining before the horizon (i.e., the option's expiration date). As the horizon date approaches, the curve

EXHIBIT 5:
OPTION-BASED PORTFOLIO INSURANCE

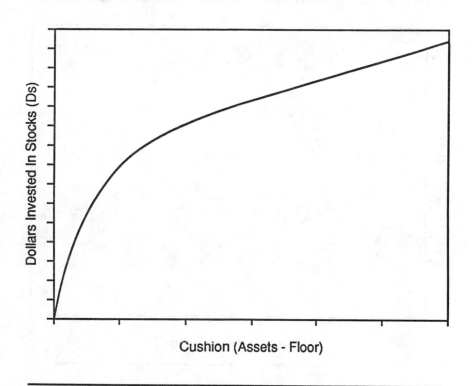

relating asset mix to the cushion moves, reaching an extreme just before the horizon in which assets are invested entirely in one class or the other, depending on whether assets are equal to the floor or above it.

Many have objected to this *time-variant* nature of option-based port-folio insurance strategies. In particular, such a characteristic seems inappropriate for an ongoing pension fund with a very long (or infinite) horizon.

More recent approaches to portfolio insurance are *time-invariant*. In particular, the curve relating the amount invested in the risky asset to the size of the cushion remains stationary from period to period.

For an important example of a time-invariant approach, see Black

EXHIBIT 6:
CONSTANT PROPORTION PORTFOLIO INSURANCE

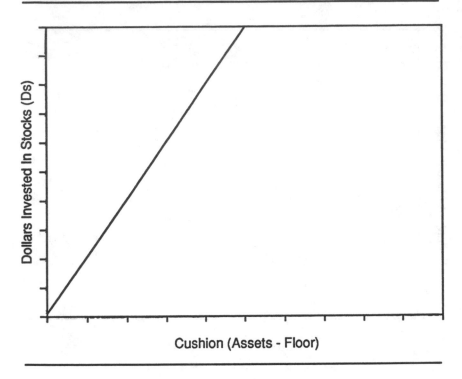

Cushion (Assets - Floor)

and Jones.[1] The foundation on which the approach is based was provided by Merton.[2] Following Perold[3] we will term the approach *constant proportion portfolio insurance* (CPPI).

CPPI uses a simple rule of the type shown in Exhibit 6: the dollar
amount invested in the risky asset should equal a constant times the size
of the cushion (asset value minus floor value), with the constant greater
than 1.

---

[1]Fischer Black and Robert Jones, "Simplifying Portfolio Insurance," *The Journal of Portfolio Management* (Fall 1987).

[2]Robert C. Merton, "Optimum Consumption and Portfolio Rules in a Continuous Time Model," *Journal of Economic Theory,* 3 (1971).

[3]André F. Perold, "Constant Proportion Portfolio Insurance," Harvard Business School, August 1986.

Formally, portfolio insurance approaches assume that asset expected returns, risks and correlations remain the same over the period during which the insurance is "in force" (although some *ad hoc* procedures have been developed to deal with unexpected changes in risk). This is portrayed by the absence of a connection between boxes C1 and C3 in Exhibit 4.

While portfolio insurance strategies are normally analyzed in terms of a relationship such as that shown in Exhibit 6, they are motivated by a relationship of the type shown in Exhibit 7. As before, the horizontal axis plots the level of the asset cushion, but the vertical axis now indicates the investor's absolute risk tolerance. Risk tolerance is zero when assets reach the minimum value at which the floor can be assured. As asset value increases, so does the investor's risk tolerance.

EXHIBIT 7:
A LINEAR RISK TOLERANCE FUNCTION

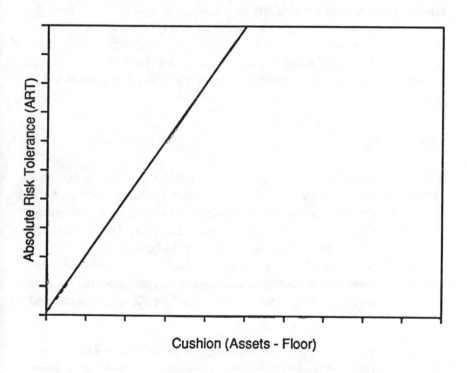

Cushion (Assets - Floor)

The relationship between the decision rule (see Exhibit 6) and the investor's underlying risk tolerance function (see Exhibit 7) is especially straightforward when one of the two assets is riskless. As shown earlier, in such a case:

$$D_s = k_1 ART$$

Thus Exhibits 6 and 7 differ only by the "scaling factor" k_1, since:

$$ART = \frac{D_s}{k_1}$$

Exhibit 7 plots the basis for constant proportion portfolio insurance: the investor's one-period absolute risk tolerance is assumed to be proportional to the size of the asset cushion. Merton[4] showed that such a policy is optimal if the investor's overall utility function displays linear absolute risk tolerance relative to wealth at a specific horizon date or relative to consumption at many dates.

Different portfolio insurance approaches imply different relationships of the type shown in Exhibit 7. Some are time-variant; some are not. Some give linear relationships; some do not. However, all can be viewed as implicit specifications of the investor's *risk tolerance function*.[5]

CONCLUSIONS

As shown throughout this book, asset allocation is typically the most important task an investor undertakes. Other chapters document the extensive effort devoted to the development and application of procedures for policy, tactical, and insured asset allocation. However, much of this work has been unnecessarily limited in scope.

As understanding of the interrelationships in this crucial area increases, the somewhat fragmented analyses can be expected to give way to a more complete approach. Investors, investment managers and

---

[4]Merton, "Optimum Consumption and Portfolio Rules in a Continuous Time Model."

[5]Further analysis of such relationships is provided in André F. Perold and William F. Sharpe, "Dynamic Strategies for Asset Allocation," *Financial Analysts' Journal* (forthcoming).

those who provide investment services share one goal: to *integrate* all aspects of asset allocation.

APPENDIX: CONDITIONS FOR AN OPTIMAL ASSET MIX

Assume that an investor's utility is related to net worth at the end of a relatively short decision period by the function:

$$U = f(W)$$

where W represents net worth at the end of the period.

Pratt[6] defines *absolute risk aversion* as:

$$ARA = -\ \frac{dU / dW}{d^2U/dW^2}$$

The reciprocal is termed *absolute risk tolerance:*

$$ART = -\ \frac{d^2U / dW^2}{dU/dW}$$

Since the time period is short, the range of possible values of W will be small. And, over a small range of values of W, the investor's actual utility function can be adequately approximated by another function displaying constant absolute risk tolerance. Such a function can be written as:

$$U = 1 - e^{-cW}$$

with:

$$ART = \frac{1}{c}$$

---

[6]John W. Pratt, "Risk Aversion in the Small and in the Large," *Econometrica*, January–April, 1964.

Since the time period is short, changes in net worth can typically be assumed to follow a normal distribution without excessive loss of precision.

Following Von Neumann and Morgenstern,[7] assume that the investor's objective is to maximize expected utility of wealth. As shown by Lintner,[8] if returns are normally distributed and the investor has constant absolute risk tolerance, expected utility can be written as:

$$EU = -e^{-c(E_w - \frac{c}{2} V_w)}$$

To make this as large as possible, one should maximize:

$$E_w - \frac{c}{2} V_w$$

or:

$$E_w - \frac{1}{2ART} V_w$$

where E_w and V_w are the expected value and variance of end-of-period wealth, respectively.

Assume that the investor's current wealth is W_0. Let R_i be asset i's *value-relative:* the ratio of end-of-period value to current value. Let D_i represent the current (dollar) value of asset or liability i (since a liability is a "negative asset," it will have a negative value of D_i). Clearly, end-of-period wealth will equal:

$$W = \sum_i D_i R_i$$

[7]J. Von Neumann and O. Morgenstern, *Theory of Games and Economic Behavior,* 3rd Ed. Princeton University Press, 1953.

[8]John Lintner, "The Market Price of Risk, Size of Market and Investor's Risk Aversion," *Journal of Business,* April, 1968.

Since the sum of the D_i values must equal W_0 optimality requires that an additional dollar invested in asset i must contribute as much to the objective function as an additional dollar invested in asset j. That is:

$$\frac{\partial E_w}{\partial D_i} - \frac{1}{2ART} \frac{\partial V_w}{\partial D_i} = K \text{ for all assets i}$$

Substituting equations for the partial derivatives gives:

$$E_i - \Sigma \, D_i \sigma_i \sigma_i \rho_{ij} = K \text{ for all assets i}$$

where:

E_i = the expected value of R_i

σ_i = the standard deviation of R_i

ρ_{ij} = the correlation between R_i and R_j

Note that although the equations hold only for assets, the summation (over j) includes assets and liabilities.

In the case of two assets (S and B), this implies:

$$D_s = k_0 W_0 + k_1 ART$$

where:

$$k_0 = \frac{V_B - C_{BS}}{V_S + V_B - 2C_{BS}}$$

$$k_1 = \frac{E_S - E_B}{V_S + V_B - 2C_{BS}}$$

and:

$$V_B = \sigma_B^2$$

$$V_S = \sigma_S^2$$

$$C_{BS} = \sigma_B \sigma_S \rho_{BS}$$

Note that in the text the value of W is written without a subscript, since the distinction between beginning and end-of-period values does not need to be emphasized there.

CHAPTER 8

Asset Allocation Optimization Models

H. GIFFORD FONG
PRESIDENT
GIFFORD FONG ASSOCIATES

FRANK J. FABOZZI
VISITING PROFESSOR
SLOAN SCHOOL OF MANAGEMENT
MASSACHUSETTS INSTITUTE OF TECHNOLOGY
AND MANAGING EDITOR
THE JOURNAL OF PORTFOLIO MANAGEMENT

In this chapter we shall describe several asset allocation models. We begin with the two-asset class problem and introduce the notion of an efficient portfolio and an efficient frontier (or efficient set). The asset allocation model with more than two asset classes is then explained and extended to (1) provide supplementary measures of risk, which we refer to as the *risk-of-loss*, (2) multiple scenarios, and (3) short-term/long-term asset allocations.

The basic inputs for the asset allocation models discussed are the expected returns, expected yields, risk estimates, and correlations (or covariances) for each asset class included in the analysis. The appropriate source for these inputs is the asset manager, since he is most directly concerned with these factors on a day-to-day basis. Additional insights can be achieved by using historical estimates, either from a lengthy past period or from more recent experience. The objective is to use the proxy that will best represent the future horizon of interest.

Typically, the asset manager will use his own return expectation in conjunction with historical risk measures based on the variance and co-variance from a historical series. Of course, other inputs may include constraints such as target minimum or maximum concentration con-straints of individual or group-of-asset types and corresponding yield constraints on part or all of the portfolio.

TWO-ASSET CLASS ALLOCATION MODEL

In order to introduce the concept of an efficient set (frontier) let us consider the asset allocation model when funds are to be allocated between only two asset classes, stocks and bonds. Exhibit 1 summa-rizes the expectational inputs (expected return, variance, standard devi-ation and correlation of returns). Exhibit 2 presents the formulas for calculating the portfolio expected return and variance of a two-asset class portfolio. When the two assets are combined to form a portfolio, the expected return for the portfolio is simply the weighted average of the expected return for the two asset classes. The weight for each asset class is equal to the dollar value of the asset class relative to the dollar value of the portfolio. The sum of the two weights, of course, must equal one. Unlike the portfolio's expected return, the portfolio's vari-ance (standard deviation) is not simply a weighted average of the variance (standard deviation) of the two asset classes. Instead, the portfolio variance depends on the correlation (covariance) between the two asset classes.

EXHIBIT 1:
EXPECTATIONAL INPUTS FOR TWO ASSET CLASSES

Asset Class	Expected Return	Variance	Standard Deviation
Stocks	.13	.0342	.185
Bonds	.08	.0036	.060

Correlation between stocks and bonds = .20

EXHIBIT 2:
FORMULAS FOR EXPECTED RETURN AND VARIANCE FOR A TWO-ASSET CLASS PORTFOLIO

Portfolio expected return

$$E(R_p) = W_1 E(R_1) + W_2 E(R_s)$$

where

$E(R_p)$ = expected return for the portfolio
$E(R_1)$ = expected return for asset class 1
$E(R_2)$ = expected return for asset class 2
W_1 = percentage of the portfolio invested in asset class 1
W_2 = percentage of the portfolio invested in asset class 2

and

$$W_1 + W_2 = 1$$

Portfolio variance

$$Var(R_p) = W_1^2 \, Var(R_1) + W_2^2 \, Var(R_2) + 2W_1 W_2 \, Covar(R_1,R_2)$$

where

$Covar(R_1,R_2)$ = covariance between the returns for asset classes 1 and 2
$Var(R_1)$ = variance of return for asset class 1
$Var(R_2)$ = variance of return for asset class 2

In terms of correlation:

$$Var(R_p) = W_1^2 \, Var(R_1) + W_2^2 \, Var(R_2) \\ + 2W_1 W_2 \, Std(R_1)Std(R_2) \, Corr(R_1,R_2)$$

where

$Corr(R_1, R_2)$ = correlation between asset classes 1 and 2
$Std(R_1)$ = standard deviation of asset class 1
$Std(R_2)$ = standard deviation of asset class 2

The portfolio expected return, variance, and standard deviation for different allocations of funds between the two asset classes using the input in Exhibit 1 and the formulas in Exhibit 2 are shown in tabular form in Exhibit 3. Exhibit 4 graphically portrays the portfolio expected return and standard deviation presented in Exhibit 3. With respect to Exhibit 4, the following should be noted.

EXHIBIT 3:
PORTFOLIO EXPECTED RETURN, VARIANCE, AND STANDARD DEVIATION FOR DIFFERENT ALLOCATIONS OF FUNDS BETWEEN STOCKS AND BONDS*

Allocation		Expected Return	Variance	Standard Deviation
W_1	W_2	$E(R_p)$	$Var(R_p)$	$Std(R_p)$
.0	1.0	.080	.0036000	.0600000
.1	.9	.085	.0036570	.0604769
.2	.8	.090	.0043820	.0661978
.3	.7	.095	.0057740	.0759872
.4	.6	.100	.0078330	.0885054
.5	.5	.105	.0105596	.1027600
.6	.4	.110	.0139532	.1181240
.7	.3	.115	.0180141	.1342160
.8	.2	.120	.0227421	.1508050
.9	.1	.125	.0281375	.1677420
1.0	.0	.130	.0342000	.1849320

*Asset class 1 = stocks.
Asset class 2 = bonds.
See Exhibit 1 for the expectational inputs for these two asset classes.

1. Every point on XYZ denotes a portfolio consisting of a specific allocation of funds between stocks and bonds. Not all of the portfolios are shown in Exhibit 3. We filled in the gaps when we plotted the results.
2. XYZ represents all possible portfolios consisting of these two security classes. XYZ is therefore called the *investment opportunity* or the *feasible set.*[1]

[1] The portfolios on XYZ include portfolios in which there is short selling of either asset class.

3. It would never be beneficial for an investor to allocate funds between stocks and bonds to produce a portfolio on that portion of XYZ between Y and Z (excluding portfolio Z).[2] The reason is that for every portfolio on segment YZ there is a portfolio that dominates it on the XY segment of the investment opportunity set. By *dominates*, we mean that for a given portfolio standard deviation (risk level), an investor can realize a higher portfolio expected return. This can be seen on Exhibit 4 by examining portfolios A and A'. Portfolios A and A' have the same portfolio

EXHIBIT 4:
INVESTMENT OPPORTUNITY SET AND EFFICIENT SET FOR TWO-ASSET CLASSES (STOCKS AND BONDS)

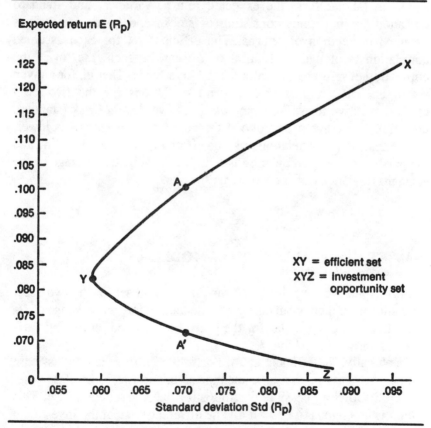

___
[2]The portfolio represented by point Y is the minimum variance that can be obtained by holding these two asset classes in any combination.

standard deviation; however, the expected return for portfolio A is greater than that for portfolio A′. Consequently, all portfolios on XY of the investment opportunity set dominate the portfolios on YZ of the investment opportunity set. XY, therefore, is called the *efficient set* or *efficient frontier*. We use these two terms interchangeably. A portfolio in the efficient set is said to be an *efficient portfolio* or an *optimal portfolio*.

The efficient set indicates the expected trade-off between return and risk (standard deviation) faced by the investor. Just which portfolio in the efficient set the investor selects depends on the investor's preferences.

To see the impact of the correlation on the efficient set, Exhibit 5 shows in tabular form the expected return, variance, and standard deviation for portfolios consisting of stocks and bonds for various assumed correlation of returns. The efficient set for each assumed correlation is plotted on Exhibit 6. As can be seen, the lower the correlation of returns, the better off the investor is. That is, for a given set of expected returns and standard deviations for the two asset classes, the investor will be exposed to a lower level of risk (standard deviation) for a given portfolio if the correlation of returns is lower. Notice that, if the correlation is 1, the efficient set is a straight line and the portfolio standard deviation is therefore a weighted average of the standard deviations of the two asset classes.

N-ASSET CLASS ALLOCATION MODEL

The principles we have discussed for the efficient set for the two-asset class allocation model can easily be extended to the general case of N-asset classes. The formulas for the portfolio expected return and variance are shown in Exhibit 7.

Graphically, the efficient set of portfolios in the N-asset class case can be portrayed in the same manner as in the two-asset class case. Exhibit 8 shows all possible portfolios for the N-asset class case. This exhibit is analogous to Exhibit 4. The difference is that the investment opportunity set in the two-asset class case does not include points

EXHIBIT 5:
PORTFOLIO EXPECTED RETURN AND STANDARD DEVIATION FOR DIFFERENT CORRELATIONS BETWEEN THE TWO ASSET CLASSES (STOCKS AND BONDS)*

Weight for Each Asset Class		Expected Return	Portfolio Standard Deviation If the Correlation Is:				
W_1	W_2	$E(R_p)$	0.2	0.0	0.2	0.5	1.0
0.0	1.0	.080	.0600000	.0600000	.0600000	.0600000	.0600000
.1	.9	.085	.0534654	.0570789	.0604769	.0667560	.0724932
.2	.8	.090	.0544230	.0605970	.0661978	.0761736	.0849865
.3	.7	.095	.0625295	.0695845	.0759872	.0873967	.0974797
.4	.6	.100	.0755168	.0822679	.0885054	.0998180	.1099730
.5	.5	.105	.0913258	.0972111	.1027600	.1130430	.1224660
.6	.4	.110	.1087330	.1135250	.1181240	.1268210	.1349590
.7	.3	.115	.1270820	.1306980	.1342160	.1409900	.1474530
.8	.2	.120	.1460200	.1484320	.1508050	.1554430	.1599460
.9	.1	.125	.1653440	.1665470	.1677420	.1701070	.1724390
1.0	0.0	.130	.1849320	.1849320	.1849320	.1849320	.1849320

*Asset class 1 = stocks.
Asset class 2 = bonds.

(portfolios) in the interior of XYZ. In the *N*-asset class case, interior points are also feasible portfolios. However, as in the two-asset class case, the portfolios represented by the segment XY dominate portfolios in the interior of the investment opportunity set.

Although the efficient set for the simple two-asset class case can be easily determined, the computation of the efficient set when funds are to be allocated to more than two asset classes becomes more difficult. Fortunately, the efficient set for the *N*-asset class problem can be solved using a mathematical programming technique called quadratic programming. This algorithm can also accommodate other constraints that might be imposed, such as limitations on the concentration of funds in a given asset class.

EXHIBIT 6:
COMPARISON OF EFFICIENT SET FOR DIFFERENT CORRELATIONS
BETWEEN TWO ASSET CLASSES (STOCKS AND BONDS)

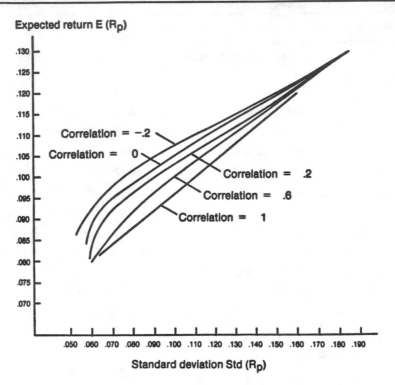

Let us now illustrate the three-asset class allocation model. Assume that an investor wishes to allocate available investment funds among the following three asset classes: stocks, bonds, and Treasury bills. Exhibit 9 presents the annual expected return, expected yield, standard deviation, and correlations for the three asset classes for two scenarios. (We will discuss the two scenarios later.) The expected yield component of the expected return is the amount of the return attributable to dividends in the case of stocks, and interest payments in the case of bonds. The difference between the expected return and expected yield is therefore the return attributable to capital appreciation.

Using quadratic programming, the efficient set can be determined.

EXHIBIT 7:
FORMULAS FOR EXPECTED RETURN AND VARIANCE
FOR AN *N*-ASSET CLASS PORTFOLIO

Portfolio expected return

$$E(R_p) \; = \; \sum_{i=1}^{N} E(R_i)W_i$$

where

$E(R_i)$ = expected return for asset class i
W_i = percent of the portfolio invested in asset class i

and

$$\sum_{i=1}^{N} W_i = 1$$

Portfolio variance

$$Var(R_p) \; = \; \sum_{i=1}^{N} W_i^2\, Var(R_i) \; + \; \sum_{i=1}^{N} \sum_{\substack{j=1 \\ \text{for } i \neq j}}^{N} W_i W_j\, Covar(R_i, R_j)$$

In terms of correlation:

$$Var(R_p) \; = \; \sum_{i=1}^{N} W_i^2 Var(R_i) \; + \; \sum_{i=1}^{N} \sum_{\substack{j=1 \\ \text{for } i \neq j}}^{N} W_i W_j Std(R_i)\, Std(R_j)\, Corr(R_i, R_j)$$

The results for scenario 1, assuming a one-year horizon and no constraints, are shown in Exhibit 10 while the results for scenario 2 are shown in Exhibit 11. For each identified level of portfolio expected return, the corresponding standard deviation, yield component of total return, and minimum risk concentrations (weights) of each class are shown on both exhibits. The columns under the heading *Probability of Annual Return of Less than* will be explained shortly.

EXHIBIT 8:
INVESTMENT OPPORTUNITY SET AND EFFICIENT SET IN AN *N*-ASSET
CLASS PORTFOLIO CASE

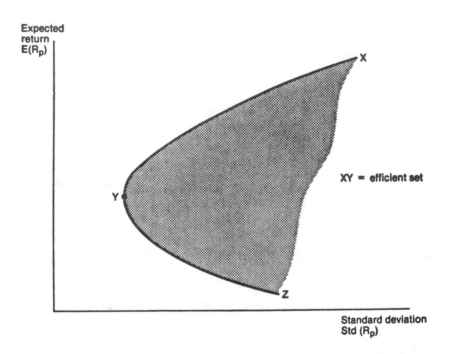

To make sure you understand the two exhibits, let's interpret one of the results. For scenario 1, the minimum risk (standard deviation) that the investor will be exposed to if he seeks a 9% return for the 12-month period is 6.552%. There is no other allocation producing a 9% return with a standard deviation less than 6.552%. The asset mix associated with this efficient or optimal portfolio is 24.8% in stocks, 64.2% in bonds, and 10.9% in Treasury bills. (The total does not equal one because of rounding.) The annual expected return of 9% will have an expected yield of 7.04%. Therefore, 1.96% of the total annual expected return will be attributable to capital appreciation.

EXHIBIT 9:
EXPECTATIONAL INPUTS FOR THREE-ASSET CLASSES
FOR TWO SCENARIOS

Asset Class	Expected Return	Expected Yield	Variance	Standard Deviation
Scenario 1:				
Stock	.13	.05	.034200	.185
Bonds	.08	.08	.003600	.060
Treasury bills	.06	.06	.000016	.004
Scenario 2:				
Stock	.15	.05	.034200	.185
Bonds	.08	.08	.003600	.060
Treasury bills	.05	.05	.000016	.004

	Correlations for Both Scenarios		
	Stocks	Bonds	Treasury bills
Stocks	1.00	.20	−.15
Bonds	.20	1.00	−.12
Treasury bills	−.15	−.12	1.00

EXTENSION OF THE ASSET ALLOCATION MODEL TO RISK-OF-LOSS

In the portfolio risk-minimization process, the variance (standard deviation) of returns was the proxy measure for portfolio risk. As a supplement, the probability of not achieving a portfolio expected return can be established. This type of analysis would be useful in determining the most appropriate mix from the set of optimal portfolio allocations.

We refer to this analysis as the *risk-of-loss*. A technical description of the analysis is described in Appendix A. The columns under the heading *Probability of Annual Return of Less than* in Exhibits 10 and 11 show the results of the risk-of-loss analysis for four annual return

EXHIBIT 10:
OPTIMAL ASSET ALLOCATION FOR SCENARIO 1: SAMPLE PORTFOLIOS IN THE EFFICIENT SET (12-MONTH HORIZON)

Annual Expected Return	Annual Standard Deviation	Annual Expected Yield	Probability of Annual Return of Less than				Minimum Risk Asset Mix		
			0.0%	5.0%	7.0%	10.0%	Stocks	Bonds	T-Bills
6.00%	0.400%	6.00%	0.9%	0.9%	99.1%	100.00%	0.0%	0.0%	100.0%
6.04	0.389	6.02	0.0	0.5	99.0	100.0	0.3	1.0	98.7
6.50	1.097	6.18	0.0	9.7	66.7	99.8	4.1	10.9	84.9
7.00	2.174	6.35	0.1	19.2	50.0	90.0	8.3	21.7	70.0
7.50	3.271	6.52	1.3	23.5	44.3	76.0	12.5	32.4	55.1
8.00	4.368	6.70	3.8	25.8	41.5	66.4	16.6	43.1	40.3
8.50	5.462	6.84	6.6	27.3	39.9	60.0	20.7	53.7	25.6
9.00	6.552	7.04	9.3	28.3	38.8	55.6	24.8	64.2	10.9
9.50	7.649	7.09	11.6	29.0	38.1	52.4	30.4	69.6	0.0
10.00	8.918	6.79	14.1	30.0	37.7	50.0	40.5	59.5	0.0
10.50	10.356	6.48	16.5	31.0	37.7	48.2	50.5	49.5	0.0
11.00	11.895	6.19	18.8	31.9	37.8	46.9	60.5	39.5	0.0
11.50	13.497	5.89	20.8	32.7	37.9	46.0	70.4	29.6	0.0
12.00	15.142	5.59	22.5	33.3	38.0	45.2	80.3	19.7	0.0
12.50	16.813	5.29	24.0	33.9	38.2	44.6	90.2	9.8	0.0
13.00	18.500	5.00	25.2	34.4	38.3	44.2	100.0	0.0	0.0

EXHIBIT 11:
OPTIMAL ASSET ALLOCATION FOR SCENARIO 2: SAMPLE PORTFOLIOS IN THE EFFICIENT SET (12-MONTH HORIZON)

Annual Expected Return	Annual Standard Deviation	Annual Expected Yield	Probability of Annual Return of Less than				Minimum Risk Asset Mix:		
			0.0%	5.0%	7.0%	10.0%	Stocks	Bond	T-Bills
5.00%	0.400%	5.00%	0.0%	50.1%	100.0%	100.0%	0.0%	0.0%	%100.0%
5.06	0.389	5.03	0.0	44.3	100.0	100.0	0.3	1.0	98.7
5.50	0.784	5.24	0.0	27.2	96.5	100.0	2.8	7.9	89.3
6.00	1.501	5.47	0.0	26.3	73.5	99.3	5.5	15.7	78.7
6.50	2.248	5.70	0.2	26.3	58.3	92.6	8.3	23.5	68.2
7.00	3.003	5.94	1.2	26.4	50.0	82.3	11.0	31.2	57.7
7.50	3.757	6.17	2.6	26.4	45.0	73.1	13.8	38.9	47.3
8.00	4.509	6.40	4.3	26.5	41.8	65.9	16.5	46.6	36.9
8.50	5.258	6.63	5.9	26.5	39.5	60.4	19.2	54.2	26.6
9.00	6.005	6.85	7.4	26.5	37.8	56.1	21.9	61.8	16.3
9.50	6.750	7.08	8.8	26.6	36.5	52.7	24.6	69.4	6.0
10.00	7.505	7.13	10.0	26.6	35.5	50.0	29.1	70.9	0.0
10.50	8.374	6.91	11.5	26.9	34.9	47.8	36.4	63.6	0.0
11.00	9.345	6.69	13.0	27.4	34.6	46.1	43.6	56.4	0.0
11.50	10.386	6.48	14.5	28.0	34.4	44.8	50.7	49.3	0.0
12.00	11.478	6.26	15.9	28.5	34.4	43.7	57.8	42.2	0.0
12.50	12.605	6.05	17.3	29.0	34.4	42.9	64.9	35.1	0.0
13.00	13.756	5.84	18.5	29.5	34.4	42.2	72.0	28.0	0.0
13.50	14.927	5.63	19.6	29.9	34.5	41.6	79.1	20.9	0.0
14.00	16.109	5.42	20.5	30.3	34.5	41.1	86.1	13.9	0.0
14.50	17.302	5.21	21.4	30.6	34.6	40.7	93.0	7.0	0.0
15.00	18.500	5.00	22.2	30.9	34.7	40.4	100.0	0.0	0.0

levels. The interpretation of the results for the 9% expected return for scenario 1 (Exhibit 10) is as follows. There is a 9.3% probability that the annual return will be negative, a 28.3% probability that the annual return will be less than 5%, a 38.8% probability that the annual return will be less than 7%, and a 55.6% probability that the annual return will be less than 10%.

EXTENSION OF THE ASSET ALLOCATION MODEL TO MULTIPLE SCENARIOS

In Exhibit 9 the expected return and expected yield are shown for two assumed scenarios. Each assumed scenario is believed to be an assessment of the asset performance in the long run, over the investment horizon. If a probability can be assigned to each scenario, an efficient set can be constructed for the composite scenario. Appendix B explains the procedure for computing the optimal asset allocation when there are multiple scenarios which are discrete or mutually exclusive and each scenario can be assigned a probability of occurrence.

Assuming a probability of 50% for each of the two scenarios in Exhibit 9, Exhibit 12 displays the optimal asset allocation for the composite scenario for a 12-month investment horizon. Exhibit 13 provides the minimum risk portfolio for specified return levels for the composite scenario results for a 60-month horizon. In both exhibits, the risk-of-loss analysis results are also shown.

Let's take a closer look at these results to see how useful they can be in the asset allocation decision. Exhibit 14 is an illustration of the optimal mixes for the 12-month horizon for the composite scenario. The vertical height of each of the three lines represents the amount that would be allocated to an asset for a given expected return level shown on the horizontal axis. For example, Exhibit 14 has the optimal concentrations for an expected return of 8% of about 12% stocks, 45% bonds, and 38% Treasury bills, corresponding to the results shown in Exhibit 12 of 16.6% stocks, 45.2% bonds and 38.3% Treasury bills. (As noted earlier, the optimal mix may not equal one because of rounding.)

The yield component of the optimal mixes is shown for each scenario and the composite scenario in Exhibit 15. As explained earlier, the yield is the amount of return attributable to dividends and interest payments for the range of optimal portfolios. For the 8% expected

EXHIBIT 12:
OPTIMAL ASSET ALLOCATION FOR COMPOSITE SCENARIO: SAMPLE PORTFOLIOS IN THE EFFICIENT SET (12-MONTH HORIZON)

Annual Expected Return	Annual Standard Deviation	Annual Expected Yield	Probability of Annual Return of Less than				Minimum Risk Asset Mix		
			0.0%	5.0%	7.0%	10.0%	Stocks	Bonds	T-Bills
5.50%	0.422%	5.50%	0.0%	24.8%	99.5%	100.0%	0.0%	0.0%	100.0%
5.55	0.412	5.53	0.0	21.8	99.4	100.0	0.3	1.1	98.6
6.00	0.918	5.71	0.0	16.7	82.4	100.0	3.3	9.2	87.5
6.50	1.777	5.92	0.0	21.3	59.9	96.3	6.6	18.3	75.1
7.00	2.666	6.13	0.6	23.8	49.7	84.8	10.0	27.3	62.8
7.50	3.560	6.34	2.1	25.2	44.5	73.9	13.3	36.2	50.5
8.00	4.452	6.55	4.1	26.2	41.5	65.8	16.6	45.2	38.3
8.50	5.342	6.75	6.3	26.8	39.5	59.9	19.8	54.0	26.1
9.00	6.228	6.96	8.3	27.3	38.1	55.6	23.1	62.9	14.0
9.50	7.113	7.16	10.0	27.6	37.1	52.4	26.3	71.7	2.0
10.00	8.063	6.98	11.8	28.1	36.4	49.8	33.9	66.1	0.0
10.50	9.168	6.73	13.7	28.7	36.1	47.8	42.3	57.7	0.0
11.00	10.377	6.48	15.6	29.5	36.0	46.4	50.7	49.3	0.0
11.50	11.655	6.23	17.4	30.2	36.0	45.2	59.0	41.0	0.0
12.00	12.981	5.98	19.0	30.8	36.1	44.3	67.3	32.7	0.0
12.50	14.338	5.73	20.5	31.4	36.2	43.6	75.5	24.5	0.0
13.00	15.715	5.49	21.7	31.9	36.3	43.1	83.7	16.3	0.0
13.50	17.110	5.24	22.9	32.3	36.4	42.6	91.9	8.1	0.0

EXHIBIT 13:
OPTIMAL ASSET ALLOCATION FOR COMPOSITE SCENARIO: SAMPLE PORTFOLIOS IN THE EFFICIENT SET
(60-MONTH HORIZON)

Annual Expected Return	Annual Standard Deviation	Annual Expected Yield	Probability of Annual Return of Less than				Minimum Risk Asset Mix		
			0.0%	5.0%	7.0%	10.0%	Stocks	Bonds	T-Bills
5.50%	0.422%	5.50%	0.0%	23.7%	100.0%	100.0%	0.0%	0.0%	100.0%
5.55	0.412	5.53	0.0	17.3	100.0	100.0	0.3	1.1	98.6
6.00	0.918	5.71	0.0	4.0	95.3	100.0	3.3	9.2	87.5
6.50	1.777	5.92	0.0	4.5	70.2	100.0	6.6	18.3	75.1
7.00	2.666	6.13	0.0	5.8	49.4	98.8	10.0	27.3	62.8
7.50	3.560	6.34	0.0	6.8	38.0	92.3	13.3	36.2	50.5
8.00	4.452	6.55	0.0	7.7	31.6	81.8	16.6	45.2	38.3
8.50	5.342	6.75	0.0	8.3	27.6	71.3	19.8	54.0	26.1
9.00	6.228	6.96	0.1	8.8	25.0	62.4	23.1	62.9	14.0
9.50	7.113	7.16	0.2	9.2	23.1	55.3	26.3	71.7	2.0
10.00	8.063	6.98	0.4	9.7	21.9	49.6	33.9	66.1	0.0
10.50	9.168	6.73	0.7	10.6	21.4	45.2	42.3	57.7	0.0
11.00	10.377	6.48	1.2	11.5	21.3	41.9	50.7	49.3	0.0
11.50	11.655	6.23	1.8	12.4	21.3	39.4	59.0	41.0	0.0
12.00	12.981	5.98	2.6	13.2	21.4	37.5	67.3	32.7	0.0
12.50	14.338	5.73	3.3	14.0	21.6	36.0	75.5	24.5	0.0
13.00	15.715	5.49	4.1	14.7	21.7	34.8	83.7	16.3	0.0
13.50	17.110	5.24	4.9	15.4	21.9	33.9	91.9	8.1	0.0

EXHIBIT 14:
RISK-OF-LOSS ANALYSIS: MINIMUM-RISK CONCENTRATIONS

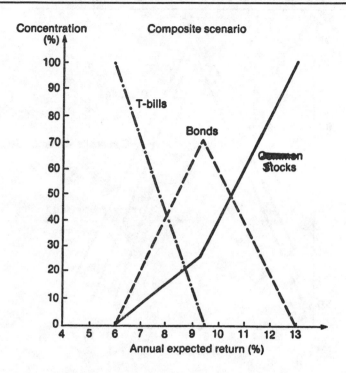

return level, Exhibit 15 indicates that the yield component is 6.55%, which leaves 1.45% as the return attributable to capital appreciation.

Exhibit 16 depicts the risk of loss or probability of not achieving the specified return benchmarks of 0, 5, 7, and 10% over a one-year horizon for the composite case. From the expected return range on the horizontal axis, the probability of not achieving a given benchmark can be determined by proceeding vertically to the return benchmark curves. For example, if the 8% expected return optimal portfolio were assumed, there would be a 4% probability of not achieving a positive percent return over the next year (probabilities on the vertical axis). From Exhibit 12 the tabular results reveal the more precise value of 3.8%. Exhibit 17 graphically characterizes the risk-of-loss for the composite scenario for the five year horizon results shown in Exhibit 13.

EXHIBIT 15:
RISK-OF LOSS ANALYSIS: YIELD OF MINIMUM-RISK PORTFOLIOS

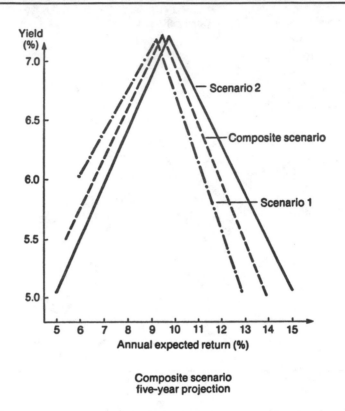

Composite scenario
five-year projection

The comparison between Exhibit 16 and Exhibit 17 is particularly interesting. The influence of the passage of time is illustrated by comparing the 12-month horizon of Exhibit 16 and the 60-month horizon of Exhibit 17. The most striking difference is the significant downward shift of all risk-of-loss curves for the longer time horizon. This is consistent with the return increasing at a greater rate than risk over time. The greater the time horizon, the greater the incentive to seek higher expected return/higher expected risk portfolios. The effect of the high risk associated with high return portfolios is most significant during short time horizons. If the risk exposure over short horizons is important, it is apparent that lower return portfolios are appropriate. In

EXHIBIT 16:
RISK-OF-LOSS ANALYSIS: PROBABILITY OF LOSS FOR
MINIMUM-RISK PORTFOLIOS

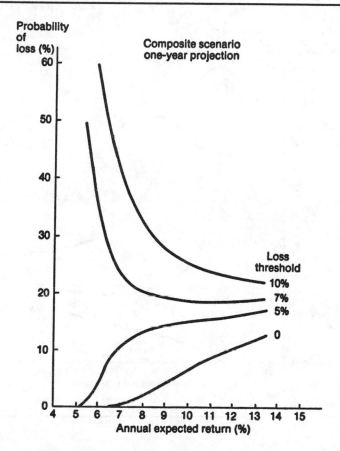

other words, if the investor is concerned with near-term portfolio fluctuation, a portfolio consisting entirely of common stock (highest expected return and risk class in our example) is clearly not fitting. As the relevant horizon increases, however, a higher proportion of stocks is possible and even desirable to achieve higher return.

In practice, there probably will be a trade-off between short-term risk tolerance and long-term return desirability. How much short-term risk is tolerable may therefore control the proportion of higher return assets and hence the expected return attainable. Using formats such as

EXHIBIT 17:
RISK-OF-LOSS ANALYSIS: PROBABILITY OF LOSS FOR
MINIMUM-RISK PORTFOLIOS

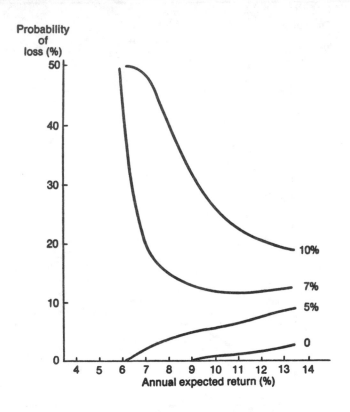

Exhibit 16 and Exhibit 17 and their supporting tables, Exhibits 12 and 13, can assist the investor in choosing the most desirable return/risk trade-off.

As an alternative to visual inspection of the return/risk trade-off, the mathematically best trade-off in terms of the most return per unit of risk can be calculated. This procedure involves the evaluation of a chosen risk-of-loss curve for the point along the curve where the second derivative of the curve is zero (i.e., where its slope is steepest). This provides the greatest decrease in risk-of-loss for an increment of expected return.

EXTENSION OF THE ASSET ALLOCATION MODEL TO SHORT-TERM/LONG-TERM ASSET ALLOCATION

In the multiple scenario case just described, it was assumed that the investor has certain expectations about the performance of the asset classes in terms of expected returns, expected yields, standard deviations, and correlations of return for each scenario. These values are used to assess, under various scenarios, the asset class performance in the long run, over the investment horizon.

It is often the case, however, that the investor expects a very different set of values to be applicable in the short run, say the next 12 months. For example, the investor may estimate the long-term expected annual return on stocks at 12%, but over the next year his expected return on stocks is only 5%. The investment objectives are still stated in terms of the portfolio performance over the entire investment horizon. The return characteristics of each asset class, however, are described by one set of values over a short period and another set of values over the remainder of the horizon.

In such a case, the investment strategy may involve investing in one portfolio over the short period and another portfolio over the remaining horizon. Naturally, the investor is mostly interested in the short-term portfolio since this addresses the current task of asset allocation. It is necessary to take into consideration the subsequent allocation as well, since both relate to the total horizon investment objectives.

To explain this point further, suppose that the investor wants to achieve a certain level of return, say 10%, with minimum risk over a five-year horizon. The 10% expected overall return may be accomplished by being very conservative in the first year and more aggressive over the remaining four years, or aggressive in the first year and more conservative thereafter. For the asset allocations in the two periods, there is a spectrum of choices that would produce the same 10% overall expected return. Not all of these choices, however, would have the same overall risk, as measured by the standard deviation of total returns. As a matter of fact, there would be one combination of the asset allocations over the first and the second periods that would have the minimum risk and overall expected return of 10%. Such a strategy represents a point on the overall efficient set. By varying the required total expected return, one can generate the whole efficient set for the investment horizon.

A procedure to identify the overall efficient frontier and characterize the investment strategies which comprise it has been developed by Gifford Fong Associates. Notice that in this context we refer to optimal strategies, rather than optimal asset allocations, because each strategy consists of two asset allocations over the two separate periods of the horizon.

This extension of basic asset allocation has considerable flexibility. It allows an investor to specify different values for the short period and for the remainder of the horizon for any of the basic data required for the asset allocation model. The investor can also specify different portfolio constraints in the two periods. In fact, it is even possible to consider different asset classes in the two periods comprising the horizon.

The techniques involved in the generation of the efficient strategies and their characterization in terms of return and risk, as well as probabilities of meeting threshold returns (risk-of-loss analysis), for the horizon and the two subperiods are fairly complex. Since the model simultaneously optimizes over two periods, quadratic programming alone is no longer sufficient. A detailed description of the computational procedure is beyond the scope of this chapter. Briefly, the approach used is as follows. For a given level of the total expected return, the overall standard deviation is expressed as a function of the first period expected return. This is possible since a value of the first period expected return determines the second period expected return necessary to generate the given overall return expectation required. Two separate quadratic algorithms give the two one-period minimum standard deviations corresponding to the one-period returns. These standard deviations are then combined by an appropriate formula to provide the overall standard deviation. Once the total standard deviation is expressed as a function of the first period return expectation, this function is minimized to obtain a point on the overall efficient set.[3] The above process is repeated for different values of the total expected return in the feasible range to generate the whole efficient set. The optimal asset allocation strategies are obtained in the process. No assumptions beyond serial independence of returns are necessary for the calculation of the mean/variance efficient strategies. Lognormality

---

[3]The method used for the minimization of this function is the three-point Newton iteration method.

of the return distributions is assumed for calculation of the probabilities of exceeding threshold returns.

To illustrate this extension of the asset allocation model, the following are assumed:

1. There are six asset classes over which funds are to be allocated. They are: (1) government/agencies, (2) intermediate-term industrials, (3) long-term corporates, (4) S&P 500 stocks, (5) AMEX stocks, and (6) Treasury bills.
2. The investment horizon is 60 months.
3. The investor has expectations for a 12-month horizon that differs from the 60-month horizon.
4. The basic expectational values for the 60-month (long-term) and 12-month (short-term) horizons are shown in Exhibits 18 and 19, respectively.
5. Minimum and maximum concentration constraints are imposed for each subperiod as shown in Exhibits 18 and 19.
6. The minimum yield for both subperiods is set at 6%.

Exhibit 20 displays the optimal strategies for the 12-month horizon. Exhibit 21 shows the optimal strategies for the residual term horizon of 48 months. The optimal composite statistics for the 60-month horizon based on the optimal strategies shown in Exhibits 20 and 21 are displayed in Exhibit 22.

APPLICATION FOR INVESTMENT STRATEGY

Implicit in the use of the model in making strategy decisions is the capability of providing capital market expectations with greater precision than using a historical average. Along with expected return judgments, it is assumed that the risk estimates are also capable of refinement. For example, over periods of less than a year the normal relationship between return and risk for the highest expected return assets will be masked by the magnitude of their expected risk (variance). Hence, unless this risk can be specified to be much lower than the historical average, the model will consistently choose the lowest-return, lowest-risk asset mixes for the short horizons. This is intuitively proper, since, if a short-term perspective is important and there is no

EXHIBIT 18:
LONG-TERM/SHORT-TERM ASSET ALLOCATION: LONG-TERM SPECIFICATIONS (60-MONTH PERIOD)

Name	Annual Expected Return	Annual Expected Yield	Annual Standard Deviation	Correlation with					
				G/A	ITI	LTC	S&P500	AMEX	T-bills
G/A	8.00%	8.00%	4.00%	1.000					
ITI	9.00	9.00	6.00	0.974	1.000				
LTC	10.00	10.00	12.00	0.965	0.965	1.000			
S&P500	15.00	5.00	16.00	0.353	0.401	0.387	1.000		
AMEX	20.00	5.00	25.00	0.281	0.356	0.327	0.845	1.000	
T-bills	6.00	6.00	1.00	0.611	0.560	0.508	-0.032	-0.097	1.000

Constraints:

Minimum concentration (percent)				20.00	0.0	0.0	0.0	0.0	0.0
Maximum concentration (percent)				100.00	100.00	100.00	80.00	80.00	60.00
Minimum yield (percent)				6.00					

Key: G//A = government/agencies
    ITI = intermediate term industrials
    LTC = long-term corporates
    S&P500 = Standard & Poor's 500
    AMEX = American Stock Exchange Index
    T-bills = U.S. Treasury bills

EXHIBIT 19:
LONG-TERM/SHORT-TERM ASSET ALLOCATION: SHORT-TERM SPECIFICATIONS (12-MONTH PERIOD)

Name	Annual Expected Return	Annual Expected Yield	Annual Standard Deviation	Correlation with					
				G/A	ITI	LTC	S&P500	AMEX	T-bills
G/A	15.00%	8.00%	4.00%	1.000					
ITI	13.00	9.00	4.00	0.965	1.000				
LTC	25.00	10.00	6.00	0.972	0.970	1.000			
S&P500	10.50	5.00	10.00	−0.200	−0.200	−0.300	1.000		
AMEX	5.00	5.00	12.00	−0.100	−0.200	−0.200	0.848	1.000	
T-bills	7.00	7.00	0.0	0.0	0.0	0.0	−0.0	−0.0	1.000

Constraints:

	G/A	ITI	LTC	S&P500	AMEX	T-bills
Minimum concentration (percent)	20.00	0.0	0.0	0.0	0.0	0.0
Maximum concentration (percent)	100.00	100.00	100.00	80.00	80.00	100.00
Minimum yield (percent)	6.00					

Key: G/A = government/agencies
    ITI = intermediate term industrials
    LTC = long-term corporates
    S&P500 = Standard & Poor's 500
    AMEX = American Stock Exchange Index
    T-bills = U.S. Treasury bills

EXHIBIT 20:
LONG-TERM/SHORT-TERM ASSET ALLOCATION: OPTIMAL INITIAL STRATEGY (12-MONTH PERIOD)

Strategy	Annual Expected Return	Annual Standard Deviation	Annual Expected Yield	Probability of Annual Return Less than					Minimum Risk Asset Mix					
				0.0 Percent	8.0 Percent	10.0 Percent	12.0 Percent	20.0 Percent	G/A	ITI	LTC	S&P500	AMEX	T-Bills
1	8.66%	0.784%	7.17%	0.0%	20.0%	95.7%	100.0%	100.0%	20.0%	0.0%	0.0%	1.6%	0.0%	78.4%
2	10.10	1.214	7.34	0.0	4.0	46.9	94.1	100.0	20.0	0.0	7.5	4.2	0.0	68.2
3	12.49	1.938	7.66	0.0	0.9	9.9	40.4	100.0	20.0	0.0	20.2	7.3	0.0	52.5
4	14.92	2.680	7.98	0.0	0.4	3.1	13.7	96.9	20.0	0.0	33.1	10.4	0.0	36.5
5	17.41	3.440	8.32	0.0	0.2	1.3	5.5	77.6	20.0	0.0	46.3	13.6	0.0	20.1
6	19.96	4.216	8.66	0.0	0.1	0.7	2.6	51.1	20.0	0.0	59.8	16.9	0.0	3.3
7	21.69	4.861	9.15	0.0	0.1	0.6	2.0	37.0	20.0	0.0	71.0	8.0	0.0	0.0
8	23.00	5.581	9.60	0.0	0.2	0.7	2.1	30.1	20.0	0.0	80.0	0.0	0.0	0.0
9	23.00	5.581	9.60	0.0	0.2	0.7	2.1	30.1	20.0	0.0	80.0	0.0	0.0	0.0
10	23.00	5.581	9.60	0.0	0.2	0.7	2.1	30.1	20.0	0.0	80.0	0.0	0.0	0.0
11	23.00	5.581	9.60	0.0	0.2	0.7	2.1	30.1	20.0	0.0	80.0	0.0	0.0	0.0
12	23.00	5.581	9.60	0.0	0.2	0.7	2.1	30.1	20.0	0.0	80.0	0.0	0.0	0.0
13	23.00	5.581	9.60	0.0	0.2	0.7	2.1	30.1	20.0	0.0	80.0	0.0	0.0	0.0
14	23.00	5.581	9.60	0.0	0.2	0.7	2.1	30.1	20.0	0.0	80.0	0.0	0.0	0.0
15	23.00	5.581	9.60	0.0	0.2	0.7	2.1	30.1	20.0	0.0	80.0	0.0	0.0	0.0
16	23.00	5.581	9.60	0.0	0.2	0.7	2.1	30.1	20.0	0.0	80.0	0.0	0.0	0.0
17	23.00	5.581	9.60	0.0	0.2	0.7	2.1	30.1	20.0	0.0	80.0	0.0	0.0	0.0
18	23.00	5.581	9.60	0.0	0.2	0.7	2.1	30.1	20.0	0.0	80.0	0.0	0.0	0.0
19	23.00	5.581	9.60	0.0	0.2	0.7	2.1	30.1	20.0	0.0	80.0	0.0	0.0	0.0
20	23.00	5.581	9.60	0.0	0.2	0.7	2.1	30.1	20.0	0.0	80.0	0.0	0.0	0.0
21	23.00	5.581	9.60	0.0	0.2	0.7	2.1	30.1	20.0	0.0	80.0	0.0	0.0	0.0
22	23.00	5.581	9.60	0.0	0.2	0.7	2.1	30.1	20.0	0.0	80.0	0.0	0.0	0.0
23	23.00	5.581	9.60	0.0	0.2	0.7	2.1	30.1	20.0	0.0	80.0	0.0	0.0	0.0
24	23.00	5.581	9.60	0.0	0.2	0.7	2.1	30.1	20.0	0.0	80.0	0.0	0.0	0.0

EXHIBIT 21:
LONG-TERM/SHORT-TERM ASSET ALLOCATION: OPTIMAL RESIDUAL STRATEGY (48-MONTH PERIOD)

Strategy	Annual Expected Return	Annual Standard Deviation	Annual Expected Yield	Probability of Annual Return Less than					Minimum Risk Asset Mix					
				0.0 Percent	8.0 Percent	10.0 Percent	12.0 Percent	20.0 Percent	G/A	ITI	LTC	S&P500	AMEX	T-Bills
1	6.80%	2.023%	6.80%	0.0%	88.5%	99.8%	100.0%	100.0%	40.0%	0.0%	0.0%	0.0%	0.0%	60.0%
2	6.86	2.031	6.78	0.0	87.2	99.8	100.0	100.0	39.2	0.0	0.0	0.6	0.1	60.0
3	6.91	2.042	6.76	0.0	86.1	99.8	100.0	100.0	38.8	0.0	0.0	0.8	0.4	60.0
4	6.95	2.056	6.75	0.0	85.0	99.8	100.0	100.0	38.3	0.0	0.0	1.0	0.7	60.0
5	6.99	2.072	6.74	0.0	83.8	99.8	100.0	100.0	37.9	0.0	0.0	1.2	0.9	60.0
6	7.03	2.091	6.73	0.0	82.7	99.8	100.0	100.0	37.5	0.0	0.0	1.4	1.1	60.0
7	7.26	2.246	6.66	0.0	75.2	99.3	100.0	100.0	35.2	0.0	0.0	2.4	2.4	60.0
8	7.58	2.589	6.56	0.0	63.6	97.0	100.0	100.0	31.9	0.0	0.0	3.8	4.3	60.0
9	8.19	3.415	6.72	0.0	46.9	86.1	98.7	100.0	41.7	0.0	0.0	5.3	6.2	46.7
10	8.80	4.266	6.99	0.0	36.8	72.6	93.6	100.0	56.8	0.0	0.0	6.5	7.7	29.0
11	9.41	5.125	7.27	0.0	30.6	60.9	85.3	100.0	71.9	0.0	0.0	7.7	9.1	11.3
12	10.02	5.997	7.38	0.0	26.6	51.9	76.1	99.9	79.2	0.0	0.0	9.5	11.3	0.0
13	10.63	6.951	7.24	0.1	24.1	45.3	67.5	99.6	69.6	3.7	0.0	12.1	14.5	0.0
14	11.24	7.946	7.36	0.2	22.4	40.4	60.3	98.6	41.2	28.2	0.0	14.4	16.3	0.0
15	11.85	8.956	7.39	0.3	21.3	36.8	54.5	96.7	20.0	44.7	0.0	16.5	18.8	0.0
16	12.47	10.018	7.14	0.5	20.5	34.1	49.8	93.9	20.0	38.5	0.0	18.0	23.5	0.0
17	13.08	11.134	6.89	0.8	20.1	32.1	46.1	90.4	20.0	32.2	0.0	19.6	28.3	0.0
18	13.70	12.290	6.63	1.1	19.9	30.7	43.2	86.6	20.0	25.9	0.0	21.1	33.0	0.0
19	14.31	13.474	6.38	1.5	19.8	29.5	40.9	82.7	20.0	19.6	0.0	22.7	37.7	0.0
20	14.93	14.682	6.13	2.0	19.8	28.7	39.0	79.0	20.0	13.2	0.0	24.3	42.5	0.0
21	15.55	15.917	6.00	2.4	19.8	28.1	37.5	75.5	20.0	10.0	0.0	19.1	50.9	0.0
22	16.16	17.217	6.00	3.0	20.0	27.7	36.4	72.2	20.0	0.0	8.0	12.7	59.3	0.0
23	16.78	18.573	6.00	3.6	20.3	27.5	35.5	69.2	20.0	0.0	8.0	0.4	71.6	0.0
24	16.80	18.613	6.00	3.6	20.3	27.5	35.5	69.1	20.0	0.0	8.0	0.0	72.0	0.0

EXHIBIT 22:
LONG-TERM/SHORT-TERM ASSET ALLOCATION OPTIMAL COMPOSITE STATISTICS (60-MONTHS HORIZON)

Strategy	Annual Expected Return	Annual Standard Deviation	Annual Expected Yield	Probability of Annual Return Less Than				
				0.0 percent	8.0 percent	10.0 percent	12.0 percent	20.0 percent
1	7.17%	1.848%	6.87%	0.0%	84.7%	100.0%	100.0%	100.0%
2	7.50	1.903	6.89	0.0	72.8	99.8	100.0	100.0
3	8.00	2.024	6.94	0.0	50.8	98.6	100.0	100.0
4	8.50	2.182	7.00	0.0	31.2	93.9	100.0	100.0
5	9.00	2.368	7.05	0.0	17.7	83.3	99.8	100.0
6	9.50	2.573	7.11	0.0	9.9	67.7	98.5	100.0
7	10.00	2.847	7.16	0.0	6.0	51.2	94.4	100.0
8	10.50	3.268	7.17	0.0	4.5	37.8	85.4	100.0
9	11.00	3.859	7.30	0.0	4.2	29.3	73.1	100.0
10	11.50	4.518	7.52	0.0	4.3	24.1	61.5	100.0
11	12.00	5.214	7.74	0.0	4.5	20.8	52.1	100.0
12	12.50	5.941	7.82	0.0	4.7	18.6	44.8	99.7
13	13.00	6.751	7.71	0.0	5.2	17.3	39.5	99.0
14	13.50	7.607	7.81	0.0	5.7	16.6	35.6	97.4
15	14.00	8.484	7.83	0.0	6.1	16.1	32.7	94.8
16	14.50	9.412	7.63	0.0	6.7	15.8	30.5	91.5
17	15.00	10.390	7.43	0.0	7.3	15.8	29.0	87.6
18	15.50	11.405	7.23	0.1	7.9	15.9	27.8	83.6
19	16.00	12.448	7.03	0.1	8.5	16.1	27.0	79.6
20	16.50	13.511	6.82	0.2	9.1	16.3	26.3	75.9
21	17.00	14.599	6.72	0.4	9.7	16.6	25.9	72.4
22	17.50	15.744	6.72	0.5	10.3	16.9	25.6	69.2
23	18.00	16.937	6.72	0.8	11.0	17.4	25.5	66.4
24	18.01	16.973	6.72	0.8	11.0	17.4	25.5	66.3

insight as to expected return and risk other than a historical average, the lower return and risk allocation would be most appropriate for this time horizon from a risk-of-loss standpoint.

Multi-outlook analysis is especially important concerning capital market expectations. While the individual scenario distributions of return may narrow, the prospect of alternative cases may become apparent and even compelling.

Over the short run, confident return projections are extremely difficult, especially for the high expected return assets. On the other hand, if the projection is not expressed with strong conviction in the form of a relatively small expected risk, the allocation process will consistently call for low-risk allocations. Therefore, a multi-scenario projection allows a range of outcomes to be evaluated, and the probability-weighted composite provides a consensus outcome. The important result is the sensitivity of the outcome under alternative assumptions. A more effective perspective for decision-making is consequently achieved.

In the context of setting strategy for a pension fund that already has a long-term policy established, the value of the probability of loss for the desired return benchmark over the long-term horizon can be used as the maximum value for the short term. For example, if the long-term policy has a 15% probability of loss for 0% return, the mix may be changed over the short run, as long as the probability of loss of the new mix has a maximum of 15%. Therefore, by taking advantage of short-term expectations to maximize return, the integrity of the long-term policy is retained.

A floor or base probability of loss is therefore established that can provide boundaries within which strategic return/risk decisions may be made. As long as the alteration of the portfolio mix does not violate the probability of loss, increased return through strategic judgment can be pursued. Ultimately, the value of the judgment must be reviewed, but the mechanism for translating the judgment into decision-making boundaries is served through an asset allocation framework.

APPENDIX A: RISK OF LOSS ANALYSIS FOR ASSET ALLOCATION

In the process of locating points on the efficient frontier for the asset allocation optimization model we described in this chapter, the standard deviation of the optimal portfolio at each point can also be obtained. These values form the basis for determining the probabilities of loss associated with these mixes. In this appendix we shall explain this process which we called *risk of loss analysis.*

If the optimal mixes associated with M values of R are called χ_m $(m = 1, 2, \ldots, M)$, associated with R_m, the corresponding minimum standard deviations can be called σ_m. Using matrix notation, these are related according to

$$R_m = r'\chi_m$$

and

$$\sigma_m = \sqrt{\chi'_m \Sigma \chi_m}$$

Thus R_m and σ_m represent the total expected return and total standard deviation, respectively based on the individual components r and Σ given for a single time period.

The probability of not achieving the expected return level L with the constrained optimal portfolio with an expected return of R_m,

$$Q = \Pr\{R \leq L | \chi_m\},$$

may now be determined.

This computation requires some assumption about the shape of the distribution of periodic returns R.

Assume that the periodic portfolio returns are lognormally distributed with mean R_m and variance σ_m so that the variable z given by

$$z = \ln(1 + R)$$

will be normally distributed with mean

$$\mu_{z_m} = \ln(1 + R_m)$$

and variance

$$\sigma_m = \ln\left[\frac{\sigma_m^{\,2} + (R_m + 1)^2}{(R_m + 1)^2}\right]$$

Under this assumption, the probability of loss for this optimal mix (expected return R_m) with the loss threshold L may then be obtained as follows:

$$Q_m = PR\{ z_m \equiv \ln(1 + R) \leq \ln(1 + L)|\chi_m\}$$

$$= \frac{1}{2} + \frac{1}{2}\text{erf}\left[\frac{\ln(1+L)-\mu_{z_m}}{\sqrt{2}\sigma_{z_m}}\right]$$

where "erf" is the error functional defined as

$$\text{erf}(x) = \int_0^x e^{-t^2} dt$$

The probability of loss of t time periods can be obtained using the random walk assumption discussed in this chapter. It will be

$$Q_m(t) = \frac{1}{2} + \frac{1}{2}\text{erf}\left[\frac{\ln(1+L)-\mu_{z_m}t}{\sqrt{2t}\,\sigma_{z_m}}\right]$$

which represents the probability of not achieving at least the total return L in t time periods using the optimal mix χ_m, which has a total expected return R_m (or tR_m for t time periods) and standard deviation σ_m (or $\sigma_m\sqrt{t}$).

APPENDIX B: MULTIPLE SCENARIO EXTENSION FOR ASSET ALLOCATION MODEL

In this chapter, we described how the basic asset allocation model could be extended to multiple scenarios. In this appendix, we shall describe this approach.

Suppose the forecast of the course of future events is to be expressed in terms of N possible scenarios, which are discrete or mutually exclusive and to each of which a probability of occurrence, P_n, $n = 1, 2, \ldots, N$, is assigned, Suppose, in addition, that the joint distribution of asset returns under each of these possible scenarios is given by $f_n(z)$, where z is the vector of future returns of the J assets over the time period of the forecast. Just as in the case of a single scenario, the expected return of the nth scenario, $\hat{R}_n$, given its occurrence, will be

$$\hat{R}_n = E_n(R(z)) = \int\int\ldots\int x'z f_n(z)dz_1 dz_2 \ldots dz_j$$
$$= x' E_n(z)$$

and its standard deviation will be

$$\hat{\sigma}^2_{R_n} = E_n\left[\left(R(z)-\hat{R}_n\right)^2\right] = \int\int\ldots\int\left(R_n(z)-R_n\right)^2 f_n(z)dz_1 dz_2 \ldots dz_j$$
$$= x'\sum_n x$$

where χ is a column vector whose elements are the allocation of the portfolio to security i, and where Σ_n is the covariance matrix among the J assets given the occurrence of the nth scenario. Consider the unconditional distribution (i.e., without knowledge of which scenario will occur), which can be called the composite distribution and identified with the scenario subscript denoted by an asterisk (*). Since the scenarios are assumed to be mutually exclusive, the composite joint distribution may be written merely as a superposition of the joint distributions of the individual scenarios:

$$f_*(z) = \sum_n P_n f_n(z)$$

This yields immediately the unconditional (or composite) expected return:

$$\hat{R}_* = \int\int\ldots\int x'z\left[\sum_n f_n(z)\right]dz_1 dz_2 \ldots dz_j$$
$$= \sum_n P_n \hat{R}_n$$

The variance of the composite distribution requires slightly more effort but may be reduced to

$$\hat{\sigma}_*^2 = E\left[\left(R - R_*\right)^2\right]$$

$$= \int\int\dots\int\left(\sum_{j-1}^{J}x_jz_j - \hat{R}_*\right)\left(\sum_{k=1}^{J}x_kz_k - \hat{R}_*\right)$$

$$\times\left[\sum_n f_n(z)\right]dz_1\,dz_2\dots dz_j$$

$$= \sum_n P_n\sum_{j=1}^{J}\sum_{k=1}^{J}x_jx_k\left[\text{cov}_n\left(z_j,z_k\right) - \left(\hat{z}_{jn} - \hat{z}_{j*}\right)\left(\hat{z}_{kn} - \hat{z}_{k*}\right)\right]$$

where $\text{cov}_n(z_j, z_k)$ represents the conditional covariance between the assets j and k given the occurrence of scenario n. $\hat{z}_{jn}$ represents the mean return of the jth asset with the nth scenario, and $\hat{z}_{j*}$ is the mean return of the jth asset with the composite scenario, or

$$\hat{z}_{j*} = \sum_n P_n\hat{z}_{jn}$$

The quadratic form $\hat{\sigma}_*2$ may now be minimized to obtain the constrained optimal mixes at each return level or the composite scenario just as for a single scenario.

The unconditional probability of loss may be readily estimated if the assumption that the distribution of total portfolio returns for each scenario is lognormal is again made. Since the scenarios are mutually exclusive, the distribution of portfolio returns will be the sum of the conditional distributions weighted by the probability of occurrence of each:

$$g_*(z) = \sum_n P_n g_n(z)$$

It follows immediately from the expressions derived for the individual scenarios that the probability of not achieving at least the total return L in t time periods using the optimal mix (for the composite scenario) χ_{m*}, which has a total expected return tR_{*m} and standard deviation $\sigma_{*m}\sqrt{t}$, will be

$$Q_{*m}(t) = \frac{1}{2} + \frac{1}{2}\sum_n P_n \,\text{erf}\left[\frac{\ln(1+L) - \mu_{nz_m} t}{\sqrt{2t}\,\sigma_{nz_m}}\right]$$

where

$$\mu_{nz_m} = \ln\left(1 + \hat{R}_{nm}\right)$$

and

$$\sigma_{nz_m} = \ln\left[\frac{\hat{\sigma}_{nm}^2 + \left(\hat{R}_{nm} + 1\right)^2}{\left(\hat{R}_{nm} + 1\right)^2}\right]$$

$\hat{R}_{nm}$ represents the portfolio expected return level for the nth scenario assumptions using the mth optimal mix for the composite portfolio and $\hat{\sigma}_{nzm}$ the corresponding portfolio return standard deviation.

SECTION TWO

Optimization and Surplus Management

CHAPTER 9

Portfolio Optimization within a Surplus Framework*

MARTIN L. LEIBOWITZ
MANAGING DIRECTOR
SALOMON BROTHERS INC*

ROY D. HENRIKSSON
VICE PRESIDENT
SALOMON BROTHERS INC

WILLIAM S. KRASKER
VICE PRESIDENT
SALOMON BROTHERS INC

An investor's asset allocation decision is typically examined as a trade-off between risk and return. Achieving a higher expected return usually requires the investor to bear a higher level of risk, risk generally being measured by the standard deviation of the portfolio return. The portfolio optimization process can be thought of as maximizing the expected return of a portfolio, subject to a risk constraint.

*Copyright © 1988 by Salomon Brothers Inc. The authors wish to thank John Plum, Margo Urbany, and Peter G. Brown for their assistance in the preparation of this chapter.

The optimization process has traditionally focused on asset returns. In many cases, however, the purpose of an investor's asset portfolio is to fund a specified schedule of liabilities. The "portfolio" subject to optimization should, therefore, comprise liabilities as well as assets. By the same token, the appropriate measure of portfolio performance is the surplus—the difference betweeen the market value of the assets and the present value of the liabilities. Thus, it becomes necessary to take account of both asset and liability returns, where liabilities act as a fixed short position.

Optimization from a surplus perspective can result in a portfolio solution that differs radically from the solution that would emerge from an assets-only perspective. The inclusion of liabilities can dramatically change the relevant risk characteristics of the different asset classes. An asset such as cash that would typically reduce the riskiness of a portfolio of assets may actually increase the riskiness of a portfolio that includes liabilities. The change in perspective will, therefore, often lead to striking differences in the optimal asset mix. With the appropriate adjustments, however, many of the procedures developed in the traditional assets-only framework can be carried over to the surplus framework.

Before developing the carry-over, however, it will be worthwhile to introduce an important refinement to the analysis of the assets-only framework that has usually been omitted from previous applications of mean-variance optimization. In such applications, the dimensions of the problem have been greatly restricted by the assumption that "bonds" can be represented as a single asset "point." That single asset is usually chosen to be a capitalization-weighted index, such as the Salomon Brothers Broad Investment-Grade Bond Index (Broad Index).

In this chapter we discuss the implications of this simplification, and then present and analyze a more realistic model of the fixed-income market. Some of our findings corroborate the conclusions of earlier analyses. For example, we demonstrate that bonds are an important component of an efficient portfolio, because their longer durations more closely match the duration of the liabilities and thereby reduce the investor's exposure to interest rate risk. For clarity, we have adopted a relatively simplistic formulation. Practical applications should be addressed with a comprehensive modeling of liabilities (including inflation and economic sensitivities), an expanded investment universe, and a more realistic consideration of the multiple objectives and risk dimensions that are associated with an ongoing concern.

Our main conclusion is that it is essential to model the full range of available yields and maturities. Portfolio optimization that incorporates the full set of available assets along the yield curve will lead to a much better risk/return trade-off than will the conventional approach, which assumes that bonds are a single asset. This conclusion is particularly important in a surplus-oriented framework where the liabilities are taken into account.

TRADITIONAL PORTFOLIO OPTIMIZATION

In traditional portfolio optimization only assets are considered, and the focus is consequently on the trade-off between asset risk and asset return. In general, one must bear more risk to achieve a higher expected return. Conversely, to reduce the risk one must typically accept a lower expected return. There is an important exception to this rule: by combining certain assets in a portfolio, some of the riskiness of one asset can be counterbalanced by the nature of the variability associated with another. This occurs because different asset values do not always change in a similar manner. Sometimes the return from one asset will be positive when the return from another asset is negative, and vice versa. This counterbalancing means that the variability, or riskiness, of a diversified portfolio will be less than the weighted sum of the variability of its constituent individual assets. Yet, this canceling will not affect the expected return, which will still be the weighted sum of the individual asset expected returns.

The reduction in portfolio risk depends on the degree of co-movement between the two assets. If the asset values always change together in the same manner, they are perfectly (positively) correlated. If they usually (but not always) move together, they are positively correlated. If there is no relationship between the two value changes, they have zero correlation. If the changes tend to be in opposite directions, they have negative correlation. With perfect (positive) correlation, it is not possible to reduce risk without also lowering the expected return of the portfolio. The potential benefits from diversification increase as the correlation decreases; the potential risk reduction is greatest when the correlation is negative.

Determining the optimal asset mix is a two-stage process. In the first stage one achieves the maximum risk reduction through diversification for every feasible expected return. In the second stage the investor's attitude toward risk is incorporated so that the optimal trade-off can be chosen between risk (standard deviation) and expected return.

The basic principles of asset-only risk/return optimization can be demonstrated by considering two risky assets (say equities and bonds) and a riskless asset (cash). A hypothetical example of the trade-off between the expected return and the standard deviation of returns for the three assets is shown in Exhibit 1. In the example, bonds and cash are assumed to have the same expected return, and equities are assumed to have both a higher expected return and a higher standard deviation.

Exhibit 2 presents the risk/return trade-offs available from portfolios comprising different combinations of the assets. The curved line, which represents the potential trade-offs between equities and bonds,

EXHIBIT 1:
THE BASIC RISK/RETURN TRADE-OFF

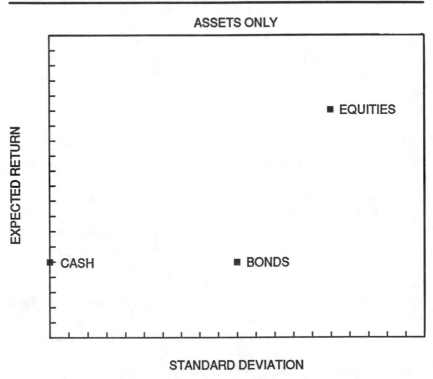

shows the effects of diversification. As equity is added to an all-bond portfolio, one moves along the curved line toward the point representing a portfolio made up entirely of equity. In the example, adding equity to the all-bond portfolio initially increases its expected return and reduces its riskiness. The initial risk reduction is a result of the low correlation between returns on equities and returns on bonds. After the equity proportion reaches a certain limit, however, the riskiness of the portfolio begins to rise more and more rapidly with increasing expected return. The portfolio becomes more of a stock portfolio, its correlation with equities rises, and the benefits of added diversification through a further increase in the equity percentage are reduced.

Now consider the role of cash. Because cash is assumed to be riskless, it is a powerful risk reducer in any portfolio mixture. The

EXHIBIT 2:
THE CASH/EQUITY LINE OF OPTIMAL MIXES

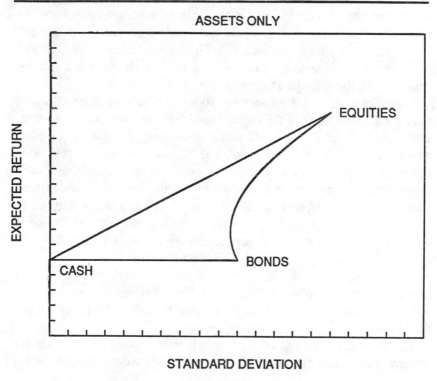

greater the amount of cash in the portfolio, the lower the portfolio risk. Moreover, cash reduces the standard deviation of the portfolio in direct proportion to the cash percentage. Thus, varying proportions of cash and equities trace out a straight line in the risk/return diagram.

BONDS AS A CONTINUUM OF ASSETS

The fixed-income market provides an unusually wide spectrum of potential investment opportunities. To examine the full potential role of bonds across this spectrum, it is helpful to begin with a model that extends the example we have just discussed in the simplest possible way. In this model one assumes that the yield curve is flat, or in other words that all bonds have the same expected return and that all shifts of the yield curve are parallel. Thus, all of the bonds in the model are perfectly correlated with one another. The risk/return diagram for stocks and bonds in such a model is shown in Exhibit 3. The expected return and standard deviation for each bond lie somewhere along the horizontal line in the exhibit, where the standard deviation risk of each bond is proportional to its duration. This graph indicates the relative positions of bonds with the same duration as the Broad Index and the Salomon Brothers Large Pension Fund (LPF) Index.

If a risky bond is mixed in a portfolio with varying proportions of equity and the returns of the two are positively but not perfectly correlated, the risk/return trade-off is a curved line (Exhibit 4). In other words, diversification is beneficial. If the single bond in the portfolio is the riskless bond with zero duration (that is, cash), then, as noted above, the risk/return trade-off is simply the straight line segment connecting that bond with stocks. As both Exhibits 2 and 4 suggest, in the model of the flat yield curve riskless cash "dominates" risky bonds as long as the bond returns are positively correlated with those of equity. No matter what standard deviation is chosen, the highest possible expected return is obtained by a portfolio consisting only of stocks and cash. Under the simplified conditions considered here, it could never make sense for a portfolio manager to hold risky bonds unless they offered a higher expected return than cash.

To examine the effects of risky bonds with returns higher than the returns of cash, one must begin to relax the restrictive assumptions of the

EXHIBIT 3:
RISK/RETURN TRADE-OFF FOR FLAT YIELD CURVE

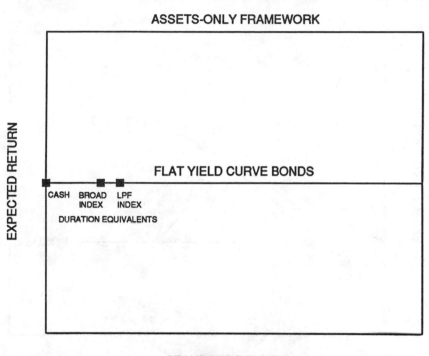

flat yield curve model. Consider a series of STRIPS, the single-payment, zero-coupon Treasury bonds with maturities of from one to 30 years. A recent STRIPS yield curve is shown in Exhibit 5; the two STRIPS with durations that are equivalent to the Broad Index and the LPF Index are identified in the exhibit. If the expected return of a STRIPS issue is assumed to be its yield and the yield curve shifts are assumed to be parallel, then the standard deviations of the STRIPS will be nearly proportional to their maturities. A typical risk/return diagram for STRIPS and equity is given in Exhibit 6. Because cash has a lower expected return than do risky STRIPS, a portfolio made up only of stocks and a single STRIPS issue can realize a better risk/return trade-off than that achievable with only stocks and cash (see Exhibit 7).

EXHIBIT 4:
EQUITY/BOND MIXTURES WITH FLAT YIELD CURVE

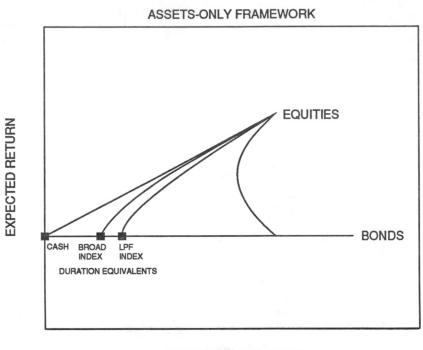

ASSETS-ONLY FRAMEWORK

EXPECTED RETURN

EQUITIES

BONDS

CASH   BROAD   LPF
       INDEX   INDEX

DURATION EQUIVALENTS

STANDARD DEVIATION

Still better results may be possible by forming portfolios that combine stocks with more than one STRIPS issue (although if all yield curve shifts are parallel, no more than two STRIPS issues will be needed). If STRIPS of all maturities are available, the full efficient frontier will be a smooth curve, as shown in Exhibit 8.

EQUITY DURATION

In most allocation studies, stocks and bonds are assumed to have a positive correlation between 0.3 and 0.4. In other words, stocks, like bonds, are assumed to exhibit positive returns when interest rates

EXHIBIT 5:
STRIPS YIELD CURVE

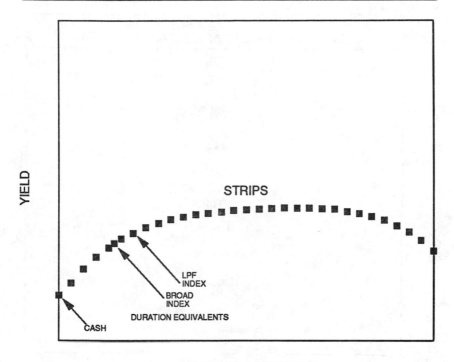

decline. The interest rate sensitivity of equities corresponds to a duration of from two to six years, depending on the estimates of relative
volatility for stocks versus bonds. The wide range reflects the statistically derived nature of the concept of equity duration. By contrast, the
concept of bond duration is far more analytical, and hence a more
reliable gauge of interest rate sensitivity.

If stocks and bonds are positively correlated, both will have positive
duration and will tend to reenforce each other's exposure to interest rate
risk. Thus one can see from a slightly different vantage point why cash
can diversify a portfolio more efficiently than any risky bonds along a
flat yield curve: cash is simply uncorrelated with equities.

EXHIBIT 6:
RISK/RETURN TRADE-OFF FOR EQUITIES AND STRIPS OF ALL
MATURITIES

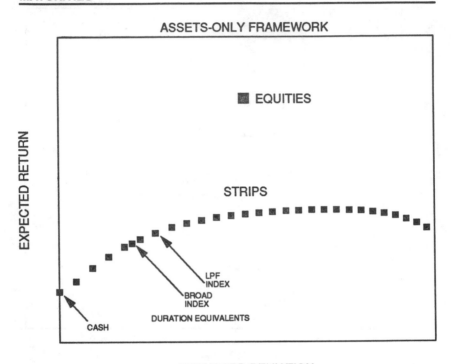

THE NEGATIVE CORRELATION CASE

Although the correlation between stock and bond returns is usually assumed to be positive, it is most instructive to examine the implications of a negative correlation. In other words, suppose that stocks tended to respond to interest rate changes in the direction opposite to bond movements—that stock prices tended to fall with declining interest rates and rise when interest rates rose. Historical evidence notwithstanding, this supposition is not entirely farfetched. In fact, it closely corresponds to an earlier "classical" view of stock behavior. However,

EXHIBIT 7:
OPTIMAL MIXES OF CASH, EQUITIES AND SINGLE STRIPS

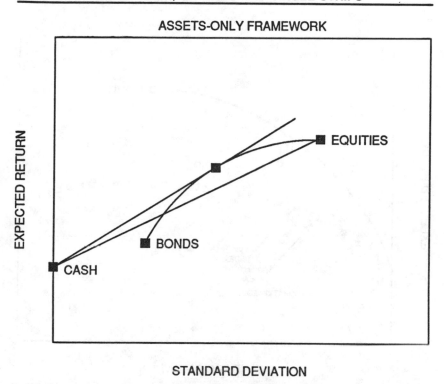

ASSETS-ONLY FRAMEWORK

our purpose here is not to argue one theory or the other, but simply to illustrate the intriguing behavior of two negatively correlated assets.

The influence of correlation on portfolio risk can be seen in Exhibit 9. For a given asset mix the portfolio risk is always less for a negative correlation than it is for a positive one.

Return for a moment to the world of flat yield curves and recall that holding bonds in a portfolio is desirable only if they offer the potential for greater risk reduction than cash. Such potential is present if equities and bonds are negatively correlated (see Exhibit 10). In the figure there are combinations of equities and bonds that offer more favorable trade-offs between portfolio expected return and risk than can be achieved from any combination that includes only equities and cash. The inves-

EXHIBIT 8:
EFFICIENT FRONTIER

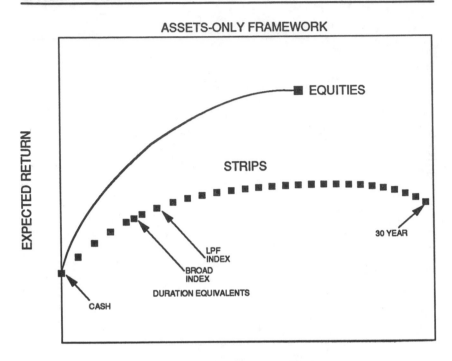

tor can lower the overall portfolio risk for the same expected return, because combining the negatively correlated bonds with equities in a portfolio has allowed the investor to neutralize or reduce the interest rate risk of the equities. This negative correlation creates a particularly valuable opportunity for reaping the benefits of diversification.

THE SURPLUS FRAMEWORK

The same approach can be carried over to the surplus framework, in which asset returns are transformed into their returns (or changes in value) relative to the changes in value of the relevant liabilities. In this framework the relevant portfolio is expanded to include both assets and

EXHIBIT 9:
DIVERSIFICATION THROUGH NEGATIVE CORRELATION

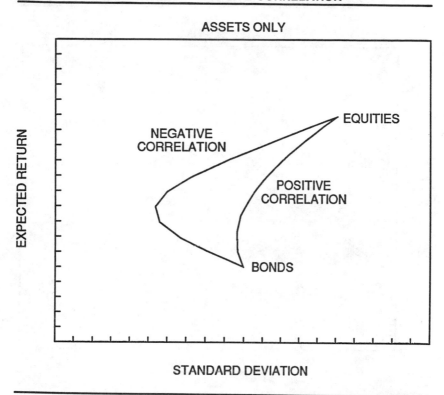

liabilities. Intuitively, the pension liability cash flows can be regarded as a fixed short position in a portfolio of single-payment bonds such as Treasury STRIPS (see Exhibit 11). The size of the short position (the negative weight) is the present value of the liabilities. Liability returns are calculated from value changes just as they would be for any asset. [1] Returns and riskiness can then be measured with respect to changes in the asset-liability surplus. Exhibit 12 shows a hypothetical risk/return trade-off for individual assets in which, for simplicity, we have assumed that all of the variation in liability values can be explained by

---

[1]See Martin L. Leibowitz, "Liability Returns: A New Perspective on Asset Allocation," in Frank J. Fabozzi and T. Dessa Garlicki (editors), *Advances in Bond Analysis and Portfolio Strategies* (Chicago, IL: Probus Publishing, 1987).

EXHIBIT 10:
THE NEW FRONTIER WITH NEGATIVE CORRELATION

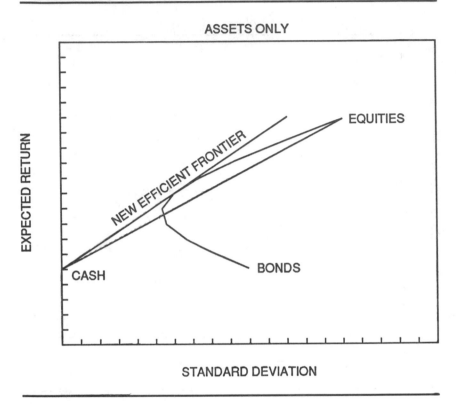

ASSETS ONLY

changes in interest rates. In this spirit, it is also assumed that the investor can create an "immunized bond portfolio" that precisely funds the liabilities.

In this new framework, the immunized portfolio becomes the riskless asset. By contrast, cash can be highly risky in the surplus framework—perhaps even riskier than equities. The seemingly paradoxical relationships among cash, bonds, and immunzied portfolios can be clarified as follows: Exhibit 13 shows the duration gap—the difference between asset duration and liability duration—for bond portfolios of varying duration values. Since variations in the bond returns and in the liabilities are assumed to be driven solely by interest rates, the surplus risk of a bond portfolio is proportional to its duration gap.

Thus, first consider cash. With a duration of zero, cash does nothing

EXHIBIT 11:
ANNUAL LIABILITY FLOWS

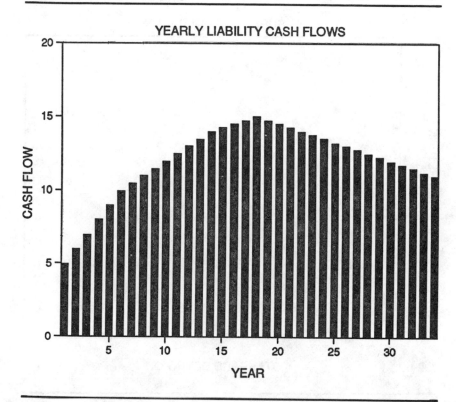

to offset the interest rate risk of the liabilities. For example, if the duration of the liabilities is 12 years, an all-cash portfolio has a significant duration gap of −12 and a correspondingly high level of surplus risk (see Exhibit 14). As the duration of the bond portfolio increases, the (negative) duration gap shrinks and the surplus risk declines. When the bond portfolio duration matches the duration of the liabilties, the duration gap becomes zero, the surplus risk vanishes, and the portfolio is immunized. Thereafter, as the bond duration continues to lengthen, the duration gap becomes increasingly positive and the surplus risk, or the standard deviation of surplus changes, rises once again (see Exhibit 14).

The risk/return trade-offs for positively correlated assets in the surplus framework show a pattern similar to the pattern in the assets-only

EXHIBIT 12:
RISK/RETURN TRADE-OFFS IN A SURPLUS FRAMEWORK

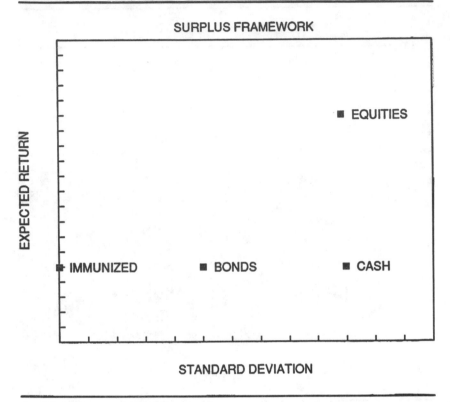

framework. In the surplus framework, the immunized fund plays the role of cash in the assets-only framework; that is, the role of a riskless asset whose returns are perfectly correlated with interest rates (see Exhibit 15). The trade-off between expected return and standard deviation traces out a straight line as the proportions of immunized fund and risky assets in the portfolio are varied. The greater the amount of immunized fund in the portfolio, the lower the risk of the portfolio in the surplus framework.

The correlations among equities, bond, and cash are positive as long as the effective durations of these assets are all less than or all greater than the effective duration of the liabilities. The risk/return trade-offs available with differing mixes of bonds and equity or equity and cash trace out slightly curved lines (see Exhibit 15). Just as in the assets-only framework, there is no demand for risky assets (in this case, bonds

EXHIBIT 13:
DURATION GAP WITH ASSETS OVER LIABILITIES

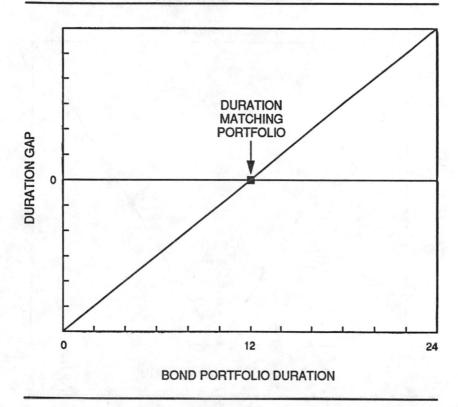

BOND PORTFOLIO DURATION

or cash) if they are positively correlated with equities and do not offer a higher expected return than the riskless asset (here, the immunized fund). The optimal portfolio in the surplus framework with a flat yield curve is made up of some combination of the immunized fund and equities.

NEGATIVE CORRELATION WITHIN THE SURPLUS FRAMEWORK

For a typical pension fund, the effective duration of equities and cash is almost always shorter than the duration of the fund liabilities.[2] Never-

---

[2]See Martin L. Leibowitz, *Surplus Management: A New Perspective on Asset Allocation*, Salomon Brothers Inc, September 1986.

EXHIBIT 14:
SURPLUS RISK VERSUS BOND PORTFOLIO DURATION

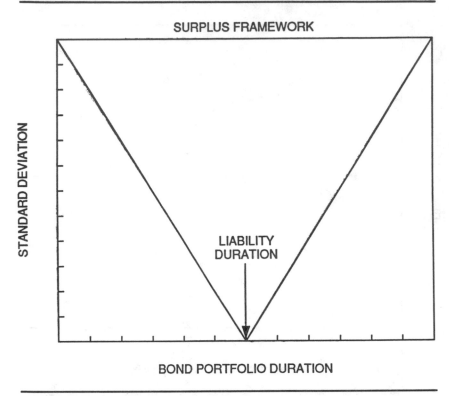

theless, it is often possible to construct a bond portfolio whose duration is longer than that of the liabilities. When rates decline, the value of such a long-duration portfolio increases faster than the value of the liabilities, and so the surplus grows. In contrast, bonds of shorter duration and cash both generate surplus losses when interest rates decline. Equities also tend to generate losses when interest rates drop because their duration is short.

Thus, the effects of long-duration bonds on the surplus are opposite to the effects of cash or equities. With respect to their impact on surplus values such long bond portfolios are *negatively correlated* with equities. There is excellent opportunity for significant benefit from diversification when asset-return correlations are negative. The potential benefit from a negative correlation between stocks and bonds, which

EXHIBIT 15:
POSITIVE CORRELATION WITHIN THE SURPLUS FRAMEWORK

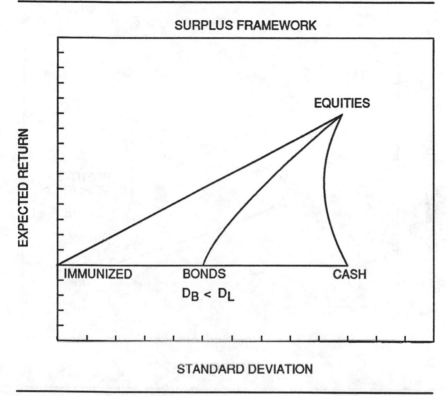

can be achieved when the bond duration is longer and the equity duration is shorter than the duration of the liabilities, is illustrated in Exhibit 16.

THE EFFICIENT FRONTIER WITHIN THE SURPLUS FRAMEWORK

Negatively correlated assets can be assembled into portfolios whose risk/return trade-offs lie above the line representing mixes of equity and immunized fund (see Exhibit 17). Every such portfolio yields more than the mix of equity and immunized fund for the same risk level. Remember that the equity/immunized-fund line serves as the efficient

EXHIBIT 16:
NEGATIVE CORRELATION WITHIN THE SURPLUS FRAMEWORK

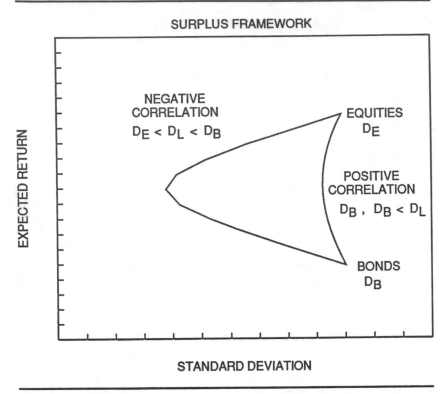

frontier—the set of optimal trade-offs between risk and return—for positively correlated assets. Thus, since mixes of negatively correlated long bonds and equity lie above this line, negative correlation opens up new territory for the efficient frontier.

The immunized fund has no risk in the surplus framework. Hence, various proportions of the immunized fund, mixed with any given portfolio, trace out a straight line on the risk/return diagram in the surplus framework. For example, consider the line from the immunized-fund point to the tangent point on the curve traced out by mixtures of equity and (negatively correlated) long bonds (see Exhibit 17). This tangent line would appear to push the efficient frontier back even farther. One can show that the portfolio mix at the tangent point has an effective duration just matching that of the liabilities. This portfolio

EXHIBIT 17:
THE DURATION-MATCHING MIXTURE OF EQUITIES AND LONG BONDS

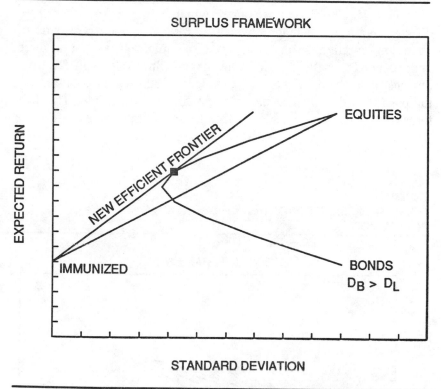

SURPLUS FRAMEWORK

mix is similar to the immunized portfolio in that the interest rate risk is entirely removed. Nevertheless, the two portfolios differ in that the "tangency" portfolio includes a certain proportion of equities. The equities account for higher expected return of the portfolio as well as its clear element of risk, which is quite separate from the risk of interest rate volatility.

For any given percentage of equities in a portfolio, one can theoretically match the effective duration of the liabilities.[3] One need only (!) find a bond portfolio whose duration is long enough so that when the bonds are combined with the equities, the effective duration of the

[3]See Martin L. Leibowitz, *Total Portfolio Duration: A New Perspective on Asset Allocation*, Salomon Brothers Inc, February 1986.

resulting mixed portfolio is equal to that of the liabilities. Such a mixture eliminates interest rate risk with no loss in expected return.

Exhibit 18 shows optimal duration-matching portfolios for three different equity percentages, which require long-bond portfolios of increasing duration. From the diagram one might guess that all three optimal portfolios lie on the same tangent line. Although far from obvious, it can be proved that the envelope of all such duration-matching portfolios does in fact plot along a single tangent line. This line turns out to be the new efficient frontier of optimal mixes.

EXHIBIT 18:
THE NEW EFFICIENT FRONTIER OF DURATION-MATCHING PORTFOLIOS

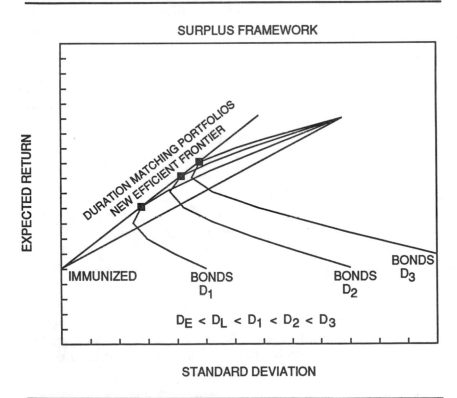

DURATION-MATCHING PORTFOLIOS

It might seem that the technique of portfolio optimization being described requires adjustments in the proportions of three assets—stocks, long bonds and immunized fund. In fact, however, there are only two major elements that must be considered: the desired amount of equity exposure and the duration match of the assets and the liabilities. Because the effective duration of equities is usually shorter than that of the liabilities, the greater the proportion of equity in the portfolio, the greater the required duration of the remaining position in bonds and immunized fund.

For example, as Exhibit 19 shows, if the investor wants to allocate 25% of a portfolio to equities, the combined effective duration of bonds and immunized fund must be 15 years, if the duration of the assets is to match the duration of the liabilities. This can be accomplished by holding 18.75% of the portfolio in bonds with a duration of 24 years and 56.25% in the immunized fund. Of course, it can also be achieved by holding 75% in bonds with a duration of 15 years, or by many other possible combinations.

If the investor wants to have 50% of the portfolio's assets in equities, the combined duration of bonds and immunized fund must be 21 years. This can be accomplished by holding 37.50% in bonds with a duration

EXHIBIT 19:
DURATION MATCHING IN A SURPLUS FRAMEWORK

Initial Assets Value = 100
Initial Liability Value = 100

		Portfolio Weights	
	Effective Duration	*Portfolio 1*	*Portfolio 2*
Liability	12	−100	−100
Equities	3	25%	50%
Long Bonds	24	18.75	37.50
Immunized Fund	12	56.25	12.50
Combined Duration of Long Bonds and Immunized Fund		15	21
Combined Duration of Assets		12	12

of 24 years and 12.50% in immunized fund. It can also be accomplished by holding 50% in bonds with a duration of 21 years, or many other possible combinations.

Duration matching reduces portfolio risk without loss in expected return, and there are many fixed-income combinations that can carry it out. In practice, the investor would simply choose the cheapest and most liquid combination among them. Such a choice is just one more example of seeking the highest expected return for a given level of risk.

A REALISTIC YIELD CURVE IN THE SURPLUS FRAMEWORK

In our discussion of the surplus framework so far, we have tacitly assumed a flat yield curve. Under more realistic circumstances, in which the investor is generally compensated with a higher expected return for buying risky bonds, the role of the yield curve becomes crucial. A convenient way to visualize how duration matching can minimize interest rate exposure along a realistic yield curve is to plot the expected returns and standard deviations of the pension surplus for equities and for each bond in the STRIPS yield curve (see Exhibit 20). The STRIPS issue whose maturity most closely matches the duration of the liabilities is a (nearly) immunized fund, and its interest rate risk is (nearly) zero in the surplus framework. STRIPS with either longer or shorter durations are risky. STRIPS with shorter durations are represented by the points along the lower part of the curve in Exhibit 20; the STRIPS with longer durations are plotted along the upper part.

It may be worth noting that the relation between duration and risk for points plotted in Exhibit 20 is exactly as it was plotted for the flat yield curve in Exhibit 14. The V in Figure 14 is reflected in the curved horizontal "V" in Exhibit 20. If the STRIPS curve were flat, of course, all the STRIPS would lie on the same horizontal line; as duration increased from zero to 30 years, the plotted points would move from right to left until the STRIPS issue matching the duration of the liabilities was reached. As duration continued to increase the plotted points would reverse direction and move from left to right (compare also Exhibit 15 and Exhibit 17).

The efficient frontier for the surplus—representing the highest expected surplus that can be attained for each surplus standard deviation—is shown in Exhibit 21. This curve simultaneously takes into

EXHIBIT 20:
RISK/RETURN TRADE-OFF IN SURPLUS FRAMEWORK

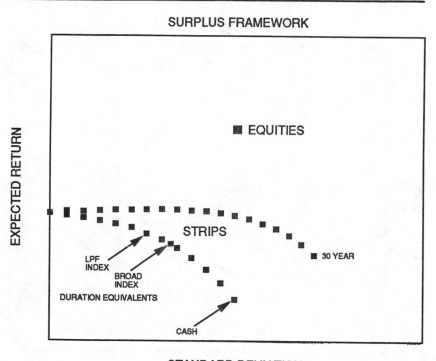

SURPLUS FRAMEWORK

EXPECTED RETURN

STANDARD DEVIATION

account two effects of the STRIPS yield curve on the surplus returns: first, the negative correlations between equity and bonds whose duration is longer than the duration of the liabilities; second, the variation of expected return in the surplus framework among different STRIPS issues. Again it is clear that the efficient frontier represents a significant gain over what could be obtained with any single asset. By combining stocks with long-duration bonds, the pension fund manager can achieve a considerable reduction in risk without sacrificing too much return.

The example illustrated in Exhibit 21 actually understates the potential for risk reduction from long bonds. Indeed, as we noted above, for virtually any given percentage of equities in a portfolio one can theoretically match the effective duration of the liabilities with long bonds.

EXHIBIT 21:
EFFICIENT FRONTIER IN A SURPLUS FRAMEWORK

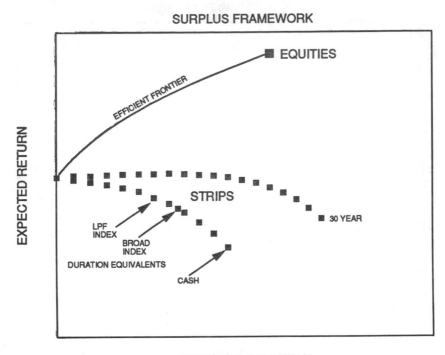

Because the longest existing STRIPS have a duration (and maturity) of 30 years, however, the investor might have to bear interest rate risk (through a mismatch in duration) in order to hold the desired amount of equities. For example, suppose the effective duration of the equities is three years and the duration of the liabilities is 12 years. In that case, the investor cannot allocate more than two thirds of the portfolio to equities and still match the duration of the liabilities with an asset portfolio of equities and STRIPS. (On the other hand, if a fund can buy Treasury bond futures, it can build a longer-duration portfolio than it can with STRIPS alone.)

Duration matching is the optimal strategy in the STRIPS example because an investor does not receive significantly higher expected return for bearing substantial interest rate risk. The investor always wants to eliminate any uncompensated sources of risk from the portfolio; conversely, he is willing to bear interest rate risk only if such risk offers an increase in portfolio expected return. For example, if the investor expects yields to increase, he might want to hold assets with a total portfolio duration less than the duration of the liabilities, because the expected return of the surplus will thereby increase. The optimal portfolio would depend on the desired risk/return trade-off.

In the same spirit, equities offer the opportunity to increase the expected return—and the riskiness—of the portfolio. The duration-matching process hedges against that portion of the equity and liability risk caused by interest rate changes. Investors must bear the remaining market risk to obtain the higher expected returns.

NONPARALLEL YIELD CURVE MOVEMENTS

All of the preceding discussion has been based on the assumption that shifts in the yield curve are always parallel and that, consequently, all STRIPS are perfectly correlated. This assumption implies that all of the uncertainty of bonds can be explained by parallel shifts in the yield curve and that the riskiness of a bond is entirely determined by its duration. If, as is actually the case, STRIPS of different maturities are not perfectly correlated, one could obtain some further reduction in overall portfolio risk.

APPLICATION IN PRACTICE

The main purpose of this report is to introduce a surplus framework into the traditional analytical procedure of comparing risk with expected return. This can be done in a straightforward manner, and the tradition- al optimization problem can be formulated in a familiar way. For the hypothetical formulation presented here, one can even apply the standard mean/variance optimization techniques to determine the optimal portfolios.

We must point out, however, that we have adopted this relatively simplistic surplus formulation only for illustrative purposes. For realistic applications, one would have to provide a much more detailed representation of the asset classes that we have touched on here. One would also want to include other available asset classes such as international equity, international fixed income, real estate, and so forth. In practice, the typical surplus problem may have several critical dimensions of liability that require a far more intricate formulation of the risk. In addition, there may be a number of other important considerations that must be incorporated into a realistic solution—multiple benchmarks, inflation effects, short-term versus long-term horizons, and the like. Shaping a comprehensive allocation policy amidst these factors may call for the use of non-standard combinations of optimization and simulation. The optimum solution in such practical situations may differ substantially from the solutions described above.

The surplus framework is immediately applicable to pension funds: it permits the new accounting factor required by Financial Accounting Standards Board Statement 87 (FASB 87) to be examined in a familiar risk/return context. Accordingly, much recent work has focused on the implications of FASB 87. Nevertheless, the surplus framework can be applied far beyond FASB 87. Most investment funds are motivated by the need to meet some liability, which may or may not be explicitly defined. In principle, the surplus optimization approach can be extended to such institutions as thrifts, insurance companies, property/casualty companies, and endowment and foundation funds. The surplus framework can also be applied to certain managed funds in which performance is determined relative to a well-defined benchmark index.

Indeed, the surplus framework is a more general formulation than the assets-only framework. It can be viewed as the assets-only framework expanded to allow for short positions. The surplus framework then takes on the character of a general arbitrage framework, and the consideration of assets alone can be construed as a relatively narrow special case in which the liability is defined as a zero payout. Thus, the surplus framework leads to a broader and more flexible characterization of the optimal asset allocation problem for a variety of institutional applications.

CHAPTER 10

Dynamic Hedging and Asset Allocation Strategies*

RICHARD M. BOOKSTABER
PRINCIPAL
MORGAN STANLEY & CO., INC.

Dynamic hedging is a name given to a wide variety of strategies used to control investment risk and to meet asset/liability objectives in both equity and fixed income portfolios. The most widely-used dynamic hedging strategy, portfolio insurance, replicates option payoffs in order to provide protection against loss without imposing equal limitations on the opportunities for appreciation.

Dynamic hedging provides a means of creating synthetic options. For example, it can provide a synthetic put option that gives a prespecified floor level of downside protection while still allowing the portfolio to share in any future market appreciation. This payoff meets the objectives of many pension funds.

Dynamic hedging also provides a means for creating and hedging many other complex payoffs, such as those generated by the carefully tailored annuity products of the life insurance industry, or the variable rate liabilities of many corporations and thrift institutions.

---

*This chapter is based on Chapter 7 of Richard Bookstaber, *Option Pricing and Investment Strategies*, (Chicago, IL: Probus Publishing, 1987).

193

HOW DYNAMIC HEDGING WORKS

A typical portfolio insurance strategy is depicted in Exhibit 1. The floor in this example equals the current portfolio value of $100 million. The unhedged portfolio will follow the equity market one for one, as indicated by the dotted line. The payoff portfolio insurance provides at the end of the year is shown by the solid line. The payoff equals the floor less the hedging cost if the market is below the floor at year end, and equals the payoff of the market less the hedging cost if the market rises above the floor.

As this example shows, portfolio insurance gives a payoff that is the same as adding to the portfolio a put option with an exercise price equal to the desired floor. If the portfolio drops below the floor value, the put option will give a payoff equal to the difference between the final portfolio value and the floor. This will compensate for the loss on the underlying portfolio.

The option is not bought in the market; it is created through the dynamic trading strategy. The strategy for replicating options adjusts the holding of the underlying portfolio to equal the delta of the option

EXHIBIT 1:
PORTFOLIO INSURANCE

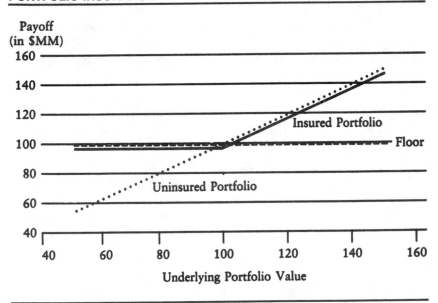

being replicated. (The delta of an option is the dollar change in the value of an option caused by a one-dollar change in the value of the underlying asset. For example, a delta of .5 means the dollar value of the option will move half as much as the value of the underlying asset.) Because the value of the option moves with a change in the underlying portfolio by an amount equal to the delta, by holding this amount in the underlying portfolio we are creating the same price sensitivity as would exist if we held the actual option itself. This replicates the option, because we adjust the portfolio exposure to mimic the price sensitivity an option on the portfolio would have. A person observing how our position value changes day by day could not tell the difference between the change in the position value induced by our dynamic hedge and the price change of an option purchased in the market.

In portfolio insurance strategies, the position that is replicated is long the portfolio and long a put option on the portfolio. The delta of a put option is between 0 and −1. It drops to −1 as the put option goes further into the money, and goes to 0 as the underlying asset increases in value and the put option goes out of the money. Because the delta of the underlying portfolio is always equal to 1, the position delta, the sum of the put delta and portfolio delta, will be between 0 and 1.

Operationally, the dynamic hedge works by increasing the size of the hedge as the portfolio value decreases, and decreasing the size of the hedge as the portfolio value increases. Exposure is reduced as the market falls, limiting the downside loss, and exposure is increased as the market rises, providing upside potential. As any trader knows, gradually selling the portfolio off as it moves down and gradually buying it back as it rises in value does not come without a cost. The cost is a slippage in portfolio value, because not all the gains of the market will be realized, nor will the portfolio be completely insulated from the market declines. This slippage from this dynamic adjustment of the position is what leads to the strategy cost. It is what gives rise to the cost of the option. The central feature of the dynamic hedge is that this cost, because it is the cost of an option, can be predicted at the start of the program.

The Dynamic Adjustment Procedure

Exhibit 2 illustrates the trading process in dynamic hedging. First, a floor return and time to expiration for the strategy are set. These decision parameters represent the investment objectives of the fund. The current portfolio value, time remaining to expiration, interest rate levels, and volatility of the market are then put into the model. The model then provides the position delta, which determines the correct asset allocation based on these inputs and the decision parameters.

EXHIBIT 2:
DYNAMIC HEDGE POSITION ADJUSTMENT PROCEDURE

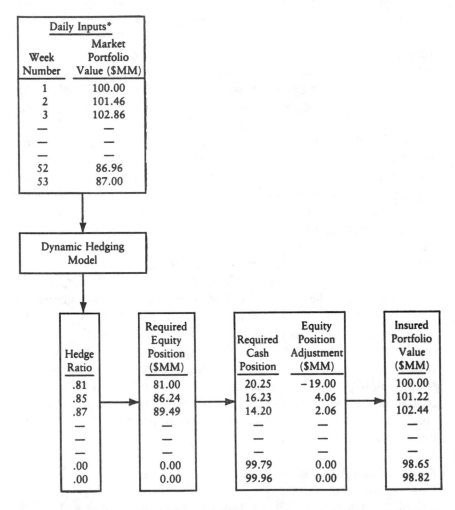

Daily Inputs*	
Week Number	Market Portfolio Value ($MM)
1	100.00
2	101.46
3	102.86
—	—
—	—
—	—
52	86.96
53	87.00

Dynamic Hedging Model

Hedge Ratio	Required Equity Position ($MM)	Required Cash Position	Equity Position Adjustment ($MM)	Insured Portfolio Value ($MM)
.81	81.00	20.25	−19.00	100.00
.85	86.24	16.23	4.06	101.22
.87	89.49	14.20	2.06	102.44
—	—	—	—	—
—	—	—	—	—
—	—	—	—	—
.00	0.00	99.79	0.00	98.65
.00	0.00	99.96	0.00	98.82

*Floor = $100MM; Time Period = 1 Year; Estimated Option Premium = $1.25MM.

The key to the asset allocation is the model-determined *delta,* also called the *hedge ratio.* The delta will determine the percent of the portfolio that should be held at a given point in time to create the desired payoff. For example, a delta of .7 means that 70% of the fund should be invested in the underlying portfolio, and the remaining 30% should be held in the riskfree asset. The delta thus determines the dollar allocation of the fund. As we already know, the delta, and hence the portfolio allocation, changes over time, and also changes as the underlying portfolio value changes. The delta needs to be recomputed on an ongoing basis and the appropriate portfolio position calculated. This is compared to the current allocation, and any required adjustment is made. Because of the continued monitoring and adjustments, this strategy is called a *dynamic* hedging strategy.

The operation of this procedure over the full year is illustrated in Exhibit 3. This exhibit presents weekly computations of the portfolio value, the delta, and the resulting allocation. The objective presented in this table is identical to that of Exhibit 2: a 0% floor return and a floor of $100 on a portfolio that is currently worth $100. The hedge period is one year.

The exhibit first lists two of the key inputs, the time remaining to expiration and the current price of the portfolio. The volatility is determined in this example with the benefit of foresight by estimating the volatility over the 53-week price series. The next column gives the delta of the portfolio. In the first period, the delta is set at .81. On a $100 million fund, initially $81 million is held long in the risky portfolio, the remainder in cash. This delta is computed using an option model.

The required cash position shown in column 5 also includes the cost of the strategy. This cost, equal to the cost of a put option with an exercise price of $100 and a year to expiration, is $1.25 in this example. The total cash position is therefore ($100 − $81) + $1.25 = $20.25. Note that we have only put up $100 for this strategy. We are not actually paying for the option cost up front. As a result, the strategy will move forward as if we had borrowed the money to pay for the option, and the cost of the strategy at the end of the year will give us the better of the floor or the upside of the portfolio less the future value of $1.25, which in this example is $1.35.

In week 2, the portfolio value rises to $101.46, and the proportion of assets held in the portfolio rises as well, to .85. This rise in the hedge ratio means a change in the required position. As column 4 shows, the

EXHIBIT 3:
DYNAMIC HEDGE WEEK-BY-WEEK POSITION SUMMARY

Week Number	Market Portfolio Value	Hedge Ratio	Required Equity Position	Required Cash Position	Current Equity Position	Equity Position Adjustment	Insured Portfolio Value
1	100.00	0.81	81.00	20.25	100.00	−19.00	100.00
2	101.46	0.85	86.24	16.23	82.18	4.06	101.22
3	102.86	0.87	89.49	14.20	87.43	2.06	102.44
4	99.92	0.81	80.94	20.20	86.93	−6.00	99.89
5	98.57	0.76	74.91	25.17	79.84	−4.93	98.84
6	98.09	0.75	73.57	26.19	74.55	−0.98	98.52
7	95.70	0.66	63.16	34.86	71.78	−8.61	96.78
8	98.18	0.74	72.65	27.05	64.80	7.85	98.47
9	97.23	0.70	68.06	30.98	71.95	−3.89	97.81
10	97.01	0.69	66.94	32.00	67.91	−0.97	97.71
11	95.04	0.61	57.97	39.66	65.58	−7.60	96.40
12	92.64	0.50	46.32	49.92	56.51	−10.19	95.01
13	92.46	0.48	44.38	51.85	46.23	−1.85	95.01
14	90.86	0.40	36.34	59.21	43.61	−7.27	94.33
15	89.90	0.35	31.47	63.81	35.96	−4.50	94.05
16	89.72	0.33	29.61	65.71	31.40	−1.79	94.10
17	90.78	0.37	33.59	62.19	29.96	3.63	94.56
18	91.63	0.40	36.65	59.54	33.90	2.75	94.98
19	91.82	0.40	36.73	59.64	36.73	0.00	95.16
20	92.64	0.43	39.84	56.96	37.06	2.78	95.59
21	91.42	0.36	32.91	63.46	39.31	−6.40	95.17
22	92.23	0.39	35.97	60.80	33.20	2.77	95.57
23	90.81	0.31	28.15	68.17	35.42	−7.26	95.12
24	90.50	0.28	25.34	71.01	28.06	−2.71	95.14
25	91.52	0.32	29.29	67.47	25.63	3.66	95.55
26	89.57	0.22	19.71	76.54	28.66	−8.96	95.05

DYNAMIC HEDGE WEEK-BY-WEEK POSITION SUMMARY

Week Number	Market Portfolio Value	Hedge Ratio	Required Equity Positon	Required Cash Position	Current Equity Position	Equity Position Adjustment	Insured Portfolio Value
27	90.04	0.23	20.71	75.77	19.81	0.90	95.28
28	88.70	0.16	14.19	82.11	20.40	-6.21	95.11
29	87.83	0.12	10.54	85.77	14.05	-3.51	95.11
30	85.81	0.06	5.15	91.06	10.30	-5.15	95.02
31	85.55	0.05	4.28	92.07	5.13	-0.86	95.16
32	85.03	0.04	3.40	93.08	4.25	-0.85	95.30
33	84.77	0.03	2.54	94.09	3.39	-0.85	95.45
34	84.54	0.02	1.69	95.10	2.54	-0.85	95.61
35	85.52	0.03	2.57	94.40	1.71	0.86	95.79
36	87.12	0.04	3.48	93.69	2.61	0.87	96.00
37	86.37	0.02	1.73	95.57	3.45	-1.73	96.13
38	87.41	0.03	2.62	94.87	1.75	0.87	96.32
39	87.26	0.02	1.75	95.90	2.62	-0.87	96.48
40	86.86	0.01	0.87	96.93	1.74	-0.87	96.63
41	86.62	0.01	0.87	97.10	0.87	0.00	96.80
42	83.85	0.00	0.00	98.10	0.84	-0.84	96.94
43	84.41	0.00	0.00	98.27	0.00	0.00	97.11
44	82.33	0.00	0.00	98.44	0.00	0.00	97.28
45	81.64	0.00	0.00	98.61	0.00	0.00	97.45
46	81.98	0.00	0.00	98.77	0.00	0.00	97.62
47	83.08	0.00	0.00	98.94	0.00	0.00	97.79
48	83.00	0.00	0.00	99.11	0.00	0.00	97.96
49	84.63	0.00	0.00	99.28	0.00	0.00	98.13
50	82.48	0.00	0.00	99.45	0.00	0.00	98.30
51	84.45	0.00	0.00	99.62	0.00	0.00	98.48
52	86.96	0.00	0.00	99.79	0.00	0.00	98.65
53	87.00	0.00	0.00	99.96	0.00	0.00	98.82

required position increases from $81 to $86.24. While the initial position of $81 has increased somewhat with the market rise, an additional adjustment of $4.06 is necessary to achieve the desired portfolio exposure. The trade necessary to make this adjustment is shown in column 7. The final column of Exhibit 3 shows the week-by-week value of the hedged position placed in cash.

As the portfolio value declines, the delta declines as well. By week 30, with the underlying portfolio at $85.81, the delta is down to 6%; 94% of the portfolio value now resides in the reserve asset. In week 30, the hedged portfolio value is $95.02. This is well below the end-of-year target of $98.65. The value can drop below the target because the funds invested in the reserve asset are growing at the riskfree rate. A look at column 8 shows that the hedged portfolio value is growing toward the floor week by week.

The net result of the strategy is a payoff of $98.82. Taking the future value of the $1.25 initial cost of the option into account, the payoff is very close to its objective.

Futures: A Tool for Noninvasive Allocation

Adjustments in portfolio exposure can be made directly in the cash market, but adjustments are often done by using futures contracts. Both bond and stock index futures are attractive for their liquidity and low transactions cost. Futures also make the dynamic strategy noninvasive. The cash portfolio does not need to be traded to facilitate the hedging strategy. For the plan sponsor, this means no limitations need to be made on the managers' stock or bond selections. The managers can continue to hold the plan funds, while the sponsor executes the appropriate asset allocation shifts through futures transactions. The noninvasiveness of the strategy also means less liquid instruments, such as GICs or private placements, can be used in the construction of the underlying portfolio.

The potential for noninvasive asset allocation permits the separation of the risk and active management components of the investment decision. The risk objectives of the fund can be established and protected while the active manager is still free to maximize return within those risk constraints.

A short position in the futures contract can be used to reduce the portfolio exposure. Selling short futures against the portfolio position is equivalent to selling off the portfolio and putting the funds into cash. As the portfolio value falls, requiring a lower position in the market, the short futures position is increased. The proceeds that accrue to the short futures position compensate for losses in the cash portfolio. The aggregate value of the cash-futures position allows the floor to be retained. As the portfolio rises, the short position is reduced. The loss from the short position as the market goes up gives rise to the option cost. As we have already mentioned, the central feature of the dynamic hedge is that this cost can be closely estimated at the outset.

While low transaction costs make futures an attractive hedging medium, the basis risk between the cash and the futures—unexpected price movements between the cash asset and the futures—introduces tracking errors. The futures market does not follow its cash market counterpart precisely. Furthermore, few portfolios exactly match the cash security or index on which the futures are based.

Using Options to Create Options

Options bear a nonlinear relationship to the underlying security. An option varies markedly in its relationship to the underlying asset as the price of that asset changes—as measured by the option's gamma—and as the time to expiration approaches—as measured by the option's theta.

Using the underlying asset to replicate the option is like trying to form a curve with a series of lines. Without minute adjustments along the entire path, the curve will be only poorly approximated. An alternative to replicating the option with the underlying asset is to use other options. Because other options share the same properties of curvature, they can provide a more accurate vehicle for creating the desired option payoff. A simpler and more accurate way of creating the curve would be to fit it with other, similar curves. That is, a set of options can construct the price characteristics of another option. Earlier we discussed the value of using options as the delta-neutral arbitrage instrument. The same concepts apply when the objective is option replication for dynamic hedging and portfolio insurance applications.

At any point in time, a dynamic hedge is determined by the model-determined delta. If a portfolio of $100 million is being dynamically hedged and the delta is .8, $20 million of the portfolio must be sold off or shorted out. One way of shorting out that exposure is by selling $20 million of futures. Because the short futures position will move one-for-one in the direction opposite that of the portfolio being hedged, the net result will be the desired reduction in exposure.

The Use of Options: Delta/Gamma Hedging Suppose there is an option in the market that has a delta of .5, and therefore moves in price by $.50 for each dollar move in the portfolio. As an alternative to shorting $20 million of futures, one could write $40 million of the option to hedge out the $20 million of portfolio of exposure. The net result for the dynamic hedge would be the same.

What is the difference between using this option—or, for that matter, any option—rather than the futures contract in the hedge? When is one better than the other? By construction, we know they are identical when the hedge is started. Their comparative performance is judged by how well they meet the hedging needs as time progresses and as the price of the underlying portfolio changes.

Exhibit 4 shows the payoff curve of a dynamic hedge for various times remaining to expiration. The payoff curves steepen gradually around the floor as time to expiration approaches. For portfolio values below the floor, the payoff becomes flat and the payoff profit reaches a slope of 45 degrees, moving one-for-one with the market as the market rises. The curvature of the payoff increases as the time to expiration approaches, becoming kinked at expiration. This curvature is called its gamma. The greater the curvature, the greater the gamma. A straight line having no curvature has a gamma of zero.

The greater the gamma of the profile, the more demanding a futures-based hedge will be. Small changes in the portfolio value will lead to frequent hedge adjustment, because the straight-line futures hedges will need to be drawn frequently to fit the steep curvature. The higher the gamma, the greater the exposure of the hedge to gaps in the market price or loss of liquidity in the hedging vehicle. In an option hedge that itself has a high gamma, options can be used to match better the curvature of the hedge portfolio payoff profile. Exhibit 5A illustrates the use of both futures and shorter-maturity options. The objective in this figure is to replicate the payoff of a protective put strategy with three months remaining. With such a short period remaining to expiration, the gamma is high, and a market option with two months to expiration better matches the curvature than does the linear futures hedge. Exhibit 5B illustrates the other possibility, that the curvature of

EXHIBIT 4:
THE CURVATURE OF A CALL OPTION

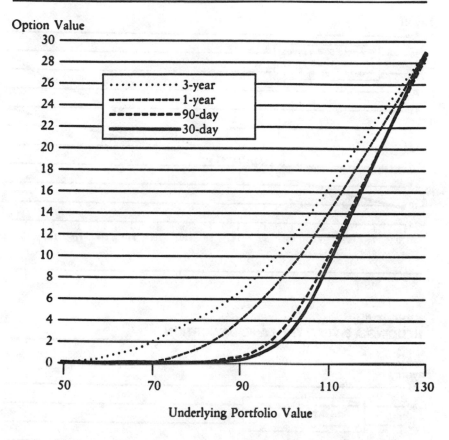

the dynamic hedging strategy is better matched by the futures. In this case, the dynamic hedge has three years to expiration, and the gamma of the market option is too severe to make it an attractive hedging vehicle.

As these two cases illustrate, it is the curvature of the hedge that dictates the desirability of using an option-based hedge. Because the gamma is a decreasing function of time, the comparatively short-maturity market options will be less useful in hedging, the longer the time to expiration of the hedge. Furthermore, because the gamma sinks lower the further the portfolio value moves from the exercise price,

EXHIBIT 5A:
HEDGING A 90-DAY WITH A 60-DAY OPTION

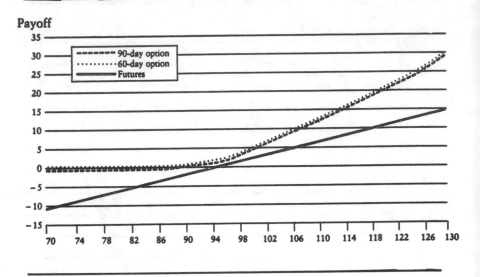

EXHIBIT 5B:
HEDGING A 3-YEAR WITH A 60-DAY OPTION

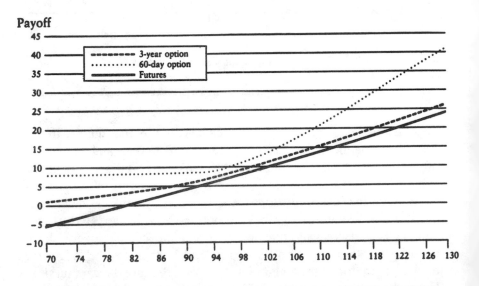

options will be less useful the further the portfolio value moves from the floor. Exhibit 6 lists the gamma of options with various times to expiration for a range of portfolio values. Because the gamma of a futures is zero, if the gamma of the hedge is less than half that of the option being contemplated as the hedging vehicle, the curvature of futures will better match the hedge.

EXHIBIT 6:
OPTION GAMMA—THE CURVATURE OF OPTIONS AS A FUNCTION OF TIME TO LXPIRATION

Portfolio Value	3-Year Option	1-Year Option	60-Day Option	30-Day Option
95	0.0101	0.0195	0.0430	0.0501
96	0.0100	0.0195	0.0456	0.0571
97	0.0099	0.0193	0.0475	0.0629
98	0.0098	0.0192	0.0486	0.0670
99	0.0096	0.0190	0.0490	0.0692
100	0.0095	0.0187	0.0487	0.0692
101	0.0093	0.0184	0.0476	0.0672
102	0.0092	0.0181	0.0459	0.0633
103	0.0090	0.0177	0.0436	0.0580
104	0.0089	0.0173	0.0408	0.0516
105	0.0087	0.0169	0.0377	0.0448

Assumptions Exercise price = $100; Volatility = .20

Unless an option in the market has the same exercise price and time to expiration as the portfolio insurance program, it will not match both the required delta and gamma. An option or futures position can be adjusted to give the right delta, but it will still deviate in curvature. The hedge will therefore need to be adjusted as the market changes. If more than one hedging instrument is used (an option and a futures, for example), both the hedge ratio and the curvature of the hedge position can be matched. We now have two instruments and can choose the proportion of each in order to solve for two objectives: delta and gamma. Such a strategy is called a delta/gamma neutral hedge. By adding even more hedging instruments—using a number of different options in the hedge, for example—an even better fit can be obtained. Such hedges are used in the large-scale exposure management of option trading positions, and with some judgment they can be applied success-fully in dynamic hedging applications.

Some Problems with Rolling Options to Create Longer-Term Options The use of options as a tool for creating the required position delta, and as a means of reducing the risk of mistracking toward the end of the portfolio insurance program, are both valid. While listed options are not liquid until a few months before their expiration, they are useful for unwinding the dynamic hedge as the time to expiration approaches. It is one of the happy coincidences of the world of finance that the last few months of a dynamic hedge, when the time the risk of tracking error is the greatest, is also the time that listed options become a viable alternative to the dynamic strategy.

The validity of a third frequently cited option strategy—that of rolling shorter-term options to replicate a longer-term option—is not so clear-cut. For example, suppose an investor were interested in a $100 floor for a security price for one year, and put options exist with three months to maturity. The investor might buy a three-month put, with an exercise price of $100, and upon expiration of that put, buy another three-month put with the same exercise price. At the end of six months the position would be liquidated, a new three-month option purchased. The procedure would be repeated again at the end of nine months. If the option expired out of the money, there would be no proceeds from the strategy, and more funds would be necessary to roll over the strategy. If the security dropped below the floor, the put option would return the difference between the floor price and the security price, covering the loss and providing the intrinsic value for buying the next contract.

The strategy will not replicate the one-year option. It is a path-dependent strategy; that is, its cost will differ not only according to the end-of-year value of the underlying security, but also according to the price path the security takes over the course of the year. The uncertain cost will be a source of risk to the hedging strategy.

Furthermore, rolling options will lead to a higher expected cost for the hedge. The reason for the higher expected cost of rolling options is not difficult to see. Rolling options provides the same floor at the end of the hedging period as does holding a single option with a time to expiration equal to the hedging period, but it provides other features as well. In particular, rolling options provides reset opportunities along the way, opportunities to change the strategy, and ones to obtain a defined payoff. These opportunities can be valuable, but they also make the strategy more costly.

To expand on this, consider a security currently priced at $100, and a call option purchased on the security with an exercise price of $100. Suppose a six-month option cost $10, while a three-month option cost $6. If the security is again at $100 when the three-month option expires, a second $6 option will need to be purchased, and the total cost of the rolling over strategy will be $12—$2 more than the cost of the six-month option. If, on the other hand, the stock drops to $80 in three months, the price of the call option for the next three months will be far less, because the option is now $20 out of the money. The next option may cost only $1, leading the rolling over strategy to be less costly. The same will be true if the security rises substantially, to, say, $120. The first of the three-month options will then pay off $20 at expiration, and the second option, being in the money, will have a small premium, selling for, say, $21. The total cost of the rolling over strategy will then be $7, compared to the $10 cost for the straight six-month option.

The Hedge Adjustment Period

In the example in Exhibit 3, the hedge was executed weekly. In practice, the hedge is monitored frequently—ideally throughout the day—and the frequency of the hedge is determined according to market conditions, rather than being based on the passage of time.

Option models are generally constructed to assume continuous revisions of the delta. In practice, of course, dynamic hedge positions are not adjusted continuously. In part, transactions costs dictate the frequency of hedge adjustments. However, there is a more important factor in gauging the market movement that triggers an adjustment in the delta of the position: the trade-off between the delta and the gamma of the strategy.

A failure to adjust the hedge to match the delta leads to tracking errors. If the position delta should be .80, and the hedge is kept at a delta of .82, the position will mistrack by 2% of any move in the underlying portfolio. On the other hand, adjustments increase the cost of the option because of the impact of volatility on the option price. This is the gamma impact of the hedge. Because portfolio insurance strategies involve a long put option, they are negative gamma strategies. The whipsawing of trading in a high-volatility environment will increase the cost of the hedge. The use of other options to better fit the payoff objective will help minimize hedge adjustment and reduce this risk.

Interest Rates

In the dynamic hedging example, the interest rate was assumed to be known and constant for the hedging period. The hedged portion of the portfolio which was invested at that rate grew toward the target value by the end of the year. In practice, interest rates change over time, and their change is uncertain.

Without a proper treatment for interest rates in the option model upon which the dynamic hedge is based, the cash position may not be sufficient to attain the target floor. For longer term hedges—hedging programs of three or more years—the impact of an incorrect treatment of yield curve effects can be more severe than the impact from volatility misestimation. When futures are used to facilitate the hedge, the implied interest rate will be the cost of carry for the futures. This short-term rate may differ from the interest rate for the time period the hedge is to be held. Shifts in the yield curve can lead to a mismatch between the holding period interest rate and the short-term carrying rate, affecting the tracking of the floor. The problems of uncertain interest rates are particularly acute for portfolio insurance and dynamic hedging of fixed income portfolios.

Liquidity Costs

Strategies that allocate assets based on a dynamic trading rule demand liquidity from the market. Thus, for example, a drop in the market that requires hedgers to reduce their asset positions will lead to a greater discount in the market price order to elicit buyers for the hedgers selling demand.

The greater the amount of assets being hedged, the greater this discount will be. Similarly, an increase in the market price will lead to a premium as the hedgers come back into the market. The net result of the liquidity demand will be to accentuate the volatility of the market—the market will rise more than it would otherwise rise, in response to the hedgers buying, and will decline more than it would otherwise decline, in response to the hedgers' selling pressure. As a result, the cost of hedging will be greater the greater the number of hedgers in the market. This liquidity cost means that the cost of dynamic asset alloca- tion programs cannot be determined without an understanding of the other strategies being employed in the market. In particular, a dynamic hedging program will become increasingly costly, and decreasingly effective, the larger the segment of the market that is pursuing similar strategies.

Full-Information Hedging

While the previous example treated a simple one-year hedge with a straightforward floor, many hedging programs require a more complex design. The floor of the hedge may be ratcheted up as the market moves up, leading to a variable floor. Or, investment needs may require that the floor not be violated by increases in volatility or in tracking error.

These aspects of the hedging design present important information that should have an impact on how the hedging model is constructed and how the hedge is executed. In the first case, the option model must be adjusted in a manner similar to the adjustments made for an Ameri- can option to minimize the cost of the ratcheting feature. In the second case, the tracking error of the hedge must be continually monitored and adjustments made to preserve the size of the reserve asset position necessary to obtain the floor. The design of specific programs and in the implementation of the hedge presents the greatest challenges to dynamic hedging and places demands on hedging expertise.

ASSET/LIABILITY MANAGEMENT

The conventional application of dynamic hedging is asset-based. It provides a cash floor on a portfolio of assets. This asset-based approach may not meet the risk control needs of a number of financial institu- tions.

A more complete framework for dynamic hedging is *asset/liability* based. To show this, we will study corporate pension plans. A pension fund consists of more than assets. It also faces a liability exposure. The liabilities themselves are uncertain, and indeed may have a greater risk than the assets that the fund managers so painstakingly allocate and monitor. The risk of the pension plan is not the risk of the asset returns, it is the risk of failing to meet the liabilities. The proper role of hedging for the pension plan is therefore to protect against this possibility. In the asset/liability context of the pension plan, the manifest risk is the plan surplus, the difference between plan assets and plan liabilities.

Pension Liabilities

Pension liabilities can be broken up into two components. The first component is the *accumulated benefit obligation (ABO)*. The ABO is composed of the future cashflows required to meet the pension obligations accrued for service to date. The second component is the incremental liability. The incremental liability is composed of the liabilities that will accrue for the current workers as their years of service and level of compensation grow. The cashflow stream for the ABO may look like that in Exhibit 7. Because the older employees typically have higher compensation levels and will be receiving their benefits earlier, most plans have the peak for the ABO in the earlier years. Because of this, the greatest concern in meeting the ABO is, justifiably, in the near future.

EXHIBIT 7:
ACCUMULATED LIABILITIES

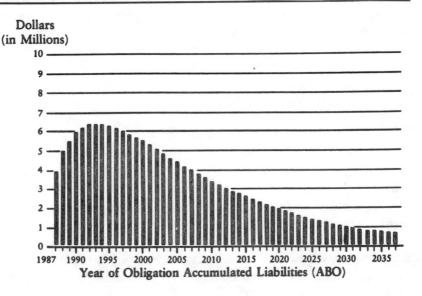

Year of Obligation Accumulated Liabilities (ABO)

The ABO is the only liability for retired employees and vested terminated employees, and is the major liability for employees near retirement. The ABO can be actuarially estimated in constant dollar terms, and therefore it can be closely matched by a dedicated or immunized portfolio.

The *incremental liability* is the major liability for younger active employees and is also the primary component of any surplus buffer the pension wishes to maintain. While the ABO is a fixed constant dollar obligation, the incremental liability is affected by inflation and economic growth. Employee benefits are usually set according to compensation level. Inflation and labor productivity both increase salary levels and therefore increase benefits.

Exhibit 8 illustrates a path for the incremental liabilities over time. The incremental liabilities follow far different dynamics than do the ABOs. Incremental liabilities are initially small, because current compensation levels are unlikely to change dramatically in short periods of time. The employees with the largest pension benefits have little impact on the incremental liabilities, because they are near the peak of their compensation levels, or have already retired or otherwise left the firm. It is the younger segment of the workforce, whose liabilities are

EXHIBIT 8:
INCREMENTAL LIABILITIES

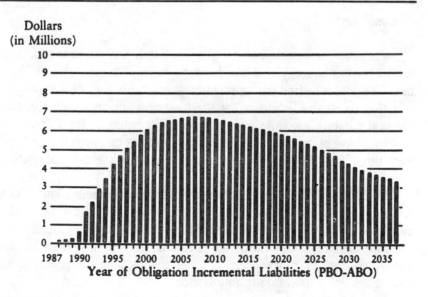

Dollars
(in Millions)

Year of Obligation Incremental Liabilities (PBO-ABO)

currently relatively small, that bring the greatest impact to the incremental liabilities.

The incremental liabilities grow at a compounding rate over time, because of the compounding effect of inflation and economic productivity. It is therefore most important far in the future. Indeed, as a comparison of Exhibit 7 and Exhibit 8 shows, the incremental liabilities dwarf the ABO 20 and 30 years into the future. The economic nature of the incremental liability strongly suggests that equity and real estate will provide a better long-run asset/liability match than will bonds.

The composition of the pension fund liabilities depends on the time frame we adopt. If a plan sponsor takes a look at the pension liabilities, goes to sleep for the night and, upon waking up the next morning, looks at how the liabilities have changed, the liabilities will look like an interest-sensitive cashflow. If, on the other hand, he falls to sleep for 20 years and then wakes up to look at the liabilities, they will have grown like equity claims because of the cumulative effect of past productivity and inflation.

It is the sum of the accumulated liabilities and incremental liabilities that make up the obligations of the pension plan. The role of surplus management, and indeed of asset allocation in general, is to meet this full liability picture, depicted in Exhibit 9.

Pension Assets

Knowing the composition of the pension liabilities, the next task is to see what asset strategy will best help the pension to meet these liabilities. The goal is to find the most efficient asset mix for doing this—the mix that meets the liabilities for the least cost, or, alternatively, that meets the liabilities while giving the highest potential for surplus.

As we have seen, pension plans operate against two time frames, and each time frame leads to a particular emphasis in the asset allocation decision.

The first is the need to meet the immediate obligations. This fills a relatively short time frame: three to five years into the future. The cashflow needs begin to blur after that point as actuarial assumptions and the financial condition of the firm change. The emphasis in this short-term case is on fixed income instruments, and the strategies of choice are dedication and immunization.

EXHIBIT 9:
TOTAL LIABILITIES

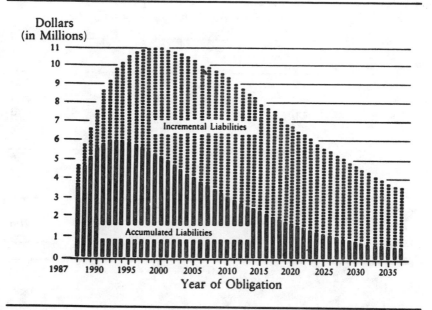

Dollars
(in Millions)

The second time frame involves the need to maximize long-term return. The emphasis in this case is on equity and real estate investments, because, at least historically, these provide a far higher long run expected return than do bonds.

Unhedged: An All-Equity Portfolio Consider the asset/liability return matrix shown in Exhibit 10. This exhibit is based on a simplified plan with interest sensitive liabilities and equity assets. It shows the surplus of a portfolio for various combinations of returns on the assets and liabilities. Initially the plan shows a surplus of $100 million, with $500 million in assets and $400 million in liabilities.

As the first matrix shows, assets may vary through the impact of both the equity market and the fixed income market. In the case of a pure equity portfolio, the only relevant variable is the equity market return. A drop of 20% in the equity market will leave assets at $400 million, while a 20% increase in the market will bring asset value up to $600 million.

The accumulated liabilities are only affected by interest rates. The

EXHIBIT 10:
UNHEDGED: AN ALL-EQUITY PORTFOLIO

	Interest Rate Change (in basis points)		
	−200	0	+200
Equity		Assets	
−20%	400	400	400
0%	500	500	500
20%	600	600	600
		Liabilities	
	500	400	300
Equity		Surplus	
−20%	−100	0	100
0%	0	100	200
20%	100	200	300

second section of the exhibit shows the current liabilities of $400 million rising to $500 million if rates decline by 200 basis points, and dropping to $300 million if rates increase by 200 basis points.

The surplus is simply the difference between the assets and liabilities for the particular market and interest rate level. Depending on conditions in the equity and interest markets, the asset vary from $400 million to $600 million, and the liabilities vary from $300 million to $500 million, resulting in surplus values that may lie anywhere between $−100 million and $300 million.

Not all elements in the matrix have equal probability. The assets contain a natural hedge for the liability position, because the assets and liabilities both share an interest rate component. For example, the upper left-hand figures' outcome, showing high liabilities and low assets, would require interest rates to drop while asset values declined. This is not very likely, because equity markets tend to be negatively correlated with interest rates.

Similarly, the lower right-hand figures' outcome, with high interest rates and high asset values, is unlikely. The dominant outcomes are covered by the Southwest/Northeast diagonal, depicting a negative correlation between interest rate levels and asset performance.

Fully Hedged: A Dedicated Portfolio Exhibit 11 shows the other extreme: a fully hedged position. Here a dedicated bond portfolio is created to match the cashflow characteristics of the accumulated bene-fit obligation. The ABO liabilities will be met under all circum-stances—indeed, a dollar floor to the surplus is established.

EXHIBIT 11:
FULLY HEDGED: A DEDICATED PORTFOLIO

	Interest Rate Change (in basis points)		
	−200	0	+200
Equity		Assets	
−20%	600	500	400
0%	600	500	400
20%	600	500	400
		Liabilities	
	500	400	300
Equity		Surplus	
−20%	100	100	100
0%	100	100	100
20%	100	100	100

While a fully hedged portfolio is an efficient means of meeting the ABO, as its low expected return demonstrates, it is not the best way to capture favorable market moves or to build up the surplus in response to the incremental liability obligations, because it does not take advan-tage of the long-term return potential of equities.

Asset Hedge: Portfolio Insurance

An alternative to the full hedge is a conventional portfolio insurance hedge. By creating a put option on the plan's assets, such a hedge will protect the assets against favorable market moves, while still allowing the assets to participate in market gains. Exhibit 12 shows the impact of portfolio insurance. The portfolio insurance is an at-the-money pro-gram, with a floor equal to the current asset value of $500 million. We assume the hedge costs $25 million. The portfolio insurance hedge provides a floor to the upper row of the matrix, because the asset value cannot drop below $375 million (the floor minus the hedging cost).

EXHIBIT 12:
ASSET HEDGE: PORTFOLIO INSURANCE

	Interest Rate Change (in basis points)		
	−200	*0*	*+200*
Equity		*Assets*	
−20%	500	500	500
0%	500	500	500
20%	600	600	600
		Liabilities	
	500	400	300
Equity		*Surplus*	
−20%	0	100	200
0%	100	100	200
20%	100	200	300

Hedging Cost = $25

This matrix illustrates, in simple form, the limitations of conventional portfolio insurance in meeting asset/liability needs. Portfolio insurance provides a payoff for drops in the equity market, but does not take into account simultaneous changes in the liabilities. The surplus is protected for the conditions depicted by the upper right and upper center elements of the matrix—a decline in the equity market with interest rate levels unchanged or increased—but does not provide adequate protection for the recession scenario of the upper lefthand element, where the decline in equities coincides with a drop in interest rates. A minimum value is set for the assets. However, the impact of interest rate declines on the liabilities is still unmanaged.

Liability Hedge: Liability Insurance Symmetry suggests a liability alternative to portfolio insurance—liability insurance—which gives a ceiling to liabilities in the same way portfolio insurance gives a floor to assets. Liability insurance, while not widely used by pensions funds, is a popular strategy in other institutional applications. Interest rate caps, which give a ceiling to the interest payments on floating rate debt, are one example of liability insurance.

Exhibit 13 illustrates a liability insurance strategy. Here the liability is capped at its current value of $400 million. The cost of the liability hedge is $15 million, so the left-most column shows a surplus value that is $85 million greater than it would be without the hedge. On the other hand, there is no protection against a decline in surplus if asset values drop. The result is an unusually high payoff if equity values rise while interest rates decline, and less-than-sufficient protection if equity values drop while interest rates decline.

EXHIBIT 13:
LIABILITY HEDGE: LIABILITY INSURANCE

	Interest Rate Change (in basis points)		
	−200	0	+200
Equity	Assets		
−20%	500	400	400
0%	600	500	500
20%	700	600	600
	Liabilities		
	500	400	300
Equity	Surplus		
−20%	0	0	100
0%	100	100	200
20%	200	200	300

Hedging Cost = $15

Surplus Hedge: Surplus Insurance The asset and liability hedges do not provide complete protection, because they are each hedging only a part of the pension fund exposure. If the objective of the hedge is to provide a floor on surplus, then the hedge should be directed to that surplus.

Exhibit 14 shows the effect of surplus insurance. This strategy is designed to provide a floor equal to the current surplus value of $100 million. In cases where the liabilities grow beyond their current value without a similar increase in assets or where the assets fall without a commensurate drop in liabilities, surplus insurance provides the specified floor. On the other hand, when assets outstrip liabilities, as occurs in the lower right section of the matrix, the surplus insurance allows the equity exposure that is necessary to meet the incremental liabilities. By addressing both the short and long term liability exposure of the pension fund, surplus insurance creates the liability asset.

EXHIBIT 14:
A SURPLUS HEDGE: SURPLUS INSURANCE

	Interest Rate Change (in basis points)		
	− 200	0	+ 200
Equity		Assets	
− 20%	600	500	400
0%	600	500	500
20%	600	600	600
		Liabilities	
	500	400	300
Equity		Surplus	
− 20%	100	100	100
0%	100	100	200
20%	100	200	300

Hedging Cost = $20

A Dominated Strategy: Combining Options on Liabilities and Assets At first glance, it would appear that surplus insurance is simply a combination of the prior two strategies of placing a floor on the assets and a ceiling on the liabilities. However, such a combination is an inefficient means of achieving the floor objective for the surplus. A portfolio of an asset put and liability call will be more expensive than the single surplus hedge, because the surplus insurance can take advantage of the interaction between the assets and liabilities, while the two options cannot. The asset hedge costs $25 million and the liability hedge costs $15 million, a total cost of $40 million compared to the $25 million cost for the surplus insurance hedge.

This cost is higher than the cost of surplus insurance because it is providing payoff characteristics the pension plan does not need. As Exhibit 15 (which presents the payoff to the combination of the asset and liability hedges) shows, this strategy gives a surplus of $200 million when interest rates rise and equity falls. Both of the hedges are binding in the upper right-hand element of the matrix. However, such a degree of protection is not needed in this case, because there is a natural hedge between the drop in the asset value and the decline in the liability exposure. A surplus insurance strategy can take this asset/liability interplay into account, and reduce the hedging cost accordingly.

EXHIBIT 15:
AN OVERINSURED STRATEGY: COMBINING ASSET AND LIABILITY INSURANCE

	Interest Rate Change (in basis points)			
	−200	0	+200	
Equity		*Assets*		
−20%	600	500	500	
0%	600	500	500	
20%	700	600	600	
				Hedging Cost = $25 (Asset)
		Liabilities		
	500	400	300	
				Hedging Cost = $15 (Liabilities)
Equity		*Surplus*		
−20%	100	100	200	Total Hedging
0%	100	100	200	Cost = $40.
20%	200	200	300	

THE EVALUATION OF DYNAMIC HEDGING STRATEGIES

Care must be taken in evaluating portfolios with return distributions altered by dynamic hedging strategies. Methods of performance evaluation that depend on mean and variance measures of returns—as all of the common methods do—cannot be applied to portfolios resulting from dynamic strategies for the simple reason that those portfolios depend on more than mean and variance. These option strategies mold the return distributions, bringing the higher moments, such as skewness and kurtosis, into play.

For example, portfolio insurance leads to a truncation of the left tail of the portfolio return distribution, and a leftward shift of the distribution. The truncation reflects the protection from downside loss, and the shift reflects the cost of the insurance. Exhibit 16 shows the distribution of the underlying portfolio, with the familiar normal distribution, and the distribution that results when a put option is created on that portfolio. In contrast to this strategy, consider the distributional effect of writing a covered call option on the same underlying portfolio, effectively "selling" insurance. The covered call has the opposite effect of portfolio insurance. It truncates the righ tail of the distribution while

EXHIBIT 16:
RETURN DISTRIBUTIONS FOR PORTFOLIO INSURANCE (BUYING PROTECTIVE PUT OPTIONS)

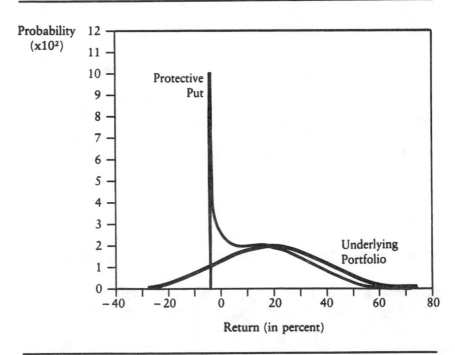

shifting the distribution to the right. The truncation is the result of selling off the upward potential, and the shift reflects the premium received from the sale. Exhibit 17 compares the distribution of covered call writing with that of the underlying portfolio.

Even a cursory reference to Exhibits 16 and 17 demonstrates that distributions resulting from dynamic, option-related strategies cannot be understood by looking at the mean and variance alone. Indeed, in this particular case, an analysis based solely on expected return and variance of return will make selling insurance appear superior to buying insurance. The two strategies have much the same effect on expected return. The expected return drops from 18% for the underlying stock portfolio to 13.6% for the portfolio fully covered by a call option, and to 14.5% for the portfolio fully covered by the protective put. But the standard deviation of returns drops from 20% for the underlying portfolio to only 16.7% for the put strategy, while it is cut to

EXHIBIT 17:
RETURN DISTRIBUTIONS FOR SELLING INSURANCE (WRITING COVERED CALL OPTIONS)

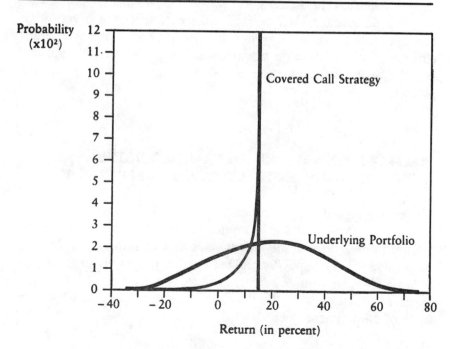

5.8% for the covered call strategy. The put strategy has a standard deviation that is nearly three times higher than for call writing. If standard deviation or variance is used as a proxy for risk, writing a covered call will be preferred to buying a protective put.

However, variance is not a suitable proxy for risk, because the option strategies reduce risk asymmetrically. The call truncates the right-hand side of the distribution, and thereby reduces the desirable upside variance. The put, on the other hand, reduces the variance on the undesirable left-hand portion of the return distribution. It is natural, then, for a reduction in variance to be compensated for differently in the two strategies.

This example illustrates the shortcomings of evaluation methods that rely on summary statistics such as mean and variance in dealing with these more advanced strategies. By trading off between the mean and the higher moments of the distribution, many unusual mean-variance relationships are possible. For example, it is possible to construct a strategy with both a higher expected return and a lower variance than the underlying portfolio. Or, it is possible to construct a strategy that yields the same return floor as a protective put but with a higher expected return. (This strategy will give a high probability of achieving only the floor return, and a small chance of receiving a very high return). Such a strategy may not, in fact, lead to a desirable return structure. But strictly on a mean-variance basis, it certainly appears superior to the conventional insurance strategy of using a protective put.

PORTFOLIO INSURANCE, DYNAMIC HEDGING, AND OTHER DYNAMIC ASSET ALLOCATION STRATEGIES

The example of portfolio insurance presented in Exhibit 3 seeks to place a floor on the portfolio by replicating the payoff of a put option on the portfolio. There are other strategies that will provide a floor on asset value without explicitly replicating a put option. Indeed, this can be accomplished with any hedging strategy which adjusts the asset exposure in a way that assures the asset value remains above the present value of the terminal floor.

For example, a strategy called Constant Proportionality Portfolio Insurance (CPPI) takes the difference between the portfolio value and the present value of the floor, and maintains a market exposure equal to some prespecified multiple of this difference. If a portfolio has $100 million in assets, and the present value of the floor is $86 million, there is a $14 million surplus available to invest in the risky asset. If we assume a multiple of 3, then the hedge will have $42 million invested in equity, with the remainder in the riskless asset. Unlike an option-based strategy, a CPPI program does not have a natural expiration date. Because of this it is sometimes referred to as a perpetual or a time-invariant strategy. And, unlike an option-replication strategy, the cost of a CPPI hedge cannot be closely specified beforehand.

Whatever the specifics of the strategy, a dynamic hedge will sell as the market drops and buy as the market rises. Other dynamic strategies are possible that adjust the asset mix in other ways, and some of these strategies have longstanding application.

Consider the strategy of buying as the market drops and selling as the market rises. This is the opposite of dynamic hedging strategies, and could be thought of as "selling" portfolio insurance. The widely-used constant-mix strategy, where the asset mix is periodically rebalanced to maintain a constant bond/stock ratio, is such a dynamic asset allocation strategy.

Like the CPPI strategy, a constant-mix strategy does not replicate a specific option payoff, and therefore cannot be priced. However, we can compare the general characteristics of the CPPI and constant-mix strategies.

The value of these two strategies will depend on both the volatility and the trend of the market. While dynamic hedging becomes more costly in a highly volatile market, the constant-mix strategy will do the best in a volatile but trendless market. While hedging cost for a dynamic hedging strategy diminishes in relative terms as the market trends up or down, providing downside protection on the one hand and an increasing share of upside potential in the other, the cost of the constant-mix strategy is greatest in these circumstances.

If a dynamic hedge is analogous to buying a protective option on the portfolio, the constant-mix strategy is similar to writing a covered option. The constant-mix strategy will do better than a buy-and-hold strategy if the option being written has a large premium—if the market volatility is high—and if option expires out of the money—i.e., if the market does not have an adverse trend.

CONCLUSION

Although they provide option-like payoffs, the payoffs provided through dynamic hedging strategies are not directly obtained by buying options. The protection comes through a hedging strategy that seeks to match the market exposure of the option being replicated as the market value and time to expiration vary. The resulting dynamic adjustment of the hedge over time and with changes in the underlying portfolio value warrants calling this a dynamic hedge.

Because it is a hedging program rather than a guarantee, the payoff specified by other dynamic hedging programs requires that the hedging strategy itself be properly executed. The design and monitoring of the dynamic hedge, as well as its execution, are, therefore, important considerations.

The dynamic hedge is often implemented by using futures contracts. For example, rather than selling a portion of the portfolio as the portfolio drops in value, a futures position can be sold against the portfolio. The use of futures allows the strategy to be noninvasive. The assets under management are unaffected by the strategy. This allows the risk control and the active asset management functions to be separated. The portfolio managers do not have to alter their investment style, and the plan sponsor does not need to pull assets away from the managers in order to execute the hedge. Using futures does subject the hedge to the cash-futures basis risk and the liquidity of the futures market.

Dynamic hedging is an alternative to buying guaranteed coverage through the option market when that coverage is available. A firm that offers an over-the-counter option must hedge its exposure. Because the hedge is not perfect, it must add a risk premium to the option, increasing the option's cost. The risk premium will be especially high for longer-term protection and for protecion on atypical portfolios. Dynamic hedging allows the investor to create the hedge directly, and leaves the investor to absorb any residual risk from imperfections in the hedge. This will be desirable for the investor who is more willing to absorb the residual risk than pay the risk premium.

The dynamic hedge is an efficient hedging technique. It cannot, however, lead to a payoff that unambiguously dominates other strategies. It is not designed as a strategy to enhance total returns, nor is it designed to provide a guaranteed minimum return under all market conditions. Rather, it is a risk control tool that molds payoff characteristics to meet investment and asset/liability objectives.

CHAPTER 11

Surplus Protection and Portfolio Insurance

GARY L. GASTINEAU
VICE PRESIDENT
SALOMON BROTHERS INC

An insured portfolio is one in which investors place part of their wealth in a portfolio of risky assets, typically common stocks, and use the remainder to buy or otherwise create synthetic put options on that portfolio. If the value of the portfolio on the date the put option "expires" is less than the striking price of the put, investors exercise the put and expect at least a predetermined minimim value for the portfolio. If the value of the portfolio on the expiration date is greater than the striking price, the put will expire. Investors typically obtain only part of the upside potential of the portfolio. In return for the put premium, investors expect to avoid a catastrophic loss.

Portfolio insurance has been used primarily by large pension funds and other large pools of capital. Insured portfolios are offered to small investors by mutual funds and banks. The fund approach or the account pooling capability of a bank is necessary because it is difficult to offer a customized insured portfolio to small investors on an economical basis. Large pools of money are necessary to keep transaction costs at a reasonable level. Because portfolio insurance is a complex topic to explain to the typical investor, insured portfolios are unlikely to become a major product for the retail market.

Particularly in the wake of Black Monday, investors often ask, "Will portfolio insurance do what they say?" Part of the answer obviously hinges on "what they say." Rather than attempt to analyze the validity of myriad claims for portfolio insurance, we will try to give a balanced appraisal of what is and is not possible and what is probable. Most of the literature available on portfolio insurance was written either by academicians with an intellectual (or even financial) stake in the acceptance of portfolio insurance or as sales literature promoting the services of specific portfolio insurance advisors or brokers. In spite of the bias inherent in these sources, most discussions of portfolio insurance are not drastically one-sided.

Portfolio insurance is neither the greatest scourge to afflict the financial markets in recent years nor the solution to every problem of stock market risk. Because the case for portfolio insurance has been made frequently and eloquently, portfolio insurance has been oversold to a number of actual and potential users.

The purveyors of portfolio insurance describe their product with great care. The terms used include "insurance," "assurance," or "minimum assured return." Many readers of portfolio insurance literature express concern over the absence of the word "guarantee" except in a few programs offered by banks and insurance companies. The question which naturally arises is, "Does portfolio insurance really work? Are we assured with absolute certainty that we will get at least the minimum results called for under the program?" The answer to this question is complex; but there is relatively little chance that the return will fall more than a few percentage points below the minimum called for in the program. Skeptics would do better to ask if the portfolio will participate adequately in a rising market; if costs are reasonable; if the risk-adjusted returns from an insured portfolio will be adequate; or if the market can accommodate every investor who wants to use portfolio insurance.

THE MECHANICS

Describing portfolio insurance as a put on the portfolio is often useful, but it may be more complex than necessary. The typical investor understands portfolio insurance best if most discussion of options is avoided. Although there are many variations, the typical insured portfolio is divided between two assets: usually common stock and actual or synthetic Treasury bills. A set of decision rules, going by the grandiose name "dynamic hedging," controls the asset allocation. Assume that the return on Treasury bills is 6% and the return on a common stock portfolio is unknown and variable. If an investor puts a bit more than 94% of assets in 6% 1-year Treasury bills and the remainder in common stocks, the portfolio cannot decline in value over a 1-year period even if the stocks become worthless. Dynamic hedging calls for a larger (typically 50 to 70%) initial commitment to stocks and for reduction of the stock position if early losses on stocks make a greater commitment to Treasury bills necessary to assure the minimum required return by the end of the insurance period. The key to achieving the minimum return is to maintain a large enough commitment to the low-risk asset and to be able to shift from the poorly performing high-risk asset to the low-risk asset to avoid an unacceptable loss. As stocks drop in value, batches of them are sold or "neutralized" (turned into synthetic Treasury bills) by selling stock index futures. If stocks drop sharply early in an insurance period, exposure to stocks will be reduced. The reduced exposure will prevent returns below the minimum assured return. If the initial decline is sharp and is followed by a sharp advance, the insured portfolios may be stopped out and may not participate significantly in the subsequent rise. The pattern of insured portfolio returns may not correlate well with common stock returns because the pattern and timing of trades required by the dynamic hedging algorithm may lead to superior performance in some markets and disappointing performance in others.

The minimum return set for an insured portfolio can be almost as high as the Treasury bill return. The higher the minimum return, the smaller the commitment to stocks and the greater the likelihood that the insured portfolio will substantially underperform the stock market on the upside. The insurance period also has important implications for how much of the market's upside the insured portfolio will capture. In general, an insurance program designed to assure at least a zero return over 3 years will capture more of the upside than a program designed to assure at least a zero return over 1 year.

A warning on the vocabulary of portfolio insurance is in order. Often an advocate of portfolio insurance will state that a program will provide a specific minimum return and 90 to 98% "capture" of the equity results on the upside. One might be justified in assuming that 95%

capture of a 20% equity return would mean an average of 19% in a 20% up year. Chances are that a return capture figure as high as 95% means 95% of the final portfolio value of 120 or 114 for a 14% expected return when the market gains 20%. It pays to ask for a definition.

A typical portfolio insurance program is really nothing more than a set of rules for switching a portfolio between common stocks and Treasury bills (or their equivalents) to assure that the Treasury bills (or equivalents) provide at least the minimum required return even if the stock market collapses. In practice, most insured portfolios rarely use Treasury bills, and are essentially fully invested in common stocks at all times. Portfolio insurers have found that by selling stock index futures against part or all of the stock portfolio they can create a synthetic Treasury bill that will often have a higher return than the real thing. If selling futures is not attractive, the insurer can always sell stocks and buy actual Treasury bills.

There is some controversy over what the preferred hedging vehicle for portfolio insurance transactions should be. Prior to the 1987 market crash, the clear choice was the S&P 500 futures contract. The primary reasons behind the choice of the S&P 500 futures contract lie first in the fact that this was the first contract available on a broad-based, widely used stock market index and second in lower transaction costs. Furthermore, the S&P 500 is the standard reference for most institutional performance measurement. Standard and Poor's 500 index options are also available. In deference to the portfolio insurance market the S&P 500 contracts have been made into European options, so the put purchaser need not pay extra for the early exercise privilege of an American option. Early exercise is unlikely to be of material value to a portfolio insurer who would like to keep the position on for the life of the option and would prefer not to worry about early-exercise values and opportunities.

Unfortunately, the S&P 500 European-style option is an SEC-regulated option. While that is a plus for most participants in the securities industry in that they can trade it with less regulatory hassle than they can trade index futures, it is a negative consideration for most portfolio insurers as a result of the position limits imposed on the exchanges by the SEC. Unless and until position limits are eliminated, the S&P 500 index option cannot rival the S&P 500 futures contract for portfolio insurance business. Most portfolio insurers operate on a large scale, and the maximum position limit available on the S&P 500 index option is simply too small to make using it worth their while. Furthermore, position limits reduce trading activity, increasing bid-asked spreads relative to those available in the futures market. If position limits could be eliminated, the S&P 500 index option might ultimately dominate the portfolio insurance market. As things are, the index option may be an appropriate vehicle for smaller portfolio insurance participants.

THE RISKS

A moment's thought will suggest that achieving the required minimum return by maintaining a large enough position in the risk-free asset should not be difficult. The only factors that might cause a shortfall are tracking error due to poor correlation between the stock portfolio and the index futures contract and discontinuities due to poor timing of portfolio adjustments. If the portfolio to be insured differs materially from the Standard & Poor's 500 stock index, there can be a tracking error in which the behavior of the underlying portfolio does not closely parallel the index. Ordinarily, responsible insurance managers will be able to deal with any tracking error quickly and effectively. The insurance manager will either take corrective steps to increase the "insurance" (Treasury bills or equivalents) purchased or point out to the client that the composition of the portfolio is too different from the index for effective hedging.

The other risk, discontinuity, is a direct consequence of the dynamic hedging technique. Dynamic hedging calls for the use of index futures markets to create synthetic Treasury bills at a higher effective yield after transaction costs than a switch to actual Treasury bills could provide. When a synthetic Treasury bill is created using stocks and index futures, the timing of transactions is directed by a computer program that describes how the manager should increase or decrease futures positions in response to changes in the value of the portfolio. The stock market does not always move continuously from one level to another. A major development overnight, over a weekend, or even during the course of a trading day can cause a significant discontinuous rise or fall in the value of the portfolio and in the price of the index.

Ordinarily these discontinuities will not have a dramatic effect on results, but the market crash of 1987 demonstrated that a substantial effect is possible. Some insurance managers reassure the client that in the event of a discontinuity the manager will exercise judgment and wait for the discontinuity to be offset, at least in part, by a reversal of the market. Given what portfolio insurance is designed to accomplish, reliance on the trading judgment of the insurance manager does not seem very reassuring. Most investors will prefer a trading rule that relegates the trader's timing judgment to decisions on when to order lunch. Before October, 1987, most observers accepted the argument that tracking errors and discontinuities are manageable, but expressed concern over the impact of portfolio insurance on the market and concern over portfolio insurance's tendency to *create* discontinuities. We will return to these points.

THE COST

The net cost of portfolio insurance (that is, the effective cost of the synthetic put) may be greater and the average portfolio return may be less than the owner of the portfolio expects. Portfolio insurance is often sold on the basis of simulations of returns from applying the proposed technique to historic data.[1] One of the greatest weaknesses of portfolio insurance simulations is that they are based on stock price data from the 1970s and the first half of the 1980s, a period of generally high interest rates and occasional sharp market declines. Just as high interest rates increase the cost (value) of a call, they reduce the cost (value) of a put. If the late 1980s are a period of low interest rates, the cost of portfolio insurance, measured in terms of the impact of the cost of the put on the return of the portfolio, will be greater than the costs suggested by simulations from the 1970s and early 1980s.

Another aspect of "dynamic hedging" that can create some unantici-pated results is that the cost of the put is not known precisely at the time the insurance program is undertaken. A change in interest rates or a change in volatility can lead to a significant change in the cost of the put. Specifically, a decline in interest rates or an increase in volatility can lead to a higher cost for the synthetic put than was anticipated at the beginning of the program. This increase in cost will not keep the program from obtaining the minimum return, but it will reduce the

---

[1]These simulations are subject to most of the weaknesses ascribed to simulations of option strategies. See Chapter 10 of Gary L. Gastineau, *The Options Manual*, McGraw-Hill, 1988, pp. 277–300.

probabilities of doing much better. The interest rate impact will be a one-time surprise as interest rates fall, and it will be reversed when they rise again. The effect of underestimating volatility can be as much as 1 to 2% of assets in an extreme case in continuous markets. The effect can be even greater in the event of major discontinuities such as the market crash of 1987.

The valuation of index futures contracts can also affect the cost of the program. Index futures contracts may appear to be leading the market up or down until they reach a degree of mispricing that will permit index arbitrage traders to move in and restore equilibrium. Portfolio insurers will *tend* to be particpants on the buy side of index futures contracts when these contracts are relatively overvalued and to be sellers of these contracts at times when they appear undervalued. Often, an index arbitrage program trader will be the party on the opposite side of an index futures transaction by the portfolio insurer. To the extent that there is a significant range of indeterminant value between the minimum and maximum futures price at which the market will clear, the effective transaction cost for a portfolio insurer could be more than the combination of heavily discounted commissions and a modest bid-asked spread suggests. The significance of this cost element for the long-term performance of insured portfolios is hard to quantify in the aftermath of Black Monday, but it could reduce the average return by as much as several hundred basis points in an extreme case. The limiting factor will be the cost of doing dynamic hedge transactions in stocks and Treasury bills rather than in the futures markets. Analyzing costs of making portfolio adjustments in each of several ways should help bracket the impact of transactions costs. Obviously, a major discontinuity could further increase costs.

THE RISK-RETURN TRADE-OFF

The most important concern to be addressed in reaching a portfolio insurance decision is basic to most investment decisions: What is the appropriate portfolio risk structure? Portfolio insurance is designed to truncate the return distribution so that large losses are eliminated. The "cost" of eliminating these large losses is lower probable returns in a rising market. Basically, the cost of the put determines the probable size of the return reduction. Two questions that need to be expolored in deciding for or against an insured portfolio are: (1) Will eliminating most downside risk lead to an equal or even higher long-term return? and (2) How will insured portfolios behave under various circumstances?

Various analysts have argued that an investor will be better off in the long run with a somewhat lower average return if the standard deviation or variability of the return is also lower. A highly variable return with large losses in some years offset by larger gains in others *can* lead to a lower average return in the long run. The key to how this works is the relationship between the average return and its standard deviation or variability. The Ibbotson-Sinquefeld study of long-term investment returns demonstrated that even though common stock returns have been more variable than returns on other assets, in the long run the common stock investor has enjoyed superior results. Ibbotson and Sinquefeld show that from the beginning of 1926 (when the study period began), through 1986, the average arithmetic return for common stocks was 12.12% with a standard deviation of 21.21%. Because of this volatility, the compound return fell just over 2% to 9.98% for the 61-year period.

Among both sophisticated and unsophisticated users of equity portfolio risk-reduction strategies, great misunderstandings stem from exaggerated concern over the relationship between risk (volatility of return) and the expected level of long-term return. The most common rationale for risk-reduction strategies goes something like this: "If you use (insert name of strategy), you may not have as good a return in a great year in the stock market; but you will avoid large losses (or have smaller losses), and the greater consistency of return will give you a higher return in the long run." On the reasonable assumption that annual stock market returns are approximately lognormal, it is a relatively simple matter to measure the relationship among average (arithmetic) return, risk (standard deviation), and compound (long-term) return. Exhibits 1 and 2 show this relationship for the average return on stock prices over the past 61 years and a range of risks. As indicated above, the average annual S&P 500 total return for 1926–1986 was 12.12% The standard deviation for the period was 21.21 and the compound return was 9.98%. An examination of Exhibit 1 indicates that a 21% standard deviation should produce a compound return of 10.1%. Apart from any other analysis, this suggests that the lognormal approximation is close enough for this purpose. Exhibit 1 also suggests that the standard deviation has to rise to about *double* the historic level before the compound return from stocks would drop as low as the compound return on bonds. To put this in further perspective, the annual return percentage has fallen outside the two-standard-deviation interval only twice during the 61-year period. There is no doubt that compound returns *are* lower if the arithmetic or average return is fixed and volatility increases. However, volatility within the range experienced in the stock market does not reduce the compound return below levels obtainable from lower-risk portfolios.

EXHIBIT 1:
COMPOUND RETURN FROM A 12.12 PERCENT ARITHMETIC RETURN AT VARIOUS STANDARD DEVIATIONS

Standard Deviation, %	Compound Return, %
0	12.12
10	11.56
12	11.36
15	11.01
20	10.26
25	9.31
30	8.19
35	6.90
40	5.48
45	3.93
50	2.27
55	0.53

If the reader is as persuaded as this author that Exhibit 1 demonstrates the folly of *most* arguments for improving compound return by reducing risk, why are risk-reduction strategies (in general) and loss truncating strategies (in particular) so popular? A complete answer would involve a longer discourse on utility theory, on the mathematics of investment returns, and on the motivations of investors, corporate directors, pension plan administrators, portfolio managers, and employee benefit consultants than most readers would tolerate. A few observations should suggest where a comprehensive analysis would lead.

1. While each individual is different, most students of utility theory and utility preferences would agree that most investors take less

EXHIBIT 2:
COMPOUND RETURN FROM A 12.12% ARITHMETIC RETURN AT
VARIOUS STANDARD DEVIATIONS

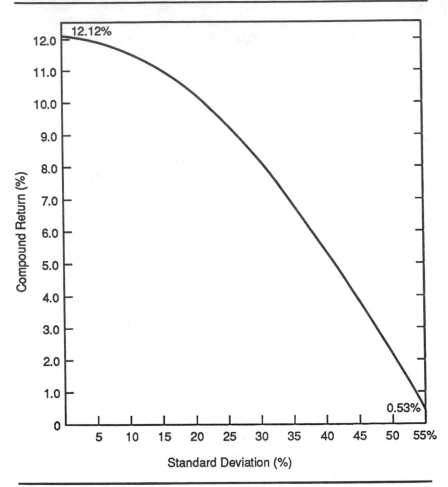

risk than their stated attitude toward risk would suggest. Furthermore, most investors say they are not willing to pay the penalty in
terms of expected return to eliminate all risk of loss when the
costs and benefits are priced realistically.

2. Many risk-return trade-off decisions are made on the basis of
imperfect or inaccurate information. The relationship in Exhibits
1 and 2 will come as a surprise to most professional investors.
Most of them realize that the additional return is worth the risk of

investing in common stocks, but few of them realize how extreme
the risk must be to bring the compound return down significantly.
Supplementary return information in Exhibit 3 computes the
probability of loss after 1 year in an Ibbotson-Sinquefield universe at 30.13%. After 10 years, the probability of loss has
dropped below 5%, and the expected value of $100 has com-
pounded to $258.90

EXHIBIT 3:
PROBABILITY OF LOSS IN A MARKET PORTFOLIO BASED ON
IBBOTSON-SINQUEFIELD RESULTS FOR 1926–1986

Arithmetic return	12.12%	
Compound return	9.98%	
Annual standard deviation	21.21%	

	Probability of loss	Expected value $100 compounded
After 1 year	30.13%	$109.98
After 5 years	12.22%	$160.90
After 10 years	4.98%	$258.90

3. Many risk-return trade-off decisions are made for the ultimate
   beneficiary by decison makers with motivations different from
   those of the individuals whose utility preferences should be con-
   sulted. Pension plan risk is borne jointly by employees and share-
   holders. Management, bondholders, and the Pension Benefit
   Guaranty Corporation typically have minor stakes. Investment
   policy decisions are made by pension fund administrators, corporate financial officers, and boards of directors. The result of the
   disparity of motivations implied here led the editors of *Pensions
   & Investment Age* (February 23, 1987) to refer to portfolio insurance as "job insurance" for pension executives.
4. If historic equity and fixed-income risk-return relationships bear
   any implications for the future; if complex "return-pattern" strategies are evaluated properly in terms of their fixed-income and
   equity components; and if the costs of exotic programs are accurately described and evaluated, there will be a lot less return-
   pattern truncation and, probably, less risk reduction.

5. More tentatively, common stock returns have been too high on a risk-adjusted basis. Perhaps future returns will be lower because of slower growth, or perhaps the relationship of earnings-price ratios to interest rates needs to move to a new, semipermanently lower level. Perhaps the higher volatility of late 1987 is an indication of things to come and a justification for high common stock returns. Time will tell.

Even after the volatility of October, 1987, there is ample evidence that stock market volatility has declined from the levels experienced in the first 20 years covered by the Ibbotson-Sinquefield study. Even if the risk premium equity investors enjoy in future years is less than it has been in the past, it seems clear that under all but the most extreme conceivable circumstances, the long-term return of an uninsured portfolio will be superior to the long-term return of an insured portfolio. The insured portfolio is, after all, only a mixture of common stocks and Treasury bills. Historic results may or may not be persuasive to the would-be portfolio insurer, but any investor who embarks on a portfolio insurance program with the expectation that long-term average results will be better than outright ownership of common stocks is almost certain to be disappointed.

Insured portfolio performance is certain to be a topic of frequent debate. As noted above, the simulations used to sell potential users on the merits of portfolio insurance typically cover the early 1970s, a period with the kind of sharp market declines that make puts and portfolio insurance more valuable.

A recent simulation by Garcia and Gould[2] examines annual returns for subperiods designed to overcome some of the weaknesses of traditional portfolio insurance simulations. Though it is hard to endorse any option-oriented simulation, the Garcia and Gould work provides some useful insights. For the period they studied, insured portfolios showed a lower average simulated return than uninsured portfolios. This is a marked contrast to simulations which show lower risk *and* higher average return for insured portfolios. Garcia and Gould found some instances in which portfolio insurance would have provided embarrassing results. Insurance advocates stress the possibility of modest positive

---

[2]C. B. Garcia and F. J. Gould, "Characteristics of Portfolio Insurance—Empirical Facts and Fallacies," *Financial Analysts Journal*, July–August 1987, pp. 44–54.

returns during periods of market collapse. Garcia and Gould found such results; but they also found occasional near-zero returns during periods of sharply rising markets. The pattern of insured portfolio results is heavily dependent on the pattern of returns day by day or month by month. Some of the Garcia and Gould findings are summarized in Exhibit 4. The entire article should be read by would-be portfolio insurance users.

EXHIBIT 4:
SUMMARY OF GARCIA AND GOULD EMPIRICAL STUDY OF PORTFOLIO INSURANCE

	S&P 500 Portfolio	1-Year Insured Portfolio	
		−5% Floor	0% Floor
Arithmetic return	9.63%	8.19%	7.08%
Compound (geometric) return	8.41	7.58	6.71
Annualized standard deviation	16.22	11.80	9.33
Long-run yearly cost (arithmetic)		1.44	2.55
Average shortfall in years the S&P 500 beat the insured portfolio		3.85	7.19
% of time insured portfolio underperformed Treasury bills		48	63

Notes: Period covered by the simulation 1963–1983—240 overlapping years of data. Assumed one-way transaction cost: 0.5%. Rebalance criterion: 10% change in hedge ratio.

WHO SHOULD USE PORTFOLIO INSURANCE?

Most investors are probably not attracted to portfolio insurance because they have illusions that the long-term results will be superior to outright holdings of common stocks. One hopes that few sophisticated investors really believe that. The attraction of portfolio insurance is the avoidance of large losses. The opportunity to avoid down years is a persuasive argument. There may be funds that cannot invade principal, and the idea of having at least something to spend each year has appeal. There are undoubtedly institutional situations in which something approximating portfolio insurance is practically mandated by structural, tax, or reporting considerations. Likewise, there are undoubtedly a few individuals whose utility functions require avoidance of large losses. In evaluating whether or not to undertake a portfolio insurance program, every entity should consider the utility functions of the ultimate beneficiaries and/or the ultimate contributors to the fund involved. Traditional forms of portfolio insurance may have a place in (1) pension plans of companies in trouble or (2) public pension plans where the local economy is weak and shows little sign of recovery, virtually foreclosing the possibility of a tax increase. The appropriate market for portfolio insurance is undoubtedly large. Many noninsurers should be using it. Conversely, many current users should not be using it.

Corporate pension planners will rarely find the traditional form of portfolio insurance to be attractive if the corporation is healthy and the pension plan is an ongoing program. Recently effected (1986), FAS No. 87 imposes standards of solvency and asset-liability matching on corporate pension plans for the first time. This pronouncement of the Financial Accounting Standards Board (FASB) eliminated many of the opportunities for juggling actuarial assumptions that have led to dramatic changes in the apparent degree of over- or underfunding of pension funds. FAS No. 87 gives some impetus toward a duration-matched bond portfolio which would increase in value when interest rates decline and would fall in value when interest rates rise. Because liabilities would also be discounted at current rates, the coverage of liabilities should remain roughly constant if the plan is funded with a duration-matched dedicated bond portfolio.

Under FAS No. 87 a type of portfolio insurance that divides the portfolio between common stocks and bonds—increasing the stock commitment when stocks have done well, but switching more heavily to bonds to protect the fund's minimum surplus of assets over liabilities—would seem more appropriate than the traditional common stock-Treasury bill variety of insurance. The form of portfolio insurance that is designed to handle asset-liability matching problems is often called *equity-enhanced dedication*. It, too, has its place; but it cannot protect a pension fund surplus as certainly as traditional portfolio insurance can promise a minimum return. Insurance companies may offer portfolio management products that guarantee a corporation's pension surplus using equity-enhanced dedication techniques. Depending on the competitive environment, these products may be either overpriced, leading to extraordinary profits for the insurer, or very cheap and risky to the insurer.

HOW MUCH PORTFOLIO INSURANCE IS AVAILABLE?

Portfolios committed to insurance programs had been growing by billions of dollars per month, in early 1987. Insurance transactions had market impact on high-volume, high-volatility days, but until October the impact seemed manageable. When the October, 1987, crash came, portfolio insurance and related strategies designed to reduce exposure to common stocks were clearly major factors in the speed and extent of the decline. The possibility that portfolio insurance might contribute to market volatility and, in particular, accentuate a market decline, had been noted over a year earlier by Arnott and Boling.[3] Their description of the destabilizing effects of portfolio insurance erred only in underestimating the growth rate of the commitment to dynamic hedging.

Ironically, an August 1987 paper by Sanford Grossman[4] had just highlighted the risk that dynamic hedging to implement portfolio insurance could cause the market mechanism to break down. Grossman argues that long-term index puts must be readily available as an alternative to dynamic hedging in the future markets. Without long-term puts as a price discovery mechanism, Grossman predicted extreme market volatility as a result of portfolio insurance and related transactions. His prescience seems almost eerie.

Merton Miller has noted a paradox of market liquidity mentioned by Keynes in connection with bank liquidity.[5] Individual bank accounts and separate stock market transactions enjoy a high degree of liquidity because all depositors do not ordinarily try to make deposits or withdrawals at once, and all investors do not ordinarily try to buy or sell at the same time. In a run on the bank or an avalanche of sell orders on the stock exchange, it is the belief in continued liquidity that makes deposits and markets effectively illiquid. We may have been close to this kind of illiquidity a few times in 1986 and early 1987. We hit the wall in October 1987.

Miller suggests consideration of temporary trading halts to permit order offsets in the style of exchange opening price determinations.

---

[3]Robert D. Arnott and Richard Boling, "Portfolio Insurance's Future Rides on Futures," *Pensions and Investment Age,* September 1, 1986.

[4]Sanford J. Grossman, "An Analysis of the Implications for Stock and Futures Price Volatility of Program Trading and Dynamic Hedging Strategies," National Bureau of Economic Research Working Paper 2357, August, 1987, forthcoming in the *Journal of Business.*

[5]Merton H. Miller, "Financial Innovations and Market Volatility," University of Chicago Speech Reprint, April 1987.

Other observers have suggested maximum daily price fluctuation limits on index futures contracts. Still others believe any fluctuations attributable to portfolio insurance transactions will stimulate an equilibrating response from other market participants. We incline toward the latter view, but mechanisms to impose temporary trading halts and even index futures price fluctuation limits would provide an opportunity for the forces of stabilization to organize.

It is too soon after the crash of 1987, and this author's perspective is too limited, to provide perfect solutions to all the problems that have come to light. Nonetheless, an options-oriented perspective and an admitted free market bias suggest that revisions in the market mechanism should include the following at a minumum:

1. The capacity of automatic order entry and execution systems must be far larger than anyone would have thought necessary a few years ago.
2. Information on customer limit orders and order flow now available only to exchange specialists must be totally computerized and readily available to all interested parties.
3. Option position limits must be eliminated. If position limits had been scrapped before October, 1987, and long-term puts had been available, the crash might have been much less severe.
4. The requirement that short sales be made only on price upticks should be scrapped. It delays price equilibrium and contributes to the chaos of a selling panic.

Hopefully, these revisions will be included among the inevitable structural changes which the crash has initiated. If these changes are included, the market's capacity to provide portfolio insurance will equal the demand. The price of index puts will reflect the risk of relying on dynamic hedging. Market forces will balance supply and demand; and Adam Smith will have been proved right once again.

CHAPTER 12

Achieving the Best Return In Asset Allocation Without Forecasting

H. GIFFORD FONG
PRESIDENT
GIFFORD FONG ASSOCIATES

OLDRICH A. VASICEK
CONSULTANT
GIFFORD FONG ASSOCIATES

This chapter introduces a new type of asset allocation strategy, the objective of which is to achieve a return on the total investment equal to the return on that one of several assets that performed the best, less the predetermined strategy cost. The strategy does not require the manager to make any judgments about the expected returns of the individual assets in order to achieve this goal. In comparison with a mean/variance asset allocation, which provides a return equal to a weighted average of the separate asset returns, this strategy assures, after costs, the highest of the individual asset returns over the given investment horizon.

OVERVIEW OF STRATEGY

Consider, as an example, an allocation of investment funds among stocks, bonds and foreign equities. If stocks happen to perform the best of the three, the return on the strategy will be that of the stock portion less the known cost. If bonds perform better over the investment horizon than domestic and foreign stocks, the investment return will equal the return on bonds less some cost. If foreign stocks do better than domestic stocks or bonds, the investor will realize the return, after costs, of the foreign stock portfolio on his total investment.

If one of the assets has a fixed return over the investment horizon, this strategy guarantees a specified minimum return in addition to assuring the best of the remaining asset returns. This minimum guaranteed return is the return on the safety asset less the known cost. Thus, if the portfolio includes a zero-coupon bond maturing at the end of the investment horizon in addition to stocks, bonds and foreign stocks, the strategy will yield an assured minimum return even if stocks, bonds and foreign stocks all perform poorly.

Portfolio insurance is a special case of the best return strategy. Portfolio insurance allows the investor to invest in a risky target asset while guaranteeing a specified minimum return. It can be viewed as a strategy that assures the better of two asset returns (after costs): the target asset and a safety asset, such as a Treasury bill. If the target asset is a balanced portfolio consisting of stocks, bonds and foreign equities, the insurance then applies to the total fund and depends only on its total performance. In contrast, the best return strategy can assure the upside potential of each of the individual components and deliver the return on the best of these.

There is no restriction on the number of assets used in the best return strategy. It can be applied to individual securities (such as getting the best of several individual stock returns), to portfolios (for example, assuring that the return achieved by the best—or luckiest—of several portfolio managers is realized on the total plan), or to whole markets (for instance, obtaining the best performing of several foreign equity markets). The cost of the strategy, of course, increases with the number of assets involved. In addition to the number of assets, the cost depends on the riskiness of the assets (the riskier the assets the higher the cost), the correlations among the assets (the higher correlated they are, the lower the cost), and the length of the investment horizon (the cost per year decreases with increasing horizon length).

The strategy is implemented by a dynamic allocation of the investment funds among the several assets. The proportions of the total investment allocated to the individual assets are continuously monitored and adjusted, depending on their performance to date and on the time remaining to the horizon date. Of fundamental importance is the ability to achieve the best return without making any judgment on expected return.

THE ANALYSIS

Traditional asset allocation through the mean variance analysis focuses on the tradeoff between expected returns and risks. In contrast, strategies based on option pricing theory do not require specification of expected returns. This is the direction in which the best return strategy approaches the asset allocation problem.

Consider a strategy with an objective described as

$$R_P = \max (R_1 - c_1, R_2 - c_2) \tag{1}$$

where R_P is the total investment portfolio return, R_1 and R_2 are the returns on two assets, and c_1, c_2 are the implied costs expressed as return differentials. All returns are assumed to be continuously compounded.

In this simple formulation, the goal is to achieve the return of the better performing of two assets. As the asset values change over time, an option pricing model can be used to rebalance the portfolio between the assets to achieve the objective described in equation (1). This arrangement—in which one of the assets has an assured return over the horizon of interest—is essentially what has been called portfolio insurance.

For example, if one of the assets was a risky target asset and the other was represented by a zero-coupon bond or an immunized portfolio, the option pricing model would allow an ongoing rebalancing between these two assets such that the final portfolio return would be represented by the higher of the two asset returns less some return differential or cost. Since the immunized portfolio has an assured return at the end of the horizon, the following result would emerge:

$$R_P = \max (R_1 - c_1, R_{min}) \qquad (2)$$

where R_{min} is some desired minimum return. This minimum return must be less than the assured return of the immunized portfolio,

$$R_{min} < R_2 \qquad (3)$$

and the implied cost associated with the safety asset is then

$$c_2 = R_2 - R_{min} \qquad (4)$$

The insurance cost c_1 in equation (2) can be determined from the Black/Scholes[1] option pricing formula if interest rates are deterministic and constant, and from Merton's[2] extension of that formula if the variability of interest rates is independent of their level. Margrabe[3] has provided a formula for two risky assets, and Stulz[4] derived an equation for two risky assets and one riskless asset. In general, the insurance costs will depend on the risk structure of the two assets throughout the horizon (i.e., their instantaneous covariance matrix as a function of time and state variables) and the length of the horizon.

The best return strategy is a generalization of portfolio insurance to multiple assets. Its objective can be stated in the form

$$R_P = \max (R_1 - c_1, R_2 - c_2, \ldots, R_n - c_n) \qquad (5)$$

where R_P is the total portfolio return; n is the number of assets in the asset allocation problem; $R_1, R_2, \ldots, R_n$ are the individual asset

[1]Fischer Black and Myron Scholes, "The Pricing of Options and Corporate Liabilities," *Journal of Political Economy* 81, 1973, 637–659.

[2]Robert Merton, "A Rational Theory of Option Pricing," *Bell Journal of Economics and Management Science* 4, 1973, 141–183.

[3]W. Margrabe, "The Value of an Option to Exchange One Asset for Another," *Journal of Finance* 33, 1978, 177–186.

[4]Rene Stulz, "Options on the Minimum or the Maximum of Two Risky Assets," *Journal of Financial Economics* 10, 1982, 161–185.

returns; and c_1, c_2, . . ., c_n are the strategy costs attributed to the individual assets. The goal is to get the best of multiple risky asset returns, less the corresponding cost. Thus, multiple assets such as domestic and foreign stocks, bonds, bills and other asset types can be simultaneously considered. The strategy is equivalent to purchasing an option that allows the investor to choose the asset to call. Note that if one of the assets has a fixed return over the investment horizon, say R_n, then the strategy also guarantees a minimum return of $R_{min} = R_n - c_n$.

DETERMINING THE COST

The strategy costs c_1, c_2, . . ., c_n associated with each asset class are given by a valuation equation for the multiple asset option. Since this is a single equation for the n costs, it means that $n - 1$ of them can be independently chosen (subject to feasibility constraints) and the remaining one is residually determined.

The valuation formula depends on the number of assets, the covariance matrix of the n-dimensional stochastic process that characterizes each asset over the horizon and the horizon length. For diffusion processes, the valuation formula involves $(n - 1)$-dimensional cumulative normal distribution functions with covariance matrices that are transformations of the n-dimensional instantaneous covariance matrix of the assets, integrated over the horizon.

Choosing the appropriate cost is subject to evaluating the tradeoff among the relative importance of the assets to the investor. Less relevant assets can be made to bear higher costs than assets whose performance is more essential.

Uniform Cost Allocation

A simple alternative is to choose that the costs all be equal:

$$c_1 = c_2 = \ldots = c_n$$

In this case, the objective function of the strategy has a particularly simple form

$$R_P = \max (R_1, R_2, \ldots, R_n) - c, \tag{6}$$

where the common value c of the n costs is determined from the valuation formula. This case, which will be called *uniform cost allocation*, assigns the costs equally to all of the assets included in the objective.

As an example, consider n assets, whose stochastic behavior is described by a logarithmic Wiener process. Let the instantaneous covariance matrix be specified by standard deviations all equal to 14% annual, with correlations among the assets all equal to .3, and assume a five-year horizon. The following table lists the value c of the uniform costs, in annual percent, as a function of the number of assets:

Uniform Costs in Annual Percent

n =	2	3	4	5	6
c =	2.5	3.8	4.6	5.2	5.7

These costs are the price to be paid for getting the best out of a number of asset returns. Suppose that the values of the parameters chosen for the example are descriptive of the international equity markets. It is possible to implement a strategy whose realized return is equal to the highest of six separate national stock markets, over a five-year period, less 5.7% annual. No prediction is needed as to which of these markets will have the highest return, or for that matter, what the expected returns are of each.

The table above is an extract from Exhibit 1 which lists the values of the uniform costs as a function of the number of assets and of the correlation among them, assumed to be the same between any pair. The investment horizon is taken to be five years and the standard deviations of the individual asset returns are assumed to be all equal to 14% per year. It can be seen that the costs decrease drastically with an increase in the correlation among the assets. The uniform costs under the same assumptions for a one-year horizon are given in Exhibit 2.

Non-Uniform Costs

The costs of the strategy do not have to be made equal. It is possible to choose them in such a way that a disproportionate part of the burden is borne by those assets in which the investor has a secondary interest. For

EXHIBIT 1:
BEST RETURN STRATEGY UNIFORM COSTS (IN ANNUAL %)

Horizon length (yrs.) : 5.0

Standard deviation (%): 14.0

Corr.	Number of Assets				
	2	3	4	5	6
.0	2.95	4.45	5.43	6.15	6.77
.1	2.81	4.24	5.17	5.86	6.45
.2	2.66	4.01	4.89	5.54	6.10
.3	2.50	3.77	4.60	5.20	5.73
.4	2.32	3.50	4.27	4.84	5.33
.5	2.13	3.21	3.92	4.43	4.89
.6	1.92	2.89	3.52	3.98	4.40
.7	1.67	2.52	3.07	3.47	3.84
.8	1.38	2.07	2.52	2.85	3.16
.9	.98	1.48	1.80	2.03	2.28

instance, consider the case of four assets with standard deviations of 12.1%, 6.2%, 13.4%, and .5%, and a correlation matrix as shown in Exhibit 3. These values correspond to historical estimates of volatilities and correlations (over the period 1/83 to 12/85) for the Standard & Poor's 500 Stock Index, Shearson Lehman Government/Corporate Bond Index, Morgan Stanley's Europe, Australia and Far East (EAFE) Stock Index, and a three-month Treasury bill Index. For a five-year horizon, the uniform costs are 3.2% annual. This means that the best return strategy applied to these four assets assures the investor a return equal to the highest of the realized annual returns over the five-year period of stocks, bonds, foreign stocks and bills, less 3.2%. For instance, if stocks turned out to do the best of these four assets with an annual return of 20%, the investor would realize 16.8% annually over the horizon. If stocks, bonds and the foreign stock portfolio all lost money, the strategy would still provide a return equal to that realized on Treasury bills less 3.2%.

EXHIBIT 2:
BEST RETURN STRATEGY UNIFORM COSTS (IN ANNUAL %)

Horizon length (yrs.)   :   1.0

Standard deviation (%): 14.0

Corr.	Number of Assets				
	2	3	4	5	6
.0	6.90	10.38	12.64	14.29	15.87
.1	6.55	9.86	12.01	13.58	15.08
.2	6.19	9.31	11.34	12.82	14.25
.3	5.80	8.72	10.62	12.00	13.42
.4	5.38	8.09	9.85	11.13	12.46
.5	4.92	7.40	9.01	10.17	11.42
.6	4.41	6.63	8.07	9.12	10.27
.7	3.83	5.75	7.00	7.91	8.95
.8	3.14	4.71	5.74	6.47	7.38
.9	2.23	3.35	4.07	4.59	5.35

Now suppose that it is essential to the investor to maintain a five-year return of no less than that of Treasury bills less 2%, while retaining as much of the upside potential of stocks, bonds and foreign stocks as possible. The costs of a best return strategy can be chosen as

$$c_1 = 3.8\%, c_2 = 3.8\%, c_3 = 3.8\%, c_4 = 2.0\%$$

(This is case #1 in Exhibit 3.) This choice of costs would assure a minimum performance of Treasury bill return less 2%, while keeping the possibility open to participate in the performance of the three riskier assets if any one of them does well.

If foreign stocks were less important to the investor than stocks and bonds, perhaps the following cost assignment would be preferred:

$$c_1 = 3.1\%, c_2 = 3.1\%, c_3 = 5.0\%, c_4 = 2.0\%$$

EXHIBIT 3:
BEST RETURN STRATEGY COSTS

Number of assets   : 4

Horizon length (years) : 5.0

Standard deviations (%):

Stocks	12.1
Bonds	6.2
Foreign	13.4
Bills	0.5

Correlation matrix:

	Stocks	Bonds	Foreign	Bills
Stocks	1.00	.42	.50	−.13
Bonds	.42	1.00	.27	.38
Foreign	.50	.27	1.00	−.22
Bills	−.13	.38	−.22	1.00

Cost (in annual %):

Case	Stocks	Bonds	Foreign	Bills
Uniform	3.2	3.2	3.2	3.2
1	3.8	3.8	3.8	2.0
2	3.1	3.1	5.0	2.0
3	2.0	7.4	7.4	2.0
4	5.0	5.0	5.0	1.0
5	4.5	4.5	5.6	1.0
6	3.5	6.0	8.0	1.0
7	6.4	6.4	6.4	.5
8	1.9	3.5	3.5	6.0

(This is case #2 in Exhibit 3.) This cost allocation would attribute lower costs to stocks and bonds than the previous case, and higher costs to the less important foreign stock portfolio.

Exhibit 3 lists a number of possible alternatives for the cost allocation. Note that these are just a few possibilities out of an infinite range of feasible cost allocations, with no particular meaning to the order in which the cases are listed.

STRATEGY IMPLEMENTATION

The strategy is executed by a dynamic allocation of investment funds among the several assets. The amounts allocated to the individual assets are maintained to be proportional to the partial derivatives with respect to the asset values of the valuation function (the same function which is also used initially to determine the costs of the strategy). The required allocation changes continuously as a function of the asset performance to date and the remaining time to the horizon.

An example of the strategy is provided in Exhibit 4. The stategy is simulated over a one-year investment horizon from 1/1/86 to 12/31/86, using the four assets described. The risk parameters are those listed in Exhibit 3 as measured over a prior period, 1/83 to 12/85. The costs, allocated uniformly, are 7.4% for each asset. The simulations assume monthly rebalancing with transaction costs of .25% round trip (a conservative estimate if the rebalancing can be executed by trading futures).

The initial allocation was 27.6%, 18.2%, 31.7%, and 22.5% among stocks, bonds, foreign stocks and bills, respectively. One month later, based on the market moves over the month, the allocation was changed to 24.8%, 16.6%, 37.9% and 20.7%, respectively, for a turnover of 5.84%. The rebalancing is continued each month until the horizon date.

For each rebalancing period, the exhibit lists the last month performance and the performance since inception of the four assets, as well as the scheduled performance of the plan (the performance, calculated from the valuation formula, that is expected from the strategy given the performance of the individual assets) and the actual performance of the plan before and after transaction costs.

The summary of the strategy performance is provided in Exhibit 5.

EXHIBIT 4:
MAP PERFORMANCE SIMULATION—PLAN #1: BEST OF FOUR ASSETS

Asset	Name	Protection Costs (%)	Title (Description)	
1	Stocks	7.38	Standard and Poor's 500 Stock Index	Inception date 1–01–86
2	Bonds	7.38	Shearson Lehman Government Corporate Bond Index	Horizon date 12–31–86
3	Foreign	7.38	Morgan Stanley's Europe, Australia & Far East Stock Index	Horizon length 1.00 Yrs.
4	Bills	7.38	Three Month U.S. Treasury Bill Index	Init'l. investment 100,000
				Rnd. trip trans. costs .25%

Correlation Matrix

Asset	Name	Standard Deviation	Stocks	Bonds	Foreign	Bills
1	Stocks	12.10%		0.424	0.499	–0.131
2	Bonds	6.16%			0.267	0.376
3	Foreign	13.40%				–0.222
4	Bills	.50%				

Date	Yrs. To Horiz.	Stocks	Bonds	Foreign	Bills	Plan Sched.	Plan Actual Before Tr. Cst.	After Tr. Cst.	
1–01–86	1.00								
Required allocation		27.56%	18.22%	31.67%	22.55%				Investment value 100,000
2–01–86	.92								
Return in last period		0.57%	0.59%	2.35%	0.61%	.88%	1.15%	1.15%	Investment Value 101,146
Return since inception		0.57%	0.59%	2.35%	0.61%	.88%	1.15%	1.15%	Turnover 5.84%
Current allocation		27.40%	18.12%	32.05%	22.43%				Transaction costs 15
Required allocation		24.80%	16.58%	37.88%	20.74%				

EXHIBIT 4: (continued)

MAP PERFORMANCE SIMULATION—PLAN #1: BEST OF OUR ASSETS

Date	Yrs. To Horiz.	Stocks	Bonds	Foreign	Bills	Plan Sched.	Plan Actual Before Tr. Cst.	Plan Actual After Tr. Cst.	
3-1-86	**.84**								
Return in last period		7.45%	4.19%	10.91%	0.52%	7.56%	6.78%	6.77%	Investment value 107,992
Return since inception		8.07%	4.80%	13.51%	1.14%	8.51%	8.01%	7.99%	Turnover 20.29%
Current allocation		24.96%	16.17%	39.35%	19.52%				Transaction costs 55
Required allocation		24.80%	11.57%	59.64%	3.99%				
4-01-86	**.75**								
Return in last period		5.58%	3.54%	13.91%	0.72%	11.33%	10.12%	10.06%	Investment value 118,856
Return since inception		14.10%	8.51%	29.30%	1.86%	20.80%	18.93%	18.86%	Turnover 26.02%
Current allocation		23.78%	10.88%	61.69%	3.65%				Transaction costs 77
Required allocation		9.35%	2.69%	87.74%	0.22%				
5-01-86	**.67**								
Return in last period		-1.12%	0.45%	6.40%	0.59%	5.86%	5.53%	5.46%	Investment value 125,344
Return since inception		12.82%	9.00%	37.58%	2.46%	27.88%	25.51%	25.34%	Turnover 9.28%
Current allocation		8.76%	2.56%	88.47%	0.21%				Transaction costs 29
Required allocation		1.58%	0.62%	97.76%	0.04%				
6-01-86	**.59**								
Return in last period		5.33%	-1.98%	-4.58%	0.49%	-4.11%	-4.40%	-4.43%	Investment value 119,797
Return since inception		18.83%	6.84%	31.28%	2.96%	22.63%	19.98%	19.80%	Turnover 10.80%
Current allocation		1.74%	0.63%	97.58%	0.04%				Transaction costs 32
Required allocation		12.47%	0.41%	87.01%	0.11%				

EXHIBIT 4: (continued)

MAP PERFORMANCE SIMULATION—PLAN #1: BEST OF OUR ASSETS

Date	Yrs. To Horiz.	Stocks	Bonds	Foreign	Bills	Plan Sched.	Plan Actual Before Tr. Cst.	Plan Actual After Tr. Cst.	
7-01-86	**.50**								
Return in last period		1.70%	2.90%	6.67%	0.65%	6.19%	6.03%	6.00%	Investment value 126,939
Return since inception		20.85%	9.94%	40.04%	3.63%	30.22%	27.22%	26.99%	Turnover 8.91%
Current allocation		11.96%	0.04%	87.54%	0.10%				Transaction costs 28
Required allocation		3.43%	0.10%	96.46%	0.00%				
8-01-86	**.42**								
Return in last period		-5.59%	0.65%	6.03%	0.54%	5.91%	5.62%	5.60%	Investment value 134,130
Return since inception		14.10%	10.66%	48.48%	4.19%	37.91%	34.37%	34.10%	Turnover 3.14%
Current allocation		3.07%	0.10%	96.83%	0.00%				Transaction costs 11
Required allocation		0.02%	0.01%	99.97%	0.00%				
9-01-86	**.33**								
Return in last period		7.42%	2.64%	9.72%	0.61%	9.72%	9.72%	9.71%	Investment value 147,126
Return since inception		22.57%	13.58%	62.92%	4.82%	51.32%	47.44%	47.13%	Turnover .02%
Current allocation		0.02%	0.01%	99.98%	0.00%				Transaction costs 0
Required allocation		0.00%	0.00%	100.00%	0.00%				
10-01-86	**.25**								
Return in last period		-8.28%	-1.25%	-1.15%	0.46%	-1.15%	-1.15%	-1.15%	Investment value 145,433
Return since inception		12.42%	12.16%	61.04%	5.31%	49.58%	45.74%	45.43%	Turnover .00%
Current allocation		0.00%	0.00%	100.00%	0.00%				Transaction costs 0
Required allocation		0.00%	0.00%	100.00%	0.00%				

EXHIBIT 4: (continued)

MAP PERFORMANCE SIMULATION—PLAN #1: BEST OF OUR ASSETS

Date	Yrs. To Horiz.	Stocks	Bonds	Foreign	Bills	Plan Sched.	Plan Actual Before Tr. Cst.	Plan Actual After Tr. Cst.	
11-01-86	.17								
Return in last period		5.81%	1.45%	-6.80%	0.48%	-6.80%	-6.80%	-6.80%	Investment value 135,546
Return since inception		18.95%	13.79%	50.10%	5.81%	39.41%	35.83%	35.55%	Turnover .00%
Current allocation		0.00%	0.00%	100.00%	0.00%				Transaction costs 0
Required allocation		0.00%	0.00%	100.00%	0.00%				
12-01-86	.08								
Return in last period		2.41%	1.22%	5.65%	0.37%	5.65%	5.65%	5.65%	Investment value 143,199
Return since inception		21.82%	15.17%	58.57%	6.21%	47.28%	43.50%	43.20%	Turnover .00%
Current allocation		0.00%	0.00%	100.00%	0.00%				Transaction costs 0
Required allocation		0.00%	0.00%	100.00%	0.00%				
12-31-86	.00								
Return in last period		-2.55%	0.36%	5.19%	0.45%	5.19%	5.19%	5.19%	Investment value 150,630
Return since inception		18.71%	15.59%	66.80%	6.69%	54.93%	50.95%	50.63%	

Over the one-year horizon, the annual continuously compounded returns for the four assets were 17.2% for stocks, 14.5% for bonds, 51.2% for foreign stocks and 6.5% for bills. The scheduled return was 43.8%, equal to the best of the four asset returns (foreign stocks in this case) less 7.4%. The actual performance of the plan was 41.2% before and 41.0% after transaction costs, very close to the scheduled. The difference between the actual and promised performance is due to monthly (rather than continuous) rebalancing and to the actual risk parameters over the investment horizon differing from the assumed values (which were estimated over a previous period).

EXHIBIT 5:
MAP SIMULATION SUMMARY—PLAN #1: BEST OF FOUR ASSETS

Plan inception date	1–01–86	Horizon length	1.00 Yrs.
Plan horizon date	12–31–86	Initial investment	100,000

	Stocks	Bonds	Foreign	Bills
Protection costs	7.38%	7.38%	7.38%	7.38%
Return since inception:				
Total	18.71%	15.59%	66.80%	6.69%
Per/yr (annl. comp)	18.71%	15.59%	66.80%	6.69%
Per/yr (cont. comp)	17.15%	14.49%	51.16%	6.48%

	Plan Sched.	Plan Actual Before T/Costs	After T/Costs	
Return since inception:				
Total	54.93%	50.95%	50.63%	Investment value 150,630
Per/yr (annl. comp)	54.93%	50.95%	50.63%	Total turnover 84.30%
Per/yr (cont. comp)	43.78%	41.18%	40.97%	Total trans. costs 247

CHAPTER 13

Portfolio Optimization Under Shortfall Constraints*

MARTIN L. LEIBOWITZ
MANAGING DIRECTOR
SALOMON BROTHERS INC

ROY D. HENRIKSSON
VICE PRESIDENT
SALOMON BROTHERS INC

The asset allocation decision is often viewed as a trade-off between maximizing the expected return of a portfolio and minimizing its riskiness, with riskiness usually being measured by the standard deviation of the portfolio return. The portfolio optimization process determines the asset mix that achieves the highest expected return for a given standard deviation. The investor can then make a choice from among the resulting set of "efficient" portfolios that reflects his attitude toward risk.

Expected return and standard deviation can define the probability distribution of potential portfolio returns. The common use of standard

*Copyright © 1988 by Salomon Brothers Inc. The authors wish to express their appreciation to Ardavan Nozari, Margo Urbany and Peter G. Brown for their help in the preparation of this chapter.

deviation as a measure of dispersion facilitates portfolio comparison, but for many investors the "confidence limit" may provide a more meaningful description of the problems associated with dispersion. A confidence limit is expressed as a shortfall constraint: the minimum return that must be exceeded with a given probability. Describing the dispersion of the potential portfolio returns in this way may be particularly helpful for investors who are constrained by multiple, and potentially conflicting, objectives.

A shortfall constraint may be especially meaningful to investors who are judged relative to a benchmark portfolio, such as an index or a basket of indexes. The risk/return characteristics of potential investment portfolios and of the benchmark portfolio determine a distribution of deviations from the benchmark. The investor may then limit the portfolio optimization process to portfolios that, with high probability (say, 95%), will not underperform the benchmark by more than a specified amount (say, 5%). This constrained optimization may be particularly attractive to investors who are measured against multiple benchmarks such as market indexes, liability thresholds or normal or baseline portfolio targets, or whose flexibility to depart from existing portfolio structures is limited.

THE TRADITIONAL MEASURE OF RISK

The portfolio optimization process focuses on the trade-off between expected return and standard deviation. For any given standard deviation there is a maximum achievable expected return. The set of portfolios that attain these values of risk and return constitute the efficient frontier, the best possible trade-offs between expected return and standard deviation. Exhibit 1 presents a hypothetical efficient frontier; as it shows, the investor must accept a higher standard deviation in order to achieve a higher expected return.

The standard deviation is a measure of the dispersion of a distribution. In the special case of a normal distribution, the distribution is completely specified by its mean and standard deviation (see the Appendix). A normal distribution is symmetric about its mean, and the probability of a particular outcome is a decreasing function of the deviation from the expected value.

Exhibit 2 shows a normal distribution, reflecting the range of potential returns for a portfolio with an expected return of 8% and a standard

EXHIBIT 1:
OPTIMAL RISK/RETURN TRADEOFFS: THE EFFICIENT FRONTER

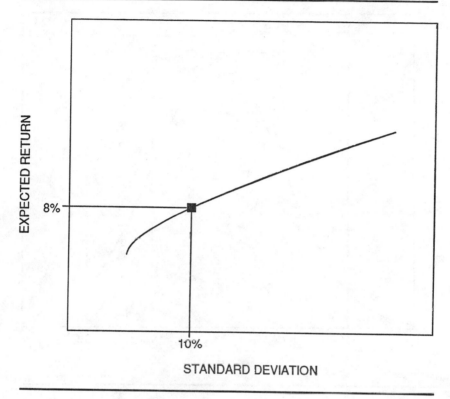

deviation of 10%. The symmetry of a normal distribution indicates that half of the potential outcomes will have a return greater than the expected value, and half will have a return less than the expected value. For a normal distribution, approximately 68% of the potential outcomes will be within one standard deviation of the expected value and approximately 95% of them will be within two standard deviations (see the Appendix).

For example, for the distribution in Exhibit 2, the realized return will be between −2% and 18% (plus or minus one standard deviation) approximately 68% of the time (see Exhibit 3) and between −12% and 28% (plus or minus two standard deviations) approximately 95% of the time (see Exhibit 4).

EXHIBIT 2:
A HYPOTHETICAL NORMAL DISTRIBUTION OF RETURNS

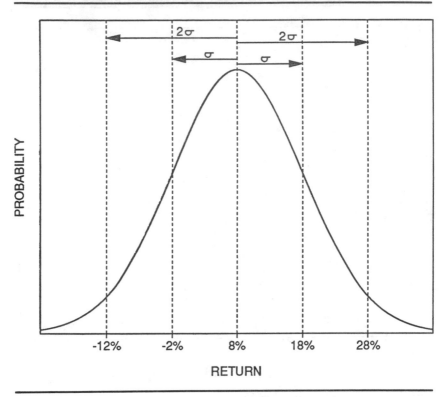

AN ALTERNATIVE MEASURE OF RISK

The use of standard deviation as a measure of risk is slightly misleading, since the potential returns on the upper tail of the distribution do
not constitute a problem. The real concern is for the below-average
outcomes in the distribution. A symmetric normal distribution can also
be completely specified, however, by its expected value and the probability that a specified minimum return level will be exceeded. The
distribution shown in Exhibit 2, with an expected return of 8% and a
standard deviation of 10%, can also be equivalently described as having an expected return of 8% and a 78.81% probability of exceeding a
return of 0% (see the Appendix and Exhibit 5).

EXHIBIT 3:
POTENTIAL OUTCOMES WITHIN ONE STANDARD DEVIATION

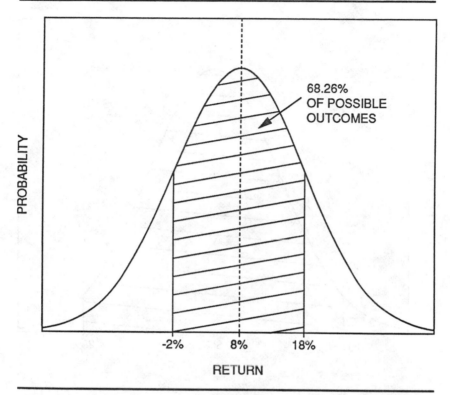

Such an approach can be extended to a more general "shortfall constraint": the minimum return the portfolio will exceed with some prespecified probability. For example, for the (8% mean/10% standard deviation) distribution, there is a 90% probability that the portfolio return will exceed −4.82% (see Exhibit 6). This result follows from the fact that for any normal distribution only 10% of the distribution represents returns that are more than 1.282 standard deviations below the mean. Since in this example one standard deviation is 10%, 1.282 standard deviations are 12.82%, and so only 10% of the distribution is less than the expected return of 8% by more than 12.82% (8.00% − 12.82% = −4.82%).

For the same distribution, there is a 95% probability that the return

EXHIBIT 4:
POTENTIAL OUTCOMES WITHIN TWO STANDARD DEVIATIONS

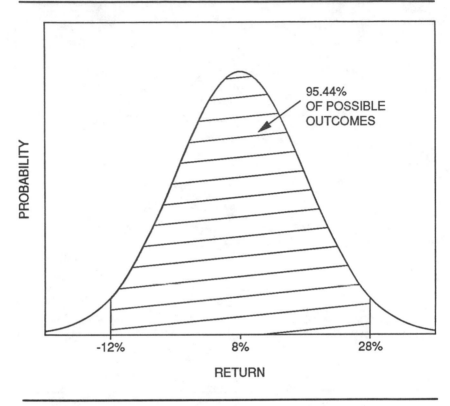

will exceed − 8.45%. Only 5% of the distribution is more than 1.645 standard deviations below the expected return (8.00% − 16.45% = − 8.45%). This minimum return can be thought of as a confidence limit—the return that will be exceeded with 95% confidence (see Exhibit 7).

SHORTFALL CONSTRAINTS IN RISK/RETURN DIAGRAMS

The preceding examples all apply to a single portfolio return distribution. How can this concept of a shortfall constraint be carried over to the universe of all possible portfolios, each having its own distinct return distribution? If one assumes that portfolio return distributions

EXHIBIT 5:
THE PROBABILITY OF POSITIVE RETURNS AS A RISK MEASURE

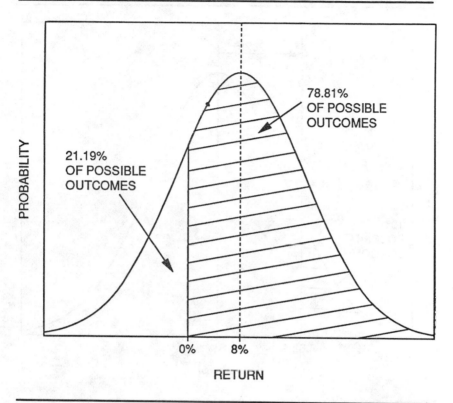

are normal, a simple formula specifies all the portfolios satisfying a given confidence limit. Recall that for any normal distribution with expected return $R_{\hat{P}}$ and standard deviation $\sigma_{\hat{P}}$, there is only a 10% probability that the return falls more than 1.282 $\sigma_{\hat{P}}$ below $R_{\hat{P}}$. Therefore, for each ($R_{\hat{P}}$, σ_P) portfolio, there is a 90% probability that the return will exceed a value $S = [R_{\hat{P}} - 1.282\ \sigma_P]$. For the (8%, 10%) portfolio, this means that there is a 90% probability that returns would exceed -4.82%.

What are the general characteristics of all portfolios having a 90% probability of beating a -4.82% return? The answer is simply that all such portfolios must have a combination of expected returns and standard deviations that satisfy the equation

$$R_{\hat{P}} - 1.282\sigma_{\hat{P}} = -4.82\%$$

EXHIBIT 6:
A 90% CONFIDENCE LIMIT

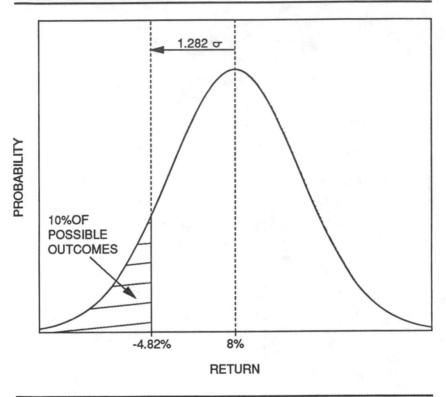

In the risk/return diagram, this includes all portfolios lying on the straight line with slope 1.282 and a Y-axis intercept of −4.82% (see Exhibit 8). All portfolios that lie above this line will have returns exceeding −4.82% with a frequency in excess of 90%.

Suppose instead that one wanted a 95% confidence limit. Exhibit 8 also plots the earlier result that the 95% confidence threshold is −8.45% for the (8%, 10%) portfolio. This minimum return value represents the intersection of the vertical axis with a straight line having a slope of 1.645 and passing through the point representing the (8%, 10%) portfolio.

Although most risk-related confidence limits of any interest to the investor will have high probabilities, it is instructive to consider the

EXHIBIT 7:
A 95% CONFIDENCE LIMIT

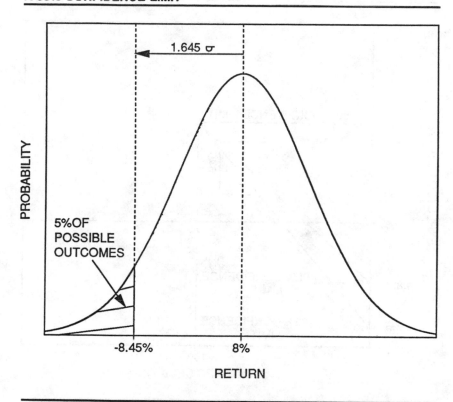

50% limit. Because of the symmetry of the normal distribution, there is a 50% probability that the actual returns will exceed 8%, which is the expected return. In other words, the 50% threshold is just zero standard deviations away from the expected return, and so the formula for portfolios that provide a 50% confidence of exceeding 8% becomes:

$$\hat{R_P} - 0\hat{\sigma_P} = 8.00\%.$$

This equation depicts a horizontal line through the 8% expected return level. For all portfolios lying above this line one has more than 50% confidence that returns will exceed 8%.

As one would expect, the minimum return for a given confidence

EXHIBIT 8:
THE SHORTFALL CONSTRAINT IN A RISK/RETURN DIAGRAM

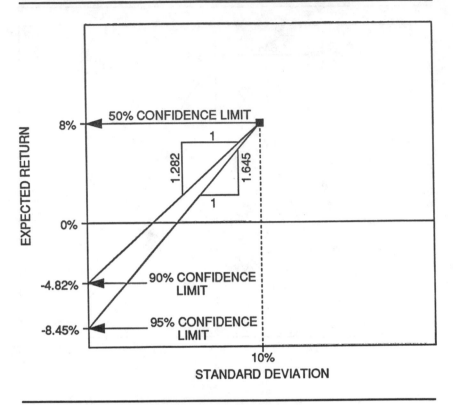

level will increase as the expected return increases (holding the standard deviation constant) and will decrease as the standard deviation increases (holding the expected return constant). Exhibit 9 shows that for every increase of 1% in the portfolio's expected return (say, from 8% to 9%) the 95% confidence limit increases by 1% (say, from −8.45% to −7.45%). Similarly, for every decrease of 1% in the portfolio's expected return (say, from 8% to 7%) the 95% confidence limit decreases by 1% (say, from −8.45% to −9.45%). Exhibit 10 shows that an increase of 1% in the portfolio's standard deviation (say, from 10% to 11%) will cause the 95% confidence limit to decline by 1.645% (say, from −8.45% to −10.095%), and a decrease of 1% in the portfolio's standard deviation (say, from 10% to 9%) will cause the

EXHIBIT 9:
THE IMPACT OF EXPECTED RETURN ON THE CONFIDENCE LIMIT

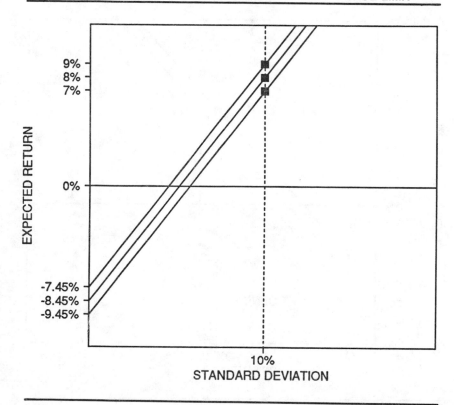

95% confidence limit to increase by 1.645% (say, from -8.45% to -6.805%).

CONSTRAINING RISK THROUGH A CONFIDENCE LIMIT

The concept of a confidence limit is similar to that of a floor in dynamic hedging or portfolio insurance. The floor, which is the minimum allowable return, limits potential losses to investors. In theory, the floor represents the 100% confidence limit for the specified dynamic strategy. In practice, the limits of discrete trading make it possible for the realized return to be lower than the floor. The floor also acts as a constraint on the portfolio. The higher the floor—that is, the higher the

EXHIBIT 10:
THE IMPACT OF STANDARD DEVIATION ON THE CONFIDENCE LIMIT

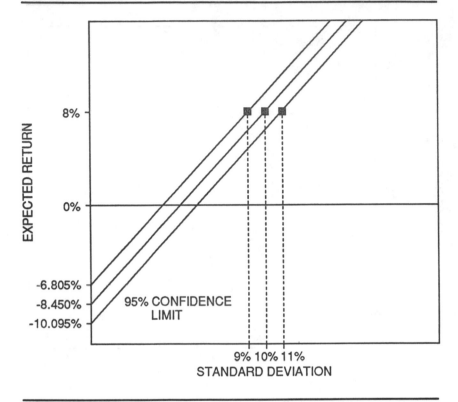

minimum allowable return—the lower the expected return of the dynamic strategy. By reducing the risk of the portfolio return, the dynamic strategy also limits the expected return that can be achieved.

A required confidence limit acts as a potential constraint on the investor's expected return. The confidence limit implies there is an acceptable but nonzero probability that the realized return will fall below the prespecified limit. The role of such a constraint on the portfolio decision is shown in Exhibit 11 for one of the examples discussed above (a minimum return of − 8.45% with 95% confidence). The shortfall constraint classifies portfolios according to the combination of their expected returns and risks. Portfolios below and to the right of the line violate the constraint; their realized returns do not

EXHIBIT 11:
CONSTRAINING RISK THROUGH A CONFIDENCE LIMIT

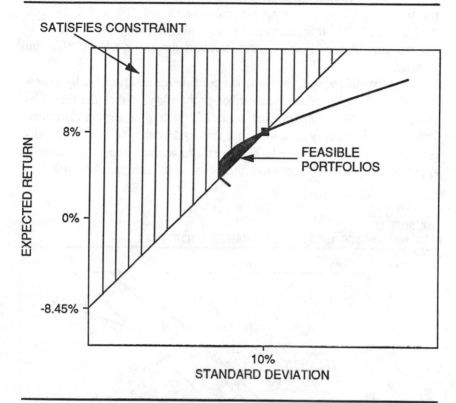

exceed −8.45% with 95% confidence. Portfolios above and to the left of the line will actually lead to returns higher than −8.45% with a 95% confidence.

Of course, only portfolio risk/return trade-offs on or below the efficient frontier are feasible. As Exhibit 11 shows, the set of feasible portfolios satisfying a shortfall constraint may be quite limited. The set of portfolios to be considered in the optimization decision is limited to the small shaded area of portfolios that are feasible and also satisfy the specified shortfall constraint.

Given the hypothetical efficient frontier from the example above, the highest achievable return with a 95% confidence limit is −6.89% (see Exhibit 12). This return is attained with the "tangency portfolio," which is derived from the "highest" point of contact between the efficient frontier and a straight line with a slope of 1.645. The tangency portfolio in Exhibit 12 has an expected return of 5.8% and a standard deviation of 7.7%. It is interesting to note that this tangency portfolio is not the portfolio with the lowest standard deviation on the efficient frontier.

As one would expect, lowering the confidence limit, either by lowering the required return or the required probability, makes the limit less constraining and qualifies portfolios with a higher expected return. Exhibit 12 demonstrates that if the required return for a 95% confidence limit is lowered to − 12%, a portfolio with an expected return of approximately 10.3% can meet the constraint, compared with an al-

EXHIBIT 12:
THE INFLUENCE OF THE ALLOWABLE SHORTFALL

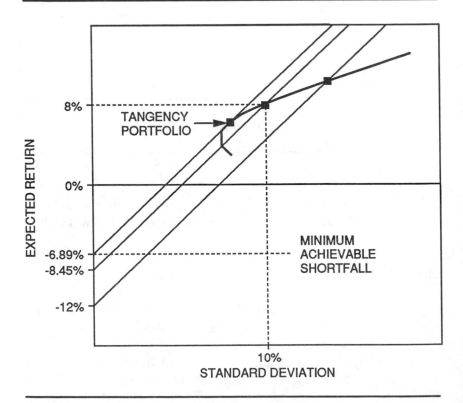

lowable expected return of only 8% when the required return is
−8.45%.

Exhibit 13 shows the effect of varying the required probability, while
holding the required return constant. Continuing with the same example as in Exhibit 11 (a required return of −8.45% with 95% confidence), the maximum expected return allowable is 8% for the hypothetical efficient frontier. If the required probability is reduced to 90%,
the straight line will have a slope of only 1.282, and a portfolio with an
expected return of 11.43% is allowable. If the probability is increased
to 97.5%, the straight line will have a slope of 1.96, and none of the
portfolios on the efficient frontier will be able to achieve the return of
−8.45% with the required 97.5% confidence.

EXHIBIT 13:
THE EFFECT OF CHANGING THE REQUIRED PROBABILITY

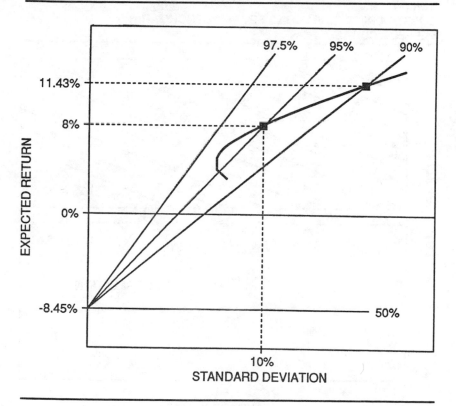

CONSTRAINT RELATIVE TO BENCHMARK PORTFOLIO

The concept of a confidence limit can also be used to examine the returns of candidate investment portfolios relative to a benchmark portfolio. The simplest example is a comparison with a riskless benchmark portfolio. This case is equivalent to the situation discussed above, in which portfolios are considered that can provide a given confidence level of exceeding some prescribed minimum return.

In the more general case, the portfolio returns are compared with those of an index or a basket of indexes. The confidence limit might be the probability of surpassing an allowable shortfall from the index. Since the return of the benchmark index is uncertain, the portfolio return corresponding to an allowable shortfall depends on the benchmark return. For example, for an allowable shortfall of 5%, a minimum

EXHIBIT 14:
CONSTRAINING DEVIATIONS FROM A BENCHMARK:
PERFECT CORRELATION

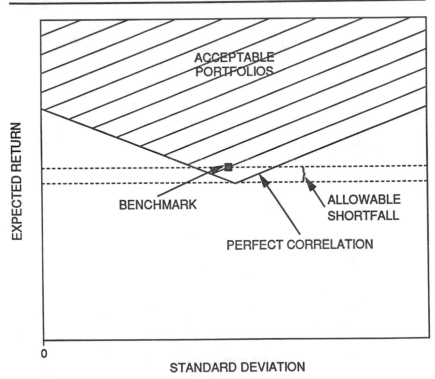

portfolio return of –5% would be required if the actual benchmark return were 0%, whereas a minimum portfolio return of 15% would be required if the benchmark return were 20%.

The expected return required to achieve the shortfall constraint depends on the standard deviation of the portfolio and its correlation with the benchmark (see the Appendix). If the portfolio is perfectly correlated with the benchmark, the required expected return to achieve an allowable shortfall will increase linearly with the difference between the standard deviation of the portfolio and the standard deviation of the benchmark (see Exhibit 14). As the correlation declines, the required expected return for a given standard deviation will increase to compensate for the greater dispersion *between* the portfolio and the benchmark returns (see Exhibit 15).

The importance of the correlation increases with the standard devi-

EXHIBIT 15:
THE ROLE OF CORRELATION IN CONSTRAINING DEVIATIONS

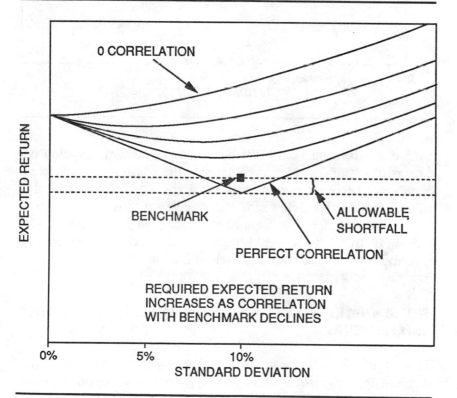

EXHIBIT 16
REDUCING THE VOLATILITY OF THE BENCHMARK

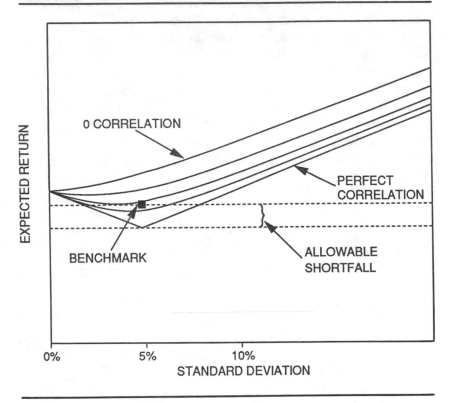

ation of the benchmark. As the benchmark's standard deviation decreases, the "bundle" of curves defining the constraint for different correlations becomes more narrow (see Exhibit 16). For benchmarks whose volatility approaches zero, the "bundle" of constraints collapses into the same straight line for *all* correlation values (see Exhibit 17). This is exactly what one would expect, because a risk-free benchmark is equivalent to the constraint shown in Exhibit 11.

THE SIMILARITY BETWEEN A SHORTFALL CONSTRAINT AND HEDGING

This use of a shortfall constraint is similar to the "arbitrage" strategies followed by many traders who try to exploit a relative mispricing of an

EXHIBIT 17:
CONSTRAINT LINE FOR THE RISKLESS BENCHMARK

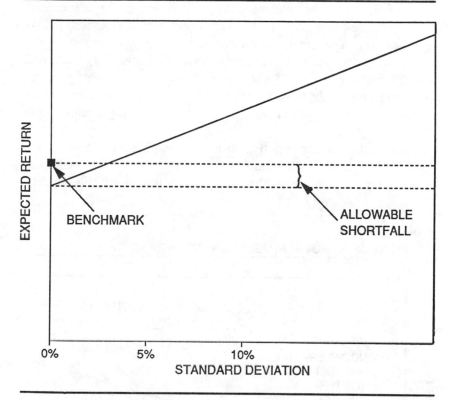

asset (or portfolio of assets) without having to bear all of the asset risk. By taking an offsetting position in similar but fairly priced assets (or in assets mispriced in the opposite direction), an investor can potentially reduce the risk of the position and still capture the targeted incremental return. The effectiveness of the offsetting asset in hedging or reducing the risk of the investor's position depends on its correlation with the mispriced asset. The higher the correlation, the better the hedge and the greater the risk reduction.

The dispersion of the differences in return between a portfolio and the benchmark is a function of their respective standard deviations and the associated correlation. For a given pair of standard deviations, the dispersion of the return deviations will increase as the correlation declines. This means that the probability the portfolio will underperform the benchmark will increase as the correlation decreases. Hence, in order to satisfy a given shortfall constraint, a portfolio having a lower correlation with the benchmark will require a higher expected return in order to overcome the greater dispersion of the differences. The same trade-off must be faced in the evaluation of enhanced indexing strategies. The greater the deviation of the portfolio from the structured characteristics of the index, the more uncertainty there will be in the tracking process. A successful enhancement strategy presumably compensates the investor with a higher expected return. This incremental return helps to reduce the probability of a significant shortfall.

A shortfall constraint relative to a benchmark portfolio acts as a stochastic constraint on the traditional process of optimizing mean and variance. Optimizing the stochastically constrained portfolio requires

EXHIBIT 18:
VIOLATION OF THE BENCHMARK CONSTRAINT

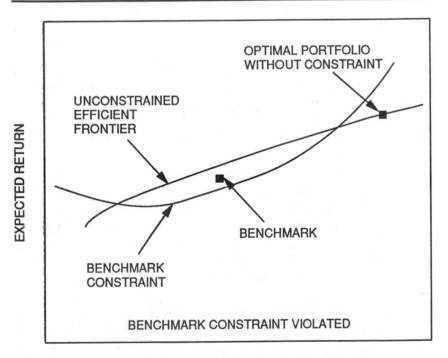

an iterative methodology: the simultaneous examination of the optimization objective and the shortfall constraint.

Whether or not an "optimal" portfolio will satisfy a particular shortfall constraint depends on the relative expected returns, the relative standard deviations and the correlation between the "optimal" portfolio and the benchmark. Exhibit 18 shows a case in which the "optimal" portfolio violates the required shortfall constraint; Exhibit 19 highlights a case in which the constraint is satisfied. (In both cases, the constraint shown is based on an assumed correlation of the unconstrained "optimal" portfolio with the benchmark.) Because the correlation with the benchmark will be different for alternative portfolios on the unconstrained efficient frontier, each portfolio will be subject to a different constraint curve. In general, the shortfall-constrained optimal

EXHIBIT 19:
SATISFYING THE BENCHMARK CONSTRAINT

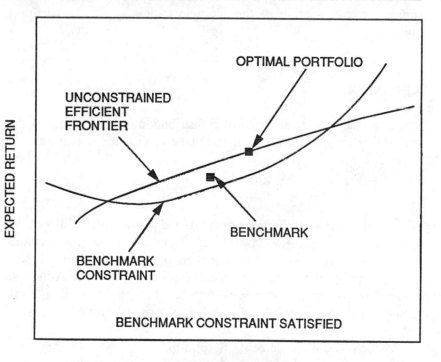

portfolio may lie below the unconstrained efficient frontier.

There are many possible applications of mean/variance optimization in the context of shortfall constraints. For example:

1. An investor may wish to constrain the potential portfolio performance relative to a normal or long-term benchmark.
2. An investor may wish to optimize with respect to his asset/liability surplus, while constraining his portfolio relative to some assets-only benchmark, or vice versa.[1]
3. An investor may wish to constrain the inflation-adjusted performance of the portfolio.

In many cases, such multiple objectives may conflict, which can lead to limited choices for the optimized portfolio or require the shortfall constraint to be quite large.

In all cases, the approach indicated by adopting a shortfall constraint can serve a valuable role in the asset allocation process by allowing for *simultaneous* evaluation of the multiple trade-offs among portfolio objectives.

APPENDIX

The expected return, or mean of a distribution of returns, R_p is the probability weighted average of the range of possible outcomes:

$$(1) \quad E(\tilde{R}p) = \sum_{Rp=-\infty}^{\infty} p_i \, Rp_i = \bar{R}p$$

Where $E(\ )$ is the expectations operator and p_i is the probability of the realized return being Rp_i. As the set of possible outcomes becomes large, the discrete probability distribution used in Equation 1 will approach a continuous distribution and Equation 1 can be rewritten as:

$$(2) \quad E(\tilde{R}p) = \int_{-\infty}^{\infty} \tilde{R}p \, f(\tilde{R}p) \, d\tilde{R}p \quad \text{where the probability p is replaced}$$

by the probability element $f(\tilde{R}p) \, d\tilde{R}p$.

---

[1]See Chapter 9.

The variance of $\tilde{R}_P$ is defined as:

(3) $\sigma_p{}^2 = E\left[(Rp - \bar{R}p)^2\right] = E\left(Rp^2\right) - \bar{R}p^2$

The standard deviation of the distribution of returns will simply be the square root of the variance:

(4) $\sigma_p = \sqrt{\sigma_{p^2}}$

A normal distribution can be completely described by its mean and standard deviation. The normal density function is defined as:

(5) $f(\tilde{R}p) = \dfrac{1}{\sqrt{2\pi}\,\sigma_p} \exp\left[-\dfrac{1}{2}\dfrac{(\tilde{R}p - \bar{R}p)^2}{\sigma_{p^2}}\right]$

and the distribution of cumulative density function is the integral of the density function, specifying the probability of a specified return, Rp^* not being exceeded:

(6) $p(\tilde{R}p < Rp^*) = \displaystyle\int_{-\infty}^{Rp^*} f(\tilde{R}p)\, d\tilde{R}p$

The probability of an outcome being within one standard deviation of the mean will be:

(7) $p\left(\bar{R}p - \sigma_p < \tilde{R}_p < \bar{R}p + \sigma_p\right) = \displaystyle\int_{\bar{R}p - \sigma_p}^{\bar{R}p + \sigma_p} f(\tilde{R}p)\, d\tilde{R}p = 68.26\%$

The probability of an outcome being within two standard deviations of the mean will be:

(8) $p\left(\bar{R}p - 2\sigma_p < \tilde{R}p < \bar{R}p + 2\sigma_p\right) = \displaystyle\int_{\bar{R}p - 2\sigma_p}^{\bar{R}p + 2\sigma_p} f(\tilde{R}p)\, d\tilde{R}p = 95.44\%$

The probability of a return exceeding a specified value, R_P^* will be:

(9) $p(\tilde{R}p > Rp^*) = \displaystyle\int_{Rp^*}^{\infty} f(\tilde{R}p)\, d\tilde{R}p$

The return that will be exceeded with 90% probability will be $\bar{R}_P - 1.282\ \sigma_P$ as:

$$(10) \quad \left(\tilde{R}_P > \bar{R}_P - 1.282\sigma_p\right) = \int_{\bar{R}_P - 1.282\ \sigma_p}^{\infty} f(\tilde{R}_P)\ d\tilde{R}_P = 90\%$$

The return that will be exceeded with 95% probability will be $\bar{R}_P - 1.645\ \sigma_P$ as:

$$(11) \quad \left(\tilde{R}_P > \bar{R}_P - 1.645\sigma_p\right) = \int_{\bar{R}_P - 1.645\ \sigma_p}^{\infty} f(\tilde{R}_P)\ d\tilde{R}_P = 95\%$$

It follows that a portfolio will exceed a minimum return, R_M with 95% probability if:

$$(12) \quad \bar{R}_P - 1.645\sigma_p = R_M$$

Similarly, all $(\bar{R}_P,\ \sigma_P)$ portfolios for which:

$$(13) \quad \bar{R}_P - 1.645\sigma_p \geq R_M$$

will exceed the minimum return with *at least* 95% confidence.

The distribution of the difference between a portfolio return, $\tilde{R}_P$, and a benchmark return, $\tilde{R}_B$, will be defined by the respective expected returns, $\bar{R}_P$ and $\bar{R}_B$, the respective standard deviations, σ_P and σ_B, and the correlation between the two returns, ρ_{PB}.

The expected return of the differences, $\bar{R}_D$, will be:

$$(14) \quad \bar{R}_D = \bar{R}_P - \bar{R}_B$$

The variance of the differences, σ_D^2, is:

$$(15) \quad \sigma_D^2 = \sigma_p^2 + \sigma_B^2 - 2\ \rho_{PB}\sigma_p\sigma_B$$

and the standard deviation, $\hat{\sigma}_D$, will be:

$$(16) \quad \sigma_D = \sqrt{\sigma_D^2}$$

Since σ_P and σ_B must be positive, it follows from (14) and (15) that the standard deviation of the return differences, $\tilde{R}_P - \tilde{R}_B$, will decline as the correlation, ρ_{PB} increases.

The distribution of deviations is simply a transformation of the returns distribution and can be constrained to exceed an allowable shortfall, S, with a prespecified probability. By applying the preceding methodology to the distribution of deviations, it follows that, for example, a 95% confidence level will be achieved by all ($\bar{R}_B, \sigma_P$) portfolios satisfying:

(17) $\quad \bar{R}_D - 1.645 \, \sigma_D \geq S$

or

(18) $\quad \bar{R}_P \geq \bar{R}_B + 1.645 \left[\sigma_{P^2} + \sigma_{B^2} - 2\rho_{PB} \, \sigma_P \sigma_B \right]^{\frac{1}{2}} + S$

SECTION THREE
Tactical Asset Allocation

CHAPTER 14

Tactical Asset Allocation: A Review of Current Techniques

CHARLES H. DuBOIS
VICE PRESIDENT
CITICORP INVESTMENT MANAGEMENT

"Asset Allocation" refers to many decisions these days, but most of these refer to either (a) establishing a longer-term "normal" asset mix consistent with objectives and attitudes toward risk or (b) periodically making changes around the longer-term asset mix to reflect apparent changes in the nearer-term return outlook for the relevant asset classes. This chapter will focus on the latter, today often referred to as tactical asset allocation (TAA).

TACTICAL ASSET ALLOCATION—WHY THE INTEREST?

TAA may be a recent addition to the lexicon of the investment business, but it is, of course, old-fashioned market timing adorned with a presumably more respectable name. In this sense, then, TAA (market timing) has been around for a long time, but it has often been dismissed as being a strategy that may not only be difficult to implement but also is risky with little likelihood of adding consistent value over the long term. However, despite the skepticism that is often expressed as to the potential of "timing" techniques, TAA has been gaining an increasing amount of acceptance in the marketplace. What are the reasons for this new-found respectability?

Importance

Most investors recognize that when a market moves in a particular direction, most of the individual securities comprising that market will move in the same direction. Reasonably diversified portfolios will almost certainly move in the same general direction as the overall market. For example, typically 85–95% of an equity portfolio's variability can be explained by general equity market movements. Only the remaining 5–15% of variability can be explained by differences from the "market" of a portfolio's exposures to common macroeconomic factors or specific industry or company developments. Consequently, the most effective way of meaningfully impacting returns is by changing exposures to the overall markets.

Risk, for most investors, relates to the chances of losing money. Money will be lost most often in a bear market. Since TAA strategies (a) address overall market exposure and (b) typically make very sizable changes in asset exposure levels, they potentially offer a much greater opportunity to reduce down-market risk than do most conventionally managed portfolios.

Lackluster Results of Traditional Management

Conventional "active" investment managers, as a group, continue to underperform the major averages. This result has increased interest in other "active" strategies, such as TAA, that may improve returns. In addition, this uninspiring management record has reduced concerns that TAA strategies may be giving up important returns by being "passive" in other dimensions. That is, while TAA techniques are not necessarily restricted to using "passive" market proxies, most such strategies have taken this route. Such vehicles as index funds, financial futures, and Treasury bonds are the most widely used instruments.

Low Transaction Costs, Available Liquidity

One of the principal historical drawbacks of TAA was the cost of transacting, particularly as asset size increased. Costs included not only commissions and fees but also the marketmaker's spread and market impact (the additional spread that might be necessary to satisfy a larger order). I have estimated that about 25–40% of the historical value-added of the more active TAA strategies could have been lost as a consequence of the transaction costs associated with trading in the traditional stock and bond markets.

Today, however, costs have been reduced in a number of ways. The list includes lower commissions, the use of index funds, and, most significantly, the availability of high volume futures markets for both stocks and bonds. Overall, current transaction costs of TAA implementations appear to be less than a tenth of those that existed, say, 10 years ago. Hence, a significant impediment to the viability of TAA strategies has been largely eliminated for today's TAA managers.

Relatedly, the relatively high liquidity and low transaction costs inherent in most TAA approaches largely eliminate asset size as a deterrent to performance. Many traditional active investment managers, who invest in individual securities, find that with larger size come less flexibility, higher transaction costs, and reduced investment returns. For these reasons, and independent of other considerations, TAA can be a particularly attractive strategy for large multi-billion dollar portfolios. Indeed, for very large ($10 billion and over) portfolios the application of TAA techniques may be the only feasible way of adding significant value over time with an "active" investment strategy.

Credible, Systematic, and "Fact-Based" Techniques

The TAA strategies which have gained the most popularity in the marketplace have been both quantitative and (primarily) "fact-based."[1] A quantitative approach systematically organizes information that can form the basis for decision making. Examples of quantitative procedures used for TAA are asset class comparisons based upon expected return levels, econometrically derived forecasts, or simple composites of several market indicators. A "fact-based" approach is a process that uses only currently available information. In contrast, a "forecast-based" process would be dependent upon a forecast of future developments. An example of a fact-based variable would be the current level

---

[1] I credit George Richvalsky, then with Richvest Management, Inc., with coining the term "fact-based," as opposed to "forecast-based."

of interest rates. An example of a forecast-based variable would be the projected rate of GNP growth.

Today's most popular strategies, being both quantitative and fact-based, simply observe the current status of one or more variables and make decisions accordingly. It's been said, "Forecasting is difficult, particularly when it concerns the future." Since a procedure of objectively observing existing data to make decisions is obviously "easier" than one which requires forecasts and/or subjective judgments, confidence in the process is greatly enhanced.

Of course, it is critical that there be a positive relationship between the status of such indicators and subsequent market performance for such a decision-making framework to add value. On this score, there appears to be both conceptual and empirical support for the types of variables being used for today's fact-based techniques. Subsequent sections of this chapter will be addressing the conceptual and statistical underpinnings of some of these variables.

Quantitative fact-based methodologies also have the advantage of being compatible with the ability to perform historical simulations. In addition, the application of disciplined implementation procedures to determine asset exposure levels is made feasible when systematic techniques are used to determine the outlooks for the financial markets involved. The discussion below elaborates on these two merits of many of today's TAA strategies.

Availability of Historical Simulations

While making investment decisions based upon qualitative assessments of future developments can be effective (it is certainly popular), such a procedure obviously does not lend itself to historical simulation. One way around this problem would be to use a more quantified "forecast-based" technique which specifies the historical relationships between the decision-making variables being considered and actual asset class performance. Indeed, such a forecast-based approach will often demonstrate excellent historical results based upon relationships of market returns to coincident and/or future economic and financial variables. However, in order to add value, an ability to forecast these variables with a reasonable amount of accuracy is necessary. Since the task of forecasting variables such as, say, corporate profits or inflation rates can be nearly as difficult as the primary objective of forecasting stock and bond prices themselves, a forecast-based approach, no matter how innovative, exhaustive, or disciplined, can be subject to serious uncertainty as to future results.

In contrast, quantitative fact-based methodologies have the advantage of not requiring forecasts of economic or financial data. Consequently, historical simulations can be performed with a relatively high degree of credibility since the historical information being used is only that which was available at the time that historical decisions were being made.

Such simulations, covering differing economic and market environments over a significant period of time, can importantly help to establish the historical accuracy and consistency of a particular TAA methodology. These simulations also can play a key role in establishing reasonable expectations for future returns, as well as aiding in evaluating "real-time" experience as it develops. For example, during the inevitable periods of sub-par performance, it would be assuring to demonstrate that the shortfall was well within the bands of an historical experience which, overall, was quite good.

In sum, while there is no substitute for "real-time" results, the availability of the perspective provided by simulated historical results can be an important aid in establishing the credibility of a TAA process.

Disciplined Implementation Procedures

Even if a sufficient degree of satisfaction and comfort is reached with respect to forecasting accuracy (the hard part), there remains the problem of converting forecasts into above-average returns for actual portfolios. Without sufficient rigor in this step, there is a real danger of not fully capturing the predictive ability of the forecasting technique being used. Fortunately, the quantitative nature of most of today's most popular forecasting approaches lends itself to the development of a systematic linkage between readings of a forecasting procedure and actual market exposures. These "rules of the game" usually also cover investment vehicles, "neutral" benchmarks, ranges of exposures, aggressiveness of implementation, frequency of rebalancing, and so on. Relative to a less well-defined process, imposing such discipline increases confidence in a number of ways:

- The speed and efficiency of decision making is greatly enhanced.
- Objectivity is increased. One of the possible drawbacks of traditional market timing is the subtle intrusion of our emotions and

biases which, too often, are unduly influenced by recent market movements or, relatedly, economic or political events which already may be reflected in current market prices.

● Communication between manager and client is improved. For example, the status of and reason for current asset exposures can be easily communicated. Performance attribution can also be reviewed in a straightforward manner.

In short, investment professionals who are attracted to disciplined forecasting techniques will want the same systematic thinking applied to achieving and reporting results. The attractiveness of TAA strategies can be increased if such issues are adequately addressed by those involved in this process.

"Real-Time" Track Records

Last, but not least, have been the encouraging results of those who have used disciplined TAA strategies. The earliest advocates of such techniques have been active for about 15 years, with actual funds in some cases being managed for about a decade. The results have been quite impressive. Other "quantitative" TAA managers apparently also have been quite successful in adding value for their clients. In short, in addition to the historical simulations referred to previously, favorable real-time results over a fairly long period of time have significantly enhanced the reputation of TAA disciplines.

Investment Implications

In sum, the increased interest in TAA appears to be soundly based. As with all investment strategies, there will be difficult periods—TAA forecasting techniques have been and always will be far from perfect. However, even a moderate amount of forecasting ability, properly implemented, can produce returns well above average. Thus, for those willing to commit their time and thought to developing appropriate procedures and realistic objectives, the potential rewards should be well worth the effort.

VALUATION APPROACHES TO TACTICAL ASSET ALLOCATION

Assets should generally be purchased when cheap and sold when expensive—this statement meets with little debate. Most investors would also agree that any useful "valuation" technique should both make sense and possess demonstrable and significant predictive accuracy. However, agreement is not as clear-cut as to which, if any, measures of value best meet these criteria. Consequently, this section will review and analyze the application of specific valuation concepts to forecasting stock and bond returns.

Premium or Spread Technique

The TAA valuation method in widest use today is the "Premium" or "Spread" approach that simply compares expected return proxies for the markets involved and makes decisions accordingly.[2] For example, if the expected return of equities compared to bonds appears to be above average, an above-average allocation to stocks *vis-á-vis* bonds would be indicated by this method. The asset classes used most frequently are equities, long-term bonds and Treasury bills.

The acceptance of this methodology has been in part due to its straightforward rationale. What could be more direct and sensible than to increase or decrease relative exposure to an asset class as the expected relative return increases or decreases? An investor who does so is presumably coolly and systematically taking advantage of the periodic opportunities offered by the emotional swings of the financial markets. In contrast, a less straightforward "market timing" approach probably would not have been accepted as quickly or as broadly as has been the case for the Premium technique.

Derivations The expected returns used for the Premium approach are typically determined as follows:

Equities: Creating an expected return for equities is equivalent to determining the equity market discount rate or cost of equity capital.

---

[2]William Fouse, then with the Wells Fargo Bank, is credited with being the first to derive and use a formal "Premium" approach to Tactical Asset Allocation.

While entire books have been devoted to the determination of the cost of equity, relatively simple approaches can achieve very satisfactory results without sacrificing theoretical appeal. The most popular approaches to calculating an expected equity return fall into the "bottoms-up" and "top-down" categories:

- *"Bottoms-up"*: This return is an average (usually "market-value" weighted) of individual company returns and hence comes from the "bottoms-up."

    The individual company returns are usually determined from a dividend discount model and hence are a function of current stock prices and estimates of future earnings and dividends. Larger investment organizations can obtain such estimates from internal security analysts. Others without such resources can obtain the necessary projections from a number of data sources. I noted in the previous section that most TAA approaches are primarily "fact-based," that is, they do not require estimates or projections of future events. The principal exception is in this case, where the expected return for equities is determined from the bottoms-up.

- *Top-down"*: Individual company analysis can be foregone by using data and assumptions for the overall market and economy to arrive at a "top-down" expected equity return.

    Some top-down approaches simply add an estimate of future earnings or dividend growth to the current dividend yield of the overall market to arrive at an expected return. This technique has strong conceptual appeal since it can be demonstrated that the expected long-run return of the equity market at any point in time is equal to the market's dividend yield plus the future growth rate of earnings or dividends.

    A second popular method is to invert the equity market's price-to-price earnings ratio to create an "earnings yield." While an earnings yield is conceptually equivalent to an expected return only under special circumstances,[3] it has been effectively used as a reasonable proxy for expected return.

---

[3]Through manipulation of the "Gordon-Shapiro" equation, where Price equals Dividends divided by: the Discount Rate (Expected Return) minus the Growth Rate, it can be shown that the Earnings/Price ratio equals Expected Return when Payout Ratios are 100% or, more realistically, when Return on Equity equals the Discount Rate. Manipulation of the same equation also demonstrates that Expected Return equals Dividend Yield plus the Growth Rate, as asserted in the preceding paragraph.

With either of these top-down approaches (yield plus growth or earnings yield), there are a relatively large number of choices available with respect to calculating the more difficult-to-determine variables, i.e., future growth for the former calculation and market earnings for the latter.

Bottoms-up or top-down? The primary advantage of the bottoms-up approach is that it reflects the current expectations of actual people in contact with real companies, as opposed to the more theoretical top-down calculation. Consequently, the proponents of the bottoms-up approach point out that since expectations determine prices, a measure of the actual expectations of market participants should be the preferred method of calculating an expected return.

However, despite the appeal and popularity of the bottoms-up technique, the advantages of the top-down calculation should not be ignored. First, because of the nature of the input requirements of the bottoms-up approach, data are available from the early 1970s, at most. While evaluating such data up to the current time is certainly useful and meaningful, a mechanically derived top-down return can be constructed as far back as desired, thus providing additional insights with respect to the effectiveness of an approach. In addition, a top-down approach can be performed by one person. And if that person is unavailable, another can perform the same calculation. In contrast, the bottoms-up approach may require greater resources with less continuity. Finally, it can be argued that the top-down technique, being "fact-based" rather than "forecast-based," may be less biased and more consistent over time. For example, security analysts appear to show a substantial lag, often measured in years, in revising their nominal growth rates for changes in secular inflation expectations.

In any case, it is my opinion that, regardless of the approach used to generate an expected equity return, the results have and will differ somewhat over the short run, but be broadly similar over the long run. The latter assumption is dependent on any bias in a particular calculation being either persistent or random and not being systematically related to economic or market cycles in a counterproductive way. For most methods used to calculate the expected equity market return, this assumption appears to be valid.

Bonds: In contrast to the many variations to constructing an expected equity return, the proxy for an expected bond return is usually the yield-to-maturity of a current coupon bond. Typically, an issue with a long maturity is used, with Treasury bonds often preferred.

The current yield-to-maturity of a bond can differ significantly from the return actually realized, even if held to maturity, because of reinvestment of the coupon income at interest rates that differ from current levels. Nevertheless, the implicit assumption that reinvestment yields will be equal to current yields appears to be a reasonable and practical assumption with respect to expectations at a point in time.

Cash: The "cash" return is the return available from fixed-income securities with relatively short maturities, usually 3-12 months. 3-month Treasury bill yields are typically used to represent cash returns because of their short maturities, "risk-free" credit status, and historical data availability. In actual practice, short-term funds may be invested in private credit market instruments that carry higher yields than Treasury bills. However, the historical studies reviewed in this chapter will use 3-month Treasury bills and, consequently, will refer to "cash" as "bills."

Historical Analysis—Definitions: The previous section indicated a number of choices available for deriving expected returns. Therefore, before presenting the past record of the Premium approach, I will first specify the definitions of the expected returns used for the analyses to be presented in this chapter:

Equities: Because it is conceptually equal to expected return and possesses an empirical record as good or better than other choices, the yield plus growth approach is used to determine the expected equity return. This expected return is the sum of the current annualized yield of the S&P 500 plus the expected annual growth rate of earnings or dividends. The expected nominal growth rate, in turn, is the sum of inflation expectations and real growth expectations.

Inflation expectations are defined as an annualized 20-quarter exponentially weighted moving average of the GNP implicit price deflator, with an adjustment factor for the recent trend in wholesale prices. An exponential moving average is simply a fancy way of expressing the fact that more recent observations are weighted more heavily than more distant observations in the calculation. The adjustment for the trend in the more sensitive wholesale price index attempts to correct for the tendency of the reported GNP deflator to lag changes in inflation expectations. The overall result is a mechanically derived number that, in my experience, does an excellent job of tracking the survey-based measures of longer-term "embedded" or secular inflation rates.

As suggested by Estep and Hanson,[4] real growth expectations are assumed to be somewhat below the average assumption when inflation expectations are high, and somewhat above average when inflation expectations are low. The average expectation for real growth is assumed to be 2.8% annually.

Bonds: The expected return for bonds is defined as the current yield-to-maturity of a 20-year current coupon Treasury bond.

Bills: The expected return for T-bills is equal to the bond-equivalent yield of a 3-month Treasury bill.

Thus, the "Premiums" used to determine relative asset class attractiveness are:

- *Stock/Bills Premium*—Expected return for equities minus expected return for Treasury bills.
- *Bonds/Bills Premium*—Expected return for bonds minus expected return for Treasury bills.
- *Stocks/Bonds Premium*—Expected return for equities minus expected return for bonds.

Results—Stocks/Bills Premium Exhibit 1 shows the historical results of the Stocks/Bills Premium, as defined above, for forecasting subsequent returns of stocks versus bills. The first column shows historical ranges of the Stocks/Bills Premium. The next indicates the number of month-end observations that have occurred within the specified ranges over the 1951–85 period. Shown in the next 3 columns are the average actually realized equity returns (versus bills) for each Premium range. Results are shown for the subsequent 1-, 3-, and 12-month periods. The final 3 columns indicate the percentage of observa-

---

[4]Tony Estep and Nick Hanson, "The Valuation of Financial Assets in Inflation," in Frank J. Fabozzi (editor), *Selected Topics in Investment Management* (Cambridge, MA: Ballinger Publishing, 1988).

EXHIBIT 1:
STOCKS/BILLS PREMIUM* AND SUBSEQUENT PERFORMANCE
STOCKS VS. BILLS 1951-1985

Premium Range	#Mo. Obs.	Avg. Subsequent Excess Return			Probability of Positive Excess Return		
		1 mo.	3 mo.	12 mo.	1 mo.	3 mo.	12 mo.
>10	10	2.5%	6.8%	26.1%	80%	80%	100%
8-9.9	64	1.9	4.8	16.7	66	78	89
6-7.9	102	0.5	2.0	6.1	57	63	63
5-5.9	62	0.7	1.3	4.6	61	69	66
4-4.9	91	0.1	1.0	2.8	57	59	64
2-3.9	74	(0.2)	(1.1)	0.9	42	36	55
<2	16	(1.9)	(3.6)	(8.6)	31	19	38
	420	0.5	1.4	5.7	56	60	66

*Long-term expected equity return minus 3-month T-bill yield.

tions within each range that were followed by positive excess returns for the 1-, 3-, and 12-month periods.

For example, Exhibit 1 tells us that very high Stocks/Bills Premiums of above 10% have occurred on only 10 occasions over this period, on a monthly basis. Subsequent to these very favorable readings, stocks have returned well above the historical average, subsequently, with the 12-month equity return averaging a handsome 26% over the bill return. Stocks outperformed bills 80% of the time (8 out of 10) for the subsequent 1 month and 3 months while, for the 12-month period, stocks outperformed bills in every case. Following this example, the returns and probabilities of positive returns for other Premium ranges can readily be observed.

Overall, Exhibit 1 demonstrates the quite meaningful differences in future returns that have been associated with different levels of this straightforward measure of equity market attractiveness.

Similar data could be presented for the Bonds/Bills Premium and Stocks/Bonds Premium. However, to keep the amount of data in this chapter at a reasonable and comprehensible level, I will now discuss the effectiveness of the Premium indicators, as well as other forecasting measures to be subsequently reviewed, with the use of "Information Coefficients." As will be seen, such an approach allows us to summarize a considerable amount of information with relatively little data.

The tradeoff is that detailed information, such as that shown in Exhibit 1, will not be presented. (However, the appendix includes graphs of the key measures covered in this chapter versus the relevant market indexes. Historical perspective can be obtained from these.)

Information Coefficients What matters, of course, are the subsequent returns associated with various levels of a forecasting variable. However, this chapter will evaluate the predictive accuracy of forecasting techniques reviewed by showing the "Information Coefficients" or "ICs" between a forecasting variable and subsequent returns.[5]

The IC is simply a correlation coefficient between forecasts and outcomes. If there were a perfect relationship between an indicator reading and subsequent returns, the IC would be 1.00. An IC of -1.00 would be perfectly terrible (of course, such a perverse relationship, and negative ICs in general, could be made useful by inverting the forecasting variable, assuming a solid rationale existed for doing so). An IC of 0.00 or in the vicinity of 0.00 would be consistent with the efficient market or random walk theories; that is, no significant relationship between forecasts and actual subsequent returns exists.

ICs have a number of merits. First, as noted, they summarize with one number a considerable amount of information, thereby vastly simplifying analysis and the presentation of results. Second, ICs provide perspective on the degree of forecasting power that a technique possesses on a linear scale of 0 (no forecasting power) to 1 (perfect forecasting power). This insight is often not addressed with return analyses. Third, if the ICs of two or more forecasting approaches are known, along with their correlations to each other, it is a relatively easy matter to calculate how well the approaches should work in combination. Without this ability, determining the value of combining techniques would be a particularly thorny problem. Finally, ICs also lend themselves to tests of statistical significance. The "luck or skill" question can therefore be addressed.

Concerning statistical significance, Exhibit 2 provides a reference to establish the significance of the ICs to be reviewed in this chapter. Presenting this exhibit is preferable to constantly indicating the signifi-

---

[5]Keith Ambachtsheer, then with Canavest House, Ltd., had much to do with popularizing the "IC" concept. He has written a number of articles on the subject; for example, see: "Where Are the Customers' Alphas?" *Journal of Portfolio Management* (Fall 1977), pp. 52-56.

EXHIBIT 2:
IC LEVEL NECESSARY FOR SIGNIFICANCE LEVEL OF AT LEAST:

Period Covered in Analysis	90%	95%	99%	99.9%	99.99%
1951–65	.10	.13	.17	.23	.27
1966–85	.09	.11	.15	.20	.23
1951–85	.07	.08	.12	.15	.18

cance level of all of the ICs to be reported. The data are based upon the standard Student's t Distribution.

For example, it will be seen in Exhibit 4 that the 1-month IC of the Stocks/Bills Premium is .21 for the 1951-85 period. This IC, therefore, is significant at the 99.99% level, since .21 is above .18.

Although the exhibits containing IC data in this chapter show ICs of a forecasting technique generally increasing over time, the 1-month ICs actually have the most relevance. This is because active TAA strategies recognize that the long term is a series of short terms. Consequently, for today's TAA strategies that quickly respond to changing conditions (by rebalancing, say, monthly), shorter-term predictive accuracy is, in effect, being compounded over time to achieve optimal long-term results. For example, it can be demonstrated that a TAA process that rebalances monthly and possesses a 1-month IC of .20 will generally achieve a return equivalent to a process that once a year capitalizes on a forecasting technique that has a 1-year IC of .68.[6] For these reasons, most of the subsequent evaluation of predictive accuracy will focus specifically on the 1-month results.

The 3-month and 12-month results still play an important role in the evaluation of TAA strategies, and therefore are included in many of the initial exhibits reviewing predictive accuracy.

The 3-month results would be of most significance to those who

---

[6]Return variability increases approximately with the square root of time, e.g., if 1-month stock market volatility is 4%, then expected annual volatility would be about 14% (4 times $\sqrt{12}$). Consequently, ICs should increase with the square root of time in order to maintain a *constant* degree of value-added, excluding transaction costs. The .68 1-year IC cited in the text is equal to .20 times $\sqrt{12}$.

make TAA decisions on approximately a quarterly basis. This may be a reasonable assumption for many investment committees.

Longer-term results, such as over 12 months (or longer), are also useful for two reasons. First, a technique that was effective over 1 month or 3 months but not over 12 months would probably necessitate large and frequent changes in asset exposure levels that not only could unsettle clients and managers but also, through higher transaction costs, reduce returns. Second, most of the methodologies being used for TAA, such as the various "valuation" techniques, are considered longer-term approaches to forecasting the financial markets. Therefore, relatively high ICs over longer time horizons validate the conceptual underpinnings of these forecasting methods.

It was noted previously that what counts are returns. One way of demonstrating the relationship between ICs and returns is shown in Exhibit 3. Exhibit 3 indicates that for a 1-month IC level of .10, the annualized added return that can be expected for particular percentile

EXHIBIT 3:
RELATING ICs TO RETURNS

Status of Current Forecast within Historical Range of Observations	1-Month IC of .10 Theoretical Annualized Expected Return (Relative to Avg. Return)		
Percentile Range	Stocks/Bills	Bonds/Bills	Stocks/Bonds
1– 5%	9.7%	6.1%	10.1%
6– 15	6.2	3.9	6.4
16– 35	3.3	2.1	3.3
36– 65	0.0	0.0	0.0
66– 85	(3.3)	(2.1)	(3.3)
86– 95	(6.2)	(3.9)	(6.4)
96–100	(9.7)	(6.1)	(10.1)
Memo:			
Average Excess Return	5.6	(1.0)	6.6
Standard Deviation	4.0	2.5	4.1

The return standard deviation shown is monthly.
All other return data are annualized.

ranges of a forecasting variable. Since the relationship between added return and the IC level is linear, returns associated with other 1-month IC levels can then be readily determined.

For example, assume that we possess a forecasting technique for stocks versus bills that possesses a 1-month IC of .20. Exhibit 3, which refers to data for an IC of .10, indicates that if such a forecasting variable were currently in the 6th to 15th percentile of its historical range, then stocks, on average, should actually outperform bills by about 12.4% (6.2×2) annually[7] over the historical average return spread during the periods that such a forecast would be in effect.

Exhibit 3 contains comparable information for the remainder of the forecast spectrum for stocks versus bills. Similar information is provided for bonds versus bills and stocks versus bonds. These theoretical returns, then, provide insight into the return significance of ICs reviewed in this chapter. Actually realized returns have, for practical purposes, closely matched these conceptual returns.

Results Exhibit 4 shows ICs for the Stocks/Bills, Bonds/Bills and Stocks/Bonds Premiums versus the comparable excess returns for the subsequent 1, 3 and 12 months.[8] The results are based upon monthly data from 1951 to 1985 (since performance was measured for periods of up to 12 months subsequent to the forecasts, the market returns used extended to the end of 1986). Results are also shown for the 1951-65

---

[7]The derivation of, for example, the 6.2% shown in Exhibit 3 and of the 12.4% referenced in the text was based upon:

  a. An historical (1951/85) standard deviation of 1-month returns for stocks versus bills of 3.97%.

  b. In the normal distribution, the forecast in the 6th to 15th percentiles represent observations which, on average, are 1.3 standard deviations above a mean forecast.

  c. If we were clairvoyant and possessed a 1-month IC of 1.00, our expected monthly excess return, in this example, would be 1.3 standard deviations above the mean return or 3.97 times 1.3 = 5.16%.

  d. However, since the assumed IC of Exhibit 3 is .10, not 1.00, the expected monthly excess return is 5.16% times .1 or 0.52%.

  e. 0.52% can be annualized by multiplying by 12 = 6.2%, the number shown in the exhibit. (We can multiply by 12 because the 0.52% is a logarithmic excess return—see footnote 8).

  f. For an IC of 0.2, the expected relative performance would be twice as large as the result for a 0.1 IC, or 12.4%.

[8]In all of the analyses presented in this chapter, the natural logarithms of relative wealth ratios were used to represent subsequent excess returns, rather than simple arithmetic differences. This procedure properly treats, for example, a relative gain of 100% as having the same economic significance as a relative loss of 50%.

EXHIBIT 4:
PREMIUM APPROACH INFORMATION COEFFICIENTS

1 Mo. Horizon	Stocks/Bills[a]	Bonds/Bills[b]	Stocks/Bonds[c]
1951–65	.16	.00	.09
1966–85	.20	.17	.16
1951–85	.21	.16	.16
3 Mo. Horizon			
1951–65	.28	(.02)	.17
1966–85	.24	.26	.26
1951–85	.30	.24	.27
12 Mo. Horizon			
1951–65	.50	(.06)	.39
1966–85	.22	.43	.42
1951–85	.40	.39	.47

Actual Subsequent 1-Month Return Difference (Annualized)
For Each 1% Difference of Premium Forecast

	Stocks/Bills	Bonds/Bills	Stocks/Bonds
1951–85	4.4%	3.7%	3.8%
Memo:			
Premium-Avg.	5.7	1.0	4.7
Std. Dev.	2.3	1.2	2.1

[a]Expected equity return minus T-bill yield versus excess returns of stocks to bills.
[b]Treasury bond yield minus T-bill yield versus excess returns of bonds to bills.
[c]Expected equity return minus Treasury bond yield versus excess returns of stocks to bonds.

and 1966-85 periods. Beginning in 1966, the U.S. economy and the financial markets have experienced significantly greater volatility than was the case over the generally calm 1951-65 period. Thus, I felt that the mid-sixties represented a useful division of results.

As can be seen, the ICs for the Premium measures have been generally positive—there has been, in fact, a positive correlation between Premium levels and subsequent returns. The 1-month IC's all fall in the same very significant area of .16 to .21, with the exception of the

Bonds/Bills Premium for 1951-65 (zero IC) and the Stocks/Bonds Premium for the same period (.09).

The 3-month and 12-month ICs are, of course, generally even higher. However, since they represent overlapping observations, their statistical significance is somewhat reduced.

An additional insight is gained from data shown at the bottom of Exhibit 4, which presents the average annualized rate of excess return associated with each 1% change in the level of the Premium forecasts. For example, a 1% increase (decrease) between the expected return for stocks and the T-bill yield has resulted in actual subsequent returns of stocks versus bills increasing (decreasing) by 4.4% annualized.[9]

Investment Implications

In sum, the information provided in Exhibit 4 offers strong statistical support for the Premium approach. There have been significant and meaningful historical relationships between straightforward measures of relative market attractiveness and subsequent relative market returns.

"True" Long-Term Value—The Expected Real Return Approach

The Premium approach seems sensible, with proven results. One conceptual criticism, however, has been that the expected return used for both stocks and bonds are long-term expected returns, while the return used for the "cash" alternative, such as the 3-month Treasury bill yield, is for the very short term. This short-term yield does not necessarily, and often clearly does not, represent investor expectations for "cash" returns over a longer time horizon. Hence, in this sense, the Stocks/Bills and Bonds/Bills Premiums may be good measures of current competitive pressures but may not represent comparable long-term expected return differentials. (This is not to say that the Premium approach is not superior—more on that issue later). Therefore, this section will review the construction and forecasting record of "true" long-term value measures for stocks and bonds.

Investors are compensated for the risks they take by being provided

---

[9]This result was determined from a simple regression of Premium levels versus subsequent 1-month excess returns.

with "real" returns, i.e., returns after inflation. Consequently, in theory, the long-term real return being offered by an asset class should be the basis for determining whether or not an asset is attractively priced.

Expected real returns, as was the case for the expected nominal equity return used in the previous section, are not directly observable. Consequently, for the purpose of analysis, I will construct what I would consider to be reasonable estimates of real return expectations.

Definitions:
1. *Expected Equity Real Return*—the expected long-term equity return (identical to the yield plus growth formulation described in the previous section) minus the expected rate of inflation. As noted previously, inflation expectations are defined as an annualized 20-quarter exponentially weighted moving average of the GNP deflator, with an adjustment factor for the recent trend in wholesale prices.
2. *Expected Bond Real Return or Real Bond Yield*—the yield-to-maturity of a current coupon 20-year maturity Treasury bond minus the expected rate of inflation.

In essence, the above comparisons differ from the Premium analysis by comparing expected nominal returns for stocks and bonds to inflation expectations instead of Treasury bills. The results, then, will vary because of differences between estimates of long-term inflation rates and Treasury bill yields.

This section will include no analysis for stocks versus bonds *per se* since a real return comparison for stocks versus bonds is identical to the nominal return comparisons of the previous section.

Results Exhibit 5 is similar to Exhibit 4. Exhibit 5 shows the ICs between the Expected Equity Real Return and the subsequent performance of stocks versus bills and between the Expected Bond Real Return (Real Bond Yield) and the future returns of bonds versus bills. The 1-, 3- and 12-month time horizons are included.

As was the case with the Premium analysis, the results are encouraging. The ICs indicate that both stocks and bonds have offered significantly more rewarding returns when long-term real returns appeared high than when they have appeared low. Each 1% change in the Expected Real Return for equities has, on average, resulted in a 7.4%

EXHIBIT 5:
REAL RETURN APPROACH INFORMATION COEFFICIENTS

1 Mo. Horizon	Stocks/Bills[a]	Bonds/Bills[b]
1951–65	.11	.05
1966–85	.16	.18
1951–85	.15	.14

3 Mo. Horizon		
1951–65	.19	.07
1966–85	.27	.33
1951–85	.25	.26

12 Mo. Horizon		
1951–65	.41	.13
1966–85	.51	.59
1951–85	.48	.48

Actual Subsequent 1-Month Return Difference (Annualized)
For Each 1% Difference of Real Return Forecast

	Stocks/Bills	Bonds/Bills
1951—85	7.4%	2.4%
Memo:		
Real Return-Avg.	7.0	2.2
Std. Dev.	0.9	1.8

[a]Expected equity return minus expected inflation versus excess returns of stocks to bills.
[b]Treasury bond yield minus expected inflation versus excess returns of bonds to bills.

(annualized) change in the performance differential between stocks and bills. For bonds, a less dramatic but still meaningful 2.4% of annualized return of bonds versus bills has been associated with each 1% change in the Real Bond Yield.

The ICs also tell us, however, that stock market excess returns have been somewhat more accurately forecast with the Stocks/Bills Premium indicator over 1 month and 3 months (Exhibit 4 presented the results) than with the Real Expected Equity Return. The Real Expected

Equity Return appears to be more effective for the longer time horizon of 12 months. With respect to forecasting bonds versus bills, the Real Bond Yield appears to possess moderately greater effectiveness than the Bonds/Bills Premium indicator over all the time horizons shown, with the one important exception of the 1-month IC for the 1951-85 period.

The final section of this chapter will attempt to reconcile and utilize the conceptual and empirical differences between the Premium approach to valuation and the Real Return valuation measures.

Traditional Measures of Stock Market Valuation

The majority of the participants in the equity market do not use the types of valuation measures which have been just discussed. Therefore, I will now comment on the relationship of more traditional measures of stock market "value" to the valuation techniques reviewed in this chapter.

The most popular stock market valuation measures are those that relate stock prices to the earnings, dividends or book values underlying these prices. All of these indicators attempt to determine the *absolute* attractiveness of the equity market, not relative attractiveness to, say, fixed-income alternatives. Therefore, these indicators are analogous to the Expected Equity Real Return calculation of the previous section, as they attempt to determine if the return the investor is receiving is commensurate with the normal risks of stock market investing.

The close relationship between the Expected Real Return of the equity market and these traditional valuation measures can be demonstrated statistically:[10]

Expected Equity Real Return
Correlation with:

S&P 500 Earnings to Price Ratio	S&P 500 Dividends to Price Ratio	S&P 400 Book Value to Price Ratio
.79	.95	.86

---

[10]This is based upon monthly data from 1951 to 1985. Earnings are trailing for 12 months. Dividends are based upon current annual rate. Book/Price ratio is for S&P 400, since book values for S&P 500 are not available.

The predictive ability of these traditional indicators can also be quantified and compared to the Real Return measure:

1 Month "ICs"—Stocks vs. Bills

Exp. Equity Real Return	S&P 500 Earnings to Price Ratio	S&P 500 Dividends to Price Ratio	S&P 400 Book Value to Price Ratio
.15	.06	.11	.11

The straightforward conclusions are that the conventional indicators of value are not only highly related to the Expected Real Return indicator but also possess generally significant but somewhat less predictive accuracy than the Real Return methodology. Consequently, it can be demonstrated that these traditional valuation techniques offer no additional predictive accuracy to that already possessed by the Expected Real Return variable. This conclusion also holds true for other variations of these traditional value indicators, such as techniques that relate stock prices to various measures of "economic" earnings, "cash flow," or "replacement cost" book value.

Therefore, the sole measure used in this chapter to determine the absolute attractiveness of the equity market will continue to be the Expected Real Return indicator, for both its conceptual appeal and its empirical validity.

A once widely followed and still popular measure of the *relative* attractiveness of stocks versus *bonds* compares the dividend yield of the equity market to long-term bond yields.

The conceptual problem with this dividend yield/bond yield "spread" is that the bond yield represents a total return while the dividend yield ignores the returns from equity ownership which result from the growth of dividends. This problem becomes very clear during periods of changing long-term inflation expectations. For example, if a 1% increase in the expected inflation rate were to occur, bond yields would increase by 1%, everything else being equal. The expected long-term nominal returns from equity ownership would also increase by about 1%, as the higher expected long-term inflation would result in a higher rate of expected nominal dividend growth. However, the spread between the current dividend yield and current bond yields would widen by 1%, creating a misleading "deterioration" in the relative attractiveness of the equity market. On this score, relative to history, the stock/bond yield spread had been significantly favoring bonds for most of the past 20 years. Thus, this observation is principally a reflection of higher inflation rates relative to history, rather than a fundamental change in the relative appeal of stocks versus bonds.

The expected equity return used for the analyses presented in the chapter resolves this problem by focusing on expectations of *total* return for the equity market. This total return then can be properly compared to a bond yield, resulting in the Stocks/Bonds Return Premium previously analyzed. Empirically, this Stocks/Bonds Return Premium outperforms the dividend yield/bond yield spread for forecasting subsequent stock versus bond performance. The comparative 1-month ICs are .16 versus .12 for the 1951–85 periood. In addition, no improvement in effectiveness is obtained by considering the traditional dividend yield/bond yield spread in combination with the Stocks/Bonds Return Premium.

In short, on both conceptual and empirical grounds, the conventional yield comparison between stocks and bonds can be safely discarded in favor of the types of measures used in this chapter.

Investment Implications

It has been demonstrated that both the Premium and Real Return valuation techniques have demonstrated a signficant level of historical predictive ability. Between the two, the Premium approach has been generally superior for forecasting stocks versus bills. Except for the one important exception cited, the Real Return technique has performed moderately better for forecasting bonds versus bills.

Traditional measures of stock market valuation offer no additional information to that which can be obtained by using the Premium and Real Return valuation measures.

In the next section, cyclical factors which can play an important role in TAA strategies will be reviewed. In the final section, the relationship between and combinations of valuation and cyclical factors will be analyzed as to their implications for TAA techniques.

CYCLICAL CONSIDERATIONS FOR TACTICAL ASSET ALLOCATION

Investment practitioners have long recognized that the cycles in stock and bond prices often are not only closely linked, but also are tied, in important ways, to the cyclical behavior of overall economic activity and the associated responses taken by the nation's fiscal and monetary policymakers. "The stock market leads the economy by six months," is one maxim. "The Federal Reserve writes the market letter for Wall Street," is another. Consequently, while previous sections discussed and evaluated concepts of value as they related to stock and bond performance, this section will review variables related to the cyclical forces which importantly and regularly impact stock and bond prices.

Historical Perspective

As an introduction, Exhibits 6 and 7 demonstrate the cyclical relationships between interest rates, stock prices and economic activity over the past 35 years. Exhibit 6 documents the dates of the troughs and peaks. Exhibit 7 shows the leads (in some cases, lags) of the sequential cyclical events of Exhibit 6.

As generally recognized, the cyclical swings of stock prices typically lead major changes in the level of economic activity. Exhibit 7, column 1 indicates that the stock market bottoms have led the trough in economic activity in every case, with the average lead being about 5 months. Column 4 shows that the stock market's lead at economic peaks has been somewhat longer, averaging about 9 months.

Columns 2 and 5 indicate that the troughs and peaks in the economy have been closely associated with troughs and peaks in interest rates, with interest rates, on average, modestly lagging the concomitant swings in economic activity.

Continuing through the cycle, columns 3 and 6 demonstrate that interest rates have always led (with the exception of one tie) the opposite turn of the stock market. That is, rising interest rates have preceded stock market peaks while interest rates have usually been falling prior to stock market bottoms. It is important to note that a relatively long period of rising interest rates, averaging about 24 months, has elapsed before stock prices have finally peaked. In contrast, the stock market

EXHIBIT 6:
STOCK MARKET, ECONOMIC ACTIVITY, INTEREST RATES—CYCLICAL TROUGHS AND PEAKS 1952–1986

(1) Stock Market Trough	(2) Economy Trough	(3) Interest Rate Trough	(4) Stock Market Peak	(5) Economy Peak	(6) Interest Rate Peak
9–53	5–54	8–54	4–56	8–57	10–57
12–57	4–58	4–58	8–59	4–60	1–60
10–60	2–61	5–61	1–66	9–66	9–66
10–66	3–67	1–67	12–68	12–69	5–70
5–70	11–70	3–71	1–73	11–73	8–74
10–74	3–75	12–76	2–80	1–80	2–80
3–80	7–80	6–80	11–80	7–81	10–81
8–82	11–82	11–82	10–83	6–84	5–84

1. Stock market peaks and troughs are based upon weekly average prices of the S&P 500.
2. Economic peaks and troughs are based upon the official designations of the National Bureau of Economic Research, with two exceptions—see note 4.
3. Interest rate peaks and troughs are based upon weekly average yields of 20-year Treasury Bonds.
4. The economic slowdown from 9-66 to 3-67 and the slowdown which began in 6-84 have not been officially classified as recessions. However, they were both accompanied by the usual cyclical responses of the financial markets. The dates used for the economic peaks and troughs are my own.
5. The major stock market peak of December 1961 has not been included as it was not primarily caused by cyclical factors, i.e., significant increases in interest rates did not occur nor did the stock market decline from 12/61 to 6/62 accompany or precede an economic recession or significant slowdown. (The market decline was apparently caused by a combination of overvaluation and supply/demand imbalances related to high levels of investor optimism and speculation in 1961.)

EXHIBIT 7:
LEADS (LAGS) OF SEQUENTIAL EVENTS OF TABLE 4

(Months)

Exhibit 6 columns	(1)	(2)	(3)	(4)	(5)	(6)	(7)	(8)
	(1)—(2)	(2)—(3)	(3)—(4)	(4)—(5)	(5)—(6)	(6)—(1)	(1)—(3)	(4)—(6)
Cycle(a)	S.M. Trough to Ec Trough	Ec. Trough to I.R. Trough	I.R. Trough to S.M. Peak	S.M. Peak to Ec. Peak	Ec. Peak to I.R. Peak	I.R. Peak to S.M. Trough	S.M. Trough to I.R. Trough	S.M. Peak to I.R. Peak
9/53-12/57	8	3	20	16	2	2	11	18
12/57-10/60	4	0	16	8	(3)	9	4	5
10/60-10/66	4	3	56	8	0	1	7	8
10/66- 5/70	5	(2)	23	12	5	0	3	17
5/70-10/74	6	4	22	10	9	2	10	19
10/74- 3/80	5	21	38	(1)	1	1	26	0
3/80- 8/82	4	(1)	5	8	3	10	3	11
8/82- 7/84	3	0	11	8	(1)	2	3	7
Mean	4.9	3.5	23.9	8.6	2.0	3.4	8.4	10.6
Median	4.5	1.5	21.0	8.0	1.8	2.0	5.5	9.5
Std. Dev.	1.6	7.4	16.2	4.8	4.0	7.0	7.8	6.9

(a) Stock market trough to trough.

has usually turned up quite quickly after interest rates have begun to fall, with the average lead being about 3 months.

Finally, columns 7 and 8 have been added to show the lead of the stock market relative to interest rates. Column 7 is simply the sum of columns 1 and 2 while column 8 is the sum of columns 4 and 5. With the exception of one tie, the troughs and peaks of the stock market have always led, over this period, the troughs and peaks of the interest rate cycle.

A large number of other relationships and observations can be derived from Exhibit 7. For example, adding columns 2, 3 and 4 (36 months) and columns 5, 6 and 1 (10 months) results in the average length of economic expansions and contractions, respectively, over this period. Or, in each of the 8 cycles, stocks spent more time rising when interest rates were in a cyclical upswing (column 3) than when interest rates were falling (column 7)! Probably of most relevance to stock and bond market strategists are columns 3, 6, 7 and 8, which suggest that observing one market may provide some insight with respect to the outlook for the other. More on this later.

These relationships, of course, are not new. As long ago as 1913, Wesley Mitchell documented such standard cyclical patterns.[11] Since then, an enormous amount of business cycle research has been accomplished, much of it under the auspices of the National Bureau of Economic Research. The purpose of Exhibits 6 and 7 is not to provide any new insights but to reaffirm and update the basic relationships, especially those concerning the financial markets, as they have existed over the recent past.

Causes and Effects

Why are these cyclical relationships and patterns observed?

Let's start with the situation when the economy begins to recover from its recession lows (column 2 of Exhibit 6). The stock market, having anticipated the turn in economic activity, is already up substantially from its cyclical bottom. Interest rates are low and liquidity is abundant, reflecting relatively low credit demands, price pressures which are still easing, and a Federal Reserve which is pursuing an expansionary monetary policy. Some of this excess liquidity finds its

---

[11]Wesley C. Mitchell, *Business Cycles* (University of California-Berkeley Press, 1913).

way into financial assets, thus providing one important reason why bonds are still performing reasonably well while the stock market is continuing to move ahead briskly.

As the recovery continues, however, and slack in the economic and financial system is reduced, some upward pressures on interest rates will occur. The increase in the price of money occurs as a consequence of increased credit demands, moderately higher inflation expectations or, typically, a combination of the two.

This initial increase in interest rates is not necessarily negative for stock prices. It is, as noted, simply the monetary response to stronger economic activity and associated improvements in pricing flexibility which, in turn, will improve corporate profitability. In addition, concerns about the economy have not yet completely disappeared and the Federal Reserve, while not as generous as earlier, is providing sufficient liquidity to sustain economic growth. Hence, stock prices continue to move forward, although the rate of gain is not as strong as that which occurred when interest rates were falling; versus bonds, which are falling in price, relative equity returns are particularly favorable at this stage of the cycle.

As the economic expansion continues, however, demands for credit will become more vigorous, reflecting the inventory and investment needs created by the stronger levels of economic activity, reduced availability of resources, and generally more optimistic assessments of the future. In addition, upward pressures on prices may increase to more worrisome levels. Consequently, the cyclical rise in interest rates becomes more pronounced. At about this time, with inflationary pressures replacing economic growth as its principal concern, the Federal Reserve will attempt to cool the economy by adopting a policy of monetary restraint that, over the short-term, will only accentuate the increase in interest rates.

It is during this latter phase of the economic expansion that the environment becomes hostile for stock prices. The increases in interest rates and related phenomena which occur at this stage are negative for stock prices for a number of reasons.

First, the strong economy, in combination with a more restrictive monetary policy, has eliminated any excess liquidity which helped boost the equity market earlier in the cycle. Hence, a key support to stock prices has been removed from the scene.

Second, with increases in the costs of labor, materials and money being combined with the lower productivity increases inherent to the latter stage of an economic expansion, unit labor costs are moving up significantly and typically cannot be completely offset by price increases. Sales growth is also slowing not only as a result of physical contraints but also because of the overall economy, which the authorities are slowing down. The combination of reduced profit margins with less ebullient sales causes corporate profits to level off, if not to decline—a negative for stocks.

Third, future business investment in plant and equipment will be reduced by the higher interest rates, as well as by the associated reduction in profitability. Since business investment is the cornerstone of future corporate earnings, this development is also a negative for the stock market.

Fourth, and perhaps of most importance, the combination of reduced investments of many types (plant, equipment, inventories, construction, consumer durables, etc.), a maturing economic expansion, and monetary restraint will typically cause the imbalances that lead to an overall economic slowdown, and, in most cases, an outright recession. Such a development will obviously have a harsh impact on both corporate profits and stock prices.

Fifth, and moving closer to the markets themselves, the increase in interest rates will reduce the competitive position of the equity market and therefore significantly reduce the demand for stocks. At the same time, carrying costs are increasing for those who have purchased equities with borrowed funds, such as the millions of investors with debit balances in their "margin" accounts.

Finally, if the market does not materially decline, at least for a while, the increase in interest rates will increase the relative value of stocks *vis-á-vis* bonds in investors' portfolios, thereby reducing any need to increase equity exposure or creating a reason to reduce equity exposure. The increase in interest rates will also decrease the present value of pension fund liabilities, everything else being equal, thereby reducing funding needs. Since pension fund flows typically have an important impact on the market's supply and demand equation, any reduction in these flows will lower the demand for equities.

For some or all of these reasons, stock prices, which often will have been trading more narrowly and erratically for several months, will peak. Economic activity will still be strong and the expectations of businessmen and a number of economists may still be rosy. Nevertheless, the seeds of an economic slowdown have been planted, and stock prices will begin to decline.

When business activity does begin to slow, interest rates sometimes will begin to fall coincidentally. However, if inflation pressures persist or a stringent monetary policy remains in place during the early stages of the economic decline, interest rates will peak somewhat after the peak in economic activity. The stock market, worried about the now clear decline in the economy, is still falling and bonds are outperforming stocks.

As the decline in output continues, however, the flip-side of the phenomena which occur at the latter stages of an economic upswing will begin to exert a positive influence on the prospects for the economy. In addition, the normal secular forces of growth will importantly aid in arresting the downswing in economic activity. Consequently, the stock market, beginning to see the light at the end of the tunnel, stops going down. A move by the Federal Reserve to aggressively promote economic growth will, at this point, send stock prices soaring. As the economy subsequently recovers, the cycle begins anew.

The above brief review of the classical description of the business cycle and the related behavior of the financial markets is, of course, a simplification, in that:

1. On a micro scale, the experiences of specific industries will differ importantly from cycle to cycle.
2. On a macro basis, the characteristics of each cycle can be significantly affected by specific events peculiar to that cycle, such as wars, financial crises, unusual monetary or fiscal policy actions.
3. Secular forces can create a more permanent change to the nature of the cycle. For example, income stabilization policies that had begun to exert their full force by the 1950s have considerably reduced the amplitude of the cyclical fluctuations of consumer income and related variables, as compared with earlier cycles. More recently, the cyclical behavior of the economy has become increasingly influenced by the "globalization" of economic forces and the sharper focus of policymakers on such forces.

For these and other reasons, the leads and lags among various economic and financial market turning points, as observed in Exhibit 7, are quite variable and, on some occasions, have not existed. Nevertheless, the regularity of the ebbs and flows of the business and financial market cycles continues to be generally operative, as Exhibit 7 clearly demonstrates.

Practical Implications

While such information is of obvious interest to students of cyclical behavior, is it useful to the investment practitioner looking for insights into where the financial markets may be headed?

In one sense, no. That is, the leads and lags documented in Exhibit 7 are, as just noted, variable and can be quite long. In addition, the peaks and troughs are observable only well after the fact. Consequently, an understanding of normal cyclical behavior doesn't assure an ability to forecast market behavior on a current basis.

However, a recognition of the normal cycle is essential to providing perspective to the daily diet of market and economic information that the investor attempts to digest. And an appreciation for typical cyclical behavior can be particularly useful from time to time. For instance, if the blanks of the following paragraph are filled with the respective words listed below the paragraph, then the market strategist usually has valuable information at the times that the specific situation exists:

If _____ have been _____ meaningfully and _____ have not yet begun to significantly _____, then it is unlikely that _____ have yet _____.

  a. stock prices, falling, interest rates, fall, stock prices, bottomed
  b. interest rates, falling, stock prices, rise, interest rates, bottomed
  c. stock prices, rising, interest rates, rise, stock prices, peaked
  d. interest rates, rising, stock prices, fall, interest rates, peaked

For example, to cite some recent history, during 1985, 1986 and early 1987, condition *c.* above existed. Stock prices were rising while interest rates were either falling or leveling off. A pronounced cyclical increase in interest rates did not occur. Therefore it was unlikely, from a cyclical perspective, that stock prices had peaked. For market analysts who fretted about the equity market for a number of reasons over this period, this simple observation provided useful information which might have improved results. As of this writing (Summer 1987), condition *d.* exists. Interest rates have increased significantly from their lows. However, with stock prices still reaching new peaks, the peak in interest rates should still be ahead of us.

Of most importance, an understanding of cyclical forces leads to the recognition that interest rates and related phenomena are importantly related to changes in the economy and the financial markets, either because of direct causality or because of their relationship with other factors which are causal. The observed historical leads and lags, *per se*, are not critical, assuming that differences in lead/lag relationships among cycles can be explained by differences among the causal variables. What is relevant to the market forecaster is the strength of the relationship between such "causal" variables and future market behavior. An analysis which addresses this need follows.

Composite Cyclical Indexes

It is well known, and supported by Exhibit 7, that movements in stock prices usually precede changes in economic activity. Therefore, in order to forecast changes in stock prices, it will do us little good to observe what is occurring with respect to current economic activity. Rather, in order to forecast stock prices, we must study events which precede turning points in the economy with a longer lead time than do stock prices themselves.

The previous discussion indicated that measures of liquidity, interest rates, Federal Reserve policy, and so on, play such an important leading role with respect to stock prices. Therefore, I have created a Cyclical Equity Index that combines measures of these types of variables—4 indicators in all.

In contrast, bond prices respond quickly and, in some cases, almost definitively to changes in various pressures in the economic and financial system (with stock prices, as noted, being affected later). Consequently, I have integrated proxies for current economic, financial, and inflation pressures, and a measure of the prospective change in these pressures, to create a Cyclical Bond Index.

Exhibit 8 shows the results of using these composite indexes to forecast subsequent returns. The format is similar to that used for the "value" measures in the previous section, as the 1-, 3-, and 12-month "ICs" are shown for forecasting stocks versus bills, bonds versus bills, and stocks versus bonds.

EXHIBIT 8:
CYCLICAL APPROACH INFORMATION COEFFICIENTS

	Cyclical Equity Index[1]	Cyclical Bond Index[2]	Equity Index Minus Bond Index[3]
1 Mo. Horizon			
1951–65	.25	.21	.23
1966–85	.28	.22	.24
1951–85	.29	.21	.25
3 Mo. Horizon			
1951–65	.41	.35	.38
1966–85	.39	.31	.29
1951–85	.42	.30	.34
12 Mo. Horizon			
1951–65	.54	.33	.45
1966–85	.38	.53	.19
1951–85	.46	.46	.32

[1]Cyclical Equity Index versus excess returns of stocks to bills.
[2]Cyclical Bond Index versus excess returns of bonds to bills.
[3]Cyclical Equity Index minus Cyclical Bond Index versus excess returns of stocks to bonds.

Generally speaking, the predictive ability of the Cyclical Indexes is higher than that of the "valuation" approaches discussed in the prior section. The key 1-month ICs for the Cyclical Indexes are higher in every case than the 1-month ICs for either the Premium or Real Return measure. While the approximate translation of ICs to returns was previously discussed, I will nevertheless, as a reminder, note that when, for example, the Cyclical Equity Index was quite positive (top 10% of all observation) stocks subsequently outperformed bills by 27% annualized, while when the Cyclical Equity Index was negative (bottom 10%), stocks subsequently underperformed bills by 24% annualized.

It is also worth recalling that these results were based upon information known at the time when the Cyclical Indexes were constructed. No forecasts were being made. The Cyclical Indexes were merely observing the "facts" as they existed at a point in time. However, as was discussed earlier, knowing what has occurred in the recent past can often provide considerable information with respect to what may occur in the future.

Investment Implications

In sum, the rationales and results presented in this section strongly indicate that measures of cyclical conditions should be considered for use in TAA strategies.

COMBINING VALUATION AND CYCLICAL INDICATORS

Previous discussion has evaluated the rationales and records of both valuation and cyclical variables for their potential to add value to TAA strategies. I will now review the relationships between these 2 classes of variables and the resulting implications for TAA techniques.

Exhibits 9, 10 and 11 first summarize the key results. Shown for the periods of interest are the 1-month ICs for the Premium, Real Return and Cyclical measures discussed in preceding sections. Exhibits 9 through 11 cover this information for forecasting stocks versus bills, bonds versus bills, and stocks versus bonds, respectively.

The information provided by Exhibit 9 indicates that each of the 3 individual approaches has been significantly related to the subsequent returns of stocks versus bills. As was noted previously in this chapter, the Cyclical Indexes have been the most effective predictors of future return. Over the 1951-85 period, the stocks versus bills forecasting accuracy of the Cyclical Index has been approximately 40% greater than that of the Premium indicator. The Premium technique, in turn, has demonstrated 40% higher predictive capability than has the Expected Real Return methodology.

It might be expected that the "value" indicators provide a view of the market outlook that is usefully separate from the message of the cyclical variables. If this were true, the use of the two techniques in combination would provide better results than those obtained by using the cyclical indicators alone.

I will first consider the Premium methodology in this combination context for stocks versus bills. Exhibit 9 shows that the combination of the Cyclical Equity Index and the Premium indicator does not add

EXHIBIT 9:
STOCKS VERSUS BILLS SUMMARY

Forecasting Excess Returns—Stocks vs. Bills

	1-Month ICs		
Technique	1951–85	1951–65	1966–85
Premium-Exp. Equity Return minus T-bill Yield	.21	.16	.20
Real Return—Exp. Equity Return minus Inflation	.15	.11	.16
Cyclical Equity Index	.29	.25	.28
Combinations			
Premium, Real Return	.22	.17	.26
Premium, Cyclical	.29	.26	.29
Real Return, Cyclical	.32	.26	.33

Correlations Between Techniques

	1951–85	1951/65	1966/85
Premium, Real Return	.50	.92	(.01)
Premium, Cyclical	.56	.27	.54
Real Return, Cyclical	.08	.11	(.02)

materially, if at all, to the results of the cyclical indicators alone. The primary reason for this result can be found among the correlations shown at the bottom of the exhibit. That is, the Premium indicator has a positive .56 correlation with the Cyclical Index. Therefore, its ability to add value to the cyclical approach is quite limited.

Now the Premium indicator for stock versus bills is equal to the expected equity return minus the current T-bill yield. T-bill yields are, of course, very sensitive to the cyclical forces which impact interest rates. Hence, the movements of T-bill yields are related to movements of the Cyclical Equity Index. This perhaps obvious observation is, then, the cause of the positive correlation between the Premium indicator and the Cyclical Equity Index.

It was noted earlier in this chapter that one criticism of the Premium technique was that it combined a measure of long-term expectations (in this case the expected equity return) with a cyclical short-term return (the T-bill yield) and, consequently, was not a measure of "true" long-term value. It can now be seen that this "shortcoming" can be, in fact, a virtue, since changes in the T-bill yield act as a (perhaps suboptimal) useful proxy for the cyclical factors which importantly impact equity market performance. On the other hand, because of this cyclical sensitivity, the Premium measure does not appear to add material value to cyclical factors and therefore would appear to be of little interest to those *directly* addressing cyclical conditions with indicators such as used in the Cyclical Equity Index.

The Expected Equity Real Return indicator, in contrast, possesses lower predictive content than the Premium indicator, but being a more valid measure of "true" long-term value, is relatively uncorrelated with cyclical indicators of the equity market. Because of this lack of correlation, combining the Real Return measure with the Cyclical Equity Index results in about a 10% increase in effectiveness (combined IC of .32 versus .29 for Cyclical alone). Therefore, in this context, the notion that valuation and cyclical variables should be combined appears to make sense.

Exhibit 10 addresses bonds versus bills. Here the same conclusions that were just reached for stocks versus bills can also be made, and for the same reasons. That is, the Cyclical Bond Index has been the most useful for forecasting bonds versus bills (for the 1951–85 period), followed by the Premium measure and then the Real Return indicator. However, the Premium indicator is relatively highly correlated with the Cyclical Index and no value added is achieved by adding the Premium indicator to the Cyclical Index. However, the effectivenss of the Cyclical approach is increased by about 10% by adding the Real Return indicator to the Cyclical Bond Index.

Exhibit 11 reviews combining valuation and cyclical variables to forecast the relative returns of stocks versus bonds. The cyclical measure of stock to bond attractivenss is simply the Cyclical Equity Index minus the Cyclical Bond Index. The 1-month IC data indicate that historically the cyclical factors have been about 50% more effective than the Premium valuation indicator for forecasting future returns of stocks versus bonds.

Since short-term yields do not play a role in the Stock/Bond Premi-

EXHIBIT 10:
BONDS VERSUS BILLS SUMMARY

Forecasting Excess Returns—Bonds vs. Bills

	1-Month ICs		
Technique	1951–85	1951–65	1966–85
Premium—Bond Yield minus T-bill Yield	.16	.00	.17
Real Return—Bond Yield minus Inflation	.14	.04	.18
Cyclical Bond Index	.21	.21	.22
Combinations			
Premium, Real Return	.20	.05	.23
Premium, Cyclical	.21	.21	.22
Real Return, Cyclical	.23	.22	.24

Correlations Between Techniques

	1951–85	1951–65	1966–85
Premium, Real Return	.18	(.13)	.23
Premium, Cyclical	.55	.46	.63
Real Return, Cyclical	.15	(.10)	.37

um indicator, there is virtually no correlation between the Premium indicator and the cyclical measure of stock to bond attractiveness. Because of this independence, the addition of the Premium valuation indicator to the Cyclical Index increases stock versus bond predictive ability by over 10%. This result is therefore similar to that obtained by adding an independent valuation technique to the cyclical variables used to forecast stocks versus bills and bonds versus bills.

This Stocks/Bonds Premium measure of value is the expected Equity Return minus the long-term bond yield. In this case of stocks versus bonds, the Premium indicator is equivalent to a Real Return indicator

EXHIBIT 11:
STOCKS VERSUS BONDS SUMMARY

Forecasting Excess Returns—Stocks vs. Bonds

	1-Month ICs		
Technique	1951–85	1951–65	1966–85
Premium—Exp. Equity Return minus Bond Yield	.16	.09	.16
Cyclical—Cyclical Equity Index minus Cyclical Bond Index	.25	.22	.24
Combinations			
Premium, Cyclical	.28	.25	.29

Correlations Between Techniques

	1951–85	1951/65	1966/85
Premium, Cyclical	.08	(.08)	(.02)

since inflation expectations are included in both the Expected Equity Return (as calculated) and the nominal bond yield (implicitly).

The conclusion just drawn from Exhibits 9 through 11 was that the best results were achieved by combining the cyclical indicators, which were the most powerful, with independent measures of "true" long-term value. Exhibit 12 details the historical weights, derived from standard regression analyses, which should have been applied to these cyclical and valuation indicators to achieve the best results. It is impressive to see, regardless of the period covered or the returns being forecasted, that the results are quite similar, with the cyclical measures assuming anywhere from 59% to 77% of the total forecasting weight.

Investment Implications

The cyclical environment for stocks and bonds is largely independent of valuation considerations, if value is defined by the Expected Real Return being offered by stocks or bonds. Consequently, adding the two approaches increases overall predictive accuracy by about 10%, versus

EXHIBIT 12:
"VALUATION" VERSUS "CYCLICAL" RELATIVE IMPORTANCE

	Forecasting Stocks versus Bills		
	1951–85	*1951–65*	*1966–85*
Valuation[1]	31%	25%	37%
Cyclical[2]	69%	75%	63%

	Forecasting Bonds versus Bills		
	1951–85	*1951–85*	*1966–85*
Valuation[3]	38%	23%	41%
Cyclical[4]	62%	77%	59%

	Forecasting Stocks versus Bonds		
	1951–85	1951–65	1966–85
Valuation[5]	38%	32%	40%
Cyclical[6]	62%	68%	60%

[1]Expected Equity Return minus Expected Inflation.
[2]Cyclical Equity Index.
[3]Bond Yield minus Expected Inflation.
[4]Cyclical Bond Index.
[5]Expected Equity Return minus Bond Yield.
[6]Cyclical Equity Index minus Cyclical Bond Index.

using the cyclical indicators alone. As a rule of thumb, the cyclical outlook should be considered about twice as important as valuation levels for determining the near-term outlook for the financial markets.

SUMMARY

Tactical Asset Allocation, for a variety of reasons, appears to be here to stay. The approach to TAA that has gained the most credence and popularity has been based upon straightforward comparisons of expected return proxies for the markets involved. This "Premium" technique has been quite effective for the practitioners that have used it.

For the purpose of forecasting stocks versus cash or bonds versus cash, the Premium approach has demonstrated significant predictive ability. Valuation measures that derive an expected real rate of return by subtracting an expected inflation rate from an expected long-term return for stocks and bonds have also been effective but have not shown as much forecasting accuracy as the Premium technique. For comparing stocks to bonds, the Premium approach is equivalent to the Real Return technique and has also been quite effective historically.

Traditional measures of stock market valuation, such as ratios of stock prices to earnings, dividends or book value, or of stock yields to bond yields, have been either inferior and/or redundant with the Premium and Real Return valuation measures reviewed in this chapter and therefore offer no additional value-added.

The cyclical swings of business and credit conditions are closely tied to the cycles of stock and bond prices. Variables that attempt to measure cyclical conditions have demonstrated predictive ability greater than that of the Premium or Real Return valuation techniques, for both stocks compared to bills, bonds versus bills, and stocks versus bonds.

The Premium valuation approach for stocks to bills and bonds to bills is actually more related to the cyclical variables than to the Real Return valuation indicators. This fact is a consequence of the cyclically sensitive T-bill yield being used in the Premium calculation. In contrast, the Expected Real Return valuation approach for stocks versus bills and bonds versus bills is essentially independent of cyclical conditions. Consequently, a combination of the Cyclical Indexes with the Real Return variables results in the most effective combination of cyclical and valuation factors.

For comparing stocks to bonds, where the Real Return variable is equivalent to the Premium indicator, a combination of the Cyclical Indexes with Real Return comparisons has also been quite useful.

Historically, the best results have been achieved when the Cyclical Indexes were weighted approximately twice as heavily as the Real Return valuation measures.

Conclusion

Many of today's TAA strategies are based solely upon "valuation" techiques. Others have included measures of the "cyclical" environment. This chapter has demonstrated the generally very significant forecasting ability of both valuation and cyclical indicators. For those who focus entirely or heavily upon valuation, this chapter also suggests that an increased consideration of the cyclical environment for stocks and bonds may offer the opportunity for further increases in the effectiveness of TAA strategies.

APPENDIX

Exhibits A-1 to A-11 graphically portray the recent history of the principal forecasting tools reviewed in this chapter. The definitions of the forecasting for each exhibit are given below:

Exhibit	*Label on Chart*	*Definition*
A-1	Stock/Bills Expected Return Premium	Expected Equity Return minus T-bill Yield
A-2	Expected Real Equity Return	Expected Equity Return minus Expected Inflation
A-3	Cyclical Equity Index	Composite of 4 Cyclical Equity Indicators
A-4	Composite Equity Index	Cyclical Equity Index (2/3) plus Expected Real Equity Return (1/3)
A-5	Bonds/Bills Expected Return Premium	Treasury Bond Yield minus T-bill Yield
A-6	Expected Real Bond Yield	Treasury Bond Yield minus Expected Inflation
A-7	Cyclical Bond Index	Composite of 4 Cyclical Bond Indicators
A-8	Composite Bond Index	Cyclical Bond Index (2/3) plus Expected Real Bond Yield (1/3)
A-9	Stock/Bonds Expected Return Premium	Expected Equity Return minus Treasury Bond Yield
A-10	Cyclical Stocks/Bonds Index	Cyclical Equity Index minus Cyclical Bond Index

Exhibit	Label on Chart	Definition
A-11	Composite Stock/Bond Index	Cyclical Stocks/Bonds Index (2/3) plus Stocks/Bonds Expected Return Premium (1/3)

Shown with each indicator history is the historical performance of the relevant index. For example, the indicators designed to forecast equity market performance are shown versus an index of the relative performance of stocks versus T-bills.

Stock returns are equal to total returns for the S&P 500. Bond returns are represented by total returns from 20-year Treasury bonds. 3-month Treasury bill returns represent the "bill" returns.

The exhibits have the following in common:

1. The top half depicts the relative performance index. The scale is logarithmic with December 1950 = 1.
2. The bottom half shows the value of the forecasting variable. For the Premium and Real Return comparisons, the actual Premiums and Real Returns are shown. In contrast, for ease of understanding and comparison, each of the Cyclical and Composite Indexes has been constructed to have a mean of 0 and a standard deviation of 5.
3. Indicator data are plotted monthly, at month-end, from January 1969 to September 1987. The relative return indexes are shown monthly through October 1987.
4. The solid line drawn through the indicator (bottom half) part of the chart represents the mean value of the series for the 1951-86 period.
5. The Composite Indexes were constructed:

	Weight
Composite Equity Index	
Cyclical Equity Index	2/3
Expected Real Equity Return	1/3
Composite Bond Index	
Cyclical Bond Index	2/3
Real Bond Yield	1/3
Composite Stock/Bond Index	
Cyclical Equity Index minus Cyclical Bond Index	2/3
Expected Equity Return minus Bond Yield	1/3

The 2/3, 1/3 weighting on cyclical and valuation factors was preferred to the "optimal" weightings of Exhibit 12 in the text, since optimal weights have the benefit of hindsight. The 2/3, 1/3 "rule of thumb" seemed preferable.

6. Generally, these charts offer pictorial support to the analyses performed in the text. While all of the histories could be reviewed extensively, I will only comment on the equity market with respect to real return valuation (Exhibit A-2) and the cyclical environment (Exhibit A-3), the purpose being to give the reader a general appreciation which can be applied to the other charts.

Comments on Exhibits A-2 and A-3

Valuation is important (Exhibit A-2). Stocks were clearly overvalued prior to the major bear markets of 1972 and 1987. 1974 and 1982 represented periods of undervaluation that led to major bull markets. On the other hand, valuation can be of little use at times. The important 1981-82 bear market began from a period of apparent "fair" valuation. The 1970-72 bull market did not begin in a particularly undervalued condition. And, as can be seen, apparent overvaluations or undervaluations can persist for a long time and even worsen before being corrected. Stocks became overvalued in 1971 and 1986. Yet the markets rolled on for 12-24 months. The undervaluations of the late 1970s persisted for many years.

It can be seen from Exhibit A-3 that cyclical conditions can explain much that valuation can not. The overvaluations of 1971-72 and 1986-87 were not corrected until the cyclical environment had deteriorated. Similarly, the undervalued markets of 1974 and 1982 did not soar until cyclical conditions had turned for the better. The bear market that began in late 1980 from a "fairly valued" condition was accompanied by very hostile cyclical forces. The favorable cyclical environment of 1970 led to a bull market that was quite strong despite not being particularly cheap to begin with. And so on. The point of course is that, despite the demonstrated importance of valuation levels, cyclical conditions, overall, often can explain more of stock market behavior than can absolute valuation levels.

EXHIBIT A-1:

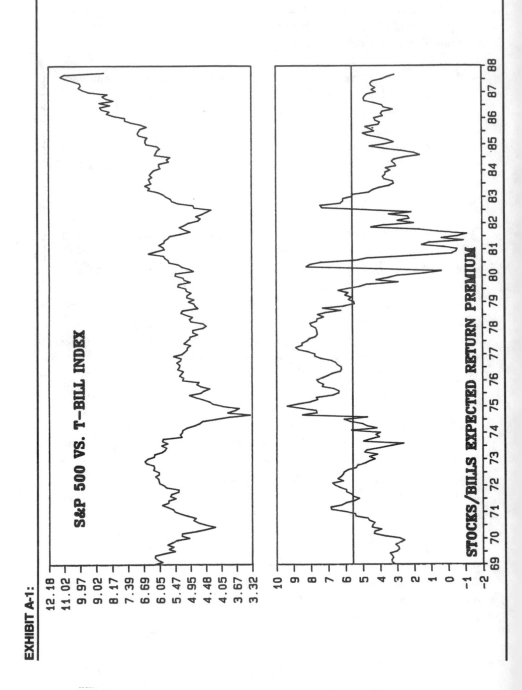

S&P 500 VS. T-BILL INDEX

STOCKS/BILLS EXPECTED RETURN PREMIUM

EXHIBIT A-2

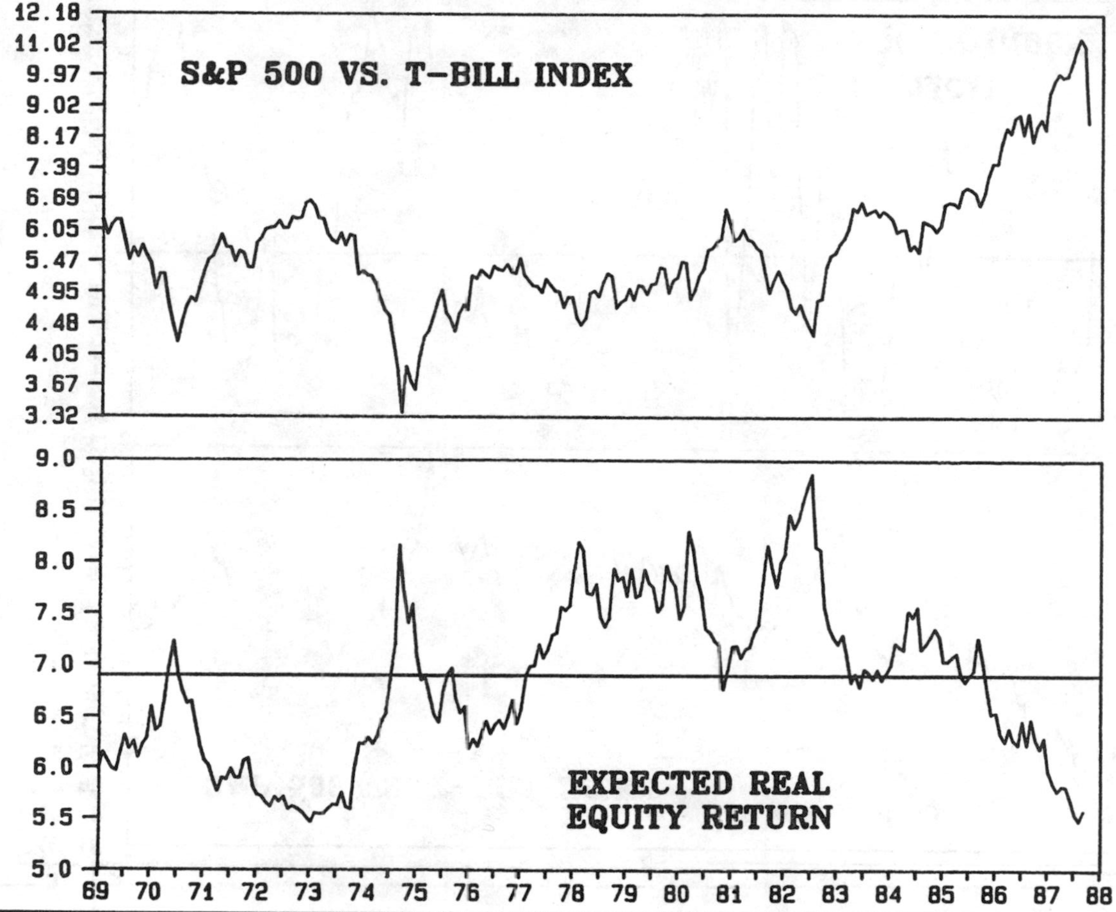

S&P 500 VS. T-BILL INDEX
12.18
11.02
9.97
9.02
8.17
7.39
6.69
6.05
5.47
4.95
4.48
4.05
3.67
3.32
EXPECTED REAL EQUITY RETURN
9.0
8.5
8.0
7.5
7.0
6.5
6.0
5.5
5.0
69 70 71 72 73 74 75 76 77 78 79 80 81 82 83 84 85 86 87 88

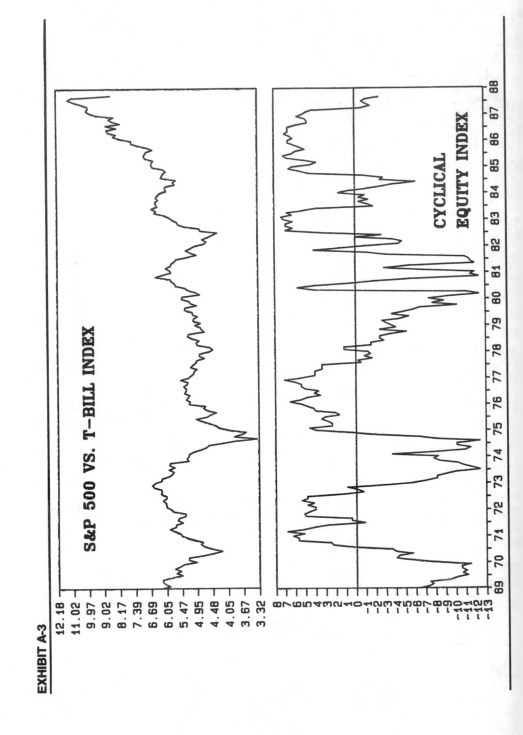

EXHIBIT A-4

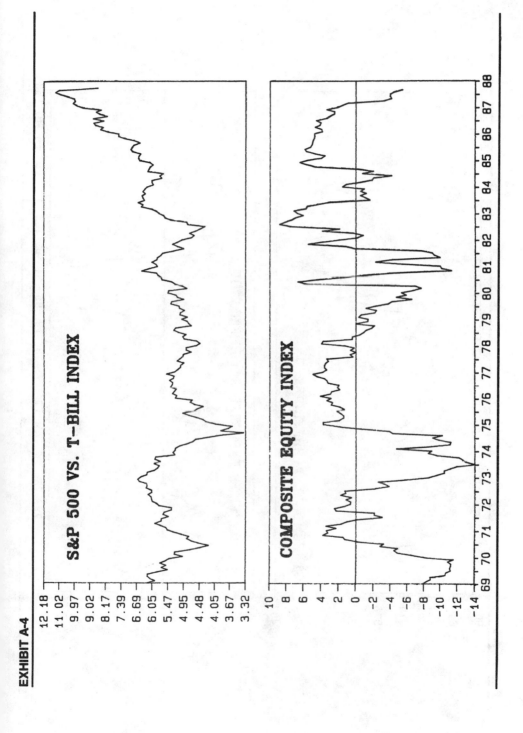

EXHIBIT A-5

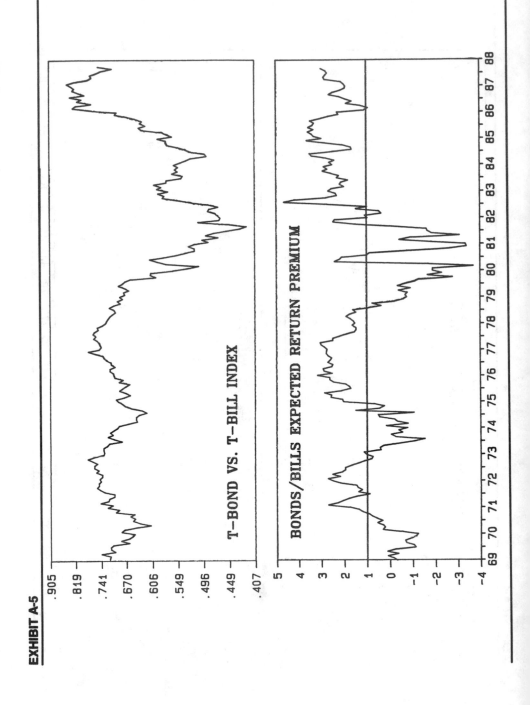

T–BOND VS. T–BILL INDEX

BONDS/BILLS EXPECTED RETURN PREMIUM

EXHIBIT A-6

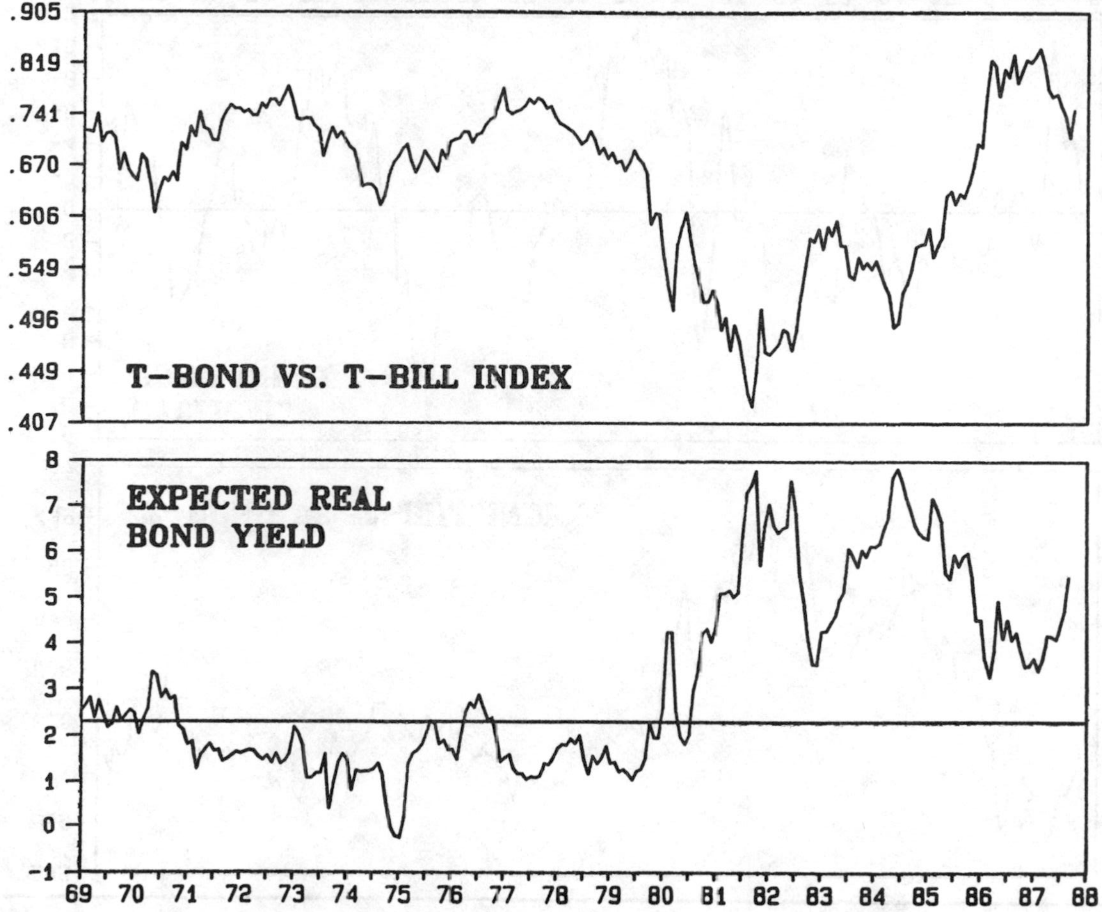
.905
.819
.741
.670
.606
.549
.496
.449
.407
T–BOND VS. T–BILL INDEX
8
7
6
5
4
3
2
1
0
–1
EXPECTED REAL
BOND YIELD
69 70 71 72 73 74 75 76 77 78 79 80 81 82 83 84 85 86 87 88

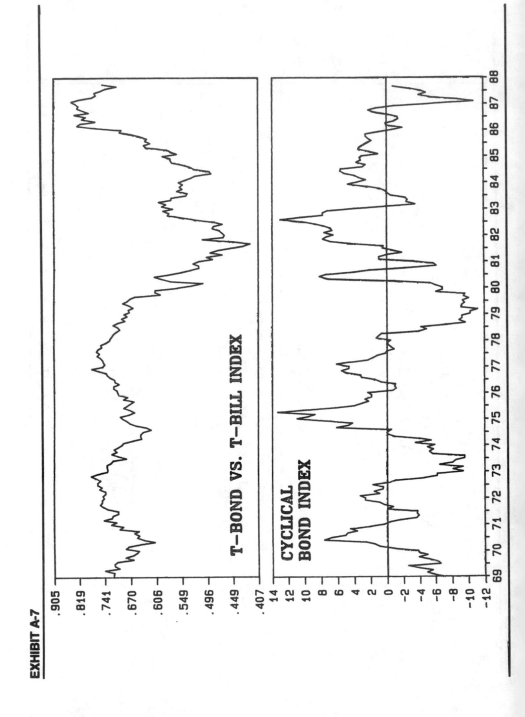

T—BOND VS. T—BILL INDEX

CYCLICAL
BOND INDEX

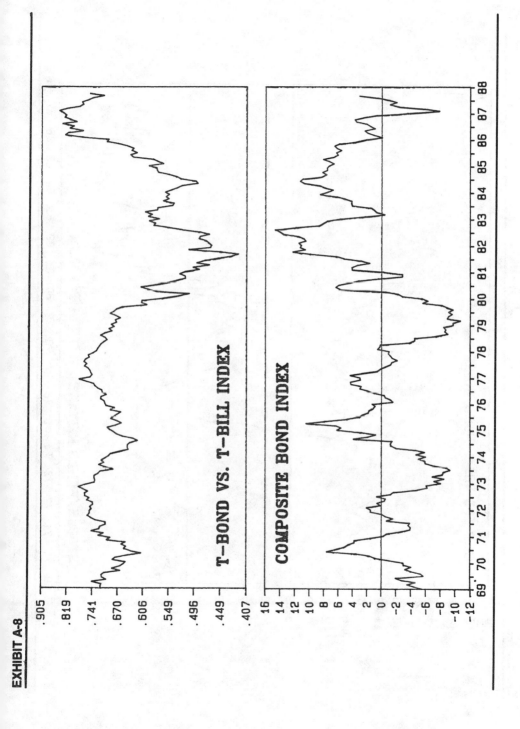

EXHIBIT A-8

T-BOND VS. T-BILL INDEX

COMPOSITE BOND INDEX

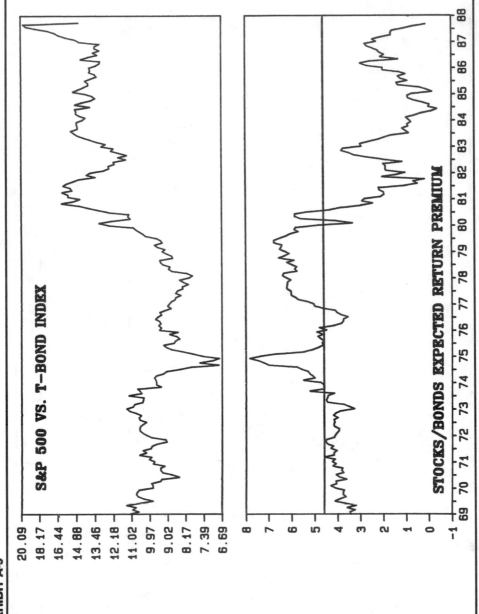

EXHIBIT A-10

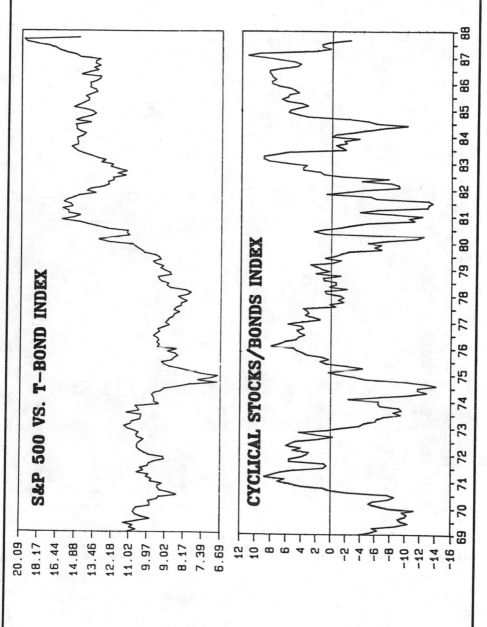

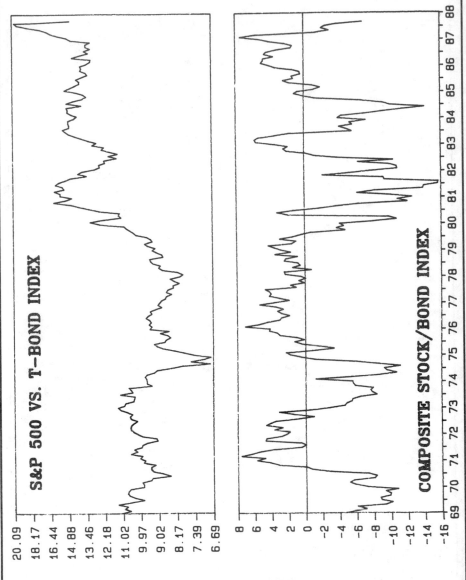

CHAPTER 15

Asset Allocation—Reward and Diversification

JEREMY J. EVNINE
SENIOR VICE PRESIDENT
WELLS FARGO INVESTMENT ADVISORS

Current conventional wisdom would have it that a pension sponsor wishing to put money into a tactical asset allocation (AA) fund should centralize his decision and have only one tactical asset allocation manager. Clearly, no one would expect a sponsor to take the same attitude toward stocks selection or asset class selection. Why then for asset allocation? Indeed, the same paradigm that we use to solve the stock selection problem can be used to solve the AA selection problem— namely, the twin concepts of added value, and added diversification.

In the case of stock selection, the added value is expected return, and the lack of perfect correlation across stocks is the reason to diversify, rather than putting all funds in the stock with the highest expected return. In the case of AA funds, the measure of value can be taken as the implied look-back option supplied by a successful fund, and the lack of correlation of successful timing across funds can be used as a measure of diversification.

The next section provides an overview of the problem at hand, and the methodology we use to analyze it. The following section discusses the concept of the value of an AA fund. The third section analyzes the effect of diversification across AA funds. The last section concludes.

OVERVIEW

Tactical asset allocation funds, or market timing funds, have presented investors with the greatest temptation, and with the greatest frustration as well. While a mispriced security can provide an investor with an opportunity to make more profit without more risk, the mispricings are usually found in assets with little market depth. Occasionally, persistent mispricings in traded assets with deep markets may allow large amounts of money to be made, such as was the case with the S&P 500 and the Treasury Bond futures contracts. But these opportunities diminished in size as more investors lined up to take advantage of them. By contrast, if one could truly discover a mispricing of one entire asset class relative to another, one could invest extremely large sums in such a timing strategy. Moreover, since such mispricings could only be discovered by an understanding of the macroeconomy, rather than violations of technical relationships (such as the cost-of-carry formula for stock index futures), one might hope these opportunities would persist for relatively long periods of time.

Unfortunately, it has been rather difficult to tell whether an AA fund was successfully doing its purported job or not, since the standard Capital Asset Pricing Model-based performance measurement methods break down in the case of a market timing fund. The CAPM states that if:

$$R_i = R_f + \beta(R_m - R_f) + e_i$$

where

R_i is the period return on stock i,

R_f is the period riskless rate,

R_m is the period return on the market portfolio, and

β is the coefficient which suggests the sensitivity of stock to market moves,

then the expectation of e_i is zero.

If β, the stock's beta relative to the market portfolio, is known, then an excess return of $\beta(R_m - R_f)$ can be obtained without skill, simply by taking an appropriate mix of cash and the market portfolio. Holding stock i in other than its capitalization weight is only justifiable if an investor knows that the expectation of e_i is different from zero. Thus, microforecasting is concerned with seeking out stocks whose residual has non-zero expectation, and then over- or under-weighting them relative to the market portfolio. If the null hypothesis is that the residuals have normal distribution with zero mean, then statistics with the t-distribution can be constructed to test the hypothesis of no forecasting ability.

In market timing, however, no stock need ever be held in other than its capitalization weights. When the stocks, as a class, are favored, wealth is moved out of some other asset class (e.g., money market funds, bonds) and into, say, the market portfolio or a proxy for it. Hence, investors may change their beta by moving money in or out of stocks, but never attempt to seek for non-zero mean residuals. This makes the CAPM of little value as a means to evaluate investment performance.

Over the last few years, AA funds have become more common, to the point where they may be viewed as commodities, rather like index funds. Those investors wishing to engage in market timing via these AA funds have therefore been faced with a decision as to how they should allocate their money across these funds.

The argument in indexing has been to centralize money into a single fund, on the grounds that many of these funds were very similar and had the same objective (e.g., track the S&P 500 index), and therefore economies of scale dictated that money not be spread around many similar funds. Typically, the deviations from the intended results in index funds are small, and most funds are affected by the same phenomena in the same way (e.g., tenders, mergers, changes in index composition). The same type of reasoning seems to have spilled over into AA funds, where there may be many funds which seek to achieve the same objective; for example, to time between the stock and bond, or the stock, bond and cash markets. However, since different funds may well use different signals to generate the allocation decision, the arguments for centralization should not be expected to hold. A model based on a dividend discount model for stocks may fail, where one based on an analysis of equity risk premia, or on an individual's intuition, may succeed. Or vice versa.

Given two tactical AA funds, most investors will find themselves obliged to treat each fund as an indivisible asset. They must simply decide how much wealth to allocate to each fund. If it were possible to combine the timing models from each fund into a single model, then it might be possible to create a "super fund," in which all the best ideas behind the most successful AA funds were combined. If so, this would obviate the need to consider the problem at hand, since all wealth would probably best be placed in the one "super fund." However, most investors will not be able to do this, and even if they had access to the paradigms underlying the models that had proved successful, it might not be at all clear how to combine different methodologies to create the single "super fund."

This being the case, a paradigm is needed that will allow investors to decide how to allocate money across AA funds. Such a paradigm can be found by looking at the paradigm used by some AA funds themselves: namely, the twin concepts of relative value and diversification.

For stocks, the measure of value is the expected period return. The risk is that there may be a residual return around this expected value, which is quantified as the variance of the stock's return. Diversification stems from the imperfect correlation of one stock with another. For example, suppose stock A has an expected return of 15% and standard deviation (square root of variance) of 25%, while stock B has an expected return of 13% and a standard deviation of 24%, on an annualized basis. Suppose further that the correlation coefficient of stock A with stock B is 0.5. Then, if we divide our money equally between stocks A and B, our portfolio will have an expected return of:

$$E = 0.5(15\%) + 0.5(13\%) = 14\%$$

The standard deviation of our portfolio will be:

$$s = \sqrt{(0.5)^2 (0.25)^2 + 2(0.5)(0.5)(0.25)(0.24)(0.5) + (0.5)^2 (0.24)^2}$$

$$= 21.2\%$$

Thus, even though we have sacrificed 1% of expected return by including stock B in our portfolio, we have reduced our risk by almost 4%. Most investors would agree that this risk/reward tradeoff is a desirable one to be able to measure, and then to make.

VALUE

The method of quantifying the value added by a market timing fund owes its origins to the work of Henriksson and Merton.[1] The general concept is to map the timing decisions of the AA fund into two components. The first is a static mix, which represents the allocation decision in a particular market environment, and the second is a look-back option to change the static mix to some other mix, in the event that a different market environment comes to pass.

By way of example, consider an AA fund which times between the stock and the bond markets by allocating money between a stock fund and a bond fund at the beginning of the month, and revisiting the decision at the beginning of the next month. A perfect market timer would always put 100% of his money into the asset class which was destined to outperform the other. This could be viewed as a static position of 100% in the bond fund (corresponding to an environment in which bonds outperform stocks), together with an option to exchange the bonds for stocks at the end of the month, in the event that stocks outperform bonds. One would pay very little to a manager for assuming a static mix, since that can be achieved without any timing skill. By contrast, the exchange option has positive value. Since the timer is essentially adding the exchange option without paying for it in the market, his added value is the value of the monthly exchange option, and this can be valued using modern option pricing theory.

In reality, no AA fund achieves perfect timing, nor do most funds take extreme positions in the asset classes. Generally a two-way fund such as the one described above would shift its exposure to the asset classes gradually, as one asset class was perceived to have better prospects than the other. In this case, the returns to the asset allocation model can be fit to the following model:

$$R_{aa2} = a + (w_s R_s + w_b R_b) + b \max (R_s - R_b, 0) + e$$

subject to

$$w_s + w_b = 1$$

[1] R. Henriksson and R. Merton, "On Market Timing and Investment Performance, II. Statistical Procedures for Evaluating Forecasting Skills." *Journal of Business*, 54 (1981), and; R. Merton, "On Market Timing and Investment Performance, I. An Equilibrium Theory of Value for Market Forecasts," *Journal of Business, 54* (July 1981).

where

1. R denotes (one plus) the returns on the 2-way AA fund, stocks and bonds, respectively

2. w represents the investment weights in stocks and bonds, respectively

3. a and b are constants

4. e denotes a residual, or "plug."

The coefficients a, b and the w's can be estimated, post factum, by linear regression methods. This model says that the AA returns are equivalent to those achieved by assuming a static mix w_s, w_b, which provides the return when bonds outperform stocks, plus b options to exchange bond return for stock return, when stocks outperform bonds. For a perfect timer, $w_s = 0$, $w_b = 1$, and $b = 1$. Note that to fit this model, we do not need to know the forecasts of the allocator; we only need to know the returns on the fund and the returns to the underlying asset classes. Thus, even the "non-quant" armed only with a spreadsheet package with linear regression, and the return series, can fit the above model. In practice, we substitute $1 - w_s$ for w_b, and rewrite the equation as:

$$R_{aa2} - R_b = a + w_s (R_s - R_b) + b [\max (R_s - R_b, 0)] + e$$

We now estimate w_s and b directly by linear regression. Evnine and Henriksson[2] describe how this methodology was applied to one such AA fund, for which the estimated coefficients were:

$$a = -0.34\%, \ b = 0.424, \ w_s = 41.83\%, \ w_b = 58.17\%$$

The R^2 from their regression was 87%, and the standard error of the residual was 1.17%. The interpretation is that the AA fund was equivalent to taking a fixed position of 41.83% in stocks and 58.17% in

[2]J. Evnine and R. Henriksson, "Asset Allocation and Options," *Journal of Portfolio Management*, 14 (Fall 1987).

bonds when bonds outperform stocks, and paying 34 basis points for an option to exchange 42.4% of the bonds for stocks when stocks outperform bonds. The exchange option was valued using a model by Margrabe[3], and found to be worth 1.797%. Thus, the value added by the market timing ability of this particular fund could be estimated at:

$$-0.34 + (0.424) (1.797) = 0.39\% / \text{month}$$

By repeating this procedure for several AA funds, an investor can produce value measures for each fund which are directly comparable.[4]

This methodology is not limited to AA funds that time between only two markets. For example, Evnine and Henriksson also consider a fund that allocates across three asset classes: stocks, bonds and cash. In this case, the returns to the AA fund are modeled as coming from:

1. a fixed cost (a);

2. a constant stock/bond/cash mix, when cash is expected to outperform stocks and bonds;

3. a number (b) of options to exchange the cash return for the maximum of the returns to stocks and bonds; and

4. a residual (e).

This can be written as:

$$R_{aa3} = a + (w_sR_s + w_bR_b + w_cR_c) + \\ + b[\max (R_s - R_c, R_b - R_c, 0)]$$

---

[3]W. Margrabe, "The Value of an Option to Exchange One Asset for Another." *Journal of Finance*, 33 (March 1978).

[4]As an aside, it is worth noting that the fund considered by Evnine and Henriksson appears to be an exception. Henriksson examined a large number of mutual funds that claimed to be engaged in market timing, and, using the above methodology, found very little evidence of successful market timing. R. Henriksson, "Market Timing and Mutual Fund Performance: An Empirical Investigation," *Journal of Business*, 57 (January 1984).

Note that:

$$\max (R_s - R_c, R_b - R_c, 0) = \max [\max (R_s, R_b) - R_c, 0]$$

so the implicit option is indeed an option on the maximum of the stock and bond returns, with a strike price equal to one plus the cash return. Using regressions, Evnine and Henriksson obtained the following estimates:

a = −0.34%, b = 0.3844
fixed stock/bond/cash mix = 38.16% / 7.18% / 54.76%

The regression had an R^2 of 80%, and the standard error of the residual was 1.48%. The interpretation of the results is similar to that of the 2-way fund, only in this case the option is harder to value, since it is an exchange option on the maximum of two asset returns. Stulz has provided a framework for evaluating options on the maximum of two assets.[5] Using his model, Evnine and Henriksson estimated the value of the option on the maximum of the stock and bond returns at 2.447% per month. From this, the added value of the AA manager could be valued at:

$$−0.34 + (0.3844) (2.447) = 0.60\% / \text{month}$$

Since a static asset mix can be obtained without engaging in market timing, an investor is in reality paying an asset allocation manager to provide him with these exchange, or look-back options; the quantity of options and the value of each option are, therefore, the determining components of the value to the allocation decision.

It is important to realize that the analysis outlined above was designed as a performance measurement tool, not as a prediction tool. It is by its nature backward-looking, and it should not be assumed that the equivalence between the fund and an exchange option tht has been established historically is necessarily a good predictor of a future equivalence between the fund's performance and an exchange option. This is similar to the problem of using historical mean returns as predictors of

---

[5] R. Stulz, "Options on the Minimum or the Maximum of Two Risky Assets: Analysis and Applications," *Journal of Financial Economics*, 10 (July 1982).

future expected returns. They tend to do an extremely poor job. However, in the case of stocks, there are alternative methodologies for predicting future expected returns, such as dividend discount models for individual stocks, or an examination of the behavior of risk premia for the stock market as a whole, or even an investor's intuition. There is, as yet, no methodology for trying to predict the future number of exchange options implicit in a tactical asset allocation fund, so an investor may have no alternative to using the estimated value for the coefficient b in the above model, and then using judgmental override to arrive at a prediction for the future value of b.

A valuation model is required to price the implicit exchange option. Margrabe's model values an exchange option between two risky assets, and is therefore appropriate to value an option to exchange bonds for stocks. If the allocation decision is between a single risky asset class and riskless cash (e.g., Treasury bills), then the Black-Scholes model is an appropriate valuation model.[6] Stulz's model values an option to exchange riskless cash for the maximum of two risky assets, and is therefore appropriate to value the exchange option implicit in asset allocation between, say, stocks, bonds and riskless cash. If the third asset class is also risky, Stulz's model may be generalized in the way that Margrabe's model generalizes that of Black-Scholes. In any event, the Black-Scholes or Margrabe models are simple to implement, requiring only univariate normal distribution values, and are frequently available in standard packages. The Stulz model requires bivariate normal distribution, which is not generally available and for which there is no readily simple approximation.

All of the above models assume that the risky assets in question follow a (joint) lognormal diffusion process. If it is felt that other stochastic processes better describe the behavior of asset prices (such as a jump process, or a jump diffusion process), then other models are available to value the exchange option. For example, real estate might be felt to be inadequately valued by a Black Scholes model, either because real estate prices may not be well modeled by the required lognormal process, or because the friction in trading real estate assets may preclude valuation by no-arbitrage arguments. This makes the option substantially more difficult to value. However, it should be

---

[6]F. Black and M. Scholes, "The Pricing of Options and Corporate Liabilities." Journal of Political Economy, 81 (May/June 1973).

noted that when comparing two tactical asset allocation funds that allocate across the same asset classes, the implicit option may not need to be valued at all, since it will be the same for both funds. It may be sufficient to compare the coefficients b for the two funds to obtain an adequate comparison of the two funds.

Models to evaluate exchange options between a greater number of asset classes would be extremely complex, and while the correspondence between an asset allocation fund and an implicit exchange option can readily be estimated (as above), the option value would be quite hard to estimate.

Whichever option valuation model is used to value the implicit exchange option, forward-looking inputs will be required. The most important inputs are the volatilities of the asset classes relative to one another. For example, in the case of asset allocation between stocks and bonds, we need the standard deviation of the difference of the logarithmic returns between stocks and bonds. In the case of an option to exchange riskless cash for the better of stocks and bonds, we need the volatilities of stocks and bonds, as well as the correlation between them. Interest rates will not be required as inputs to the valuation model. Since we are exchanging one return for another, the present value of the strike price, in a Black-Scholes sense, is exactly $1. If cash is one of the asset classes, then the interest rate appearing in either the Black-Scholes or Stulz model is precisely one plus the return to cash, which is known in advance. However, since the strike price appears in both models discounted back to the present, the interest rate will disappear from the formula. Neither do we need to worry about dividend forecasts, since if we allocate wealth to stocks, we will collect the dividends; so the exchange option is, in a sense, dividend-protected.

Volatility is the single most important input into the valuation model that cannot be directly observed. In a backward-looking analysis, we can use the actual realized volatility, measured either from daily returns intra-month, or from monthly returns, which are more likely to be easily obtainable. On a forward-looking basis, we will need to use a prediction of volatility. It should be clear intuitively that the added value of a successful asset class timer is greater when the relative volatility across asset classes is greater.

Finally, then, the investor has in hand the estimated values of the coefficients a and b in the model described above. He then applies any judgmental override which he feels appropriate. This may be indispensable if the fund in question has insufficient performance history to generate meaningful historical estimates of a and b. Next, using forward looking inputs, the investor values the implicit exchange option. He then multiplies this value by his forward-looking estimate of the coefficient b, adds the estimate of the coefficient a, and this is his valuation measure.

DIVERSIFICATION

The model used above for the returns to an AA strategy express these returns as:

AA return = fixed cost

+ static mix return

+ exchange option return

+ residual return

The static mix is neutral, in the sense that it contributes neither to the risk nor reward of the timing attempts. Any investor can assume a constant mix at virtually no cost (over and above the transaction costs of, say, monthly rebalancing). The value of the AA strategy comes from the fixed cost and the value of the exchange option. The risk in the AA strategy stems from the residual return. This has, by construction, a mean of zero, but may be positive or negative. Its value represents the amount by which the AA return differs from that of a static mix and an exchange option. If it were identically zero, then the investor would know for certain that his return would correspond exactly to that obtained from a static mix and an exchange option, and the value of that strategy is known. To the extent that the residual has a large variance around zero, this represents risk to the strategy.

If the investor's attitude towards risk were known, in the sense that he had a known risk aversion parameter, then the certainty equivalent of the risk in the residual could be computed and subtracted from the value of the exchange option. This would have the effect of making the added value of the AA manager slightly lower than it would be in the absence of residual risk.[7]

However, if the investor has the opportunity of investing in several similar AA funds, for which the residuals are not too highly correlated, then the risk in the residual can, to some extent, be diversified away. Consider the stock/bond and stock/bond/cash AA funds above that were analyzed by Evnine and Henriksson. If an investor places all his funds in the 2-way AA fund, he obtains options worth 0.39% per month, plus a residual investment with a standard deviation of 1.17% per month. If he places all his funds in the 3-way AA fund, he obtains options worth 0.60% per month, plus a residual investment with a standard deviation of 1.48% per month.

An analysis of the fitted residuals in the regressions of the 2-way and 3-way strategies yields the result that the correlation of the two sets of residuals is 0.62. Thus, we expect some possibility of diversifying the residual risk. Suppose that an investor places two-thirds of his wealth in the 3-way AA strategy, and one-third of his wealth in the 2-way strategy. The added value in the mixed strategy due to exchange options is:

$$(2/3) \ (0.60) \ + \ (1/3) \ (0.39) \ = \ 0.53\% \ / \ month$$

The variance of the residual from this mixture is given by:

$$(2/3)^2 \ (1.48)^2 \ + \ 2 \ (2/3) \ (1/3) \ (1.48)(1.17)(0.62) \ + \ (1/3)^2 \ (1.17)^2$$

which is 1.603%². Hence, the standard deviation of the residual is 1.27% per month. If the residuals had a zero correlation, then the standard deviation of the residual of the mixed portfolio would have been 1.06% per month; and if the correlation were -0.3, the residual of the mixture would have a standard deviation of 0.95% per month.

The same principle that guides us in stock selection can be made to work here too. We do not place all our funds into the single stock with the highest expected return, since the risk involved in such a strategy is unnecessarily high. By placing some of our funds into stocks with lower expected return, we will reduce the "value" (expected return) of

---

[7]See Evnine and Henriksson.

our portfolio, but this will be more than compensated for by the reduction in risk that stems from the fact that the stock returns are imperfectly correlated. This is the paradigm that underlies the Markowitz selection model[8], and also underlies the arguments above for choosing between AA funds.

This leads naturally to the question: How well do the residuals from different AA funds correlate with each other? While the modeling of the covariance of stock returns has received a great deal of attention over the last 20 years, the same cannot be said of asset allocation funds. The two funds considered above had a fairly high correlation because they were managed by the same firm and used identical methodologies, the only difference being that the 3-way strategy included cash as an additional asset. On the other hand, the fact that the two strategies were not timing identical asset classes probably reduced the correlation somewhat.

In general, many AA models use the yield-to-maturity on fixed-income assets as a proxy for the expected return on those assets. There are many models that use some form of a dividend discount model to obtain an expected return on stock. All models of this type will probably produce residuals that correlate fairly highly with one another. However, strategies that use macroeconomic models or subjective inputs to produce the asset allocation decision will probably correlate less highly with models of the first type. If histories of the strategies under consideration are available, then the regressions described may be run and the residuals explicitly computed. In this case, the correlations and standard deviations of the residuals can all be computed from the output of the same regressions. If histories are unavailable, then guesses must be made as to the degree of diversification that will be obtained from mixing strategies.

Let us assume that we now have in hand both the valuation measures of all the AA funds in our investable universe, and the standard deviations and correlation coefficients of the residuals from the look-back option model. How should we then allocate our wealth across the AA funds in our universe? A pure mean/variance approach may be misleading. The AA funds do not comprise all the available funds in which we may place our wealth. In particular, if we choose a particular

---

[8]H. Markowitz, "Portfolio Selection," *Journal of Finance*, 7 (March 1952).

portfolio of AA funds, we will implicitly obtain the corresponding portfolio of static mixes that make up the first half of the look-back option model specification. But the resultant static mix may be combined, if desired, with a completeness fund to obtain a static mix of the investor's choice. This latter may stem from a strategic asset allocation decision, choice of normal portfolio, and so on.

The real tradeoff is between the added value in the portfolio of implicit options, which has positive "utility," and the variance in the portfolio's residual, which has negative "utility." Rather than attempting a formal optimization, a better approach may simply be to examine potential combinations of the tactical AA funds, and to compare the net value of look-back options, and variance of the portfolio residual around the option mapping, until the highest level of comfort is obtained. This will allow an investor to take into consideration such factors as trust in the look-back option as a suitable description of an AA fund, the amount of money to be given to any one manager, or to any one type of AA strategy, and so on. Even if hard numbers are difficult to come by, the intuition suggested by the Markowitz selection model can still be useful in determining how to allocate funds across asset allocation managers.

CONCLUSION

We have shown that the concepts underlying the Markowitz selection model may be useful in determining how to allocate wealth across asset allocation funds. In place of expected return, the measure of value is the value of implicit exchange, or look-back, options provided by a successful timing strategy. This is the paradigm suggested by Henriksson and Merton to evaluate market timing models. The residual from their model is the risk that the investor would like to diversify away, if possible, and this may be achieved by spreading wealth across different funds, particularly those that use different methodologies to generate the allocation decision.

CHAPTER 16

Asset Allocation Using Futures Markets

ROGER G. CLARKE
MANAGING DIRECTOR
AND CHIEF INVESTMENT OFFICER
TSA CAPITAL MANAGEMENT

The area of active or tactical asset allocation has attracted enormous interest in recent years. The objective in active asset allocation is performance. The intent is to shift the asset mix to respond to changing patterns of opportunity which are available in the markets.

In one sense, active asset allocation is comparable to equity sector rotation, except that instead of rotating among the economic sectors of the equity market, portfolio exposure is rotated among the sectors of the capital markets or asset classes. It is based on a strategy which subjectively measures the likely relative returns of the major asset classes, typically stocks, bonds and cash. This strategy involves a disciplined, quantitative structure for measuring available returns. Active asset allocation is designed to exploit shifts in the relative attractiveness among these asset classes.

Developing such a model to indicate which asset classes offer the most attractive returns is the first key step in an asset allocation process. A disciplined structure for asset allocation is generally predicated on two key assumptions: first, that the capital markets indicate what rates of return are available in the various asset classes; second, that there is a normal relationship among the returns implied in the market-place. As the offered returns stray from their normal relationships, the forces of the capital markets will pull them back into line. It is this tendency to return to normal that is the profit mechanism of any asset allocation strategy.

A shift in the asset mix in a portfolio can be done either by buying and selling the actual underlying assets in the portfolio or by buying and selling futures contracts. Only within the last decade have the futures markets been well developed enough in financial futures to accommodate major volume for trading.

NATURE OF A FUTURES CONTRACT

Basically, a futures contract is an agreement for the purchase or sale of an item with the price established upfront but with settlement delayed to a future date. The concept behind a futures contract is one that we use all the time. For example, the terms of the purchase at a car dealership are often quite similar to a futures contract. The car dealer may not have on the lot the exact car the buyer wants. The buyer can purchase the car at an agreed price but may have to await delivery of the car until some future date. These terms are similar to those of a futures contract. The purchase price is agreed on, but payment for and delivery of the car does not actually take place until some future time. If car prices go up, the buyer benefits because the agreed price for the car will be less than the subsequent current market price at the time of delivery. This kind of transaction is similar to a futures contract. The buyer may have to post a small down-payment or deposit in order to ensure the car dealer that the buyer will follow through with the purchase of the car. However, actual payment for the car does not take place until the car is delivered.

Equity index and financial futures contracts work in a similar man-ner. The contracts have standardized provisions similar to those speci-fying the color, style and other options on a car. This package of standard features can then be traded on organized exchanges. They are highly liquid because one futures contract looks exactly like another. A small performance bond or initial margin is deposited at the contract origination date. No actual cash changes hands in the purchase or sale of a futures contract at the beginning except for this small deposit.

However, unlike our car example, any change in the price of stocks or bonds over time is settled on a daily basis. This process of settling daily gains and losses is called *marking to market*. The daily settlement requires that money be transferred between the investor and the broker each day to reflect these gains or losses.

The important thing about futures contracts is that the futures price moves directly with the underlying price of the commodity linked to the futures contract. This is what makes the futures contract an important investment instrument. The futures price is kept highly correlated with the cash price of the underlying instrument because of the arbitrage possibilities that are created if the futures price deviates to a great extent. As a result, transactions in the futures market can be used as a substitute for actually buying and selling the underlying assets. This close correlation between the futures price and the underlying cash instrument is illustrated in Exhibit 1 where we have plotted the price of the futures contract on the S&P 500 against the S&P 500 index. The futures price does deviate from the index itself, but these deviations are generally small.

To illustrate the investment exposure that an investor can achieve through the use of the futures market, consider the following example. Suppose an investor has a current portfolio worth $100 million, and that the current S&P 500 index is at 246.45. Each index point on the S&P 500 is worth $500. Consequently, each futures contract has a dollar equity exposure of 500 times the value of the index, or an equivalent value of $123,255 (with the index at 246.45). The number of contracts needed for equivalent equity exposure of a $100 million portfolio would be approximately 812 futures contracts.

Exhibit 2 illustrates the investment impact that futures contracts would have on an equity portfolio compared to a straight $100 million equity investment in the index. The S&P 500 index on January 2, 1987 stood at 246.45 and finished the month of January at 274.08. This movement in the S&P 500 index during the month of January would have led to an increase in a $100 million equity portfolio of $11,211,199. The purchase of 812 futures contracts would have led to a total dollar gain of $11,124,400. Though the futures contracts do not track the movement in the S&P 500 index exactly, the percentage differences are usually small. This tight linkage between the movement in the underlying commodity and the future is what makes the futures contract useful for investment purposes. If it were not so tightly linked

EXHIBIT 1:
S&P 500 FUTURES VS. S&P 500 INDEX
(JANUARY 1987–MARCH 1987)

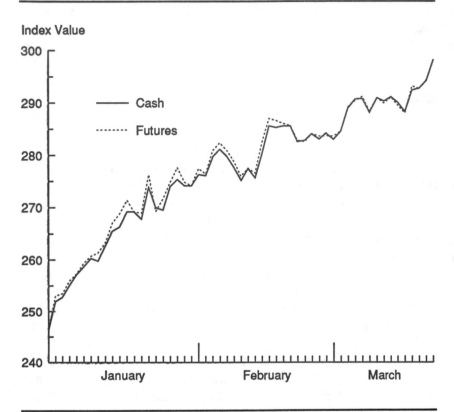

and the futures price could drift aimlessly away from the cash price, futures contracts would not be very helpful for managing asset allocation.

It is the possibility of arbitrage which keeps the S&P 500 futures closely linked to the S&P 500 index. If the futures price is too high relative to the S&P 500 index, an investor would have an incentive to borrow money, buy a market basket of stocks resembling the S&P 500 and sell the overpriced S&P 500 futures contract. During the life of the futures contract the investor would reap the rewards of any changes in the price of the stock plus the accumulated dividends from the stocks. At the expiration of the futures contract the futures price will converge

EXHIBIT 2:
EQUITY EXPOSURE THROUGH FUTURES

Current Portfolio Value	$ 100,000,000
Current S&P 500 Index	246.45
$/Contract	× 500
	$ 123,255

Contracts Needed for Equivalent Exposure	$$\frac{100,000,000}{123,225}$$	= 812 contracts

	S&P Future	S&P Index	Equity Portfolio
Jan. 30, 1986	274.15	274.08	$ 111,211,199
Jan 2, 1987	246.75	246.45	100,000,000
Net Point Gain	27.40	27.63	
$/Contract	× 500		
Total Gain/Contract	$ 13,700		
# of Contracts	× 812		
Total $ Gain	$ 11,124,400		$ 11,211,199

to the price of the stocks. Consequently, the investor is completely protected against the price movement in the stocks that have been purchased because the short futures position offsets the long cash position. The investor is then left with the dividends which accrue on the underlying stocks less the interest paid on the money borrowed initially to purchase the stocks. This spread between dividends accrued and interest paid determines the fair price of the futures.

If the futures price deviates too far from this fair price, an investor can earn above-market rates with little risk. This is the arbitrage process which keeps the S&P 500 future closely linked to the performance of the S&P 500 index. If the futures price is too high relative to its fair value, an investor can sell the future and buy stocks and earn an above-market interest rate. On the other hand, if the futures price is too low relative to its fair value, an investor can effectively borrow at below-market rates by selling stocks and buying the undervalued futures. The fair pricing of the futures contract on the S&P 500 is illustrated in Exhibit 3 using the data in Exhibit 2 and assuming that the annualized interest rate and dividend yield are 5.5 and 3.2%, respectively. With 77 days left to expiration, the fair price of the futures contract would be 247.65.

EXHIBIT 3:
FAIR PRICING OF S&P 500 FUTURES CONTRACT

$$F = I(1 + (r - d)n/365)$$

F   = Price of the S&P 500 futures contract

I   = Price of the S&P 500 Index

n   = number of days until expiration of the future

r   = annualized riskless interest rate with maturity of n days

d   = annualized dividend yield on the S&P 500 stocks

The fair price of the futures contract with 77 days to expiration, a riskless rate of 5.5%, a dividend yield of 3.2% and with the index at 246.45 would be:

$$F = 246.45 (1 + (.055 - .032)77/365)$$

$$= 247.65$$

ADVANTAGES OF IMPLEMENTATION USING FUTURES CONTRACTS

The principal disadvantage of active asset allocation without the use of futures is the size of transaction costs. Transaction costs often fall in a fairly wide range for stocks and bonds. Let's suppose that transaction costs are 200 basis points for equities and half that for bonds. A tactical asset allocation will likely force turnover amounting to perhaps 100% per annum. This means that an asset allocation discipline must add 150 basis points per annum or it is not worth employing. Most tactical asset allocation disciplines do indeed offer rewards several times that.

Therefore, tactical asset allocation does not require the use of futures. It can be implemented effectively and very profitably without resorting to the use of futures.

What about implementation through futures? As Exhibit 4 suggests, the merits of using futures in asset allocation are considerable. First, the commissions on a futures trade are trivial. A $20 round-trip commission for purchase and subsequent sale of $150,000 worth of stock market exposure in the stock market will represent less than 2 basis points. Liquidity is typically excellent and market impact is usually small, adding no more than 5 to 10 basis points. Instead of an asset allocation discipline having to add 150 basis points, it need only add 10 to 20 basis points to cover the transaction costs.

EXHIBIT 4:
ASSET ALLOCATION IMPLEMENTATION—ADVANTAGES OF USING FUTURES

1. Reduced transaction costs

2. Excellent liquidity; rapid execution

3. One-day settlement; simultaneous trades

4. Does not disrupt management of underlying assets

5. Stabilizes portfolio income stream

6. Potential for favorable mispricing

Second, these markets are very deep and liquid. Stock index futures now trade some $15 billion each day. Bond futures are the most liquid single market in the world routinely trading over $25 billion daily. As such, a $100 million asset allocation shift can be executed in minutes with relative ease and little market impact.

For example, Exhibit 5 illustrates the growth in equity index futures in recent years relative to the dollar volume of equities traded on the New York Stock Exchange. Stock index futures were first introduced in 1982. By 1983, the average daily dollar volume traded in equity index futures surpassed that traded on the NYSE itself. Now the stock index futures trade approximately twice the volume of the stocks in the NYSE.

EXHIBIT 5:
NEW YORK STOCK EXCHANGE VS. FUTURES DOLLAR VOLUME
(DAILY AVERAGE: JANUARY 1982–APRIL 1987)

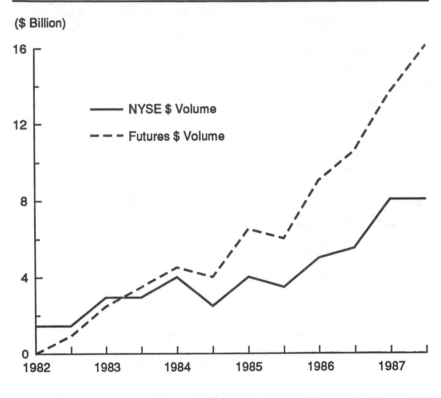

($ Billion)

NYSE $ Volume

Futures $ Volume

Third, futures permit simultaneous trades. If investors want to sell $100 million worth of bond exposure and buy $100 million worth of stock market exposure without using futures, they can eliminate the bond exposure in minutes, since the Treasury markets are highly liquid. However, on the equity side, they will have to carefully craft a buy program consistent with their investment management disciplines and have their trading desk and brokers work the order carefully—all of which can take days.

To some extent this is mitigated if the trades are managed through index funds, where a program trade can be effected quickly. But, even with index funds, the manager can run into a thorny problem with the differences in settlement times. The stocks settle in five days while Treasury bonds settle in a day. This means that there would be $100 million completely uninvested for four days in order to synchronize settlement dates. Investors can make a $100 million shift in their asset mix in minutes using futures without any concern for settlements or other operational difficulties.

Fourth, a shift in mix implemented by futures is not disruptive to the management of the underlying assets. If investors want to sell $100 million in stocks and buy $100 million in bonds, they have to carefully design a sell program which will not alter the characteristics of the equity portfolio in unintended ways. This alone can take some time. They then have to execute the trade, carefully working the order in conformity with available liquidity. Then they have to do the same thing on the bond side. The whole process could take several days. With futures, the underlying stock and bond portfolios are not disrupted. Indeed, the futures strategy can be implemented without the underlying asset manager even being aware of the trades.

This separation of the futures positions from the asset managers has another advantage. If the active asset managers are outperforming the index, the use of futures permits the investor to fully capture the value added within the asset classes. The futures only reflect the index return, while the assets are earning the index return plus something extra. Thus, any excess returns stay with the portfolio. However, the reverse is also true: any underperformance within the asset classes relative to the index also stays with the portfolio.

Fifth, for organizations where income is a consideration, the use of futures does not disrupt the income stream. If the portfolio is shifted from stocks into bonds, the income rises, which is nice. If a few months later it is shifted back to stocks, the income drops, which might be an unpleasant dose of reality. With the use of futures, the underlying asset mix need not change, and the income stream generated by those assets need not change either. However, the value of the futures will fluctuate as the markets move, resulting in gains and losses on the futures positions; but these changes might be considered more as realized capital gains than as income. When accounted for in this way, the income can remain stable though the asset mix is shifting.

Sixth, the futures may be favorably mispriced. If a futures trading strategy uses the futures mispricing as a part of the decision rule, a strategy can be designed which benefits from any ongoing pattern of futures mispricing. From time to time futures do stray from the fair value *vis-à-vis* the underlying assets.

Let's look a little closer at the issue of futures mispricing. Research suggests that many times the futures are favorably mispriced when tactical asset allocation shifts are made. But thus far, they have rarely been mispriced to an extent which would justify the transaction costs of making an asset allocation shift via the stock and bond markets. In short, the mispricing has been highly advantageous for most conventional tactical asset allocation processes.

Much of the reason why mispricing usually favors asset allocation trades is because most tactical asset allocation disciplines are inherently contrarian. It is often a buy low, sell high discipline. When equities sag, equity exposure is typically boosted. This usually happens at a time when, due to the drop in the stock market, there is a good deal of pessimism and the futures are underpriced *vis-à-vis* fair value. Equity exposure is often cut after significant market rallies. This is typically a period of euphoria in which the futures are overpriced *vis-à-vis* fair value. In short, asset allocation disciplines, because they are contrarian, often reap considerable benefit from futures mispricing.

Consider the following two illustrations of the asset allocation decision. In the first example in Exhibit 6, we accomplish asset allocation by using the underlying assets. In this case, we start with the portfolio of $50 million of equity and $50 million of bonds. If we want to shift the asset allocation mix from 50% bonds to 60% equity and 40% bonds, we would sell $10 million worth of bonds and buy $10 million worth of equity exposure. The resulting portfolio would be shifted to $60 million worth of equity and $40 million worth of bonds.

Next consider the asset allocation shift using futures. First, the use of futures requires a liquidity reserve in order to fund the margin requirements for the futures positions. In the second example in Exhibit 7, we begin with a portfolio totaling $100 million, composed of $45 million worth of equity, $45 million worth of bonds and $10 million in cash equivalents. The cash reserve is used as collateral for the futures positions. In order to accomplish the asset allocation shift, we must buy $15 million worth of equity exposure and sell $5 million worth of bond exposure. With these futures transactions, equity exposure in the portfolio would total $60 million. This is achieved by having $45 million of equity exposure in the underlying stocks and $15 million of equity exposure through the futures market. The bond exposure in the portfolio would be reduced to $40 million from the initial $45 million by the short position in $5 million worth of bond futures. As a result of the futures transactions, the total portfolio exposure has been changed to

EXHIBIT 6:
ASSET ALLOCATION SHIFT USING UNDERLYING ASSETS

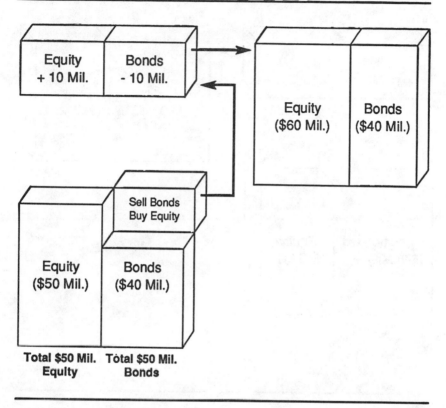

60% equities and 40% bonds, while underlying assets have been left in place.

Disadvantages of Implementation Using Futures Contracts

Though having important advantages, the use of futures for asset allocation does have some disadvantages, as noted in Exhibit 8. In the first place, even though the use of futures often allows for favorable mispricing, there is the potential for unfavorable mispricing. These periods of unfavorable mispricing will increase the cost of the asset allocation move using futures relative to making the shift using the underlying assets. However, the mispricing would have to be quite severe before it

EXHIBIT 7:
ASSET ALLOCATION SHIFT USING FUTURES

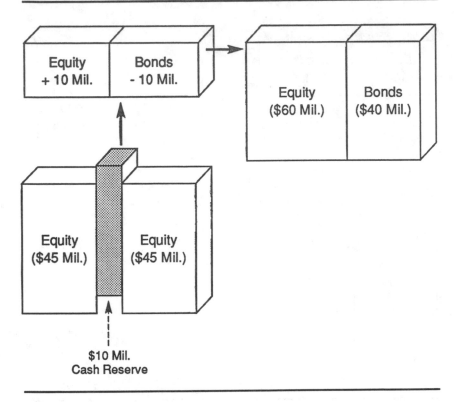

$10 Mil.
Cash Reserve

would actually be more advantageous to trade the underlying securities. With current arbitrage activity it is unlikely that such levels would occur very often.

A second disadvantage of using futures involves the potential basis risk between the underlying assets and the futures contract. Even if there is no mispricing of the futures contract, the underlying portfolio may have somewhat different characteristics than the equity market index or fixed-income security tied to the futures. Most managers will try to duration match the futures position with the underlying fixed-income assets or beta match the equity index futures with the equity portfolio, but this will not be a perfect fit. The differential performance between the futures and the actual portfolio could be positive or negative and is referred to as *basis risk*.

EXHIBIT 8:
ASSET ALLOCATION IMPLEMENTATION—DISADVANTAGES OF USING FUTURES

1. Risk of unfavorable mispricing.

2. Basis risk between futures and portfolio.

3. Liquidity reserve required to accommodate margin requirements.

4. Daily back office work required to mark to market.

5. Replaces active asset returns with index-like performance on liquidity reserve.

6. Disruption of asset management to raise cash if liquidity reserve is depleted.

A third disadvantage of using futures for asset allocation arises because of the back office work which is required on a daily basis to mark to market the futures positions. Any gains and losses in the futures contracts are required to be settled daily; this requires transfers of funds between the investor and the broker. This daily back office work requires constant attention and can sometimes be bothersome.

A fourth disadvantage of using futures is that a cash liquidity reserve is necessary to accommodate the margin requirements and daily settlement of the futures positions. Funding this liquidity reserve often forces the investor to liquidate some assets currently invested in stocks and bonds. Though the underlying reserve is invested in cash equivalents, a full investment exposure can be achieved by buying equity index or bond futures or overlay the cash position. This replaces the active asset returns which might be had from investing in actual stocks and bonds with index-like performance tied to the futures contracts. To the extent that active asset management can add value relative to the index, this differential return is sacrificed because of the necessity to fund the liquidity reserve and achieve full exposure indirectly using a futures overlay.

A final disadvantage of using futures also occurs because of the daily marking to market which forces the fund to realize the daily gains and losses. If the asset allocation decision is wrong and the differential market returns are substantial, the cash reserve can be depleted fairly quickly. If the futures positions are maintained, the cash reserve must be replenished. This infusion of cash usually requires some liquidation of underlying assets. Selling assets to raise cash will now affect the managers of the underlying assets and may interrupt their investment strategies.

CALCULATING THE FUTURES POSITIONS FOR ASSET ALLOCATION SHIFTS AND RISK ADJUSTMENTS

Once an asset allocation policy is decided and the portfolio exposure is determined, this exposure must be translated into an appropriate number of futures contracts. In this section we discuss the process to calculate the number of futures contracts necessary to alter the portfolio mix and adjust its risk characteristics.

Equity Exposure

Consider an underlying equity portfolio combined with n_s equity index futures contracts. The sensitivity of the portfolio to a change in the equity index can be represented as:

$$\frac{\Delta E}{\Delta I_s} = \frac{E\beta_s}{I_s} + n_s\beta_f \tag{1}$$

where:

E = $A_s V_0$ = the value of the current equity portion of a portfolio

V_0 = the total value of the portfolio

A_s = the actual proportion of equity in the portfolio

β_s = the current beta of the equity in the portfolio relative to I_s

I_s = the dollar value of the equity futures index (typically $500 times the index)

n_s = the number of equity futures contracts

β_f = the beta of the equity future

M_s = the target proportion of equity in the portfolio

β_T = the target beta of the portfolio relative to I_s

Equating the response of the combined equity portfolio with the futures contracts to a target portfolio with desired beta β_T gives:

$$\frac{\Delta E}{\Delta I_s} = \frac{A_s V_0 \beta_s}{I_s} + n_s \beta_f = \frac{M_s V_0 \beta_T}{I_s} \tag{2}$$

Solving for the appropriate number of equity futures contracts results in:

$$n_s = \frac{V_0}{I_s \beta_f} (M_s \beta_T - A_s \beta_s) \tag{3}$$

By rearranging terms this equation can be rewritten as:

$$n_s = \frac{V_0 \beta_s}{I_s B_f} (M_s - A_s) + \frac{V_0 M_s}{I_s \beta_f} (B_T - \beta_s) \tag{4}$$

The first term represents the number of futures contracts needed to change the current asset mix to the recommended mix at the current beta. The second term represents the number of futures contracts needed to change the recommended equity mix to the target beta from its current beta.

For example, assume an equity portfolio has the following parameters:

V_0 = \$100,000,000

A_s = .45

β_s = 1.0

I_s = \$125,000

$$\beta_f \quad = 1.0$$

$$M_s \quad = .50$$

$$\beta_T \quad = 2.0$$

The number of equity futures contracts needed to alter the portfolio exposure would be:

$$n_s = \frac{100,000,000\,(1.0)}{125,000\,(1.0)}\,(.50-.45) + \frac{100,000,000\,(.50)}{125,000\,(1.0)}\,(2.0-1.0)$$

$$= 40 + 400$$

$$= 440 \text{ contracts}$$

Changing the mix of the current portfolio from 45% equity to 50% equity would require 40 contracts to be purchased. Another 400 contracts would be required to change the resulting portfolio beta from 1.0 to 2.0 as illustrated in Exhibit 9.

Debt Exposure

The interest rate sensitivity of a bond portfolio which contains n_b bond futures contracts would be:

$$\frac{\Delta B}{\Delta i} = \frac{-BD_b}{I_b(1+i)} - \frac{n_bD_f}{(1+i)} \tag{5}$$

where:

$B \quad = A_bV_o =$ the value of the current bond portion of a portfolio

$V_o \quad =$ the total value of the portfolio

$A_b \quad =$ the actual proportion of bonds in the portfolio

$D_b \quad =$ the duration of the bonds in the portfolio

EXHIBIT 9:
RISK ADJUSTMENTS USING FUTURES

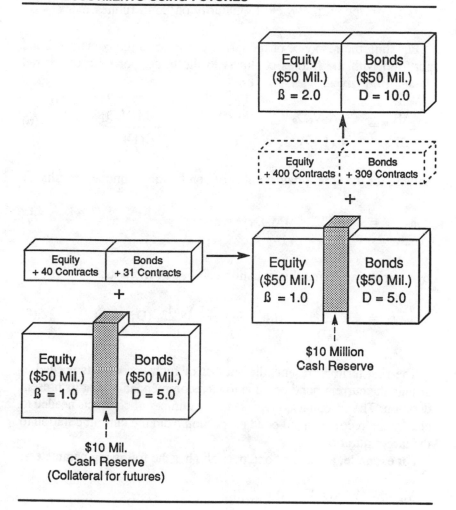

I_b = the dollar value of the bond futures index

n_b = the number of bond futures contracts

D_f = the duration of the bond future

M_b = the target proportion of bonds in the portfolio

D_T = the duration of the target portfolio

i = the current yield to maturity on bond futures index

Equating the response of the target portfolio to the combined bond portfolio with the futures contracts to the target portfolio of desired duration D_T gives:

$$\frac{\Delta B}{\Delta i} = \frac{-A_b V_o D_b}{I_b(1+i)} - \frac{n_b D_f}{(1+i)} = \frac{-M_b V_o D_T}{I_b(1+i)} \tag{6}$$

Solving for the appropriate number of bond futures contracts results in:

$$n_b = \frac{V_o}{I_b D_f} (M_b D_T - A_b D_b) \tag{7}$$

By rearranging terms this equation can be rewritten as:

$$n_b = \frac{V_o D_b}{I_b D_f} (M_b - A_b) + \frac{V_o M_b}{I_b D_f} (D_T - D_b) \tag{8}$$

The first term represents the number of futures contracts needed to change the current bond position to its recommended mix at its present duration. The second term represents the number of contracts needed to change the recommended bond proportion from the current duration to the target duration.

For example, assume a bond portfolio has the following parameters:

V_o = $100,000,000

A_b = .45

D_b = 5.0

I_b = $90,000

D_f = 9.0

$M_b = .50$

$D_T = 10.0$

The number of debt futures contracts needed to alter the portfolio exposure would be:

$$n_b = \frac{100,000,000\,(5.0)}{90,000\,(9.0)}\,(.50 - .45) + \frac{100,000,000\,(.50)}{90,000\,(9.0)}\,(10.0 - 5.0)$$

$= 31 + 309$

$= 340$ contracts

The results indicate that 31 bond contracts would be required to increase the mix of the current bond position from 45% to 50% at the current duration. An additional 309 contracts would be required to increase the resulting portfolio's duration from 5.0 to 10.0 years, resulting in a net position of 340 bond contracts needed to create the combined position. The complete set of transactions to alter both the portfolio mix and its risk characteristics is shown in Exhibit A-9.

MEASURING PERFORMANCE OF ACTIVE ASSET ALLOCATION STRATEGIES

Anyone involved in the evaluation of active asset allocation strategies, can find performance measurement a perplexing issue. No asset allocation indexes are available, nor are there established universes of asset allocation managers. The issue is further complicated by the fact that the mode of implementation often differs from manager to manager. Some use futures, others use index funds and still others use a combination of the two. Typically, the value-added by an active asset allocation strategy is measured by comparing its performance to that of a passive benchmark or "normal" mix, which is regularly rebalanced. Though this sounds simple enough, there are subtleties to consider, particularly where futures are involved.

Though not a panacea for the complexities of asset allocation performance measurement, the following framework does provide a straightforward way of evaluating the strategy's effectiveness. The first section reviews the return components of the asset allocation portfolio. The second explains how to calculate the value added by a futures overlay relative to a passive benchmark or "normal" portfolio mix. The last section illustrates the difference between value added in the portfolio and the net cash flows from futures activity.

Portfolio Return Components

The return for the total portfolio can be segregated into the return on the underlying assets plus the return from futures activity related to asset allocation shifts.

$$R_p \quad = R_a + R_f \tag{9}$$

where:

R_a = return on underlying assets

R_f = return from futures activity

= F/I

F = total dollar futures gains or losses

I = initial value of investment portfolio

The benchmark return $R*$ is the target against which the performance of the portfolio is measured.

The actual and benchmark returns can be further broken down into their components using the following symbols:

	Recommended Strategic Mix	Normal Mix	Actual Physical Mix	Actual Asset Returns	Benchmark Returns
Stocks	M_s	N_s	A_s	R_s	$R*_s$
Bonds	M_b	N_b	A_b	R_b	$R*_b$
Cash	M_c	N_c	A_c	R_c	$R*_c$

$$R_a \quad = A_sR_s + A_bR_b + A_cR_c \tag{10}$$

$$R^* \quad = N_sR^*_s + N_bR^*_b + N_cR^*_c \tag{11}$$

The total return on the underlying assets is given by the actual proportion of the portfolio in each class of assets times the return on the respective asset class. The benchmark return is given by the normal or target proportion in each asset class times the respective benchmark return.

Components of Value Added

The term *value added* (VA) is defined as total portfolio return less the return for the benchmark of the portfolio. Or,

$$VA = R_p - R^* \tag{12}$$

where:

VA $\quad$ = *value added* for portfolio

R_p $\quad$ = total portfolio return

R^* $\quad$ = benchmark return

For example, if the portfolio returns 3.9% and the benchmark returns 2.2%, the *value added* would be 1.7%.

$$VA \quad = 3.9 - 2.2$$

$$= 1.7\%$$

Substituting the components of each return into the value added equation and rearranging terms gives the *value added* as:

$$VA \quad = R_p - R^*$$

$$= R_a + R_f - R^*$$

$$= [N_s(R_s - R^*_s) + N_b(R_b - R^*_b) + N_c(R_c - R^*_c)]$$

$$\dot{} + R_f - [R^*{}_s(N_s - A_s) + R^*{}_b(N_b - A_b) + R^*{}_c(N_c - A_c)]$$

$$- [(R_s - R^*{}_s)(N_s - A_s) + (R_b - R^*{}_b)(N_b - A_b) + (R_c - R^*{}_c)(N_c - A_c)] \tag{13}$$

The first set of terms represents the *value added* by the management of the underlying assets if they had been held at the normal mix in the portfolio.

The second set of terms represents the *value added* by active asset allocation. The returns reflect the total gains from futures activity less those incurred as a result of first adjusting the portfolio mix to its normal mix. This difference represents the active bet made by the asset allocation decision and assumes that the futures generate index-like returns equal to the benchmark.

The last set of terms reflects the opportunity cost of using futures to rebalance the portfolio and bring the effective mix to its normal position before any active asset allocation bets are taken. At a minimum, a portion of the portfolio's stocks and bonds will have to be taken from the asset managers and set aside as a cash reserve to fund the futures margin. This last set of terms represents the differential returns that would have been earned by asset managers versus the index returns of the futures over this portion of assets.

It is interesting to note the value-added calculation for a portfolio whose actual assets yield index returns in each asset class so that there is no differential asset performance relative to the benchmark. In this case the value added reduces to just that added by active asset allocation:

$$VA \quad = R_f - [R^*{}_s(N_s - A_s) + R^*{}_b(N_b - A_b) + R^*{}_c(N_c - A_c)] \tag{14}$$

To illustrate the full value-added calculations, consider a portfolio with the following data and a benchmark of 50% equity and 50% bonds:

	Strategic Mix	Normal Mix	Actual Mix	Actual Asset Returns	Benchmark Returns
Stocks	.60	.50	.80	11.00	10.00
Bonds	.40	.50	.10	-3.00	-1.00
Cash	.00	.00	.10	5.00	5.00

$$R_f = -1,350,000/50,000,000 = -2.7\%$$

The three components of total *value added* would be:

$$VA = -.5 + (-2.7 - (-3.9)) + 1.1$$

$$= 1.8\%$$

The *value added* from the management of the underlying assets is $-.5\%$, while the *value added* from active asset allocation is 1.2% $(-2.7 - (-3.9))$. The net opportunity cost of having the assets managed by the asset managers who outperformed the equity market but underperformed the bond market added another 1.1%. The total of these three components gives a *value added* for the entire portfolio of 1.8%. Notice that the total futures activity resulted in a net cash drain of -2.7%. However, not all of this is due to active asset allocation. Indeed, the cash drain due to rebalancing to the normal mix amounts to -3.9%. The net effect of the two actually gives a positive value added by active asset allocation equal to 1.2%.

In simulated results of asset allocation it is usually assumed that the recommended mix (M) is held constant for the entire period and that the futures give index-like returns. The returns from futures activity can then be represented as:

$$R_f = (M_s - A_s)R^*_s + (M_b - A_b)R^*_b + (M_c - A_c)R^*_c \qquad (15)$$

This represents the return from futures activity as that earned by shifting the actual portfolio mix to its recommended mix with the incremental shift yielding index-like returns. Substituting (15) into (13) gives a slightly altered form of the value-added equation:

$$VA = [N_s(R_s - R^*_s) + N_b(R_b - R^*_b) + N_c(R_c - R^*_c)]$$

$$+ [R^*_s(M_s - N_s) + R^*_b(M_b - N_b) + R^*_c(M_c - N_c)]$$

$$- [(R_s - R^*_s)(N_s - A_s) + (R_b - R^*_b)(N_b - A_b)$$
$$+ (R_c - R^*_c)(N_c - A_c)] \tag{16}$$

The first set of terms again represents the value added by the management of the underlying assets if they had been held in the normal mix in the portfolio.

The last set of terms also reflects the opportunity cost of using futures to rebalance the portfolio and bring the effective mix to its normal position before any active asset allocation bets are taken.

The middle terms reflect the value added from active asset allocation. They are generated by the index returns of the futures as the portfolio is shifted from its normal or target mix to its recommended mix. The only difference between the two representations of total value added in (13) and (16) lies in this term. Using the actual returns from futures activity generally gives a more accurate measure of value added if the recommended portfolio mix is allowed to vary over the measurement period.

The data from our previous example, assuming that the recommended mix has been held constant, gives the total value added as:

$$VA = -.5 + 1.1 + 1.1$$

$$= 1.7\%$$

In this case, the estimate of value added from active asset allocation using a constant recommended mix is slightly less (1.1% versus 1.2%) than that calculated using the actual futures gains.

Futures Returns and Cash Flows

When futures positions are held constant over the entire measurement period, the total returns from futures activity in an asset allocation portfolio are generated by the differences in mix between the actual underlying assets in the portfolio and the recommended mix achieved by the use of futures:

$$R_f = (M_s - A_s)R^*_s + (M_b - A_b)R^*_b + (M_c - A_c)R^*_c \qquad (17)$$

The total returns from futures activity are due to two different effects. The first effect comes from the active asset allocation decision and reflects returns generated by the difference between the recommended asset mix and the normal mix used as a benchmark. The second effect captures returns caused by any difference between the mix of physical assets used in the portfolio and the normal mix of the asset allocation portfolio. These two parts can be seen by decomposing the total return from futures activity as follows:

$$R_f = [(M_s - N_s)R^*_s + (M_b - N_b)R^*_b + (M_c - N_c)R^*_c]$$

$$+ [(N_s - A_s)R^*_s + (N_b - A_b)R^*_b + (N_c - A_c)R^*_c] \qquad (18)$$

The first group of terms reflects the returns from the active bet on asset allocation. The returns from this part of the strategy will be positive if asset allocation is adding value. Positive value-added implies positive cash flows into the portfolio as the futures are marked to market.

The second group of terms reflects the returns from the rebalancing needed to bring the effective mix of the portfolio to its normal position before any active asset allocation bets are taken. For a portfolio whose physical asset mix is close to its normal mix, this latter term will generally be small and have little impact on cash flows from futures activity.

However, if the actual underlying portfolio mix deviates substantially from the normal mix, the size of futures positions required to bring the portfolio to its normal position can be large. If index returns in the market are also large, the cash flows into or out of the portfolio can be considerable. These cash flows do not reflect either value added or lost since they are offset by unrealized gains or losses in the underlying physical assets. Substantial cash flows from this segment can be troublesome, however, since they can be large enough to distort the cash flows from value added by asset allocation and give the impression that value added is different than it really is.

As an illustration, consider the following example:

	Recommended Mix	Normal Mix	Actual Mix	Benchmark Returns
Stocks	.60	.50	.80	10.00
Bonds	.40	.50	.10	−1.00
Cash	.00	.00	.10	5.00

The total returns from futures activity split into its two parts would be:

$$R_f = [(.60-.50)(10.0)+(.40-.50)(-1.0)+(.0-.0)(5.0)]$$
$$+ [(.50-.80)(10.0)+(.50-.10)(-1.0)+ (.0-.10)(5.0)]$$
$$= 1.1-3.9=-2.8\%$$

The active asset allocation decision has added 1.1% to the performance of the portfolio against the benchmark of 50% equity / 50% bonds. However, the actual mix of underlying assets is overweighted in equity relative to the benchmark, so that the cash flow from the futures position has subtracted 3.9% due to the rebalancing to normal. This 3.9% cash drain from futures positions would be offset by unrealized gains in the overweighted equity position held as actual assets so that no actual net loss has occurred from the rebalancing. Nevertheless, the net cash flow from futures activity would be negative, amounting to 2.8% of the portfolio value even though the value added from active asset allocation is positive. This negative cash flow can give the impression that asset allocation has not added value. In addition, if the futures margin reserve is to be maintained at a certain level, some cash would need to be transferred to the reserve to replenish it. This could be accomplished by selling stock and realizing some of the gains in the equities which are overweighted relative to the normal mix.

THE FUTURE FOR TACTICAL ASSET ALLOCATION

In closing, we might observe that the capital markets are exhibiting a pattern of "telescoping." The time horizon between the development of an effective concept, the translation of that concept into effective, differentiated product and the popularization of that product, is growing ever shorter. Even so, active asset allocation strategies appear to offer an intriguing opportunity. In the past five years, active allocation disciplines have moved from essentially no assets, to approximately $15–20 billion in assets in the U.S. This still amounts to less than 1% of total institutional assets.

As long as these disciplines are employed to manage a relatively small pool of assets and as long as *most* asset allocation decisions continue to be made on a somewhat *ad hoc* basis, this kind of process should continue to offer significant and relatively consistent opportunities for value-added. History suggests that this kind of discipline can add 400 to 600 basis points per annum on average. Even if the coming decade only provides half as great an opportunity, the cumulative impact of that kind of return enhancement is staggering. Indeed, it would be fair to say that an asset allocation discipline is far more important than either effective manager selection or security selection for the long-term performance of a pool of assets.

CHAPTER 17

A Disciplined Approach to Global Asset Allocation*

ROBERT D. ARNOTT
PRESIDENT & CHIEF INVESTMENT OFFICER
FIRST QUADRANT

ROY D. HENRIKSSON
VICE PRESIDENT
SALOMON BROTHERS INC

Does a disciplined approach to active asset allocation lend itself to export? Can the methods developed for the allocation of U.S. assets be applied in overseas markets? Yes. Our preliminary empirical results suggest that the same tools that have proved to be so profitable in the United States have value in the international arena.

The development of a global strategy for tactical asset allocation is a challenging task, if only because the most profitable strategy is to focus on the least comfortable asset class. With an an objective measure of prospective market returns, one can determine the relative market outlook for various asset classes, and that outlook can provide valuable

*The authors would like to thank Elizabeth Krier of MIT for her contribution to this research, and Peter Brown for his editorial contribution. Also, Morgan Guaranty Trust should be commended for the historic data which they kindly provided.

guidance on asset allocation. The markets provide objective measures of these returns. We *know* the yield for cash equivalents. We *know* the yield-to-maturity for bonds. We can estimate the approximate earnings yield or dividend discount model return for equities. These measures have been used with great success to profit from the relative performance of stocks, bonds and cash in the United States.[1] The use of a disciplined approach for including other information, such as recent inflation or the economic environment, may provide additional insight into the return prospects for each asset class.[2]

Past efforts to "globalize" the asset allocation decision have fallen prey to several kinds of error. One common misconception about the global markets is that something is fundamentally "wrong" when one market trades at several times the price/earnings ratio of another. Such differences cannot be attributed merely to differences in accounting: even after these are factored out, the residual differences in the ratios can still be very large. Nevertheless, there is nothing in investment theory to suggest that price/earnings differences between markets represent disequilibrium opportunities. Such differences are no more symptomatic of disequilibrium than are differences in bond yields.

This observation leads to a rather simple conclusion for evaluating equity markets in global asset allocation: The appropriate comparison is not between the earnings yields in one country and their counterparts in another. Rather, one should compare the earnings yield (or some other equity return measure) in one country with the cash or bond yields in the same country, thereby providing a measure of the equity risk premium in that country. These equity risk premia can then be readily compared across national boundaries.

Such comparisons can provide direct and objective measures of relative opportunities both within and between countries. There is no reason that the equity risk premia should be the same across countries. The economic risks of each country may be different. However, changes in the relative risk premium between two equity markets can provide a measure of changes in relative valuation and potentially of

---

[1]See Jeremy Evnine and Roy Henriksson, "Asset Allocation and Options," *The Journal of Portfolio Management*, Fall 1987.

[2]This approach to asset allocation was detailed, for the U.S. investor, by Robert D. Arnott and James N. von Germeten, in "Systematic Asset Allocation," *Financial Analysts Journal*, November/December 1983.

changes in the relative attractiveness of the two markets. In so doing, these risk premium changes can suggest abnormal relative opportunities within a country, and can provide a framework for asset allocation with a truly global perspective. In essence, such a framework would enable comparisons among Japanese stocks, German bonds and U.S. cash.

FUNDAMENTALS OF ASSET ALLOCATION

Pricing in any market reflects the collective judgments of all the participants in that market. By basing a measure of future asset class returns on current indications of relative opportunity, one capitalizes on this information. The assumption underlying such a model is that financial markets demand differential return premia on different asset classes.

The sophisticated investor must continually ask a critical asset allocation question: In the prevailing market environment, which assets merit emphasis? The natural tendency is to choose the comfortable answer, the answer that minimizes anxiety. The comfortable answer, however, is rarely the profitable answer. Few managers were aggressively cutting U.S. equity holdings in early 1973 or mid–1987. Few managers were doing the opposite in late 1974 or mid–1982. While these may not have been comfortable strategies, they certainly would have been profitable.

A discipline for asset allocation can provide a reasoned basis from which to confidently resist the comfortable answers when pursuit of a contrarian strategy would be most rewarding. This chapter describes such a discipline. In essence, it allows the market to indicate what future returns will be. The asset allocation decision can then be based, as it should be, primarily on the relative attractiveness of returns from the various asset classes. The allocations will change only with changing prospects for the relative return of the assets.

UNLOCKING MARKET OUTLOOK

This disciplined approach to asset allocation rests on four assumptions.

1. Prospective long-term returns for various asset classes are directly observable in the markets. We know the yield on cash; we

know the yield-to-maturity on long bonds; and the capital markets provide some crude but objective measures of long-term prospects on equities, in the form of earnings yield, dividend yield, or consensus-based dividend discount models.

2. These returns reflect the consensus view of all market participants on the relative attractiveness of asset classes. For example, if calculated equity returns are high relative to bond returns, then the market is implicitly demanding a substantial equity risk premium. Such a premium suggests that investors are uneasy about equities.

3. These relative returns tend to exhibit a normal or "equilibrium" level.

4. As future returns stray from this normal equilibrium, when measured against investment alternatives, market forces pull them back into line. Such adjustments create an asset allocation profit mechanism.

Even if one disregards the third and fourth assumptions and assumes no equilibrating mechanism in the markets, an objective approach to asset allocation can still work. If long-term equity return prospects rise by 100 basis points relative to other asset classes, the investor will expect to earn 100 basis points of excess return per year, even if there is no tendency to return to equilibrium. On the other hand, this equilibrating mechanism has been the source of impressive profits achieved by many tactical asset allocation practitioners.

For example, suppose the equity risk premium is 100 basis points too high relative to long bonds. Then either long bond yields should rise 100 basis points or stock earnings yield should fall 100 basis points in order to restore equilibrium. These adjustments require a price move in either stocks or bonds amounting to *many times* the 100-basis-point disequilibrium. While this equilibrating mechanism is not essential for successful active asset allocation, it plays a key role in providing the substantial profits that such strategies have delivered.

WHY DO CONVENTIONAL GLOBAL COMPARISONS FAIL?

As we noted earlier, one of the most obvious errors in global asset allocation is that measures of value such as dividend yields or price/

earnings ratios can be fairly compared across national boundaries. Such comparisons are the equivalent of blindly comparing yield differentials between countries for bonds or cash! Hence, it may be useful to analyze why such comparisons fail in the bond markets in order to understand why they also fail for equity valuations.

Differences in bond yield are explained by equilibrium theory by citing long-term inflation rate differences and currency shifts. If 10-year government bonds yield 10% in one country and only 5% in another country, there can still be yield parity if the currency in the high-yield country erodes 5% per year *vis-a-vis* the currency in the low-yield country. Such a differential would result in a 40% currency depreciation over the course of a decade. Currency moves of this magnitude are so commonplace as to be routine. No serious economist would suggest that international interest-rate differences run contrary to equilibrium theory.

The same point holds for rates of return in the dividend discount model. If the dividend discount model rate of return is 15% for one country and 10% for another, this difference in *nominal* returns can be fully justified by the long-term expectation of a 5% annual currency divergence. The investor from the low-return country seeking to capture the superior performance offered by the high-return country would expect to forfeit the differential performance through currency depreciation. Similarly, if the investor were to seek protection against this currency erosion by hedging in the foreign exchange markets, the foreign exchange forward markets would be priced to take away much, if not all of the differential rate of return.

Price/earnings ratios historically have tended to be rather closely correlated with dividend discount model rates of return. Hence, the same argument can be applied to price/earnings comparisons. If $100 buys $5 per year of earnings in one country and $10 per year of earnings in another, nothing in equilibrium theory suggests that this price/earnings difference should be inappropriate. Suppose the currency of the high-price/earnings country appreciates relative to the currency of the low-price/earnings country. Then the book value, the sales and the currency-adjusted earnings of companies in the low-price/ earnings country would all diminish when measured in the currency of the high-price/earnings country.

For price/earnings ratios, there are several factors other than currency risk that cloud the comparison of one country with another.

- Accounting principles differ across countries.
- Growth opportunities differ across countries.
- Different countries face different economic risks.
- Differences in political environments will influence investor's perceptions of future cash flows.

All of these considerations, and other lesser ones, could justify substantive differences in earnings yields, *even in the absence of currency considerations*.

In general, there is no theoretical support for the common arguments suggesting that countries with low price/earnings ratios, low price-to-cash-flow ratios, or low price-to-book-value ratios are inherently more attractive investment opportunities than their high multiple counterparts. The appropriate comparison will be much more complex, as many factors will impact the equilibrium relations of prices and earnings.

RETURNS AND P/E RATIOS

It is true, however, that the empirical evidence shows a weak tendency for countries with low price/earnings ratios to offer higher return prospects than countries with high ratios. There is nothing wrong with this. However, in addition to currency and interest rate considerations, differences in price/earnings ratios can also result from greater growth prospects or higher risks for one country than the other. Differences in equilibrium expected returns, in the absence of market barriers, should result from differences in risks. A riskier market will require a higher expected return, which will be accompanied by a lower price/earnings ratio.

Because P/E ratios should differ across countries, the best way to compare equity markets in different countries is to measure the equity risk premium in each country. The equity risk premia in different countries can then be compared. Regardless of any price/earnings ratio differences, if the *equity risk premium* in one country is higher than another, we might argue that the higher risk premium implies a better investment opportunity. Even here, however, there is a potential pitfall. In one country the *equilibrium* relation between earnings yield and bond or cash yields (hence the normal equity risk premium) might be higher or lower than it is in another country. Thus, since different growth rates, accounting standards, or political and economic climates can justify different price/earnings ratios, even these equity risk premiums cannot be directly compared with one another.

This observation leads to the final step in the comparative analysis. If the equity risk premium is measured in any one country and compared with the "normal" equity risk premium for that country, an *abnormal equity risk premium* can be determined. This abnormal equity risk premium is an indication of how far the equity markets of a given country have strayed from equilibrium, either above or below the normal reward opportunities. The abnormal risk premia *can* be directly compared across country boundaries.

GLOBAL ASSET ALLOCATION VERSUS CURRENCY SELECTION: TWO SEPARATE DECISIONS

The kind of framework we have described makes no naive assumptions about the normal relations between price/earnings ratios across national boundaries, and it makes no assumptions inconsistent with equilibrium theory. Importantly, such a framework separates the currency forecast from the forecast for asset class returns. In so doing, the investor is presented with an array of fully hedged investment alternatives. Forecasts of hedged asset class returns can be developed directly from measurement of risk premia. These can then be supplemented with independent forecasts of currency returns.

Distinguishing asset class expectations from currency expectations is important because it achieves two often contradictory objectives: it broadens the set of investment alternatives and it simplifies the evaluation of those alternatives at the same time. If asset class decisions are made based on fully hedged (local currency) return expectations, the resulting structure gives approximate equivalency among cash equivalents around the globe, since the forward markets are largely driven by this arbitrage. This is graphically illustrated in Exhibit 1.

This structure leads to direct comparability of the asset classes and to variance and covariance measures that are independent of the "home currency." The currency decision can then be made separately, based on whether the incremental return associated with an attractive currency would justify the incremental risk associated with lifting the hedge. In fact, the appropriate "no-forecast" allocation for investors will be

EXHIBIT 1

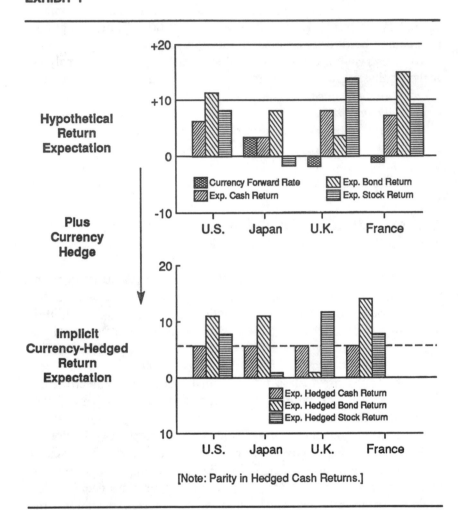

[Note: Parity in Hedged Cash Returns.]

fully hedged since the two-sided nature of the currency market makes it unlikely that the normal expected return from being unhedged is sufficiently positive to justify bearing the additional risk.

THE DECOUPLING OF ASSET ALLOCATION AND CURRENCY SELECTION

This view of the global capital markets clearly suggests that the currency decision and the asset allocation decision can and should be made independently. It is worth asking whether history supports this view. Exhibits 2 and 3 summarize the historic return and volatility of international equities. In examining historic data, we should note that historic returns tend to be poor indicators of future returns and that historic volatility tends to be a better, but still imprecise (witness October 1987), indicator of future volatility. Therefore, it is not appropriate to scrutinize the individual numbers, but the general pattern of the results is quite important.

During the three-year period ending June 1987, a hedged strategy sharply impaired the performance of a global portfolio. The reason is clear: the dollar fell relative to other world currencies far more than the forward rates used for hedging would have suggested. On the other hand, the results over a longer horizon are somewhat more encouraging. It would seem that the dollar outpaced forward-rate expectations early in the past decade by nearly as much as it underperformed in the past three years.

Without hedging, the volatility of individual equity markets around the world, denominated in U.S. dollars, all exceed the volatility in the United States. The correlations among the world markets, however, are low enough that the volatility of the world market, even on an unhedged basis, was slightly lower than that of the United States. This has been equally true over spans of three, five, or ten years.

By hedging, the investor is exposed only to the volatility of each market in local currency terms and the currency risk of the unknown change in asset value over the hedging interval. The empirical evidence supports the assertions that this second source of risk is quite small, therefore making it possible to effectively decouple market and currency risk. Here the results are striking. Over any historic time span, most individual world equity markets still exhibit somewhat more volatility than the U.S. market. With the exception of Italy, however, their volatility has only been moderately above that in the United States.

The hedged world portfolio consistently exhibits about 20% lower volatility than the unhedged world portfolio. Even though the historical correlations are slightly higher among hedged equity returns than unhedged equity returns, the lower volatilities of the hedged returns more than offsets the diminished ability for risk reduction from diversification. This result holds true even though the U.S. market represents a large portion (between 35% and 60%, depending on the year) of the world market! In other words, hedging reduces risk even more sharply than this data might suggest. When compared with a simple U.S.

EXHIBIT 2:
TOTAL RETURN OF INTERNATIONAL EQUITIES

	1-Year*		3-Year		5-Year		10-Year	
	Unhedged	Hedged	Unhedged	Hedged	Unhedged	Hedged	Unhedged	Hedged
France	32.9	13.5	51.9	33.3	40.6	33.4	24.4	20.3
Germany	16.6	(1.1)	46.5	30.7	35.4	31.4	18.3	19.2
Italy	22.4	NA	68.3	NA	43.0	NA	27.6	NA
Japan	76.3	59.5	64.2	42.7	48.6	36.5	29.2	24.9
U.K.	52.4	40.5	46.2	34.8	32.6	32.9	24.3	23.4
U.S.	23.8	23.8	30.3	30.3	27.2	27.2	16.2	16.2
World	43.4	35.0	42.2	34.0	34.1	31.1	20.5	19.9

*All periods ending 6/87; data from Frank Russell International.

EXHIBIT 3:
VOLATILITY OF INTERNATIONAL EQUITIES

	3-Year*		5-Year		10-Year	
	Unhedged	Hedged	Unhedged	Hedged	Unhedged	Hedged
France	30.2	24.8	24.9	20.6	28.1	21.9
Germany	24.9	20.5	22.7	18.2	21.7	15.7
Italy	41.4	35.7	37.8	32.6	36.4	33.4
Japan	23.9	15.3	26.5	16.2	24.2	15.0
U.K	21.0	15.8	20.8	15.0	21.7	16.4
U.S.	15.6	15.6	15.3	15.3	14.8	14.8
World	13.2	10.9	13.9	11.3	14.7	11.8

*All periods ending 6/87; data from Frank Russell International.

equity investment, the risk reduction ranges from 20% to 30%, again despite the fact that the United States is a large part of the index.

What is the cost and reward of hedging? Exhibit 4 gives some insight into the penalty that risk extracts from returns. Suppose one believed that all world markets offered an expected return of 12%. Then an investment solely in the U.S. market, with its average volatility of 15%, might be expected to deliver a compounded geometric return of 10.9%. If that risk can be reduced by a fifth (from 15% to 12%) through the use of a global hedged portfolio, then the geometric return rises by 40 basis points to 11.3%.

EXHIBIT 4:
THE PENALTY OF RISK

Average Return	Standard Deviation	Geometric Return
12%	10%	11.5%
12%	12%	11.3%
12%	15%	10.9%
12%	20%	10.0%
12%	25%	8.9%

In the wake of October 1987, if a higher standard deviation is assumed, the penalty of risk is greater still. This result follows without making any assumptions at all about active management or the ability to select countries or markets. Currency hedging on the forward markets is quite inexpensive, costing far less than this very real penalty of risk. If the disciplines described in this chapter can be effectively used to select the better performing world markets, then the reward of hedged international investing is greatly enhanced, because the penalty of currency risk is avoided. If a high currency standard deviation is assumed, the penalty of risk is greater still.

We would not advocate the automatic use of a currency hedge. If the investor believes a certain foreign currency will perform much better than its forward rates, then a hedge is not necessarily desirable. Clearly, over the past three years, a currency hedge for U.S. investments overseas would have been costly due to the plunging dollar. In the absence of a confident view on foreign currency strength, however, a currency hedge not only significantly reduces the risk of global investing, but in so doing it also actually improves the long-term expectations.

STAGE I: DO OBJECTIVE MEASURES OF FUTURE RETURNS MATTER?

The expected return on bonds can be represented by their yield-to-maturity; the expected return on cash is cash yield. Equity valuation presents a more difficult problem. Ideally, it calls for a measure of the net present value of future cash flows. In a practical international context, however, normalized earnings yields prove to be the most manageable and consistent indicator of stock performance.[3] To fully calculate total returns for equity, it is necessary to add a measure of sustainable growth. The addition of economic variables to the regressions indirectly but effectively introduces such a measure.

None of these measures differs conceptually from those now widely employed in similar models in the United States. In general, remarkably few changes were required to adapt a U.S. model to the markets of other countries.

In a "Stage I" asset allocation model, one assumes that objective measures of prospective relative return are positively correlated with subsequent actual relative returns. Is the equity risk premium versus bonds (stock earnings yield minus bond yield) positively correlated with the subsequent relative performance of stocks versus bonds? Is the equity risk premium versus cash (stock earnings yield minus cash yield) positively correlated with the subsequent relative performance of stocks versus cash? Is the bond maturity premium (bond yield minus cash yield) positively correlated with the subsequent relative performance of bonds versus cash? If the answers to all these questions are affirmative, then a Stage I model will be profitable. In essence, a Stage I model assumes that there is an equilibrating mechanism between asset classes, whereby unusual market conditions give rise to unusual subsequent relative performance.

---

[3]See also, "The Equity Risk Premium and Stock Market Performance," Salomon Brothers Inc, July 1987.

Exhibits 5, 6 and 7 give univariate regression coefficients of 15 different countries for Stage I asset allocation. In each instance we are testing the relation between objective measures of the prospective return differences and the subsequent realized return differences over a one-month horizon.

In order to better understand the information in the exhibits, consider the regression coefficient for Japan in the "Stock/Bond" column of Exhibit 5. In this exhibit, the equity risk premium is measured against bonds (stock earnings yield minus bond yield). In the "Stock/Bond" column, this risk premium measure is regressed against the subsequent

EXHIBIT 5:
STOCK EARNINGS YIELD MINUS BOND YIELD

	Coefficient of Regression with Subsequent Asset Class Relative Performance		
	Stock/Bond	*Stock/Cash*	*Bond/Cash*
Australia	−0.23	−0.76	−0.53
Austria	1.09	0.98	−0.11
Belgium	0.24	0.19	−0.05
Canada	0.33	0.28	−0.05
Denmark	0.05	−0.18	−0.23[1]
France	0.16	−0.05	−0.21[2]
Germany	0.46	0.29	−0.16
Italy	0.04	−0.05	−0.10[2]
Japan	1.39	1.36	−0.03
Netherlands	1.64[2]	0.97[2]	−0.67[1]
Spain	2.90[2]	2.79[2]	−0.11
Sweden	0.79	0.44	−0.34
Switzerland	0.86[1]	0.88[1]	0.02
U.K.	1.36[2]	0.80	−0.54
U.S.A	0.36	0.10	−0.26
Average	0.76[2]	0.54	−0.22[2]

[1]Significant at 5% level.
[2]Significant at 1% level.

Note: The data cover various time periods. For most countries, data are included from December 1972 through February 1987; for Australia, Austria, Japan, Spain, Sweden, and the U.K., however, data beginning in September 1979 or July 1981 were included.

excess returns of stocks minus bonds. The resulting regression coefficient is 1.39. In other words, for every 100-basis-point change in the Japanese stock/bond risk premium (stock market earnings yield minus 10-year bond yield) there is an average of 139 basis points difference in the relative performance of stocks versus bonds over the subsequent month.

At first glance this number might seem extraordinary. How can a 100-basis-point change in the risk premium translate into more than 100 basis points for the subsequent month's performance? The answer is found in the leverage inherent in the capital markets. Suppose the earnings yield were 4%, at a time when the 10-year bond yield was 6%. A 100-basis-point rally in stocks would depress the earnings yield by only 4 basis points (from 4.00% to 3.96%). A 100-basis-point rise in bonds would depress 10-year bond yields by only about 13.5 basis points (from 6.00% to about 5.865%). A relative performance difference of 139 basis points in a single month, stemming from a 100-basis-point stock/bond disequilibrium, could result from either a 5.5 basis point change in the stock earnings yield or an 18.7 basis point change in bond yields.

The striking finding in Exhibit 5 is that the equity risk premium versus bonds serves as a predictor for the subsequent relative returns of stocks versus bonds in 14 of the 15 countries tested–4 of them with statistical significance. The average link between the stock/bond disequilibrium and subsequent stock/bond relative performance is a strong one: every 100 basis points of measured disequilibrium translates into 76 basis points of relative performance in the subsequent month! Intriguingly, this variable is also quite powerful in suggesting future bond behavior, as can be seen in the "Bond/Cash" column. In 14 of the 15 countries tested, if the equity risk premium is abnormally high, the subsequent bond market performance is adversely affected relative to cash.

Exhibit 6 suggests that the equity risk premium versus cash (stock earnings yield minus cash yield) is a good indicator of stock excess returns versus cash in 14 of the 15 countries tested. The stock/cash risk premium is also indicative of the relative performance of stocks versus bonds in 14 of the 15 of the countries tested.

Finally, Exhibit 7 suggests that the slope of the bond market yield curve is a powerful indicator of subsequent bond performance relative to cash. If the yield curve is unusually steep (that is, if bond yields are high relative to cash yields), the outlook is good for fixed-income

EXHIBIT 6:
STOCK EARNINGS YIELD MINUS CASH YIELD

	Coefficient of Regression with Subsequent Asset Class Relative Performance		
	Stock/Bond	*Stock/Cash*	*Bond/Cash*
Australia	−0.30	−0.32	−0.03
Austria	0.25	0.42	0.16[1]
Belgium	0.11	0.18[1]	0.07[1]
Canada	0.17	0.22	0.05
Denmark	0.03	0.01	−0.03
France	0.56[1]	0.95[2]	0.40[2]
Germany	0.27	0.35[1]	0.08
Italy	0.12	0.32	0.20[2]
Japan	1.77	1.64	−0.13
Netherlands	0.60[2]	0.61[2]	0.01
Spain	0.68	0.72	0.04
Sweden	0.43	0.24	−0.18
Switzerland	0.16	0.28	0.12[2]
U.K.	0.34	0.14	−0.18
U.S.A	0.30[1]	0.37[2]	0.07
Average	0.36[2]	0.41[2]	0.04

[1]Significant at 5% level.
[2]Significant at 1% level.

returns. This relationship is statistically significant for over half of the countries tested.

This finding for the slope of the bond market yield curve flies in the face of conventional wisdom. The conventional wisdom is that a steep yield curve suggests a likelihood of rising yields. If this were true, then a steep yield curve would correspond to *weak* bond results relative to cash. The empirical evidence is quite persuasive in refuting this conventional wisdom. While the relationship is not invulnerable to error, a steep yield curve tends to correspond to stronger returns on bonds than on cash.

The implications of these three tests are relatively straightforward: market-implicit rate of return matters. If the equity risk premium is

EXHIBIT 7:
BOND YIELD MINUS CASH YIELD

	Coefficient of Regression with Subsequent Asset Class Relative Performance		
	Stock/Bond	Stock/Cash	Bond/Cash
Australia	−0.47	−0.44	0.03
Austria	0.08	0.43	0.36[2]
Belgium	0.12	0.23[1]	0.12[2]
Canada	−0.02	0.25	0.28[1]
Denmark	−0.16	0.24	+0.26[1]
France	0.20	0.54[2]	0.34[2]
Germany	0.19	0.42[1]	0.22[2]
Italy	0.04	0.28[1]	0.24[2]
Japan	−0.72	−0.81	−0.09
Netherlands	0.26	0.53[2]	0.27
Spain	−0.48	−0.34	0.14
Sweden	−0.01	0.00	0.01
Switzerland	−0.02	0.14	0.16[2]
U.K.	−0.04	−0.12	−0.06
U.S.A.	0.22[1]	0.52[2]	0.30[1]
Average	−0.05	0.12	0.17[2]

[1]Significant at 5% level.
[2]Significant at 1% level.

unusually high, it follows that most investors are averse to equities. The investor with the courage to bear that risk will tend to be rewarded. If the bond market maturity premium is high, most investors are evidently averse to interest rate risk. The investor willing to bear that risk reaps reward.

STAGE II MODELING: A CHANGING EQUILIBRIUM

Recent studies of capital markets behavior suggest that the *equilibrium relationships between asset classes can change.*[4] An obvious question

---

[4]See "Equity Risk Premium Review: Reflections on the Risk Premium," Salomon Brothers Inc, February 16, 1988.

is whether it makes sense to employ a process in which current market conditions are measured against recent, rather than long-term, equilibria.

In order to test the effects of a changing equilibrium, Exhibits 8, 9 and 10 adopt a short-term definition of equilibrium. These exhibits, rather than comparing the current risk premium with a long-term equilibrium relation, compare the current risk premium with the average value over the most recent 24-month period. For example, to measure the U.S. stock/bond disequilibrium for January 1987, the average stock versus bond risk premium (stock earnings yield minus bond yield) is calculated for January 1985 through December 1986. The risk premi-

EXHIBIT 8:
24-MONTH TREND IN STOCK EARNINGS YIELD MINUS BOND YIELD

	Coefficient of Regression with Subsequent Asset Class Relative Performance		
	Stock/Bond	*Stock/Cash*	*Bond/Cash*
Australia	−0.48	−0.70	−0.22
Austria	0.11	0.24	0.13
Belgium	0.36	0.28	−0.09
Canada	0.44	0.75[1]	0.31[1]
Denmark	0.08	0.13	0.05
France	1.18[1]	1.57[2]	0.38[1]
Germany	0.66	0.92[1]	0.26
Italy	0.14	0.47	0.33[2]
Japan	4.16[1]	3.16	−0.99
Netherlands	1.32[2]	1.00[2]	−0.33
Spain	2.58[2]	2.42[1]	−0.16
Sweden	1.00	0.78	−0.23
Switzerland	0.96	1.39[1]	0.43[2]
U.K.	1.22[1]	0.82	−0.34
U.S.A.	0.49	0.84[2]	0.35
Average	0.95[2]	0.94[2]	−0.01

[1]Significant at 5% level.
[2]Significant at 1% level.

EXHIBIT 9:
24-MONTH TREND IN STOCK EARNINGS YIELD MINUS CASH YIELD

	Coefficient of Regression with Subsequent Asset Class Relative Performance		
	Stock/Bond	*Stock/Cash*	*Bond/Cash*
Australia	−0.26	−0.26	0.00
Austria	−0.20	0.00	0.19[2]
Belgium	0.08	0.14	0.05
Canada	0.11	0.30	0.20[1]
Denmark	0.04	0.33[1]	0.29[1]
France	1.28	1.61[1]	0.34[2]
Germany	0.32[1]	0.50[2]	0.18[1]
Italy	−0.04	0.18	0.22[2]
Japan	2.11	1.90	−0.22
Netherlands	0.55[2]	0.62[2]	0.07
Spain	3.07[1]	2.97[1]	−0.10
Sweden	0.22	0.16	−0.08
Switzerland	0.24	0.41[1]	0.17[2]
U.K.	0.16	0.06	−0.07
U.S.A.	0.39[1]	0.61[2]	0.22
Average	0.47[1]	0.57[2]	0.10

[1]Significant at 5% level.
[2]Significant at 1% level.

um that existed at the beginning of January 1987 is compared with this 24-month average. Any difference is then viewed as a disequilibrium, suggesting relative opportunities between stocks and bonds.

As Exhibits 8, 9 and 10 show, this approach actually worked better than the Stage I approach for most countries. The improvement is especially noticeable for the stock/bond and stock/cash relations as the regression coefficient increases in 11 of the 15 countries. A "Stage I" approach, based on the naive assumption of static equilibrium relation, has merit and can add value. But an approach that recognizes the potential for changes in equilibrium may lead to better predictive power.

EXHIBIT 10:
24-MONTH TREND IN BOND YIELD MINUS CASH YIELD

	Coefficient of Regression with Subsequent Asset Class Relative Performance		
	Stock/Bond	*Stock/Cash*	*Bond/Cash*
Australia	−0.38	−0.34	0.05
Austria	−0.54	−0.14	0.40[2]
Belgium	0.01	0.10	0.08[2]
Canada	−0.05	0.19	0.24
Denmark	−0.02	0.24	0.26[1]
France	−0.04	0.28	0.32[2]
Germany	0.27	0.45[1]	0.19[1]
Italy	−0.12	−0.04	0.08
Japan	0.30	0.64	0.34
Netherlands	0.37	0.60[2]	0.23
Spain	−0.60	−0.50	0.10
Sweden	0.63	0.69	0.06
Switzerland	0.21	0.41	0.20[2]
U.K.	−0.10	−0.11	−0.01
U.S.A.	0.40[1]	0.60[2]	0.20[1]
Average	0.02	0.20	0.18[2]

[1]Significant at 5% level.
[2]Significant at 1% level.

REAL INTEREST RATES

In a study published in 1983,[5] the trend in real interest rates (defined as Treasury bill yields minus 12-month CPI inflation) was found to be a powerful factor in the performance of the U.S. capital markets. The results in Exhibit 11 reaffirm that relation. These results suggest that a rise in real interest rates in the U.S. leads to a substantial flight of money out of stocks. The result is significant at the 1% level, and every

[5]Robert D. Arnott and James N. von Germeten, in "Systematic Asset Allocations," *Financial Analysts Journal,* November/December 1983.

EXHIBIT 11:
24-MONTH TREND IN REAL CASH YIELD

	Coefficient of Regression with Subsequent Asset Class Relative Performance		
	Stock/Bond	Stock/Cash	Bond/Cash
Australia	−0.21	−0.11	0.10
Austria	0.69	0.47	−0.22
Belgium	0.00	−0.03	−0.03
Canada	−0.18	−0.16	0.01
Denmark	0.08	−0.01	−0.09
France	0.03	−0.08	−0.11
Germany	−0.40[1]	−0.54[2]	−0.14
Italy	−0.03	0.02	0.04
Japan	−0.76	−0.35	0.40
Netherlands	−0.42[2]	−0.46[2]	−0.04
Spain	−0.88	−0.86	0.02
Sweden	−0.29	−0.01	0.28
Switzerland	0.01	0.00	−0.01
U.K.	−0.16	0.16	0.35
U.S.A.	−0.50[2]	−0.43[2]	0.07
Average	−0.20	−0.16	0.04

[1]Significant at 5% level.
[2]Significant at 1% level.

100-basis-point rise in real interest rates translates into a one-month performance penalty of 50 basis points for stocks versus bonds!

As we seek to broaden this research, however, we find the relations between real interest rates and the markets are not consistent around the globe. We find statistical signficance for only three countries (albeit highly significant for each): namely, the United States, West Germany, and The Netherlands. Elsewhere, the relation is spotty and inconsistent at best. In short, CPI inflation appears to have only limited merit for active asset allocation decisions in the global arena.

Does this mean that the results for the United States, West Germany, and The Netherlands are spurious, stemming from random noise in the data? Or does it mean that in these countries the relations between markets and real interest rates are especially powerful? Statistical tools cannot answer these questions. Nevertheless, we are skeptical about such inconsistent relations, which do not stand up to a global evaluation. We are inclined to ignore models, such as the trend in real yields, that show only intermittent statistical significance.

STAGE III MODELING: THE INFLUENCE OF THE MACROECONOMY

Capital markets do not exist in a vacuum. Asset values do not rise and fall of their own accord. Rather, they embody the views of the investment community about future macroeconomic prospects. In a world where the judgments of millions of investors shape market pricing patterns, it might seem reasonable to assume market efficiency, to assume that the macroeconomy cannot provide useful guides to future capital market performance. If the consensus views of investors fairly reflect macroeconomic factors, then the markets should be fairly priced to reflect this kind of objective information. *The empirical evidence shows this may not be the case.*

Several macroeconomic factors appear to be somewhat predictive of the subsequent performance of various assets. We studied the following variables:

1. Stock return variance.
2. Rate of change in retail sales.
3. Rate of change in producer prices.
4. Levels of employment.
5. Rate of change in unit labor costs.

Each of these variables was tested by regression analysis, in which the data were appropriately lagged to reflect reporting delays that differ from country to country. The results were surprisingly significant.

Stock return variance, as shown in Exhibit 12, simply represents the volatility of stock market performance over the preceding six months. A Salomon Brothers study[6] in April of 1987 found this variable to be a powerful indicator of future stock market performance in the United

---

[6]"Risk and Reward: An Intriguing Timing Tool," Salomon Brothers Inc, April 6, 1987.

EXHIBIT 12:
STOCK RETURN VARIANCE

	Coefficient of Regression with Subsequent Asset Class Relative Performance		
	Stock/Bond	*Stock/Cash*	*Bond/Cash*
Australia	−0.33	0.77	1.01
Belgium	0.65[1]	0.88[2]	0.23[2]
Canada	2.00[1]	2.48[2]	0.47
Denmark	0.14	0.60	0.46
France	−0.47	−0.84	−0.37
Germany	0.22	0.44	0.22
Italy	0.36	0.37	0.02
Japan	1.00	1.13	0.13
Netherlands	0.73	1.04	0.32
Sweden	2.40	2.88[1]	0.48
Switzerland	0.25	0.28	0.04
U.K	−0.18	−0.25	−0.11
U.S.A.	1.27[1]	1.83[2]	0.56
Average	0.62[1]	0.89[2]	0.27[2]

[1]Significant at 5% level.
[2]Significant at 1% level.

States. As a predictor for relative stock market returns, past volatility and subsequent reward are positively correlated relative to bonds in 11 of the 13 countries tested and relative to cash in 10 of 13 countries. This consistency suggests that stock market volatility has global relevance.

One might think that the rate of change in retail sales is a useful indicator of economic activity, and hence an indicator of equity prospects. Unfortunately, the evidence in Exhibit 13 suggests that retail sales are fully discounted in securities prices, as the regression coefficients display no consistent directional patterns. In fact, retail sales are significantly positively correlated with West German stock performance and significantly negatively correlated with British equity performance. These results would not earn the confidence of any sensible investor.

EXHIBIT 13:
PERCENTAGE CHANGE RETAIL SALES

	Coefficient of Regression with Subsequent Asset Class Relative Performance		
	Stock/Bond	Stock/Cash	Bond/Cash
Australia	0.00	0.02	0.01
Belgium	0.02	0.02	0.00
Canada	0.14	−0.09	−0.23
Denmark	0.04	0.07	0.03
France	0.04	−0.05	−0.09
Germany	0.34[1]	0.37[2]	0.03
Italy	0.00	0.00	0.00
Japan	0.34	0.12	−0.23
Netherlands	0.02	0.05	0.03
Sweden	−0.01	−0.05	−0.03
Switzerland	0.07[2]	0.07[1]	0.00
U.K.	−0.62	−0.77[1]	−0.14
U.S.A.	0.31	−0.09	−0.39[1]
Average	0.05[1]	−0.03	−0.08

[1]Significant at 5% level.
[2]Significant at 1% level.

On the other hand, the rates of change for producer prices give more promising results. Whereas the results in Exhibit 11 suggested that real yields, based on CPI inflation, are of limited value, inflation as measured in producer prices, as shown in Exhibit 14, turns out to be consistently useful. In *every single country tested,* an acceleration in PPI inflation translates into a subsequent erosion of bond performance. In 6 of the 13 countries, the relation was statistically significant, and in 5 of the 13 countries, it was significant at the 1% level.

Acceleration in PPI inflation also has a bearing on stock market performance. Accelerating PPI inflation depresses subsequent stock market performance versus cash in 9 of 13 countries. Five of 13 coefficients are statistically significant, and each of the significant coefficients is negative. In short, although CPI inflation appears nearly

EXHIBIT 14:
PERCENTAGE CHANGE PRODUCER PRICE INDEX

	Coefficient of Regression with Subsequent Asset Class Relative Performance		
	Stock/Bond	Stock/Cash	Bond/Cash
Australia	0.13	0.08	−0.06
Belgium	−0.43	−0.55[1]	−0.12[1]
Canada	2.34	1.43	−0.91
Denmark	0.60	0.13	−0.47
France	−0.14	−0.34	−0.20[2]
German	−0.98	−1.91[2]	−0.92[2]
Italy	−0.02	−0.75	−0.73[2]
Japan	0.46	0.45	−0.01
Netherlands	−0.62	−0.87[1]	−0.25
Sweden	−0.90	−1.36	−0.46
Switzerland	−1.45[2]	−1.81[2]	−0.35[2]
U.K.	0.17	−0.60	−0.78
U.S.A.	−0.18	−1.08[2]	−0.90[2]
Average	−0.08	−0.55	−0.47[2]

[1]Significant at 5% level.
[2]Significant at 1% level.

irrelevant, PPI inflation acted as a depressant on both stocks and bonds.

The final two tests gave consistent and interesting results. The first of them, Exhibit 15, is a test of unemployment. If unemployment is above average, both stocks and bonds achieve better subsequent rewards. The relation is slightly more consistent for bonds than it is for stocks: for bonds the relation holds in every country except Canada, whereas in stocks it fails to hold in three countries. However, the average impact on stocks was greater than the average impact on bonds. All of the statistically significant results point to stronger capital markets performance when unemployment is above average than it is when unemployment is below average.

Finally, if people are working and are well paid, unit labor costs can rise rapidly (Exhibit 16). Here we find a relation even more consistent than the one with unemployment rates. Rising unit labor costs hurt

EXHIBIT 15:
UNEMPLOYMENT

	Coefficient of Regression with Subsequent Asset Class Relative Performance		
	Stock/Bond	*Stock/Cash*	*Bond/Cash*
Australia	−0.96	−0.16	0.80
Belgium	0.15[1]	0.23[2]	0.08[2]
Canada	−0.11	−0.24	−0.13
Denmark	−0.42[1]	−0.07	0.36
France	0.46	0.96[1]	0.49[1]
Germany	0.26[2]	0.39[2]	0.12[1]
Japan	0.05	0.06	0.02
Netherlands	0.12	0.21	0.09
Switzerland	1.92	2.09	0.16
U.K.	0.02	0.23	0.22
U.S.A.	0.33	0.69[2]	0.35
Average	0.17	0.40	0.23[2]

[1]Significant at 5% level.
[2]Significant at 1% level.

stock market performance in each country where this statistic is available. Bonds are hurt by rising unit labor costs in all but one country (Canada) in which this data is available.

Evidently, the capital markets and the workforce operate at cross purposes. Crudely stated, if the worker is happy, the investor will be sad, and vice versa.

CONCLUSION

The most telling conclusion of this research is that the relationships successfully applied to asset allocation strategies in the United States also have promise for other countries around the globe. Although statistical significance was sometimes elusive, the consistency of the

EXHIBIT 16:
PERCENTAGE CHANGE UNIT LABOR COSTS

	Coefficient of Regression with Subsequent Asset Class Relative Performance		
	Stock/Bond	*Stock/Cash*	*Bond/Cash*
Belgium	−0.40	−0.51	−0.11
Canada	−0.08	−0.06	0.02
Denmark	0.37	−0.30	−0.67
France	−1.18	−2.03	−0.84
Germany	−0.31[2]	−0.30	0.01
Italy	−0.23	−0.40	−0.17[1]
Netherlands	−0.46	−1.16	−0.70
Sweden	0.09	−0.04	−0.13
U.K.	0.47	−0.02	−0.54
U.S.A.	0.06	−0.44	−0.50
Average	−0.17	−0.53[2]	−0.36[1]

[1]Significant at 5% level.
[2]Significant at 1% level.

results from one country to another is ample grounds for encouragement about the merit of these investment tools.

What about the investor who wants to take a disciplined approach to asset allocation on a global basis? The evidence would suggest that such a disciplined approach is not only intuitively appealing, but that it also can add value.

CHAPTER 18

International Asset and Currency Allocation

ADRIAN LEE
VICE PRESIDENT
J. P. MORGAN INVESTMENT MANAGEMENT INC.
LONDON

The focus of this chapter is on the international asset allocation issues that confront U.S. investors. These are:

1. International assets versus domestic assets.
2. International equities versus international fixed income.
3. Foreign currency exposure versus foreign asset exposure.

We will show that, when an investor considers the full opportunity set of all the world's capital markets, both equities and fixed income, his risk/reward preference as revealed by domestic asset allocation choices should also be reflected in international asset allocation choices. In other words, an investor with a balanced domestic portfolio is likely also to prefer a balanced international portfolio.

It will also be shown that, in international investment, it is appropriate to separate long-run asset allocation decisions from long-run currency allocation decisions. This suggests that investors will inevitably enhance their risk/return opportunity set by making *separately* two kinds of international allocation decisions—one concerning asset exposure and one concerning currency exposure. When these allocations differ, the use of continuously hedged international portfolios is implied.

In fact we will conclude that, in general, it is appropriate for a U.S. investor's *normal* international equity and fixed-income portfolios to be defined as fully hedged. Only under perverse assumptions about long-run currency surprises should an international investor's *normal* portfolio be exposed to foreign currency.

We will use the results of the last 10 years to illustrate the effects of these choices in the past and we shall outline a framework for how these decisions can be addressed optimally in the future.

INTERNATIONAL CAPITAL MARKET RETURNS AND RISKS

The world's investable capital markets, excluding cash and real estate, comprise some $13 trillion as of December 1986. This forms the universe for an institutional investor (see Exhibit 1). The world fixed-income markets total some $7.5 trillion, while the world equity markets total $5.6 trillion. The U.S. markets comprise less than half the total of world markets in both the case of fixed-income and equities.

EXHIBIT 1:
WORLD CAPITAL MARKETS

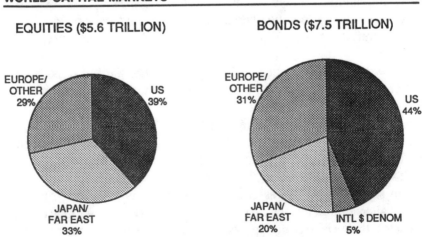

EQUITIES ($5.6 TRILLION)   BONDS ($7.5 TRILLION)

Sources: Morgan Stanley Capital International, Salomon Brothers, Inc.

The non-U.S. markets have offered significant opportunities for U.S. investors over the last 10 years. These opportunities can be seen in the form of return enhancement and risk reduction.

RETURN ENHANCEMENT

Exhibits 2 and 3 show the returns in U.S. dollars from investing in international equity and fixed-income markets over the last 10 years. For both equities and fixed-income securities, non-U.S. markets have yielded significantly higher returns than their U.S. equivalents. A market weighted average of all non-U.S. equity markets returned 21.1% per annum in U.S. dollars compared with 11.4% per annum from the U.S. equity market. Similarly, non-U.S. fixed-income markets returned 13.4% compared to the U.S. fixed-income return of 10.3%.

EXHIBIT 2:
INTERNATIONAL EQUITY MARKETS
RETURNS IN U.S. DOLLARS 1977–1986

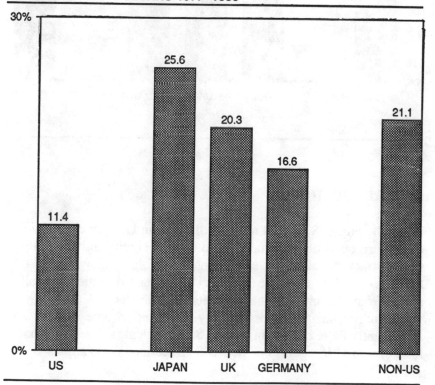

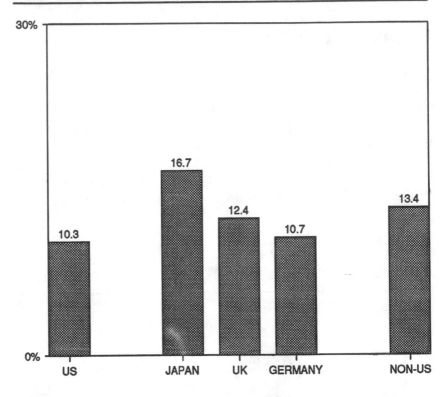

EXHIBIT 3:
INTERNATIONAL FIXED-INCOME MARKETS
RETURNS IN U.S. DOLLARS 1977–1986

RISK REDUCTION

While the non-U.S. capital markets offered the U.S. investor significant return opportunities, they did so without significantly increasing
risk. In fact, the U.S. investor's total portfolio risk was reduced.
Exhibits 4 and 5 show the annualized standard deviation of dollar
return from the international markets over the period 1977–1986.
While individual international equity and fixed-income markets are
significantly more risky than their U.S. equivalent, a diversified portfolio of non-U.S. equities or non-U.S. fixed-income securities is not

significantly more risky than the equivalent domestic market. For example, a market weighted average of non-U.S. equity markets had an annual standard deviation of dollar return of 15.6% per annum compared with 14.4% per annum for the U.S. equity market.

EXHIBIT 4:
INTERNATIONAL EQUITY MARKETS
STANDARD DEVIATION OF RETURNS IN U.S. DOLLARS 1977–1986

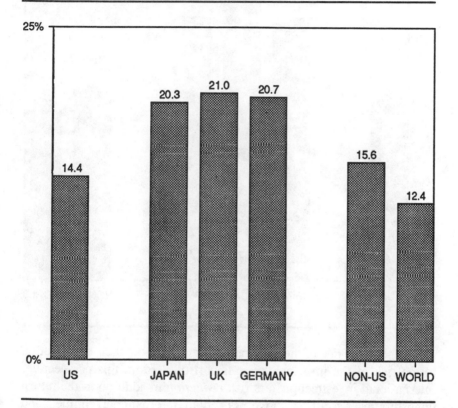

This diversification *between* international markets is significant for both equities and fixed-income securities. It is important to bear in mind that international investment for any investor, U.S. or otherwise, always offers two tiers of diversification: first, diversification out of the domestic market; second, diversification across the many markets outside the domestic market.

In assessing the risk of international investment, the relevant mea-

EXHIBIT 5:
INTERNATIONAL FIXED-INCOME MARKETS
STANDARD DEVIATION OF RETURNS IN U.S. DOLLARS 1977–1986

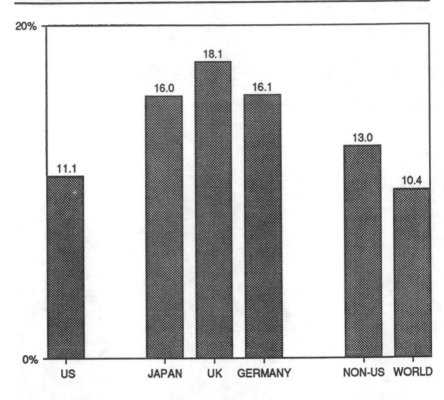

sure is not total risk of the international markets, but their contribution to the risk of the investor's overall portfolio. From this perspective, international investment offers risk *reduction* in addition to the return opportunities described above. For both international equities and fixed-income securities, a capitalization weighted world portfolio of U.S. and non-U.S. markets is less risky than the U.S. market alone. This shows that diversification into international markets in fact reduces a U.S. investor's total portfolio risk.

INTERNATIONAL ASSET ALLOCATION

Exhibit 6 illustrates the returns and risks to various asset allocation decisions over the period 1977–1986. The line joining USS and NUSS shows returns and risks to a portfolio ranging from 100% U.S. equities up to 100% non-U.S. equities. The line USB, NUSB shows portfolios ranging from 100% U.S. fixed-income to 100% non-U.S. fixed-income. The line NUSB, NUSS shows all combinations of international fixed-income securities and international equities.

EXHIBIT 6:
INTERNATIONAL EQUITY AND BOND MARKETS
RETURNS AND RISK 1977–1986

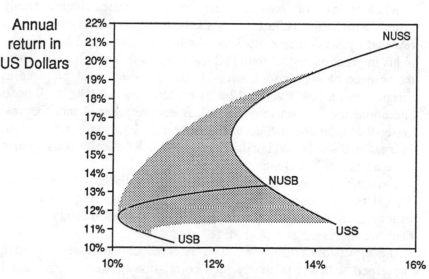

	Correlations			
U.S. stocks(USS)	1			
U.S. bonds(USB)	.42	1		
Non-U.S. stocks(NUSS)	.36	.32	1	
Non-U.S. bonds(NUSB)	.15	.44	.75	1

Exhibit 6 shows (1) that international equities and fixed-income securities add value when compared with their domestic counterparts, and (2) that they offer diversification among themselves (see frontier of the shaded area). This is the third tier of international diversification— across international equity and fixed-income.

From an asset allocation perspective, it is appropriate to consider the full spectrum of all international assets simultaneously when identifying an investor's portfolio risk/reward tradeoff. In other words, the more traditional domestic/international allocation question is more appropriately addressed in the context of simultaneous allocations across all four asset classes—U.S. equities, U.S. fixed-income, international equities and international fixed-income securities.

Of critical importance to this asset allocation problem is the correlation of diversification characteristics of all asset classes simultaneously. Exhibit 6 also gives these correlations for the period 1977–1986.

When an investor considers these four asset classes simultaneously in an optimization context, it is likely that his risk preference, as revealed by his domestic stock/bond allocation, will also be reflected in his international stock/bond allocation. In other words, say that in the absence of international investment, an investor was prepared to accept a target risk level of 12% as revealed by a 60/40 stock bond allocation; then, when international assets are allowed into the universe, the optimal portfolio at the same risk level will include both international stocks and bonds. A balanced U.S. investor is likely also to be a balanced international investor.

The exact proportions of such optimal portfolios will inevitably depend on the future expectations for risk, return and covariance. Examples of such optimal portfolios using *ex ante* equilibrium assumptions are discussed at a later stage.

U.S. investors considering such asset allocation issues are often concerned with the relatively high correlation between international equity and international fixed income. This high correlation results from both asset classes sharing very similar currency exposure—a Japanese equity and a Japanese bond imply identical exposure to the Yen.

In order to appropriately identify asset allocation policies in global investment, it is important first to separate international asset allocation issues from international currency allocation. Indeed, we shall show in the next section that the risk/reward opportunity set for a U.S. investor is greatly enhanced by considering these allocations separately, and that the high correlations of international equities and bonds can be greatly reduced when asset and currency decisions are separated.

SEPARATION OF ASSETS AND CURRENCIES—HEDGED INTERNATIONAL PORTFOLIOS

Returns to a U.S. investor in international markets derive from two separate sources of return—local assets return and currency appreciation (depreciation) versus the U.S. dollar. The local and currency returns to U.S. investment in international equities and fixed-income securities are shown in Exhibits 7 and 8.

EXHIBIT 7:
INTERNATIONAL EQUITY MARKETS
LOCAL AND CURRENCY RETURNS 1977–1986

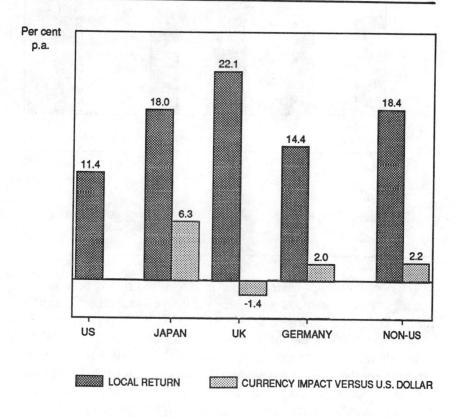

EXHIBIT 8:
INTERNATIONAL FIXED-INCOME MARKETS
LOCAL AND CURRENCY RETURNS 1977–1986

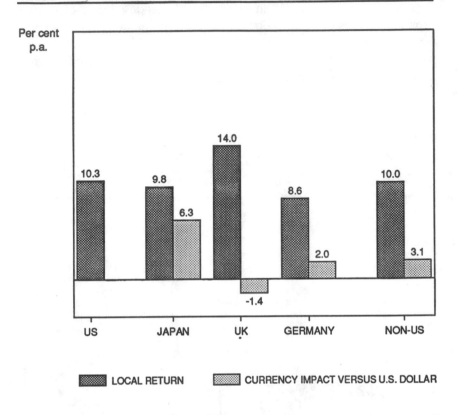

The contribution of currency return to total return has been unsystematic; for some markets it has been positive and for others negative; for diversified portfolios or non-U.S. markets it has been small.

In contrast, however, the contribution of currencies to investment risk is significant and systematically positive. Exhibits 9 and 10 separate the total risk (standard deviation of return) of international equities and fixed-income markets into risk from local return volatility and currency volatility versus the U.S. dollar. Total risk is given by the outlined bar, and component risks are given by the inner bars. It can be seen that currency risk is approximately equal to 80% of the local risk of equity markets and more than 180% of the risk of local fixed-income markets. The total risk as indicated by the outlined bar is not equal to the addition of the two component risks, because standard deviations are not additive, due to the correlations of local asset and currency returns. These correlations are indicated also in Exhibits 9 and 10.

EXHIBIT 9:
INTERNATIONAL EQUITY MARKETS
LOCAL AND CURRENCY RISKS 1977–1986

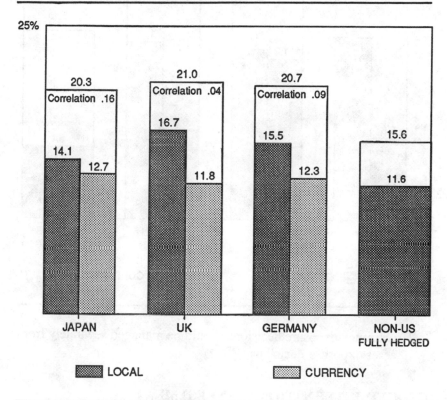

The correlations are consistently small especially for international equities. This observation, combined with the fact that currency risk is a significant source of investment risk in international portfolios suggests:

1. Currency risk should be managed and not simply assumed in international investment.

EXHIBIT 10:
INTERNATIONAL FIXED-INCOME MARKETS
LOCAL AND CURRENCY RISKS 1977–1986

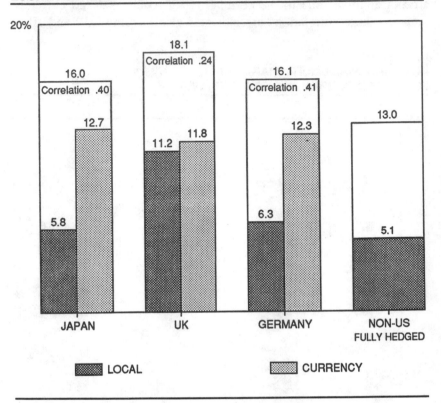

2. Currency exposure decisions should be managed separately from asset exposure decisions.

HEDGED INTERNATIONAL INVESTMENT

International portfolios that have exposure only to local asset return can be constructed by hedging the currency exposure of the underlying foreign asset back into the dollar. The risks of such hedged portfolios of all non-U.S. markets is also given in Exhibits 9 and 10. These risks show that hedged portfolios, with only exposures to international assets and not currencies, can avoid the significant currency risks associated with international investment.

Return to a fully hedged foreign investment is equal to:

local asset return + forward premium/discount[1]

Exhibit 11 plots the risks and returns to the full spectrum of asset and currency allocation choice over the period 1977–1986—U.S. stocks, U.S. bonds, non-U.S. stocks, non-U.S. bonds, non-U.S. stocks fully hedged and non-U.S. bonds fully hedged.

EXHIBIT 11:
INTERNATIONAL EQUITY AND BOND MARKETS
RETURNS AND RISKS 1977–1986

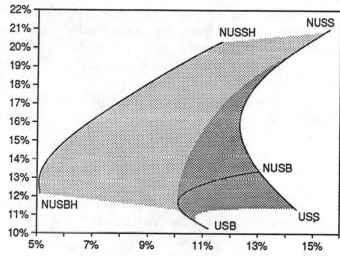

Annual return in US Dollars

Standard deviation of return in US Dollars

	Correlations					
U.S. stocks(USS)	1					
U.S. bonds(USB)	.42	1				
Non-U.S. stocks(NUSS)	.36	.32	1			
Non-U.S. bonds(NUSB)	.15	.44	.75	1		
Non-U.S. stocks hedged(NUSSH)	.42	.21	.73	.21	1	
Non-U.S. bonds hedged(NUSBH)	.27	.48	.47	.66	.36	1

---

[1]Forward premium – U.S. short-term rate – foreign short-term rate.

It can be seen that the returns to fully hedged international equities and bonds for the period 1977–1986 were roughly equivalent to their dollar adjusted equivalent. *Ex post* the hedged and unhedged returns will differ by the "surprise currency" depreciation beyond that anticipated in the forward premium. In other words, unhedged investment will outperform hedged investment only if currency appreciation is greater than that anticipated by the forward premium.

Inclusion of fully hedged portfolios in the universe of choice greatly enhanced the risk/reward opportunity set to the U.S. investor. In fact, hedged international equities and bonds dominated their unhedged equivalents in terms of return and risk; this is so because hedged portfolios had similar returns to unhedged portfolios but significantly reduced risks. Also, and importantly, hedged international equities and bonds are significantly less correlated than their unhedged counterparts − .36 versus .75, thus improving diversification between international equities and bonds. This addresses the concern raised earlier of the relatively high correlation between international bonds and equities, due to their shared currency exposure.

Hedged international portfolios have equivalent diversification characteristics to unhedged portfolios, as can be seen from the correlations of returns in Exhibit 11.

Currency exposure in international portfolios is not itself the source of international diversification. It can be shown that diversification of unhedged international investment, as measured by correlation of domestic asset return with combined return of foreign local asset and currency, can be broken down as follows:

$$R_{a+c,u} = \left(R_{a,u} \frac{S_a}{S_{a+c}} \right) + \left(R_{c,u} \frac{S_c}{S_{a+c}} \right)$$

a = foreign asset local returns
c = foreign currency returns
u = domestic asset returns
R = correlation coefficient

This says that the unhedged correlation is the weighted average of local asset correlation with the domestic asset and the correlation of the foreign currency with the domestic asset. The weights are given by the respective ratios of asset risk and currency risk to total risk.

It can be shown that hedging will not reduce diversification unless

$$\frac{R_{c,u}}{R_{a,u}} < \frac{S_{a+c} - S_a}{S_c}$$

In other words, unless $R_{c,u}$ is small and the increase in risk associated with currency exposure is large, hedging will not reduce diversification. Empirically the impact of hedging on diversification has been minimal.

However, the appropriate way to evaluate the impact of hedging is by examining its effect on total portfolio risk, i.e., its marginal impact on the risk of a portfolio of U.S. and international assets. The chapter appendix shows that hedging international investment must reduce total portfolio risk when compared with unhedged international investment—the *combined impact of diversification and international risk reduction associated with hedging is always to reduce total portfolio risk.*

LONG-RUN INTERNATIONAL ASSET ALLOCATION— A FRAMEWORK FOR A GENERALIZED SOLUTION

In order to adopt appropriate asset allocation strategies for the future, it is first necessary to identify separately the domestic and international asset classes and currencies and then to estimate equilibrium or long-run returns and risks for each category.

Equilibrium estimates are assumptions that can be expected to hold over a long period of time and are such that return and risk are balanced. Historical returns cannot be relied on as *ex ante* estimates although *relative* historical risks and covariances can provide some insight into future relationships. An illustration of such equilibrium estimates is given in Exhibit 12. These estimates assume that

- domestic assets and international assets have the same similar long-run returns;
- hedged portfolios have lower risk than unhedged ones;

- hedged portfolios have the same long-run returns as unhedged ones;[2] and
- that relative covariance characteristics of these categories will be roughly equivalent to those observed in the past.

EXHIBIT 12:
LONG-RUN ASSET ALLOCATION

Equilibrium Assumptions—U.S. Investor

	Compound Return	Annual Standard Deviation	Correlation Return
U.S. equities	10.5%	18.0%	1
U.S. bonds	7.5	9.0	.40 1
Non-U.S. equities	11.0	20.0	.35 .30 1
Non-U.S. bonds	7.5	11.0	.15 .45 .75 1
Non-U.S.equity—hedged	11.0	15.0	.40 .20 .75 .20 1
Non-U.S.bonds—hedged	7.5	4.5	.25 .50 .45 .65 .35

Using Markowitz optimization techniques, the resulting optimal portfolios, constrained to have 60% in domestic assets, are shown in Exhibit 13.

The conclusions are clear:

1. International stock/bond allocations should reflect domestic stock/bond allocations.
2. Hedged international investment of both equities and bonds is the appropriate *normal* portfolio position for the U.S. investor.

---

[2]This is equivalent to the rational expectation that currency changes do not consistently deviate over the long-run from those anticipated in the forward exchange market, or from long-run inflation differentials.

EXHIBIT 13:
LONG-RUN ASSET ALLOCATION

| | Optimal Normal Portfolios | | | | |
| | Constrained* | | | | |
	Min. Risk	B	C	D	Max. Returns
U.S. equities	2%	12%	19%	42%	57%
U.S. bonds	58	48	41	18	3
Non-U.S. equities	–	–	–	–	–
Non-U.S. bonds	–	–	–	–	–
Non-U.S. equities—hedged	–	14	30	40	40
Non-U.S. bonds—hedged	40	26	10	–	–
	100	100	100	100	100
Portfolio return	7.57%	8.35%	9.14%	10.15%	10.70%
Portfolio risk	6.45%	7.26%	9.00%	12.14%	14.39%

*U.S. equities + U.S. bonds = 60%.

By how much do unhedged portfolios have to outperform hedged ones before normal portfolios should include a currency exposure? We examined the sensitivity of the optimizations to various levels of expected "surprise currency appreciation." "Surprise currency appreciation" is the amount that foreign currencies appreciate annually over and above the forward premium. The results are shown in Exhibit 14. Unless one assumes that currencies over the long-run will appreciate by 4–6% per annum in excess of forward premia, hedging international portfolios is appropriate in defining the *normal* portfolio for the U.S. investor.

It should be stressed that defining the normal portfolio as fully hedged in no way reduces the need for or role of tactical currency

EXHIBIT 14:
CURRENCY SURPRISE FACTOR (CONSTANT RISK LEVEL)

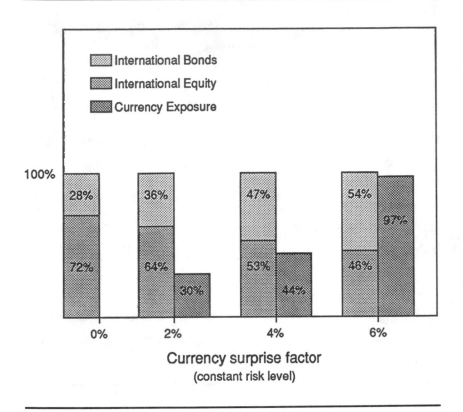

allocation; it simply rebases the neutral currency exposure to zero, from the traditional neutral position of a market capitalization weight.

SUMMARY AND CONCLUSIONS

On the basis of past data and optimization of *ex ante* expectations, we can conclude:

1. Investment in both international equities and fixed income in significant percentages will raise returns and reduce risks for U.S. investors.

2. Percentage allocations between international and equities should reflect domestic stock/bond allocation.
3. International investment should be defined as being on a fully hedged basis.

APPENDIX

The appropriate question in evaluating the case for hedged international investment is whether or not the risk of a diversified portfolio using hedged foreign securities is lower than that of diversified portfolio using unhedged foreign investment.

Assume the diversified portfolio is split w% domestic, $1-w\%$ foreign. The risk of a hedged diversified portfolio is given by:

$$\text{VAR}\left(\frac{u}{w} + \frac{a}{1-w}\right) \tag{1}$$

Risk of unhedged diversification is given by:

$$\text{VAR}\left(\frac{u}{w} + \frac{a+c}{1-w}\right) \tag{2}$$

Total portfolio risk reduction is given by:

$$\text{VAR}\left(\frac{u}{w} + \frac{a+c}{1-w}\right) - \text{VAR}\left(\frac{u}{w} + \frac{a}{1-w}\right) \tag{3}$$

$$= \frac{1}{w^2}\text{VAR}(u) + \frac{\text{VAR}(a+c)}{(1-w)^2} + \frac{2\,\text{COV}(u,a+c)}{w(1-w)}$$

$$-\left[\frac{\text{VAR}(u)}{w^2} + \frac{\text{VAR}(a)}{(1-w)^2} + \frac{2\quad\text{COV}(u,a)}{w(1-w)}\right]$$

$$= \frac{1}{(1-w)^2} [VAR(a) + VAR(c) + 2COV(a,c)] +$$

$$\frac{2}{w(1-w)} [COV(u,a) + COV(u,c)] \quad -\frac{VAR(a)}{(1-w)^2} - \frac{2COV(u,a)}{w(1-w)}$$

$$= \frac{1}{(1-w)^2} [VAR(c) + 2COV(a,c)] + \frac{2}{w(1-w)} COV(u,c)$$

$$= \frac{1}{(1-w)^2} \left[S_c^2 + 2R_{a,c} S_a S_c \right] + \frac{2}{w(1-w)} R_{u,c} S_u S$$

> 0, unless $R_{c,a}$ or $R_{u,c}$ are significantly negative.

Unless there is a significantly *negative* correlation between currency appreciation and the local or domestic asset, hedged foreign investment reduces total portfolio risk over unhedged investment.

Historically these correlations have been consistently non-negative. For U.S. and Japanese equities for 1970–1986, the empirical results are as follows, where $w = .5$. from equation (1):

$$= \frac{(.108)^2}{4} + \frac{1}{2} \times .108 [.197 \times .08 + .158 \times .04]$$

$$= .016$$

or hedging reduced the standard deviation of the diversified portfolio from 19% to 14.2% per annum.

How negative do these correlations have to be to justify unhedged investment on a risk equivalent basis?

Using the data for 1970–1986 again and assuming the correlation between local asset and currency is zero, then the Yen should have a $-.34$ correlation with the U.S. equity market. The equivalent number for bonds is $-.57$.

Index